Through
THEIR EYES

A People's View of the Global Church

Through
THEIR EYES

A People's View of the Global Church

F. DEAN LUEKING

FOREWORD BY MARTIN E. MARTY

TBC
Tyra Books
Chicago

7300 W. Division, River Forest, IL 60305

www.tyrabookschicago.com

ISBN-13: 978-0-615-37157-3

Cover and book design by Melissa C. Lucar,
Fisheye Graphic Services, Inc., Chicago

Printed in the United States of America

Tyra Books
Chicago

7300 W. Division, River Forest, IL 60305
www.tyrabookschicago.com

TABLE OF CONTENTS

FOREWORD

Author F. Dean Lueking writes clearly and compellingly, so he does not need a Foreword-writer to explain what he is about, or an introducer to interpret his chapters. Therefore, why write and publish these lines, which means, why draw attention to the book, which can stand on its own; why advertise its value and virtues? I hope that as you read these pages you will find them quite clear and compelling, as well as an attempt to advance the conversation which the author starts here. All of his books—that "all" signaling a remarkable feature of his vocation, during which for over a half century he was a full-time pastor and church leader while writing numbers of volumes—are bids for conversation. He does not blast away with noisy arguments; he invites response and extension.

His main approach, as is clear on every page here, is to tell stories. During the past generation we have read many pleas for "narrative theology" to complement biblical and systematic theology. I can't remember Lueking ever pleading for or theorizing about narrative. He just provides it, in a way that suggests how more of the interpretation of the Christian faith and endeavor should proceed in an era when readerships deal more congenially with happenings and narratives than with the abstractions which have so often helped Christians make their points, but which now also can stand in the way of comprehension.

To test this observation, dear reader, crack open a pack of small post-it notes and stick one on every page of this book where a new story begins, and see the margins of the book explode with yellow tags. Pull at any of them and you will find yourself drawn into a story which most potential readers have not anticipated but which, I picture, all will welcome. He has a gift for opening access, in an economical fewness of lines, to the variety of personalities here visited. A few more lines will tell us how the subjects dressed, appeared, gestured, and decorated their quarters. I have only visited a few peopled places pointed to here—Slovakia being an example—but would have little difficulty recognizing the face and being of his characters should I visit in person.

A waning popular magazine used to feature a column on "the most unforgettable character I've met." Dr. Lueking finds such "unforgettables" for every chapter. And what a variety they make up! While he and I inhabit the same church body, I had heard of few of his characters, mainly because on the front lines, mingled with church planners and officials, are people ordained to ministry by their baptism. Scores and scores of them. Some of them struggle their way into formal offices of ministry, but make no show of it. There is too much work to do, too little time to fuss. Again and again my own yellow post-it notes would flag what some call "pastorpreneurs," people who set up shop where no one has done Christian work or where, in Jesus' term from the gospels, "the laborers are few."

One could lift out dozens of these stories and organize them into a case book with many causes, such as:

Conversion: here are non-stereotyped stories of how people have been found by grace and, through faith, have followed the call. Most of them had someone present the case for Christ to them. We like to quote the late Cardinal Bernardin quoting St. Francis: "Preach the Gospel. Use words if necessary." Good. But one is struck by the way in all continents and the cultures described here, some person—be it parent, spouse, teacher, stranger—also in print or by voice, often a whisper, articulated the case for Christ convincingly, and then the case closed with a "pro-Christ" response.

Whether these new Christians live in Africa with its many spiritual backgrounds, in Korea where huge numbers of Christians offer precedents good and bad, in Japan where the Christian minority hangs by a toe-hold after five centuries, one thing they all have in common is diversity. In our culture some try to force conversion into a particular mold. I've heard of someone asking another: "Have you found Jesus Christ as your personal Savior?" only to get the response: "No, I believe in sharing." Throughout this book, the community of believers is active, sustaining even the lonely.

Mission. Lueking knows and wants his readers to know, often by deduction, that the concept of "foreign missions" has come to be questioned in many circles, that the impulse to inspire and propel missionaries into new zones has quieted, that the support of such by church bodies has waned. You would seldom know it from the way people in these stories, living on the various continents, have picked up on mission, improvised, found subtle and bold ways to reach those in whom the Spirit of Christ had been unknown or dimly recognized. The "converts," the people with new vocations that Lueking finds, do not sit back; they step up and imaginatively extend the mission.

Struggle. Whoever reads surveys, even in popular magazines, probably has a statistical fix: it notes that the Christian church booms in the poor world, and has declined toward death in some parts of the other world, "Euro-America," long a stronghold but now, especially in Europe, having only a weak hold on minorities of the population. Get ready for surprises: Lueking on one hand interviews many in fields where Christian churches prosper, leaders who caution against reading too much into the prosperity. He mentions problems of Christian illiteracy, sometimes even of ecclesiastical boondoggling, often recycling of converts who come in the front door and exit soon from the back. (So, what else is new?)

Many of the interviewees tell of how their parents' generations suffered under murderous regimes, and not a few of them bear scars, often emotional, from harassment, exclusion, and persecution. One will find in some chapters a virtual updating of the biblical Book of Acts, locating believers who replicate the world of the early Christians. Alongside them are narratives of fools for Christ, adventurous and audacious springers into action for the Lord and the people they love. Most find peace in the God of peace, but few can relax in the face of their near-poverty and the brutal poverty of the people they serve. Raw faith carries them through. Lueking reproduces what they say in ways that can help their responses serve as templates for those of us in more passive and taken-for-granted situations.

Diversity. Christians in cultures which offer molds and stamps and grooves into which believers must fit—think of the hackneyed distinction between "traditional" and "contemporary" worship and worshipers—will be astounded to see how diverse are the expressions of faith among the people Lueking visits and whose stories he brings home. As they reach to find languages, concepts, and policies, they offer a blurred picture, one redeemed

[margin note: clarity & fuzziness]

[margin note: paradox]

by one clearly-outlined feature: the desire to serve the Lord who has called them. Yes, there is blurring. Sometimes they risk obscuring sharp lines between Christianity and the other faiths which have dominated but often grown stale, but if the openness to existing culture is apparent, the focus of distinct faith in Christ and His church always comes through. Yes, more blur: between "clergy" and "laity." Also, sometimes the line between Lueking's home team, the Lutheran churches, and all kinds of others Christians—you'll hear about the Assemblies of God as just one sample!—is fuzzy, because leaders on both sides, all sides, grasp for Christian resources wherever they can find them, and pool such resources where such common spirit and action promote the cause.

[margin note: NB]

Readiness to learn. Here is an astonishing feature which only a close friend of the Luekings gets away with mentioning: "Dean and Bev," as we have known them for over a half century, never, *never* come across as superior, knowing, favor-imparting visitors. I have to say a word about Beverly, the wife, who makes cameo appearances on so many pages. The Martys have been in their home and home church hundreds of times, have camped and traveled with them, and even made a house call on them in Bratislava. We know a fact that has to be revealed: this mission, this narrative, could not have occurred without Beverly's co-initiative. She may inhabit an impressive suburban house in America, or donned fashionable gowns on some occasions when the Luekings drop in to Illinois between their forays "into all the world." But Beverly has carried laundry in a basket on her head when washing in the river during the experience of an earlier sabbatical in the backcountry of Kenya, or kept the unwelcome company of tarantulas and scorpions and bats and other night-visitors to their quarters

It would disturb the plot and appear a bit cloying to those who do not know this couple, had Dean, the author, staged Beverly at the center of the action where she has so often belonged. But readers can pick up clues along the way as to how Ms. Lueking's presence adds nuance to narrative, thickness to plot, elegance to description.

Apparent limits. This is not a book about all Christians; the Assemblies of God received only those few lines; Roman Catholic presences come and go. Only seventy or eighty million Christians among the two billions of people who bear the Christian name and identity are Lutherans. Yet Lutherans are on stage here, focal, visited, reported on, and scrutinized. Some may find this to be a flaw. Would not a friendly hop-skip-and jump among the thirty-to-fifty thousand identifiable Christian church bodies have provided a more ample sample? Perhaps, but all of them would be reduced to almanac-level entries, terse but not memorable. What we need next are scores of books which follow this precedent, because together they will provide a more full picture of the church today.

Along with the Lutheran identity and choice of locations comes a form or expression native and congenial to Lueking types and the men and women they visit in tiny apartment missions or large open fields. That is, they "witness," they use language which reveals how the Luther-an interpretation of Paul, the apostles, the gospels, the prophets, has been portable, and has been picked up from catechists, teachers and preachers. Lueking does not bother to translate or paraphrase, such as, "If this group were Russian Orthodox, they would witness this or that way..." His own faith and expression fade in and out, in harmony with the phenomena of the articulators he visits. I'd say he makes a virtue of his necessity to speak this pious witness-language, and readers of other Christian communities can make their own translations to complement his subjects' own.

Transcending the limits. Often I describe four vantages from which one can observe the storms, struggles, and partial victories which occur in the modern world. Picture them here, as if we are hurricane-watching:

First, we can take the satellite view, from 30,000 miles up, looking at the Christian world in ways symbolized by the silvery circles and bands shown us by weather people on television. They represent an important kind of knowledge. So we can speak of thinning circles and bands, say, in Europe—a scene that often saddens the author—and the growing spheres in the poor world. This book does some of that, manly by inference.

Second, closer to the storms, are the receptions and perceptions of data from equipped C-130's, which are in the very eye of the storm—and thus safe. Their instruments guide them when the winds get dangerously close. They impart helpful information. This is where the—shall I say "we"?—historians, statisticians, sociologists, and mission-sending agents—sit to observe. Many books represent this vantage.

Next are the up-close people who know what the vision of the satellites and C-130's impart, but who cannot flee the scene when figurative storms and winds come. They are like fire-fighters, medics, communicators, chaplains, when things turn furious. Most of Lueking's featured people are in such roles: pastors, teachers, ministers, catechists, nurses, and the like. I'd like to meet more of them personally, and cannot forget most of them, even if I've greeted them on only a half-dozen pages here.

Fourth, there are the people in the cabins and huts, the trailers and tents, or even sometimes in the mansions, which cannot be protected when the storms hit. The levees do not hold, the waves surge twenty-five feet, and the people are devastated. Lueking's book is a book that deals mainly with perspectives three and four. A scholarly historian, he wears his learning well, and provides on the ground accounts, from which others can draw ideas. His subjects are often apparent losers who turn out to be winners. They have suffered and wrestled, but not been defeated. Since the author tapes most of the conversations he enjoys, they can be checked up on. Some may be tempted to check; these Christians are authentic, surprising because of the degree of eloquence each can summon.

One of the assignments to authors of forewords is to get out of the way and let the author, his subjects, and the book speak for themselves. I so enjoyed reading the accounts, and took so many notes, that I am tempted to write more, but you can take your own notes as you read. So with what do I leave this reading, this writing, with you readers in mind?

First, to appreciate theology-by-story. Jewish philosopher Martin Buber hypothesized that God created the world because he loves stories. Alasdair MacIntyre has observed that the human:

> …is in his actions and practices, as well as in his fictions, essentially a story-telling animal. He is not essentially, but becomes through his history, a teller of stories that aspire to truth. But the key question for men is not about their own authorship: I can only answer the question "What am I to do?" if I can answer the prior question "Of what story or stories do I find myself a part?"[1]

[1] Alasdair McIntyre, "The Virtues, the Unity of a Human Life, and the Concept of a Tradition," in *Why Narrative? Readings in Narrative Theology,* ed. Stanley Hauerwas and L. Gregory Jones (Grand Rapids, Michigan: Wm. B. Eerdmans, 1989), p 101-102.

Christians of all sorts, Catholic, Orthodox, Pentecostal, Evangelical, Mainline Protestant, *even Lutheran!* have good reason, by reading the stories here, finding themselves discovering, in new ways, that they are part of the story of the hearers, speakers, and doers of the Word around the globe. I get to visit enough of such fellow-believers in my travels, which are vastly more limited than those accounted for here. But when I sing of the church around the globe, I find that I do not stay content with sweeping phrases, generalizations, theories, or abstractions. I think of different specific people in specific places, Christians about whom I've read, as I did and as you will, here.

The second verse of a favored evening hymn always calls them to mind:

We thank you that your church, unsleeping
While earth rolls onward into light,
Through all the world its watch is keeping,
And never rests by day or night.

Read on, and know that when you retire, people you will meet on these pages, in their various time-zones and climates, "unsleeping," are keeping watch, and inspiring you to take your turn when they are at rest.

— Martin E. Marty
Emeritus, The University of Chicago

INTRODUCTION

From the Hasidic tradition of Judaism comes this testimony to the power of story to convey a larger truth:

> Once, to save a life, the Baal Shem Tov went into the forest, attached a candle to a tree and performed other mystical actions and meditations, and he saved the boy, with the help of God. After the Baal Shem Tov's passing, there was a similar matter with his disciple and successor, the Maggid of Mezritch. He said, "I don't know the mystical meditations the Baal Shem Tov used, but I'll simply act, and God will help." So he lit the candle in the forest and performed other mystical incantations, and his deeds were acceptable on high and had the desired effect. In the next generation, there was a similar matter with Rabbi Moshe Leib of Sassov, a disciple of the Maggid of Mezritch. He said, "I don't even know how to do what is necessary, but I'll just tell the story of what the Baal Shem Tov did, and God will help." And so it was, with God's help. [1]

Early in my training for ministry, I learned to appreciate the point of the Baal Shem Tov legend about the power of story to connect people separated by time and space. Between my third and fourth years of seminary I was sent to Japan for a two year internship. My support came from several hundred of my fellow seminarians (who chipped in a dime a day, which meant something in 1951-1953) so that I could keep them informed on my experiences in post-World War II Japan. I quickly learned to build my reportage around what I was learning from the Japanese people themselves. Their stories, based in their lived experiences, became the slender

[1] I am indebted to Rabbi Victor Mirelman for finding this quote from *Storytelling and Spirituality in Judaism* by Yitzhak Buxbaum. This quotation may be found on the web at: http://www.hasidicstories.com/Articles/Hasidic_Theories/spirit.html , p. 7

thread of conveying a larger sphere of meaning about the course of the Gospel in a Japan struggling to rise from the ashes of a devastating defeat.

Those two years of internship and what I learned about interpreting the life of the church through the stories of people who comprised the church were more formative for the next half century of my ministry than I could have realized at the time. Following my return to complete my seminary education, I thought my future might take me back to Asia for a missionary vocation. Instead, things took another turn. I was called to a Lutheran parish in suburban Chicago where I was ordained and began my pastoral calling under a superb mentor, Otto Geiseman, who helped me gain my grounding in parish ministry and at the same time encouraged me to continue graduate study. I paired my daily work in the congregation with study at the Divinity School of the University of Chicago, where I had the stimulation of Jaroslav Pelikan, Sidney Mead, and Robert Pierce Beaver as my thesis advisors. The latter, a modest, quiet-spoken mission scholar (who was among the western missionaries interned by the Japanese army in 1943) motivated me during and after my doctoral program to stay abreast, as a parish pastor, of the momentous changes occurring in global Christianity, especially the explosive Christian growth south of the equator from the mid-1950's onward in Africa, Asia, and South America. During my pastorate the people of Grace enabled me to take two sabbaticals for a closer look at this phenomenon, the first to study congregations in Africa and Asia in 1983 and the second to do the same in the Southwest Pacific in 1991. These first hand contacts with Christians in their local milieu were rich opportunities for continued bridge-building between people afar and Grace parishioners. As the current motto puts it, we learned more about thinking globally and acting locally. Christians from abroad came to deepen our parish life as guest pastors and teachers. Our business people, students, tourists, and military personnel from Grace Church found a welcome among Christians overseas as they learned where to find them and join in worship and common works of service. They brought home stories to expand and deepen the range of what they experienced. Also, from the 1960's on through the turn of the century, my pastoral ministry was leavened by reading the works of world mission leaders such as the Germans, Walter Freytag and Hans Werner Gensichen, the Indian churchmen, Rajah

Manikam and D.T. Niles, the British missionary scholars, Stephen Neill, and Lesslie Newbigin, and more recently the books of the American, Philip Jenkins, and the Finnish mission theologian, Risto Ahonen. Robert Pierce Beaver's lasting influence prompted me to subscribe to the International Review of Missions throughout the early decades of my ministry and later to the Occasional Bulletin from the Missionary Research Library (which he founded), later known as the International Bulletin of Missionary Research. David Barrett's monumental World Christian Encyclopedia volumes have kept me abreast of the dramatic changes in the demographics of world Christianity from 1900–2000. To these and other scholars I am indebted lifelong for their discerning the broad contours of theological trends and shifting centers of the global Christian mission and its interaction with nations, cultures, and religions around the world.

What I missed in these writers, and what by the nature of their task they could not provide, was the global picture of the church presented through the lens of the individuals who gather regularly in congregations, who know the ups and downs of Christian discipleship in their daily lives in the world. This book seeks to do that. It tells of what I have learned by going personally to men and women, several hundred in number, who are scattered across thirty two nations in five continents. They are people with names and faces, young and old, lay and clergy, who succeed and fail, who know in their bone and marrow the particular life of the church in their particular place, whose stories of what they see through their eyes are woven into the larger story of God's mission in his world. Can their stories speak to readers who are not likely to read theological books on global mission? Can they, through stories, connect to readers in a way that opens ideas about meeting new neighbors down the block with different accents and skin colors, or stir the imagination to participate more fully as co-workers with God in doing justice, loving mercy, and walking humbly with him in his far-flung family?

The nudge to find out came in an unexpected time and place. In the mid-1990's, friend (since we met as seminarians in 1947) Martin Marty and I began leading summer retreats for laity and clergy. After the concluding session of the 1994 retreat, as we and our spouses were enjoying a glass of wine on the deck of the retreat house that faced onto Lake Michigan,

Marty did for me what he has done for so many. He planted the seed of an idea with a future. Through an offhand comment he suggested that I might think about revisiting Christians abroad whom I had known from previous travels and write a book based on what they had to say. He added that he couldn't think of another book of this genre. When Martin Marty observes that he doesn't know of a book on some aspect of how the Christian faith interacts with society, there's little point in second guessing him by trying to find one. It's better to write the book that can help fill the gap. And so I did. When I retired from Grace in 1998, a decade of providential opportunity opened up in continuing ministry, which took my wife, Beverly, (whose presence and partnership has been essential all the time, everywhere) and me to Slovakia for seminary teaching, and then on to further teaching residencies in Eastern Europe, Africa and Asia. I taught staff members doing development work with World Vision, Habitat for Humanity, and Opportunity International staff, and while in their countries, made additional contact with Lutheran Christians wherever possible. In addition, there were designated travels to Central and South America, the Near East, and the South Pacific to meet people who had stories to tell. Funding for it all came through the generosity of the members of Grace Lutheran Church in the Chicago suburb of River Forest, from the Wheat Ridge Ministries, and others whose prayers and cash keep us going. The considerable task of making necessary arrangements beforehand to meet people on schedule and in places where they could accommodate us was possible through the help of colleagues, missionaries, church staff people, and friends. In some instances, simply showing up in a village or city turned up serendipitous ways to meet remarkable people on the spot.

In gratitude to all of these several hundred people across the world, who were unfailing in hospitality, generous in giving their time, and discerning in sharing their insights, I dedicate this book. They take the place of footnotes. Their stories document the entry points into the larger story that I tell Many of them, reticent at first, then emboldened as they warmed to the invitation to talk about their experiences, wondered why we would come so far to seek them out, adding that they were hardly people of importance. My conviction is that now that Christ has come in the flesh that we all bear, there are no unimportant people. Everybody, everywhere, counts.

personal
"everyone" — people "who pushed back
— a spouse — 5 yr old grandson
— gay student
— a divorced man
— a centenarian who couldn't sit still
— a bishop who — a doctor who
who
dared
— a mentor who pushed ahead

It is precisely these people that I most wanted to engage as my teachers in this venture, for only they could share what their eyes have seen, their minds have absorbed, their bodies have endured, and their hearts have embraced concerning the Gospel of Christ, the community his Spirit creates, and the world God loves unconditionally.

— F. Dean Lueking, Pastor Emeritus
   Grace Lutheran Church, River Forest, Illinois

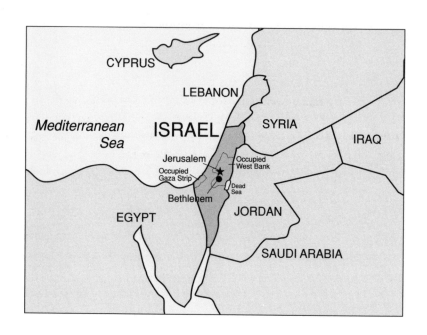

PART I

INTRODUCING PALESTINE

Despite the steady stream of news from the Near East, most of it bad, on Arab-Israeli conflicts in the Holy Land, there is reason to appreciate another reality on the ground in that beleaguered corner of the earth. Christians are there, Lutherans among them, who continue to live the faith begun with the covenant God made with Abraham and, as Christians believe, fulfilled in Jesus of Nazareth. Now, as with the first Christian believers, the church lives in the cauldron of unrelenting conflict. Christians are adversely affected by the retaliatory violence carried out by Palestinian extremists who launch rockets from Gaza onto Jewish settlements, killing Jewish children and adults, and threaten the extermination of Israel. Christians and Muslim citizens of Palestine are far more adversely affected by the Israeli military occupation, F-16 air strikes, and a wall which separates them from land they once owned but now is covered with illegal Jewish settlements which they are helpless to forestall, let alone reclaim.

How do Palestinians live under these circumstances? In hearing their responses to this question, their answers were more than we could fathom amidst the complexity of the conditions under which they have lived all their lives. Rather, they ask us to catch their spirit of hope and glimpse what it is that keeps them from despair. Look for these hints as their insights and experiences unfold in this opening chapter. They ask not for pity or for what we in America can do for them. They ask for partnership in the Gospel and interdependence as fellow members of the body of Christ as we work and pray together. This can take such practical form as visiting them personally when touring the Holy Land, sharing mutual resources through participation in service projects and conferences that inform and inspire, and—not the least—in communicating well informed pleas for justice to our own policy makers in Washington whose decisions directly affect their daily lives.

Seated comfortably at the supper table in Adel and Hala Khader's home in Bethlehem, a handsome stone residence overlooking the surrounding Judean hills, my first impression was that at least this Palestinian family was not suffering. Their house was elegantly furnished. The meal Hala prepared was superb, a sign of Arab hospitality at its best. Their grown children joined us, one an attorney, another in business (a third son was studying in the United States), and their married daughter spoke of the jewelry shop she and her husband own in the city. First impressions are deceiving, however. While the Khaders do live better than most among some 30,000 Palestinians crowded into the Bethlehem where Jesus was born, their lives are anything but an oasis of carefree affluence. They and their fellow Bethlhemites see themselves as living in a virtual open air prison, enclosed within the twenty-five foot high concrete wall that snakes its way through the city and beyond—a barrier that Israelis justify as needed protection from Palestinian terrorists and Palestinians resent as symbolic of an overwhelmingly disproportionate Israeli response. In any case, the wall does indeed separate workers from jobs (the jobless rate is 50%) families from families, friends from each other, children from schools, and seriously ill from hospitals, leaving 13% of the 660 square miles of the Bethlehem governorate available for Palestinian use. Palestinians are further aggrieved as they see Israeli settlements which they deem illegal expanding on land taken from them, bringing a total of 470,000 Israelis living in houses built since 1967. Despite these daily pressures, the Khaders have managed to survive and even flourish since coming to Bethlehem twenty years ago as refugees from Jenin, sixty miles to the north, where Adel's parents lost their ancestral land and Adel lost his first accounting business. What, I asked, keeps them above despair, bitterness or emigrating abroad?

bondage

oppression

despair

hope

Hala and Adel Khader

late

PALESTINE

A del began the answers by citing as of first importance the power of
their congregation as a staying factor in their lives. Christmas Lutheran
Church in Bethlehem is their spiritual home and anchor. Hala, a native of
Bethlehem, was baptized in this congregation founded soon after Lutherans
came from Europe in 1854 and is but a few minutes' walk from the 4th
century Church of Nativity built over the traditional site where Jesus was
born. Adel grew up in an Orthodox Christian family in Jenin, but joined
Christmas Lutheran Church when coming with Hala to Bethlehem two
decades ago. Both expressed gratitude for their pastor, Mitri Raheb, not
only for his pastoral care for them and others in the congregation, but for
the breadth of his creative ministry in the public life of Bethlehem and
beyond. "We are moderates in political matters" he said, meaning to distance

himself from Palestinians who have returned violence received with violence returned against Israelis. He put the matter simply: "when we pray 'Forgive us our trespasses as we forgive those who trespass against us' we look out the window to see what that means." He and his family have learned to live from Sunday to Sunday as doers of the Word that feeds their souls and motivates them to return evil with good. Christ's death and resurrection has broken down the worst of all walls, Adel said, the one that separates them from God. They see examples of grace at work in the lives of others at Christmas Lutheran Church whom they know and admire, helping them to stave off the inertia of self-pity that only makes bad situations worse. It is from his spiritual roots in the Gospel, well nourished in his congregation, that he has found what it takes to rebuild his life and his livelihood after losing everything as a refugee a quarter century earlier. That same source makes him an example to his children to whom he has passed on the faith and vision of overcoming evil with good as a way of life in Bethlehem.

Hala broke into the conversation with a story to illustrate how it is to live in Bethlehem as an open air prison. She told of the time when Adel suffered a near fatal heart attack and the ordeal of getting him to Amman, Jordan (60 miles to the northeast) for emergency care. They started out from Bethlehem in an ambulance with Hala doing her best to help keep her husband alive. At the first checkpoint they were allowed to go through after only a short delay. But at the second checkpoint the Israeli soldiers denied their Palestinian driver passage because of an alleged defect in his permit card. Hala begged the guard to recognize her husband's critical condition and allow them to get to Amman before he died. She quoted the Israeli soldier's response: "You're not getting through... Your husband can die right over there by the side of the road." There was nothing for her to do but call back to Bethlehem for another driver, which meant a full day of waiting in the ambulance with Adel until the new driver arrived, presented his credentials, and drove them on to Amman where Adel was admitted into the emergency room of a hospital. The return trip brought another crisis at the border crossing, making the agony of getting to and from the hospital, on top of the crisis of the heart attack, "a parable on why the temptation to hate is so strong and why the Lord's grace is the only thing stronger"—

as she put it with considerable feeling. In the light of such experiences she

4

made it clear that being moderate as Palestinian citizens does not mean calculated neutrality with no conviction, but a determined choice to disavow violence born of hate that would consume them if they gave in to it. She added, ruefully, that many in Bethlehem caught up in a similar crisis could never afford to hire transportation to get to Amman for needed medical help and would indeed die "over there, by the side of the road." (Hala's son)

Delay

The oldest son in the family, George, spoke of his experience of life as a young adult in Bethlehem. He told why it took him eight years instead of four to get his degree at the University of Bethlehem (founded in 1973 by a Roman Catholic educational order) : "The Israeli military arrested me five times during my four years as a student protesting the occupation. Each time meant three months in jail with no charge other than designating me as a person dangerous to the state." He showed me pictures from an album he kept of his jail experiences, noting that his main problem was boredom, bad food, and overcrowding. Listening to his story, I guessed that there was probably more to it than his dismissal of it as a pointless doubling of the customary four years required for a university degree. Before I could inquire further about his student activism, Hala cut off further conversation on the subject. "After he finished school we thought it better for him that he marry quickly" was her way of letting me know it was time to move on to other matters.

Haste

Persistence

Determinity

Adel took up a topic I had hoped might surface during the evening. He spoke his views on the two Palestinian "Intifada" (insurrection) episodes that have been well covered internationally through media footage of Palestinian rock-throwers confronting Israeli tanks. The first was in 1987. Adel viewed it favorably because it demonstrated a capacity within Palestinians to finally rise up in outrage against Israeli policy of outward oppression and inward humiliation. He filled out his observation with a brief overview of the complicated historical developments since the 1948 formation of the State of Israel. Instead of blaming Palestinian youth for throwing rocks at the Israeli tanks demolishing everything in sight, he wanted the footage of those events to show the world the disproportion of weaponry between the two sides as well as the most important thing—Palestinian courage to rise up as a David against a Goliath. He explained that the second Intifada occurred in 2000 after the controversial Israeli political leader Ariel

Sharon's highly provocative visit to a temple site in Jerusalem which Palestinian Muslims regard as the third holiest in Islam. Adel said that the second Intifada was not good because Yasser Arafat, the Palestinian leader, failed to unify disparate political segments of the Palestinian cause into a coordinated political response. That problem continues, he added, and thus life for Palestinians continues to be assaulted by Israeli military might (supported in large part, he reminded me "by USA tax dollars and Washington's capitulation to the Jewish lobby") as well as the indifference of the wider Arab world to the Palestinian plight. I asked him what that meant. *"It means that our larger, richer Arab brothers and sisters do not count it in their self interest to intervene in ways that would relieve us Palestinians of our role as a thorn in Israel's side"* was his answer. The evening with the Khaders held these lessons for understanding their lives and outlook: they are not free, they disavow suicide bombers killing Israelis, they can and do critique their own Palestinian leadership, their faith community is the core of their strength, they can flourish even after losing everything, hope rather than despair guides their daily lives. We would add this as well: they can provide an evening of memorable Arab hospitality coupled with illuminating conversation that places their personal experiences in a larger context. True, they are but one family among the 2.2 million Palestinians on the West Bank, one family among the three thousand Lutheran Christians of the five Lutheran congregations in the Holy Land. Yet their disavowal of violence is symbolic of the wider numbers of Palestinians who are essential to the ultimate policies that will ease this intractable Israeli-Palestinian conflict, which, since 1948, has dragged on as the longest in modern history.

They had spoken warmly of their pastor, Mitri Raheb, whose ministry at Christmas Lutheran Church since the late 1980's has been their spiritual lifeline. I was eager to renew my acquaintance with him after having met him first during one of his previous American visits. I had also become acquainted with his ministry through reading two of his books on

Mitri Raheb and Munib Younan

his life as a Palestinian pastor. My participation in an international conference in Bethlehem in 2005, my fifth visit to the region, gave me that opportunity. He welcomed me for conversation late one afternoon as we sat together in his office as the director of the International Cultural Center in Bethlehem, adjacent to Christmas Lutheran Church. He was generous in giving me his time at the end of a tiring day, and seemed to warm up quickly to the occasion when my opening question touched what was closest to his heart, being a Lutheran pastor in today's Bethlehem.

"We are a minority within a minority," he began, referring to the few thousand Lutherans as a minority among the approximately 150,000 Palestinian Christians of varied traditions, who, in turn, are a minority among the predominantly Muslim population in the land. "Our strength is not in our numbers but in the message of God's grace that we are here to demonstrate in word and action" he explained. He cited the importance of understanding the surrounding religious context that stresses acceptance before God through meritorious works. Also, he made a point of something I had not thought of before; Islam has never had a reformation comparable to that which Luther initiated in the 16th century. As a result, religious development here has long emphasized traditions and rituals which become rigidly encrusted. Martin Luther questioned and confronted something similar in his time, he noted, but this has not happened in Islam. Human traditions, both religious and cultural, stand under the Law of God and are subject to his judgment, but these cannot feed and revive people whose daily lives are dominated by tension and conflict. The liberating grace of Jesus Christ the Lord does, Raheb said, and that is what Lutherans are here to bring.

He acknowledged his own bouts with anger, frustration, and worst of all—the assault on human dignity by Israeli treatment of Palestinians as sub-human. I asked him for an example. He answered with what he endured when trying to make a trip overseas for a speaking engagement. It was an ordeal that covered four days, involved fourteen discrete episodes, and ended in futility. He took a taxi out of Bethlehem to the first check point with proper credentials in hand, was refused passage, returned to Bethlehem for a three day wait, took another taxi to the same checkpoint, given approval of the same credentials, arrived at Tel Aviv airport where Israeli security personnel rejected the approved credentials, was denied access to a telephone to reach the airport police, went by foot to the airport police office outside the terminal, was denied entrance there, again was denied phone contact to airport authorities, called Israeli military office with an appeal for their intervention, waited three hours for a response, then received this answer: "No Palestinian is allowed to leave the country today—wait till things calm down," and returned to Bethlehem with unused airline tickets to inform his overseas hosts that he could not come. "This was not Israeli security caused by Palestinian terrorists," he said with his voice rising, "but an example of Israeli denial of his personhood as a Palestinian. It is but one instance of the daily harassment that thousands of Palestinians experience and an example of why Palestinians believe that the ultimate goal behind Israeli policy is the extinction of Palestine and the emigration of Palestinians from the Holy Land altogether." He documented this perception on a broader level with references to such things as the continued encroachment of Israeli settlements on Palestinian land, the Israeli military occupation of the West Bank, and the Wall confining Bethlehemites within the 2.5 square mile area of their city. The trenches, buffer zones, barbed wire, sensors, curfews, pass requirements, and ghettoized atmosphere make life for Palestinians an *apartheid* existence. When I asked how he kept his sanity when pushed to his limits, he answered "I start a new project!" spoken with a touch of humor seeping into his deadly serious narrative. He explained that a new project did not mean busy work as a distraction, but an act of faith solidly grounded in what he called "our theology of the cross, not a theology of glory." His reference was Luther-speak for finding God's hidden power to save and renew through his crucified Son, not in a shallow theology that has no room for the scandal of the cross. His statement was all the more poignant given the context of his ministry.

Raheb walked me through an overview of three projects he had referred to as alternatives to going crazy. One was the International Conference and Cultural Center begun in 2003, a handsome multi-story building adjacent to Christmas Lutheran Church in downtown Bethlehem, funded in large by a $5 million grant from the government of Finland. The second was the Health and Wellness Center, initiated in 2003 by a generous grant from The Wheat Ridge Ministries in the United States and currently served by Rami Khader, the third son of the Bethlehem Khaders. The late Palestinian leader, Yasser Arafat, enabled the Lutherans to acquire the property, but with the stipulation that the land costs would have to be covered and the ample building paid for within one year. Both were done. The third was the combined elementary and high school opened in 2000, named Dar al-Kalima (house of the Word), with its 265 student enrollment equally divided between Christian and Muslim youth. Added to the campus of Dar al-Kalima School is Dar al-Kalima College, which I learned later was opened in 2006 with eighty students, the first Christian institution of higher learning started in the Middle East in decades. A coherent vision joins all three in a holistic ministry, Raheb emphasized, with the intention to raise up a coming generation of well trained Palestinians as exemplary citizens and leaders in all phases of Palestinian life. To that end the elementary, high school, and college serve. The International Cultural Center serves a prime Palestinian need of retaining their culture and the development of the skills to promote it. Thus it offers a full program of conferences, concerts, movies, classes in art, sculpture, music, dance, and courses to train film makers who can transmit the treasures of Palestinian culture through the public media. The Health and Wellness Center, opened in 2003, exists to serve Palestinians whose health and wellbeing suffer the results of constant tensions and violence under which they live. The Center reaches up to 4,000 people annually through fitness programs and exercise facilities designed to enable people to be proactive in taking responsibility for their health, plus clinics offering professional medical care in nutrition, endocrinology issues, hearing loss, and psychological disorders. Community health programs also are offered for elder care, young families, and an ingenious Bright Stars of Bethlehem outreach to promising youngsters to help them discover and reach their potential as productive Palestinian citizens. These three major facets are coordinated under an overarching consortium formed in 2007 to facilitate planning, administration, and funding for a holistic, ecumenical ministry. Its vision is to empower people threatened with the blight of helplessness to see themselves not as victims who react but as proactive youth and adults with a viable future and the means to shape it. As Raheb turned from the outrages of injustice to his ministry which builds lives through hope in action, I could see his whole demeanor change. He does head off going crazy by starting new projects. What he and his staff (starting with four in 1995, now numbering one hundred) have done in less than a decade is remarkable. They embody Divine grace in overcoming obstacles impossible for outsiders like me to fathom. They persevere in doing the best thing Palestinians can do as peacemakers, to build a new generation of Palestinian prepared to connect with their Israeli counterparts on the other side of the Wall as leaders who can chart their own course toward peace.

The conference that brought us together included trips to Jerusalem in which those of us who were not Palestinians were free to travel the five miles to Jerusalem to meet with Israeli peace groups who are vigorously outspoken in protesting their government's policies, who help rebuild homes of Arabs in Jerusalem demolished by Israeli bulldozers, and who find ways to slip across to Bethlehem to speak in conferences such as ours. I heard such an Israeli speaker at the conference on the day following my visit with Mitri Raheb, an articulate and courageous woman whose presentation was a high point of the meeting. For me, as one who grew up in a Christian family with endearing ties to Jews, who has visited the death camps at Auschwitz, Dachau, Buchenwald, and Theresienstadt where millions of Jews perished, and as one who has joined with neighboring rabbis in community service throughout my pastoral ministry, it was important that the Palestinians planning conferences such as the one I attended include Israeli participants. Such inclusion helps dispel the stereotype of Israel as a monolithic state of over six million Jews who support its policies uncritically.

Rehab spoke of key elements in his spiritual development. He went to Germany to earn his masters of theology degree from Hermannsburg Seminary, and later on his doctorate from the University of Marburg. He credited his primary spiritual formation, however, to his hands-on ministry under conditions of crisis in his homeland. He has learned stamina from his people of Christmas Lutheran Church where he began his pastoral ministry eighteen years ago when the congregation was a demoralized remnant of a dozen people. That has changed. It now numbers 300, with Sunday attendance for worship averaging 100 or more, despite the uncertainties of being able to even get to church in occupied Bethlehem. A deeper obstacle is the constant threat of giving up, or moving out if emigration is available as an option. That pressure is palpable daily; people experience it in trying to get to work when passing through checkpoints, when visiting relatives, getting health care (the Khader saga came to mind), and enduring the constant problem of unemployment. He said there are 1835 Palestinian families in Bethlehem who have lost their land to Israeli annexation. In Bethlehem 70% of the residents depend on personal support by families and friends from outside, mostly the USA and Europe. A nation cannot be built upon such realities, he said, and yet his pastoral calling is to defy those odds by constantly shoring up his parishioners by preaching the Word of Christ's grace on Sundays and helping them live it between Sundays.

Regarding my question about the Hamas/Jihad elements of the land, Raheb said that his ministry is not directly bothered by them, though he acknowledged the problem of lumping Palestinian terrorists together with Palestinians in general. His main point: "We attack no one and there is no reason for anyone to fear us or be afraid to come to us and see with their own eyes what we are doing and how networks of partnership can be forged. Come and see!" He meant that invitation; the conference I was attending was witness to the growing global network of those who come to see and return home to communicate what they have seen. Such encouragement from worldwide partners led him to his closing comment in summary of his ministry in all of its aspects: "Grace just happens! We don't command it. It comes as a gift, often as a surprise, always with encouragement."

Munib Younan, 55, is the bishop of the Evangelical Lutheran Church in Jordan and the Holy Land. He is an open, readily approachable man, short in stature, his face unmistakably Arabic in appearance but without the flowing beard characteristic of his Orthodox Church counterparts. If his shoulders seemed somewhat bent, I counted that as part of his credentials as one who has carried the burdens of beleaguered Palestinians of every kind and condition who have found in him one will listen and help. I spoke with him in Bethlehem at the International Cultural Center where his long term contacts with the Church of Finland helped bring it into being. I was aware of his reputation as a decidedly pastoral bishop with a full daily schedule; this made me particularly grateful for his time as well as organized in my questions about three things: his background and calling, the context for his church's work, and his hope for the future.

First, his background. He grew up in a refugee family driven from their home and property three times before he was eighteen years old. That, he said, was an essential in his childhood that helped prepare him to one day lead a church under a Lord who had nowhere to lay his head. When the State of Israel was formed in 1948 his father and the family lost their house and ancestral land in Beersheba, some forty miles southwest of Jerusalem, together with 6,500 other Arab residents in that area. Their properties and possessions in the area where Abraham and Sarah had settled two millennia before had initially been mandated by the United Nations to Beersheba to remain with their Arab owners. The Israeli army's invasion changed that. The Younans lost everything, including their right ever to return to their homes or even to visit the graves of their forbears nearby. They fled to Jerusalem where his mother's relatives took them in, and where, despite their poverty, she insisted that young Munib enter the same Lutheran elementary school in the Old City where she was educated in her youth. The Six Day War of 1967 made Munib and his family refugees once again, this time escaping within minutes of the Israeli bombing of the dwelling they had fled. With their belongings on their backs they found refuge in another village beyond Jerusalem. As Palestinians with Israeli citizenship status they filed suit for the return of the damaged family property and won their case in the Israeli Supreme Court. But the Israeli army destroyed their property once again, in defiance of the Supreme Court's decision, forcing the family to flee once more—this time to Haifa. Younan recounted this family saga of repeated loss and flight in order to underline the impact of *el Nakba,* Arabic for the Catastrophe, the word Palestinians choose in describing their fate after 1948. For Jews the world over the establishment of the State of Israel in 1948 was euphoric. For Palestinians it was catastrophic. The newly drawn borders of the new state made the Younans and thousands of Palestinians like them landless, homeless, and jobless. Yet, for Munib Younan, *el Nakba,* with all its disastrous injustice, dislocation, tears, and death, was not catastrophe alone, but a harsh pedagogy in training him to be a refugee bishop for a refugee people.

His mother's conviction that Munib would benefit from the excellence of Lutheran schools (she worked as a cleaning woman to pay the fees) was significant because the Younans were Greek Orthodox Christians and, in fact, had managed to take up residence in several rooms of the Greek Orthodox convent in Jerusalem. His father made room for Bible study every Tuesday afternoon as an alternative for neighborhood teenagers who were tempted to drink and gamble. The resident priest, aware that young Munib was increasingly active in the sessions, was not impressed and showed it by frequently turning off the electricity. Younan smiled as he recalled this early experience of ecumenism and its problems in a Jerusalem context, but it was part of his early sense of the call to ministry. He finished high school with high marks and talked to the senior pastor of Redeemer Lutheran Church in Jerusalem about becoming a Lutheran pastor.

The pastor arranged for Munib to study theology abroad since there was no opportunity for him to do so in Palestine. Germany was the most likely choice, but as plans were delayed, Munib occupied himself as a volunteer who welcomed visitors and handled messages at Redeemer Church. Among those who came was an American fundamentalist preacher who sought to convince him that what he termed the liberation of Jerusalem by the Israeli army was a glorious fulfillment of a prophecy in Daniel 7. This interpretation was one he could hardly accept as a young Palestinian, confused and smarting under the humiliation of a crushing victory by the Israeli army occupiers. However, the experience did set him off on learning Hebrew to better understand the Old Testament Scriptures. For the first time, he said, he began to think of the Scriptures as a word of God for this time and place, if not as the American fundamentalist had claimed, then how indeed to discern what God was speaking to the world around him? It was a question he had never thought about before. This quest for meaning was more than textual. It was contextual with all that meant for a young Munib Younan yearning for a vocation that could free him from the enclosure, powerlessness, and futility that Palestinians know in their bone and marrow.

Two Finnish visitors, one a pastor and the other a deacon, came to Jerusalem in the spring of 1969 seeking a student candidate to study in Finland as a Lutheran deacon. The Redeemer senior pastor, Hans-Joerg Koehler, introduced Munib as a good choice, and before he could express his choice to study for the pastoral ministry rather than the diaconate, it was decided that he should go. He went to Finland convinced that although the prospects were not exactly as he had hoped, he would trust God to fit the coming opportunity into a broader plan for his calling. Over the next three years he excelled in the diaconal school located an hour north of Helsinki, mastering not only the Finnish language but making good use of the solid Lutheran theology he learned in high school. After finishing diaconal training, he applied for continued study toward pastoral ordination and was accepted. To stay on in Finland he needed an extension by the Israeli consulate of his study visa, which, in turn, meant he had to apply in person before the Israeli ambassador in Helsinki. That prospect of meeting face to face with the Israeli official made him shake uncontrollably as he stood at the street entrance of the embassy. After summoning the courage to enter, he was told that as a Palestinian he would have to secure the visa extension in Israel rather than in Finland. Younan told me that what happened next was surely providential. An Israeli official—he remembered him by name—Michael Ben Yehuda, noticed him, asked about his purpose, and astonished him by declaring: "I am going to help you *because* you are a Christian. Years ago in Italy, Catholics hid me from the German soldiers. They did this at the risk of their lives and I have never forgotten their courage and compassion for me, a Jew. If it were not for these Christians I would not be here." The man inquired further about Munib's future, even encouraging him to go on in pastoral studies and asking for an invitation to attend his ordination when that time came. This was an unforgettable moment of meeting an Israeli whose words and actions were unlike any he had experienced before. Although Ben Yehuda could not attend his ordination in 1976, Younan met him again in 1993 at a reception at the Finnish Embassy in Tel Aviv. They remembered each other and sealed their improbable reunion with a hug. Younan told him that his kindness in granting the visa extension opened the way to seven years of theological study for both his bachelor's and master's degrees. Ben Yehuda's responded: "I am fulfilled. I played a role." That turn of events broadened Younan's experience of Palestinian-Israeli relationships because it was a rare exchange in heart and mind between a Palestinian and an Israeli. Younan drew upon it thereafter in avoiding stereotyped generalizations about those on the other side of the wall.

The Finnish years were deeply formative for Munib Younan. He learned Biblical theology and wrote his thesis on the doctrine of election based on Isaiah 40-55. Initially he hesitated to accept invitations from his fellow Arab expatriate students at the University of Helsinki to talk politics over a beer. Politics was a taboo subject, according to what had been ingrained in him as a refugee continually fleeing the violence bred by bad politics. His early Lutheran training, while sound in many ways, was weak where Lutherans are often weak, connecting theology to life in the political realm. This began to change as his Finnish years continued, however, and what Younan noticed in himself was that as he broadened his vision of God's work in the world, his Palestinian identity deepened positively. He learned more about distinguishing between political ideology and a deeper spiritual engagement with people regardless of their circumstances. Reading Martin Luther's theology taught him to interpret all Scripture from this center—*was Christum treibt*—"that which offers Christ." From the Finns he had learned to apply Scriptural theology contextually, which served him well as he returned for ministry in the Palestinian setting of his homeland. With a Gospel-centered principle of interpreting the Scriptures, enhanced by his studies in Isaiah 40-55 for a Biblical view of God's way among the nations, well grounded in Christian basics learned in Lutheran schools in Jerusalem and expanded by theological study in Finland and—not the least—deeply formed by life experiences as a refugee, he was, by his mid-20's, ready for his future as an ordained pastor of the Evangelical Lutheran Church of Jordan and the Holy Land.

politics

My second question was about the political and cultural context in which he and other Christian leaders work. He answered with six themes, warning me that each deserved more time and depth than was available. Condensing vast amounts of data from United Nations mandates and their violations, successive wars, Intifadas, failed international interventions, conflicts over land and water rights, refugee camps, and Israeli settlements into a half dozen statements, he named the following as essential in understanding daily life in Palestine: 1) Withdrawal of Israeli troops from Arab lands according to the 1949 United Nations Resolutions 242 and 338, 2) the two State solution dating from the United Nations partition plan of 1947 that has yet to be implemented, 3) international acceptance of the reality of both the Palestinian and Israeli states so that both can be free to determine their own future as neighbors, 4) an end to illegal Israeli settlements on Arab land, 5) a just settlement of the right of return for Palestinian refugees driven from their land and the dismantling of the barrier wall which separates them from their rightful homes, 6) a shared Jerusalem among Jews, Christians, and Muslims with open access to the Holy Places by all.

Knowing my own limits in grasping the complexity of these issues, I asked Younan to assess where Palestinians have obstructed their implementation. He began with the obvious, comparing how hard it is for Palestinians to look critically at themselves to asking a man beaten to a pulp by attackers what he's done lately to alleviate gang violence. As a Christian, however, he did have something to say as one who can put humility, repentance, and honesty before God to work, beginning with himself. Palestinians who resort to violence, suicide bombing, firing rockets indiscriminately into Israeli settlements and towns, offend God and defy his will. Returning violence with violence cannot be condoned by Younan or other Christians who confess their own need for daily forgiveness from God. While the Arab proverb holds true that "when you corner a cat it scratches," there can be no peace without cessation of violence on the Palestinian as well as Israeli side. Corruption in Palestinian politics was another fact that deters peace at home and viable negotiation with Israelis. The unwillingness of the wider Arab world of the Middle East to give humanitarian aid to Palestinians who have been refugees since 1948 fuels Palestinian frustration and adds to the general misery of life. Vast migration of Palestinians to other lands, many of them among the brightest most resourceful on the West Bank, has weakened the cause toward a more viable Palestinian state.

What part have Israelis played in this morass of vexing issues? They must answer for themselves, the bishop asserted, but if Israelis can put themselves in his shoes, they might be surprised by what they hear from Palestinians. It is not only the military tanks and F-16s that are the problem, but violence in the form of emotional abuse at checkpoints, the stripping away of human dignity, the violence of denying water rights, homes, and health care, the violence to the human psyche, especially children, all of which come with warfare. There is economic violence that closes people off from their means of livelihood. (United Nations estimates place Palestinian unemployment at 60%, with two thirds of the people living on less than two dollars a day.) There is violence of communication, i.e., the constant media stereotypes of Palestinians as sub-humans who send their sons and daughters off as suicide bombers to kill Israelis. The wall, the settlements on confiscated land, the occupation, are all visible signs of the inner wounding of what it means to be a Palestinian person, and underneath all the layers of injustice and abuse is human sin in the hearts of both Israelis and Palestinians. Younan did not expect people on both sides to come to this diagnosis, but it was his as one who lives under the Word of God's judgment and grace. That foundation gave him something to say about the third area of inquiry, the future and what keeps him going.

He gathered his thoughts around reflections on Christ's ministry, death, and resurrection. Witness means showing forth by word and deed the good news of God's saving work in the midst of bad situations. Such witness activates his belief that God has created all humanity with equal value in his sight and the responsibilities that go with it. His hope for the future? Its anchor is in Jesus Christ, who has made his home with us, especially among the outcast and suffering. In his prophetic ministry, sealed by the Holy Spirit's calling, Younan is a servant shepherd in a church largely composed of people who need a future governed by hope rather than the pain of what they have lost.

Younan illustrated the meaning of witness, both from his personal life and in his role as bishop. He recalled what happened when his nephew, a 38 year old carpenter and deaf mute (employed by an Israeli who held him in high regard), was killed by Arab extremists who bombed the bus he was riding one morning as he went to work in Jerusalem. It was a hopeful time for a breakthrough to peace in 1996; the Oslo accords were progressing and Yasser Arafat and Yitzhak Rabin had shaken hands on the pact at the White House. Extremists on both sides were relentless, including the Israeli who assassinated Rabin and the Palestinians who bombed the bus. Younan went to Jerusalem when he learned that his brother's son was among those killed and called the family together to form a unified, clearly Christian response to the reporters he knew would soon ask how the Younans felt about the death of their relative at the hands of Arab terrorists. Younan quoted from memory his brother's words: "The blood of my son, now mixed with the blood of Jewish children and Muslim children, is shouting for peace and justice in this country. May God forgive those who did this and killed my son." That witness resonated through the funeral service the next day when Younan preached the memorial service sermon, stressing that this was not an occasion to stir passions against the enemy but a time to lift broken hearts to God as people who can grieve in common and forgive each other.

In his role as bishop in Jerusalem, Younan made his witness to Muslims a practical matter of daily life relationships rather than occasions limited to theological dialog. An example occurred soon after he had located his office in the Lutheran Church of the Redeemer in Jerusalem. Local youths had sneaked into the building, broken windows, and when accosted by the doorkeeper gave him a beating. The senior pastor at Redeemer, a westerner, was furious over the incident and told Younan he was calling the police immediately. Younan moved to handle the incident differently, however, without police involvement. He called his Muslim friends to work the neighborhood network to find the culprits, knowing they would respect him for going to them directly. In less than twenty-four hours his friends reported that they had found the kids, and the issue was, as Younan had suspected, vandalism rather than an anti-Christian act. The Muslim friends offered to bring the perpetrators to the church to apologize, but Younan proposed that they come instead with their fathers and uncles for more than an apology. His point was that Christians and Muslims do not vandalize their houses of worship and this was an opportunity to make it not a Christian-Muslim fight but an act of witness to a mutual sense of reverence. The result was that fathers and uncles came with the offending youth who expressed their apologies—plus fifty Muslim business people from the neighborhood who appreciated Younan's understanding of what it means to work out a problem in a manner respectful of each other's traditions rather than inflaming religious tensions. He turned the apology/pardon session into something more valuable yet, further discussion on the spot about Christians and Muslims working together in mutual respect and what that meant for wider cooperation matters of civic and business responsibilities. His European clergy colleague at Redeemer learned an important lesson, one that is urgently needed in the non-Muslim world where Islam is increasingly suspect. He cited three essentials for Christians in relating to Muslims: humility, avoiding needless conflicts based in ignorance of Islam, and solidarity in times of crisis. Regarding the latter, Younan mentioned what it has meant in his ministry to attend Muslim funerals in order to personally express condolences. As he said that, emphasizing how Muslims attend funerals in large groups and as families, I thought of what I had missed when watching media footage of crowds of mourners carrying a casket through the streets. He stressed as well the critical importance of distinguishing between the majority of Palestinian Muslims who disavow the misuse of their religion and Muslim fundamentalists who use Islam for causes that are unsupported by the Koran.

Similarly, Younan emphasized how practical daily relationships and informed knowledge of Judaism permeates his witness to Jews. In contrast to his close contacts with Muslims from his childhood on, friendships and neighborly ties with Jews have been next to nil because of the barriers that have increasingly separated Christians and Jews from each other since 1948 and following. That reality was painfully clear when he literally shook with fear when speaking with an Israeli Jew at the embassy in Helsinki; that surprising outcome has strengthened his resolve to seek hopeful, positive engagement with Jews throughout the years since. Younan regretted that formal theological dialog—trialog when Islam is included—has more often begun from outside rather than inside Palestine or Israel. In Sweden, for example, the Life and Peace Institute of the Church of Sweden began a trialog that was followed up by later conferences in Switzerland under Lutheran World Federation auspices, and a third round in Greece with large international delegations attending. Such encounters are important and he acknowledged the responsibilities for faithful engagement between Christian, Jewish, and Muslim leaders of Jerusalem by the very fact of their unique geography. For example, in one square kilometer of Jerusalem known as the Old City, there are thirteen bishops of various Christian traditions, and a Muslim mufti; in nearby West Jerusalem there are two chief rabbis, one Sephardic (Oriental) and the other of the Ashkenazi (Western) strand of Judaism. Is there anyplace similar, he wondered? Younan has found that while there is a necessary theological impulse for coming together in interfaith dialog, his preferred term for it is the art of dialog. That word speaks to the imagination, gracefulness, perception, and skill needed not only to come together in dialog but stay at it as witness to the power of God to open the eyes of the heart as well as the mind.

Younan longs for the re-emergence of opportunities for closer personal ties between Palestinian Christians and Israeli Jews, reminiscent of opportunities of earlier decades when people of both traditions could come together as friends and families in their respective homes. In his memory was the time when he and his wife, Suad, had prepped their two young children to be on their best behavior when the Younans were invited as guests to a Jewish home in Jerusalem. The rabbi host and family received them with hospitable courtesy and began polite but stilted conversation—to the discomfort of adults and children alike. The Jewish hosts asked if the children might not like to play. On cue, they replied that they were just fine as they were. When the Jewish children asked if their guests might like to see their room, the artificial atmosphere was punctured and soon enough the children were laughing and playing together as children are good at doing. The adults followed the lead of the children and the evening blossomed into a wonderful enjoyment of each other's company and stories, with both mothers confessing that they had over-coached their kids for the occasion. It was the beginning of a friendship. The Younans reciprocated by inviting the Kelmans to be guests in their home, and the mutual hospitality continued into the future as seder and Easter meals were shared. The rabbi and Lutheran pastor had known each other previously as participants in formal religious dialog, but household hospitality and dinner table fellowship opened wider, deeper channels for establishing shared convictions and removing misunderstandings. This is the kind of setting for which Munib Younan is gifted. He has a keen mind and is a well trained theologian. His theological acumen has been sharpened and tested intellectually as well as experientially. But my main impression of him was his capacity to care for people as they are through the love of Christ that is real in him.

Younan has no choice, he concluded with a smile and something of a shrug, but to keep on in his calling as a witness to Christ's grace. He has known its amazing twists and turns since his earliest days as an Arab refugee lad, then as a young student who could complete his theological education in Finland through the righteousness of an Israeli Jew, and now in his years as a Palestinian pastor and bishop fully engaged with the embattled people he serves. His witness does not depend on winners and losers in the political uncertainties of Palestine and Israel but is based in the risen Lord who commissioned his church to begin its witness in Jerusalem and who promises its continuance to the ends of the earth until the end of time.

My learning what Palestinian Lutherans see through their eyes ended with participation in an act of hope. We participants in the Bethlehem conference gathered on our last day to plant trees on a hillside above the Dar al-Kalima campus. It made me think of Luther's comment about planting a tree today if he knew the world would end tomorrow. And so we did, at a place in the world where Lutherans are both as embattled and creative as any I have met anywhere, and at a time when the only seemingly sure thing about tomorrow is more violence. Against that bleak prospect, I found Palestinian Lutherans to be worthy witnesses to the Psalmist's description of the faithful: "they are like trees planted by streams of water, which yield their fruit in its season, and their leaves do not wither"(Psalm 1:3).

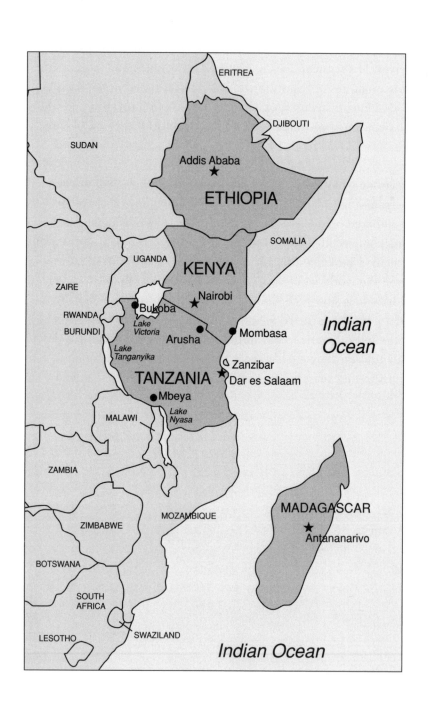

PART 2

INTRODUCING AFRICA

Media-created images of Africa are wildly contradictory. Nelson Mandela is a respected world leader; Idi Amin is a bad memory. Pandemic AIDS stalks the continent; heart transplant surgery which began in South Africa is now practiced worldwide. The heartbreak of genocide in the Congo and Darfur is numbing; the vast game preserves of Kenya and South Africa draw millions annually. No wonder there are those who are afraid to set foot on African soil and others can't wait to get there.

One contradiction, however, both reflects and vastly transcends these contradictions. It is this: despite crushing poverty, catastrophic disease, and chronic governmental dysfunction, (or is it because of them?) Christianity is growing faster in Africa than anywhere else on earth. As the World Christian Encyclopedia reports in its 2001 edition, 23,000 new converts are added *every day* to the body of believers in Jesus Christ. That means 8.4 million annually. As the current annual growth rate of 2.4% continues at a pace unmatched anywhere else in the world, by 2025 the African continent will be home to 633 million Christians, second only to Latin America as the continent with the largest aggregate number of Christians on earth.

What accounts for this? And what can be learned by non-African Christians from this seismic demographic shift in world Christianity that has occurred in the past seventy-five years? The answers are many, but the chapters following provide insights and experiences from African themselves, in this case from African Lutherans. Their testimony counts because they are making a particular contribution to the overall picture of explosive numerical growth that has been fueled largely by Pentecostal Christians. Lutherans offer growth that is inward and sustaining, much needed amidst the unprecedented pace of outward numerical expansion. Their stories often touch upon growth in faith that is essential to discipleship because it is anchored in the Gospel as the heartbeat of the Scriptures and the key to living the Word in the church and daily life in the community. They draw upon the sacraments which continue to nurture souls made weary by poverty and privation. Lutherans continue their historic tradition of establishing Christian schools that train minds for useful vocations. They extend the ministry of healing through hospitals and clinics for the care and healing of the sick.

Although there are Lutherans in countries throughout Africa, those cited here are selected from Ethiopia, Kenya, and Tanzania (as well as from Madagascar, the island off the southwest coast of Africa). It was in these three countries of sub-Sahara east Africa, plus Madagascar, that pastors and laity graciously received me, told me their stories, showed me their work, and were hospitable representatives of the much wider number of Lutherans in the other twenty-nine African countries I could not visit because of the limits of time and circumstance. Their stories remain to be told.

One more note: Beverly was not able to join me on this African trip. I had ten separate airline connections to make during the month of travel. Without her along, I missed two of them.

A daylong stopover in Nairobi, Kenya, was an all too brief break in the trip southward from Ethiopia to Tanzania. It was regrettable not to have more time for interviews and story gathering in the 75,000 member Evangelical Lutheran Church in Kenya. Adding to my frustration was the fact that my own congregation in suburban Chicago has had a long standing link with this church body and other Christians in Kenya and more time there would have been welcome. Since there are 15.2 million Lutherans scattered among thirty countries of Africa, visiting only three of them on this trip had to suffice.

Forest Park?

Chuol Simon Bhan

KENYA

The short time in Nairobi was enough time to reconnect with Chuol Simon Bhan, a young Sudanese whom I had met three years earlier in the same city. He is a refugee from Sudan who is just one among the thousands of Sudanese caught up in the tragic litany of the woes refugees must endure: the loss of family together with house and land, repeated relocation, death from wartime violence, or the slower death that comes by starvation. They live with the constant prospect of becoming non-persons, unwanted aliens, the wards of understaffed relief agencies, and largely neglected by the world community. Much of that is personalized in Simon's story as he puts a face on the plight of the anonymous millions of refugees worldwide. As a boy of 11 he and his family were driven from their village in southern Sudan by the North-South civil war that has ravaged the country for decades. They made it to Ethiopia where they lived in a refugee encampment for six years. Then came the disruption of 1991 with the ouster of the military junta that had forced communism on the country in the early 1970's. In the chaos of that changeover, Simon, now eighteen years old, was separated from his family. Through the agency of the United Nations High Commission For Refugees he was relocated to the Kakuma Refugee Camp in northern Kenya. There he came into contact with Lutheran Church—Missouri Synod mission workers from America who led him to profess Jesus as Lord and turn from the dissolute ways he had picked up in his teen years of rootless living. His chance to leave the Kakuma Refugee Camp came when a fellow refugee who was active in the Lutheran congregation resettled in Australia and sent Simon enough money to enable him to move to Nairobi as a more likely place to realize his dream of an education and meaningful future. When he arrived in Nairobi by bus, he saw a signboard outside the station with an invitation to Uhuru Lutheran Church in the downtown area of this capitol city of two million. There he found his spiritual home, but was still without a job or any means for an education.

On Easter Sunday, 2004, Beverly and I, together with a youth delegation from our Chicago suburban congregation, were at worship at Uhuru Church. During the service I noticed Simon—at 6'7" he is not hard to notice—but did not meet him till afterward when parishioners and visitors gathered for tea and coffee outside the church door. Simon stayed on the outside edge of the circle of hospitality, hesitant as a Sudanese outsider to join in. Then began a kind of dance of grace of which I was only partially aware at first. As I moved among those welcoming us, Simon moved with me from his place outside the circle, never taking his eyes away from me nor relaxing the piercing look of near-desperation on his face. His skin was the blackest of all the Africans present, made so by the Sahara sun beating down on generations of his ancestors. I have seen that look in many faces of people, especially young people, in the developing world. It carried a mixture of hope and resignation, of envy and resentment, a plea for help as well as readiness for the rejection that comes in a gesture as simple as a diverting turn of the eyes. Simon's riveting gaze my way created that split second for decision, whether to turn away or see "with the eyes of the heart," in St. Paul's poignant phrase (Eph. 1: 18)—the kind of seeing that has consequences. Divine love won out in that instant. I met Simon's eyes with my own, and moved toward him, half wanting, half not wanting to hear what was behind those eyes that would not let me go.

We found a place in which to talk. In a torrent of sentences he poured out his plea for help in realizing his dream of an education for a life that could mean something. His words were not polished but came out in a hurried tumble of saying it all at once, fearing that his appeal would be rejected. I heard him out, with no idea whatsoever of what the years of hardship and homelessness had meant to this very tall and relentlessly determined young man, but it occurred to me in that moment that there was a connection between the good news of Christ's resurrection and what Simon was begging me to consider. To be sure, my mind was focused on the dozen teens who were hungry and ready to eat before getting on with our Nairobi itinerary for the rest of the day. There was only time to say that I would be back in Nairobi after a week with our youth visiting a village high school in western Kenya and that if he was serious about further conversation he should meet me at a designated time and place.

The week passed. He met me exactly as scheduled. Plans were made for him to enter a pharmaceutical school in Nairobi that Simon had researched thoroughly among the educational options available. It was a prospect that appealed to him with promise for a medically related future vocation in his homeland. I appointed a Kenyan to be a treasurer-mentor, Peter Khamasali, whom I had known from an earlier Kenya visit and trusted with monitoring the funds made available to Simon. In one week after an Easter Sunday conversation, Chuol Simon Bhan and I bonded in a covenant of mutual commitment. My part was to provide money donated by generous people of Grace Church ten thousand miles away. His part was to use it for service according to God's leading. In less than an hour the pact was sealed and started, a venture of faith with much yet to be learned as to its outcome.

Now, two years later, there was Simon to meet me at the Nairobi airport, accompanied by his mentor and my longtime friend, Peter Khamasali. He was smiling as he wrapped me in an embrace that is memorable when delivered by a tall men with very long arms. We had emailed regularly throughout the two intervening years in accordance with my requirement that his accountability show in his studies and grades that qualified him for a pharmaceutical degree. It is gratifying to report that he has done well in his studies. He has completed his education and has returned to Sudan where he is employed by a relief agency serving those who are now where he once was as an 11 year old refugee boy nearly a quarter century ago.

His most recent letter to me ends with these words: "Let me know if Grace Lutheran Church would like to preach the gospel in south Sudan. I would gladly start a mission church in my home area if I can be of help." His idea sounded far out and unlikely as strategy. But, as African Christians repeatedly demonstrate, the faith is spread by lay persons—in this case a refugee who found his spiritual home while in exile from his homeland. In Chuol Simon Bhan's story lies a hint of why the Christian faith is spreading so rapidly in Africa, in the face of conditions of unspeakable suffering through poverty, disease, and corruption. Or, is this the point that Christians everywhere must learn, that the Good News is truly good news because it speaks so directly to people engulfed by so much bad news?

I keep a photograph of Simon nearby my desk. It was taken as he towered over the entrance to a bare-bones hut in the refugee camp where he spent six years in Kenya. The humble structure is the church where his spiritual formation began. Between its thatched roof and earthen floor are walls of dung and clay, with an artful floral design painted on, and the words: "Welcome! Merry Christmas and Happy New Year." It's hospitable message is easy to miss, even as I could have easily missed meeting and connecting with Simon on an Easter Sunday in Nairobi years before. As I look at that small picture and think about the outsized young man standing beside the door, smiling, the words of Jesus' beatitude come apply: "Blessed are the meek, for they shall inherit the earth." Blessed, as well, are those who get the message.

Ethiopia is mentioned over a dozen times in the Bible, notably in Acts 8 with its reference to the baptism of an Ethiopian eunuch from the court of the Ethiopian Queen Candace. The Eastern Orthodox Church has been established there since the fourth century of the Christian era. The Jesuits brought Roman Catholic Christianity in 1555. The first Protestants were Swedish Lutherans who came in 1866, followed by missionaries from Europe and the United States. Their seed-planting labors have borne fruit beyond their fondest dreams as missionary pioneers whose Gospel proclamation and Biblical teaching led to the establishing of congregations, schools, and medical clinics throughout the first half of the 20th century. In 1959 an indigenous church was formed from Lutheran and Presbyterian roots and given the unique name: The Ethiopia Evangelical Church Mekane Yesu, called by its acronym EECMY in these pages. Mekane Yesu means "the dwelling place of Jesus "in the Amharic language. At its founding in 1959 it numbered 20,000 members. It reached one million in 1991, then more than doubled to 2.3 million in 1997, and reached 4.5 million by 2006 (twice the size of the Episcopal and Presbyterian Church USA combined). It continues to grow annually at a rate between 10 and 15%. It is organized into 6,006 congregations, 1788 preaching places, and served by 1515 pastors and 1788 evangelists. Problems accompany such explosive growth, to be sure, and this chapter takes them into account. Yet, the sheer magnitude and rapidity of the spread of Christianity south of the equator is overwhelmingly evident in Ethiopia, where the surprises of grace at work among Ethiopian Lutherans came to me in the first moments of my arrival in the capitol city of Addis Ababa.

Geneti Wayessa

ETHIOPIA

Acceptance

"That's fine"

relationship

I was nearly twenty-four hours late due to missed connecting flights from Chicago and Europe and had no way to inform my host of the serially changing times of my arrival. When finally I did meet him at the Addis airport I wondered if his several futile trips to the airport to fetch me might dampen his welcome. As I began with apologies he interrupted in mid-sentence with a cheery "No problem" and with a handshake and warm smile steered me to the lost baggage desk of the terminal, a location he knew well from previous experience with late arriving guests.

Geneti Wayessa is a trim, wiry, man in his middle fifties, with a touch of graying hair and a strong face to go with his engaging manner. He reminded me of a younger Sidney Poitier with clerical collar. My first impression of him as one well acquainted with problems beyond airline delays was confirmed as I learned through later conversations that he was orphaned at age five, endured Communist persecution as a young pastor during Ethiopia's tumultuous decade of Marxism, and now has a major role in helping prepare a largely rural church for its mission under new conditions of urbanization. At present 85% of the Lutherans in Ethiopia live by subsistence farming on less than one acre of land, their church contributions sometimes made with grain, chickens or even a cow. Coffee is the only cash crop here, but as elsewhere in the developing world, globalization practices by large corporations deprive those who grow some of the world's best coffee from their just share of the profits. Starbucks flourishes internationally while Ethiopian coffee growers struggle to barely survive.

Wayessa told me of his early calling to teach in an elementary school of the EECMY. He then prepared for the pastoral ministry by attending the seminary in Addis Ababa. His ordination in 1981 occurred on one day, his wedding the next. This was during Ethiopia's dark era of Communist oppression, a time in which all Christian ministries were sharply curtailed, driven underground, or brutally destroyed by arrests of clergy and leading laity and destruction of church properties. He had already learned resiliency of discipleship as a seminarian in Addis Ababa where students formed underground groups for theological instruction and prayer. Theology was not abstract, he recalled, but learning with head and heart, with a dependence upon the Holy Spirit in the African way of keeping the spiritual and physical inseparable and weaving the individual believer into the community of faith. This story from his early ministry indicates how the 1980's era of a tested faith prepared the way for later decades of growth.

With no congregation assignment available after his seminary graduation, he went to an area 150 kilometers north of Addis where he knew of one family of faith in a village closed to the Gospel by Communist political leaders in the region. He arranged to stay in this household for a time, quietly gathering people for house church worship and prayer. Despite the dangers, twenty five men and women joined this underground congregation. Wayessa kept contact with pastoral colleagues and teachers in Addis, knowing he would need their help in preparing these new converts to be well grounded enough to withstand the opposition that awaited them. He drew up a plan for all of them to travel in smaller groups to the seminary for short, secret periods of instruction. Friends and families in Addis accommodated them with food and lodging during their stay, accepting the risk of discovery and arrest by the state police. This lay group finished a course of instruction in Addis and returned to underground evangelizing in an area that had been notoriously resistant to the Gospel. Today, Wayessa told me with an enthusiasm that had not waned with the passing of twenty years, that nineteen congregations now flourish in that region. The story illustrates elements of why the church has grown exponentially: conversion is inseparable from evangelizing, bold witness to the lordship of Jesus needs grounding in Scripture and sound doctrine, the community of believers participate in outreach, persecution sharpens the will to outwit the opposition, and laity rather than clergy are the main messengers of the Gospel.

His stories emphasized the mystery in the ways of the Spirit, whom Jesus likened to the wind which comes and goes with no one knowing its whence and whither. One such story told of a peasant farmer who could neither read nor write—he paused to tell me his name, Dresse Goye, who had received the Holy Spirit's gift of healing and ministered to the sick wherever he found them, people with no doctor or clinic in sight but with ready access to a village witch doctor. Wayessa had seen Goye lay hands of healing on the suffering and saw them healed. That humble peasant healer taught him that the gifts of the Spirit's are not limited to seminary graduates, a point he made without apology for his own seminary education. He added that when he speaks the Apostles Creed and comes to the words "I believe in the Holy Spirit, the holy catholic Church"—Dresse Goye comes to mind as a living reminder of what catholicity means—universal, not limited to one place or form, but wherever the Spirit is pleased to work. Wayessa and his generation of pastors learned to live "with God alone as our help," as he put it, and so he could welcome this humblest of village preacher-healers as a mentor in faith. He noted as well that persecution under Communism was neither constant nor everywhere in Ethiopia, especially in the rural places where Party operatives dismissed the poor as nobodies. Some in the government looked the other way in allowing the Gospel to be spoken, requiring only that it not be done in open opposition to the regime.

There were also prominent Lutherans who inspired Wayessa by open and public opposition to Marxism. Emmanuel Abram, was the head of the

Department of Mines under Haile Selassie's government and part time lay president of the EECMY. He was detained in prison in the late 1970's by the military dictator, Mengistu Haile Mariam. Gudina Tumsa, the General Secretary of the EECMY, was a churchman of towering strength throughout the church during the years from 1974 on when the socialist revolution turned bloody. Wayessa spoke of Tumsa as the Ethiopian Dietrich Bonhoeffer, the German pastor who was martyred in 1945 for his defiance of the Nazis. What made Tumsa particularly influential was his theological depth matched with clear social analysis in leading the church through harrowing times. Like Bonhoeffer, he chose not to seek personal safety through exile abroad as pressures against him mounted in his homeland. In 1974 he was the principal author of a bold pastoral letter addressed to the membership of the EECMY which laid out the narrow path for the church as it lived through the chaos of the Marxist Revolution. The document accepted the reality that the church had to turn over its educational and medical institutions to the government, as was anticipated from the beginning of church-state tensions, but with an appeal to all pastors, teachers, and medical workers to be faithful to Christ as peacemakers in striving for justice under the law. The motive for this is the key point of the Pastoral Letter, a copy of which Wayessa gave me as documentation of what Lutherans bring in times of national crisis. Quotes from it here are given as a tribute to Gudina Tumsa, who four years later paid for his confession of faith with his life:

> In its proclamation and prayer, the Church interprets the situation in which it lives and finds in Scripture an understanding of God's dealing with men. Through His Spirit, the Lord Jesus Christ calls for repentance and announce the coming of the Kingdom of God. It is this kingdom which we must seek above all else. In order to liberate man from the power of sin, selfishness, death and the evil one, Jesus Christ died upon the cross. God is the God of all creation, the God of history. He has called into being a people to serve Him in the world. He liberates this people from oppression, brings them into judgment, defeat and exile, and restores them time and again. God's final judgment and victory will only come after a time of distress and

upheaval. The people of God have been called to discipleship, pilgrimage, even suffering in this world, because true life is found only through suffering and death. The Church is challenged to find itself by giving itself for the true liberation of the whole man. In this, its witness to the Gospel of Christ and its service to man, it teaches that salvation as wrought by Christ must be experienced in this life, but that fullness of life is to be realized at the Second Coming of our Lord and Savior.[1]

"Ask me why and how the church in Ethiopia has grown so miraculously after the 1980's" Wayessa said, anticipating my question before I could ask it. His answer: "because Christians like Gudina Tumsa lived the faith and died for it in the 1970's." Another galvanizing event was an open debate with his brother, Baro Tumsa, a member of the government politburo and an avowed Marxist. It was a heated exchange, made all the more dramatic because it set brother against brother (Matthew 10:36) in a public debate. Although Gudina Tumsa never demanded that his words and actions become the norm for all Lutherans in their response to tyranny, the reaction by the regime to his defiant leadership brought increased persecution of Christians throughout the Western Synod, a prominent arm of the EECMY. Tumsa was imprisoned, tortured, and executed on July 28, 1979, by the Mengistu regime which was overthrown in 1991. It remains as a dark stain on Ethiopia's recent history. Tumsa' legacy lives with inspiration to the church and nation through the Gudina Tumsa Foundation.

I asked Wayessa how is it different now? With something of a sigh he lamented the fact that political freedom has provided soil for a whole new set of problems the sins of backbiting and disunity in the EECMY which are as old as the apostle Paul's problems with the Corinthians and older. Newer problems are financial dilemmas as the church increasingly moves into the cities where cash is required to buy land, build churches and maintain schools. Uniting Ethiopians of two language groups, Amharic and Omoro, is a problem akin to what American Christians know from the racial divide. And then he turned to a new challenge of outwitting a new enemy, not the communist state of the 1970's, but the pressures which urban transition imposes on pastoral marriages and families.

---

[1] Found on the web at "Thursday Theology #396"
http://www.crossings.org/thursday/Thur011206.htm (pp. 2,3)

When pastors and evangelists are worn thin by the exertions needed to reach people in new ways and places with the good news of Christ's redeeming love, what then? Who ministers to the ministers? Wayessa envisions a fresh and timely idea, and his passion has been instrumental in bringing it to church-wide approval for staffing and funding. The Christian Family Life Education program is the project he has been working on in the past several years, with the aim of training trainers for grass roots service in congregations. Initially, 1,500 instructors are needed during the coming ten years. It provides basic Biblical and theological foundations for marriage and family life, and accomplishes these goals through seminars and retreats. It established an ongoing Center for the production of materials and refinement of methods, and fosters the integration of Christian Family life ministry into existing church activities. Wayessa oversees the budget that will sustain this effort throughout the coming ten years. He is realistic about the challenge, but as his "No problem" spirit I experienced at the airport continues, this ambitious and timely program will flourish.

A Sunday in the Addis suburb of Buruyu gave me the opportunity to watch a congregation in action. Seminary faculty member Belay Guta Olam, my host for the day, picked me up early for the drive through crowded roads to our destination. En route he told me of the German missionary had begun evangelistic work in 1841 but was abruptly halted by the connivance of the local ruler and Orthodox clergy. Now, over a century and a half later, in 1992, a mission congregation was begun after careful study by the EECMY leadership. In ten years the congregation has grown to 850

Belay Guta Olam

members, funded their own temporary church structure, established two more mission congregations in adjoining areas, and laid plans for a permanent sanctuary that will house 800 on land made available by the government. The chairman of the board of elders, Mr. Negasa Deressa, neatly attired in a business suit and at ease in welcoming foreigners, gave me a three page summary of the background and present plans for the new sanctuary, a detailed analysis of the $150,500 cost, and an outline of its purpose as a base for worship, education, fellowship, and outreach to an estimated 100,000 new arrivals in the area who are without the Gospel. He stayed with me as my translator throughout the liturgy and sermon, which included something I would have easily missed—bilingual worship in both Amharic and Omoro to accommodate those who spoke one or the other language. Language differences, some eighty dialects are spoken in Ethiopia, translate directly into volatile political tensions across the cultural divide; Deressa helped me understand that bilingual worship is not to be taken for granted.

The worship was spirited with lively singing that Africans do so naturally in hymns both familiar and new to me. Among my lasting impressions of the morning worship was the fervency of the prayer offered by leader of the Sunday School children as he gathered several dozen youngsters around the altar. For a full five minutes he prayed that the Holy Spirit would not only open their minds to Christ and his truth for the hour at hand but guard them from during the week ahead from all evil in their homes and families—including homes and families are already riddled by AIDS and other woes.

Then a wonderful surprise occurred. I learned that a wedding would take place in the congregation after the members decorated the corrugated iron walls of the temporary sanctuary. The men carried the plain wooden benches outside for picnic-style seating while the women prepared the wedding meal. It was an all-out congregation event in behalf of the wedding couple, each recently baptized, each coming from distant villages too far for many from their respective families to attend. The wedding was schedule for 3 p.m. but like all weddings in the history of matrimony, it started late. The first sign of the bride and groom's arrival was the appearance of a rented Toyota slowly making its way across the open field, festooned with wedding ribbons and escorted by three riders on horseback decked out in cowboy garb and raising a hubbub that soon swept up all of us into the moment. The bride and groom were in the backseat, she looking resplendent in her white bridal gown, he looking nervous in his best

Sunday suit. The wedding service lasted at least an hour, augmented by three visiting choirs, surrounding the wedding couple in a rainbow arc of support. Vigorous singing, with all, including the bridal couple, swaying to the rhythmic beat, set the tone of infectious celebration, followed by the wedding vows exchanged in a quieter tone of reverence, followed by the wedding dinner served outside.

It was a moving demonstration of a *Mekane Yesu* moment, a congregation-become-Jesus'-dwelling place. The bridal couple, whose families lacked the means to make the trip, were embraced by their new spiritual family whose support was as palpable as the rented Toyota, horseback rider escorts, the cheering kids, the visiting choirs, the wedding dinner prepared by the women and served by the men. This couple can face their future in Addis Ababa, a sprawling city of over seven million, with their new life together well established in a spiritual home. Would that every couple everywhere could begin their life together on such solid ground and build upon it lifelong.

An afternoon of conversation with a group of seminarians of the EECMY in Addis Ababa provided a mosaic of hopes and concerns among those preparing for a pastoral future. I met first with a half dozen women of the student body who preferred a women-only setting in order to speak more freely. They were a mix of married and single women, in their twenties and thirties, each one tastefully dressed for this occasion which was a first for each of them. These summaries of two of the seminarians provide a cross-section of the experiences of all six.

Ameme Yadeta is a quiet person who spoke only after pauses to measure what she wanted to say. She spoke of growing up a sickly child in a nominally Christian household of the Orthodox Church tradition. The first time she heard anything about Jesus was from her older sister, a situation she regarded as not uncommon in the Orthodox Church which in her experience does not teach children the stories of Jesus. Her first experience of Christian faith that makes a difference came from people in her village who were active in healing prayer and evangelism outreach in the EECMY congregation. They learned of her health problems and invited her to join a women's circle of healing prayer. She has vivid memories of those intercessions which resulted, in her words, "in the disease flowing out of my body so that I could know a relief I never knew before." This pivotal moment led her to continue in the women's prayer circle in ministry to others, an experience that started her on the path to pastoral aspirations and seminary enrollment. Strangely enough, she added, it was just as these life changing events were happening to her that her mother became a Muslim. She had no way to understand it; it was one more reality with which Ethiopian Christians live in a population that is 35% Muslim.

Haile ("My Violet") Yenealem, the ninth child in a family of thirteen, is in her first year of seminary study. She was inspired to study for the pastorate by her parents, both of whom were evangelists. After high school she took on the challenge of two years as a helper to Norwegian and Finnish missionaries serving in a remote desert area of southern Ethiopia. She described how hard it was at first to adjust to primitive tribal peoples who wore nothing, where snakes and other wild animals were a constant threat, where tribesmen regularly rejected her as a woman—all formidable obstacles to a future female pastor in the EECMY. It also made me wonder where else in the world candidates apply for theological study with her credentials. When I asked her how she managed communication and living conditions, it took some coaxing on my part to get her to tell me that she mastered the tribal dialect in her first few months and made do for two years with a tiny hut with no lights, running water or toilet as her place to live. Having weathered those circumstances, my sense was that Haile, as well as her sister seminarians, will meet the obstacles of opposition to women clergy by many male pastors of the EECMY with no illusions about what's ahead. She cited examples of congregations where men ostentatiously refuse to receive the Eucharist from a woman pastor and overcrowd the communion rail where a male pastor serves to make their point. All six concurred that open discussion of the bias against women is difficult to generate in congregations, and that they will be tested as they pioneer a way forward with tact born of wisdom and a patience that comes from love. The women seminarians were neither surprised nor defeated by these realities; they saw them as part of their calling at this moment in the life of the EECMY.

After the women had their say they left the room. Waiting to enter was a group of male seminarians who took their places with some evident curiosity about what had preceded them. Their manner was respectfully courteous, however, and for all of them this was the first time that a pastoral brother had come from afar to listen more than to speak. The highlights of our hours together came in these comments from two seminarians.

Esayas Emene is 30, married and the father of a son. Like many of the ordained clergy, his earlier experience as an evangelist in the congregation was basic to seminary enrollment and his to pastoral ministry. When I asked him what posed the greatest challenge ahead, he cited the need for depth of discipleship among those recently converted, as well as his concern about supporting his family on the meager salary congregations provide—between $100 to $300 annually. He knew that most Ethiopian Lutherans are farming people with limited access to a cash economy, an obvious challenge to his commitment to God's call. It also challenges him to resourcefulness in developing a greater maturity in stewardship among those served. I asked him how as a pastor he would handle me if I was an Ethiopian who came seeking baptism—with my four wives. He studied me for a moment, wondering if I had any idea of the layers of centuries of cultural tradition surrounding the circumstance I imagined. First, he answered, I must understand that the cattle I have to support my family come from the families of my four wives. Then, if I confess Jesus and seek to live faithfully, my wives and I will be accepted together with my responsibility for the care of all four. But no more marrying, since marriage is not given by God for the purpose of increasing the herd of cattle and the income they bring. He said that his father had faced this question and resolved it by divorcing one after seeing to her maintenance, and keeping the other. He then added that the divorce rate in Ethiopia is somewhere under 5%, but that he had heard that it was ten times higher in the United States. How do I handle that? My response was—not very well—but it has to do much more with preparing rather than repairing marriages.

Tsegahun Mikore, 38, single, is a man with a bright smile and engaging manner. He spoke of his background as a Baptist Christian growing up in southern Ethiopia, where he also was an evangelist and Bible School teacher and how he found his way to a Lutheran seminary. When in his twenties he began to realize that he could not maintain the white-heat fervor of charismatic speaking in tongues and healing which are required standards of authentic faith according to Pentecostal teaching. He had come across materials which spoke to his misgivings, an eight week course written

by Herman Dominianus, a German missionary theologian of the
Hermannsburg Mission and veteran missionary in Ethiopia. That interested
me directly, since I had met Dominianus in Germany earlier, and gained
much from him in preparing for my time in Ethiopia. The contacts with
the author of Lutheran response to Pentecostal practices in Africa, plus
this conversation with one who was influenced by it, provided a unique
opportunity to see a Lutheran contribution first hand. That document was
an important influence that led him to enroll in the seminary in Addis. His
story affirmed what Lutherans have to bring to the African Christian experience, Biblical grounding for the work of God the Holy Spirit, centered in
Jesus' ministry, death, and resurrection, for the reconciliation of sinners with
God and each other in the church. This Baptist seminarian also helped me
understand the ecumenical openness of the EECMY to seminarians from
other traditions, a practice consistent with the inter-confessional beginnings
of the church nearly a half century ago.

Following a full afternoon of seminarian conversations I thought the
day had been full enough. But as I sat down for a cup of coffee at the student
kiosk, the most popular and populated place for seminarians to gather, I
met Belaynen Geshere, a 36 year old pastor who was in Addis for a pastoral conference and had stopped by the seminary to talk with the American
gathering stories for a book. I welcomed his inquiry and assured him there
was still time and energy to listen to him. Indeed there was. The sun was
setting and the cool evening air (Addis, like Denver, is at 5,000 feet elevation) settling in made for a refreshing setting as we sat together on a bench,
away from the coffee kiosk and student clatter. He rapidly took me through
his earlier years which resembled the stories others told me, born into a
nominal Orthodox family, father a farmer, who first heard of Jesus through
an EECMY evangelist. In this case, Geshere said, the evangelist intentionally
selected a prominent tree in his village as the place of worship but the
Orthodox clergy contacted the police to have the temporary shelter torn down.
Then followed something startling. The local Muslim leader, after having a
powerful dream, declared publicly that these Christians must not be forbidden a place to worship. This sequence of events moved young Geshere
to devote his life to Christ and ministry, a decision confirmed in a vision
three other believers experienced separately as assurance for his call. He

went to the seminary with support from villagers and returned to this area, trained twenty evangelists to work with him voluntarily, formed a new district of self-supporting congregations, taught the faithful to tithe their Teff crop (a grain native to Ethiopia), and told me that now, two decades later, there are 150,000 Christians in 110 congregations served by ninety-five pastors—a very high ratio of self-supporting congregations with their own pastor. Are there problems? I asked. Sure, he answered. Muslim opposition has set in despite the mullah who gave the church new life in a perilous time, and the opposition can become violent. To date five EECMY Christians have died from physical attacks. And the woeful famine of several decades back caused widespread starvation. By that time full darkness had set in and no lights were near our meeting place. We spoke our prayers and parted, leaving me grateful that our paths had crossed and I had one more glimpse of the grace of God at work among his Ethiopian children.

Itaffa Gobena is the president of the EECMY. He was elected in 2001 and is in his second four year term. I spoke with him last because I wanted to learn all I could from lay and clergy Lutherans before hearing his overview of the church he leads, as well as his joys and burdens as a leader. He is 63, married to a former teacher for thirty five years, and the father of three adult children. He has the manner of one who is at home with himself, without airs, yet he imparts a sure sense of knowing both what he knows and doesn't know about being the spiritual leader of one of the largest and fastest growing Lutheran churches in the world.

I must have surprised him at the outset of our conversation by asking him who his pastor is. He paused to think about it, then answered: "I don't really have one presently. Formerly I did, a Pentecostal layman who prayed with me at least once a week, either by phone or in person—but he's gone now and, I guess, I need one." It says something about him that he did not take offense at the question, as if a foreign guest had no business asking about such matters. I explained that I had been welcomed so fraternally since my first five minutes in Ethiopia that I felt I could approach him as a brother pastor, older than he by a decade, but aware of how much I need a pastor myself. It was a good start to an important hour together, and gracious of him to give me time on his schedule.

His spiritual beginnings fit the common pattern I had heard from many: nominal Orthodox parents, farm family, and from southwest Ethiopia where Lutherans are more numerous. When he was a boy of ten, he met a blind evangelist who told him a truth he had never heard before, the Good News from John 3:16 of God's saving love in Jesus his Son. The evangelist had walked the fifty miles from his home area, preaching the Gospel as he went. He helped Itaffa Gobena enter a mission school and high school. After graduating he was spiritually adrift, he said, but then had what he called "a spiritual course correction" through another Pentecostal evangelist who made a strong case for the empowering presence of the Holy Spirit. Later, when starting in his first calling as a teacher in a mission school, he thought about the contrast between his life and the evangelist's description of what happens when the Holy Spirit indwells the heart. He had been teaching the Book of Acts, and the 19th chapter account of the disciples of John who had never heard of the Holy Spirit gripped him and kept on gripping him until he joined yet another influential layman in Addis who prayed with him. A transforming experience of the Holy Spirit's indwelling fell upon him. He began speaking tongues. He was thereafter, in his words, "different, I can't explain it, I was just different."

By 1970, with the Marxist revolution beginning to unsettle Ethiopia, Gobena considered entry into a technical school, but then changed his mind. He worked as a carpenter till the end of 1970 when an American missionary asked him if he would join her as an interpreter and helper in preaching and teaching. During this time, in fact on a Monday night late in 1970, he felt God's call to ministry and fought it with every excuse he could think of. The crisis of it all put him in the hospital for three days. He finally gave up and gave in to the Lord's calling and after a series of further encounters with God's Spirit through prayer, preaching, and revival among youth, he came to Addis in 1975 and began seminary study. The area to which he was assigned as a student worker gave him preaching and social ministry experience, plus the all-important work of training others to evangelize. EEMCY congregations grew out of those beginnings in the mid-1970's. He estimated that there are now over 300,000 Christians in that district. In 1981 he was elected to his first church leadership post, jut as the Communist Derg (Marxist military cabal that overthrew Haile Selassie) cracked down on the churches. Gobena was accused of being a CIA agent, arrested, beaten up badly, threatened with execution, but was spared death by the sudden action by the jail warden who, without explaining why, arranged his release—an experience that to this day Gobena attributes to the intervention of angels. In 1984-85 he studied theology at Wartburg Seminary in the USA, returned as coordinator of mission and theology until 2001 when he was elected president of the church body.

He named these things as his main burdens: insufficient inward growth in soundness of faith as the church rapidly expands outwardly, conflicts in the church which come from imitating the spurious teachings of sects and self-made prophets, and the difficulty of engaging the Orthodox Church in meaningful dialog.

What gives him joy in the work? He spoke first of what I heard from every leader and lay person in some form or another: the joy of living as God's child and servant, free in Christ's grace to believe the good news and share it openly. Then he said something distinctively Ethiopian: "We of my generation have experienced so much blessing that others before us could only foresee by faith—doors opened and believers formed by Christ's Spirit in astonishing ways and numbers. Fifty years ago our parents were tortured, chained, humiliated, and in some cases murdered for the sake of the Gospel. Now we see the fruits of their faith and that is our greatest joy."

We shook hands, spoke our prayers for each other, exchanged a hug, and were off on our respective ways.

The Evangelical Lutheran Church in Tanzania, with its 3.5 million members, is the largest Protestant church body in this nation of 37.2 million. Lutheran work began at the turn of the 19th century when missionaries came from Germany and Sweden. The strong contingent of German missionaries was largely expelled during the World War I years from 1914–1918. Missionaries from the United States came to help fill that gap from 1922 on and joined with six other Lutheran mission agencies in laying the groundwork for the formation of the Evangelical Lutheran Church in Tanzania in 1963, two years after national independence was gained. The principal seminary of the church, Makumira Lutheran Seminary, was recently merged with other educational divisions of the church to become Makumira Theological College. It is located in Arusha and is the largest Lutheran seminary in Africa, serving the ELCT as well as candidates for pastoral ministry from surrounding countries and Asia. The ELCT is the one Lutheran church body in the country.

TANZANIA

Before getting to stories of Tanzanians, here are first impressions of the people scene as it unfolded before my eyes during the hour ride in from the airport to the city of Arusha. I describe this because of something learned from years of global travel: take in the first day impressions of a country but don't allow them to be off-putting. This is especially important for one like myself, coming from affluent America to the sharply contrasting sights, sounds, and smells of East Africa. The hour's drive in from the Arusha airport to the city provided a kaleidoscope of people, mostly people walking the red dirt paths on both sides of the roadway, men and women, young and old, backs perfectly straight as they carry packages, buckets, bundles, whatever—on their heads. Those not walking ride in busses filled to overflowing, or are stuffed into taxi vans with eye-catching names like God's Favor, Yesu Ni Kwama, Hot Stepper, Allah Akhbar, and so on. When the airport shuttle van gets stuck behind a battered truck trailing bluish black clouds of exhaust fumes, one must take heart that this, too, will pass. One must not miss the meaning of people, who, if not walking, are standing, sitting, or lying down, so many of them young. They are signs of those who have left farmlands worn out by overuse, who flock to towns and cities for jobs that are hard to find. There is a wonderful variety of color and style of dress: women with elaborate head wraps, men and boys with stocking caps despite the tropical heat, little kids wearing nothing or whatever is available in families living on a dollar a day, older youth in school uniforms, police men and women in their official gear, businessmen (but rarely women) impeccably dressed in suits, shirt and tie, and shoes shined. A sight to marvel over is that of women, bent over at a right angle, planting, hoeing, picking, tending the land and its yield, and other women sitting together under a shade tree or umbrella, flat on their bottoms, legs straight out, making people like me wonder how they can do that for hours. And in all this jumble of humanity, there is something deep in the African psyche, the sense that people belong to each other. People congregate for any reason or no reason, just to be together, smiling or glum, greeting each other with a hand-slap, high five, or a thumb wrapped around a thumb. These are signs of the African sense that one becomes a person by belonging in community. There are other signs that signal other realities of African life, evident in the plethora of advertisements for burglar alarms, security fences, and guard services which thrive because nothing can be left unlocked, unguarded, unwatched. A ride from the airport in to the city can be more than getting from Point A to Point B. It can be an introductory glimpse of the enormous, fascinating complexity that is Africa.

In the 1950's a medical dispensary of ten beds and limited medical services was all that was on the site that later became Selian Hospital. In 1985, when a young American graduate of Harvard Medical School, Mark Jacobson, arrived through a cooperative arrangement between Lutherans in Tanzania and the United States, he took over the dispensary which had grown to twenty beds but still had no

Mark Jacobson

electricity or running water. Instruments had to be sterilized over a hibachi stove. This was the only location offering even minimal medical services to people in the surrounding area of 200,000. When I arrived for a visit twenty years later, Selian Hospital had become a full service hospital with multiple buildings and a 120 bed capacity, situated on well-kept grounds with a full staff of Tanzanian doctors, nurses, and office personnel. I arrived early, in time to join the full hospital staff for morning devotions, wondering as I sat down among them where else in the world the entire medical staff begins the day together with prayer and Scripture led by one of their number. Jacobson presided over a morning briefing on medical matters for the day. I was introduced and welcomed, then stated briefly why I was there and brought greetings from my home congregation. With that, all were on their respective ways to the duties of the day, including Mark Jacobson who was almost out the chapel door when I reached him and asked for a time to interview him. He gave me his cell phone number (cell phones are everywhere, also in Africa) and suggested I call him for a time that fit both of our schedules a week or so later. Before parting I mentioned my relation to Wheat Ridge Ministries as a former board member and continuing advocate for this Chicago-based Lutheran agency which seeds medical and related ministries worldwide. He knew it well and I made a note to bring it up a week later when we met again for conversation in the Lutheran Guest House in downtown Arusha. He began with reflections on what it meant to him to grow up in a family where he learned from the example of his parents that responsibility goes with privilege, and service is the mark of faithful living. As a youth he was open to the pastoral calling, but after high school and acceptance at Harvard in the early 1970's, during an era of student activist protest of the Vietnam War, he turned to the study of law. He found that too impersonal and lacking in hands-on opportunities for serving people and switched to medicine. Upon graduating from Harvard Medical School, his father, active in retirement with the Gideon Bible Society, took him along on a visit to Tanzania. That proved decisive for his emerging sense of vocation which he defined as the fit between one's gifts and human need for those gifts. With a future medical mission in Africa in mind he took several years of additional study in public health at the University of Minnesota and Johns Hopkins. By 1985 he was exceptionally well prepared to return to Africa to use his gifts for meeting the needs in Tanzania he had not forgotten in the ten years since his father took him for his first visit. The Lutheran Church in America called him to begin community based health care at the dispensary in Arusha; over the past twenty years he had led the work that has made Selian Hospital a major health center in Tanzania, which together with neighboring Malawi, has the lowest number of physicians per 100,000 people in the world.

As I set out from the centrally placed chapel building for a look around the hospital grounds and buildings I had the good fortune to meet Gabriel Kimirei, an actively retired pastor of the Evangelical Lutheran Church of Tanzania (ELCT) who came regularly to minister to patients, especially those with AIDS. When he spotted me as a stranger, uncertain about directions on the hospital grounds, he took me under his wing with his welcoming manner and his fluent English. He wore a University of Oklahoma baseball cap at a jaunty angle as if to counterbalance the clerical collar and suit he was wearing. After looking in at various places in key buildings, he invited me to sit down in his office for the first of several extended interviews which provided a gold mine of seasoned insight into ministry in Tanzania.

He was born in 1940 in Arusha, of non-Christian parents. As a boy with no opportunity to go to school, he spent his time looking after his father's goats. His only association with religion was a piece of ear jewelry he was told to wear but about which he knew nothing. That odd ear adornment caught the attention of a German missionary who, upon meeting young Gabriel, yanked the symbolic jewelry off his ear and told him he should go to school. When Gabriel asked how that could happen, Missionary Reusch answered that he would take care of the school fees himself, and added without further explanation: "Don't come back till I tell you!" Thus his early life took a sudden, providential turn, initiated in one stroke by an authoritarian German Lutheran missionary, who, as he recalled, "was honored like a father and obeyed without question." He showed promise as a student in elementary and high school. Then came his call to the ministry and four years of study at the Makumira Lutheran Seminary, where he graduated in 1971. The seminary and church leaders recognize his gifts and recommended him for a scholarship and continued pastoral studies at Wartburg Lutheran Seminary in the USA for another four years.

He recalled his first Sunday in Dubuque, Iowa, where he and another African seminarian found their way to a Lutheran congregation and had their initial experience of worship at a typical midwestern Lutheran church. No sooner had they entered and taken their place in the pew alongside a couple, than the pair got up abruptly and took their seats elsewhere in the congregation. Kimirei said that he had not even noticed what had happened, let alone understood its meaning. When his fellow student whispered an explanation of what was going on, he recalled two distinct and lasting impressions. One was sadness at being rejected in a place where Christ was named Lord of all nations. The other was the determination that regardless of what this couple thought, "they'll have to get used to us." It was different among the students and faculty of the seminary, he added, where he found acceptance and lasting friendships, a sign of grace that was a welcome oasis in the desert of racial unease running throughout the United States in the volatile 1970's. He returned to Tanzania for his first pastoral assignment, followed by eight years of specialized ministry in producing Biblical and other materials for congregational use. From 1980 until his retirement in 2003 he assisted the bishop in a wide range of duties among the Arusha area congregations of the ELCT. During his 45 years of widespread pastoral experience the ELCT grew from under one million to 3.5 million. His account of what brought about such unprecented growth included these: the Gospel motive for loving people, lay leadership in evangelism, congregational emphasis on literacy at all levels, healing prayer in casting out evil spirits, the congregation as an oasis for care and preventive education regarding AIDS, Jesus' priority upon the poor as hope for impoverished people, and church hospitals such as the one in which we were meeting.

At our second meeting at a coffee shop in Arusha, he told me another story that featured Joseph Kibira, Tanzania's most famous Lutheran bishop and the first African to reach international prominence in a term as president of the Lutheran World Federation. Kimirei's eyes twinkled as he took me back in his memory to a unique experience soon after he was underway as a newly ordained pastor to students at the seminary in Makumira. He had come to know a young woman whose gifts for teaching and preaching stood out in a day when no women were in the teaching or preaching office of the ELCT. He encouraged her to enroll in the seminary and she

75

did. Word of this novel development came, first to the local bishop and through him to the general bishop and universally revered ELCT leader, Joseph Kibira. Kibira wrote a strong letter to young Kimirei, instructing him to stop Alice from any further teaching or preaching, and asking him: "who are you to encourage this Alice to do such a thing that is not allowed by the word of God?" Adding to the dilemma was the fact that Bishop Kibira sent a copy to the local bishop, Stefano Moshi. Something of young Kimirei's spunk was evident in the letter that he wrote back to Kibira, carefully avoiding any direct confrontation, but nonetheless rephrasing Kibira's question with a subtle twist: "Who am I to stop the work of the Holy Spirit in the heart of one of the faithful daughters and servants of Jesus Christ?" Before posting the letter, however, he went to Moshi for advice on how to settle a potentially explosive situation for one so recently ordained. Moshi told him he was right in recognizing the work of the Spirit in Alice, but also right in not directly confronting the general bishop of the church. He suggested this way to come to terms with Kibira, and the memory of the conversation was so vivid, Kimirei quoted the words verbatim: "This is what you do. Arrange a meeting with Bishop Kibira. Post yourself inside the door of the room where you are both to meet. When you see that he is entering, before he can say anything, kneel before him, kiss his feet, and declare your respect for him in his bishop's authority." Kimirei did as advised. He recalled Josiah Kibira's pleased response: "Now, that's better!"

Kimirei knew that this was not a resolution of the matter, but it was, in his words, an African way of dealing with a matter that could not be solved while Kibira was in office and exercising the influence that he had. Meanwhile, what happened to Alice was a detail that I forgot to ask about, as Kimirei went on to recall a moment in 1985 in Germany, when he was in the congregation as Kibira preached on the occasion of the 400th anniversary of the Augsburg Confession. Kibira noticed Kimirei and, after the Service, embraced him warmly and asked him "if he had stopped that foolishness more than a dozen years ago?" Kimirei told me that he greatly respected Kibira as a great leader with a pastoral heart, and revered him as "the walking bishop" who would readily walk to the most remote villages and go house to house, visiting, encouraging, and comforting people who were under his charge. But Kibira could also be stubborn and unbending regarding the role of women in the church, and thus, as Kimirei said with a hint of knowing humor in his eye, it would have been good for Kibira if he might have had a Nicodemus come to him at night, telling him that the Spirit of God, like the wind, blows where the Spirit wills, with no one knowing whence or whither. Before Josiah Kibira died, women were ordained in the ELCT. That was a sign of true greatness in a powerful leader, that he could remain teachable by the Holy Spirit, who is, Kimirei observed, the chief teacher in the church.

In a conversation some days later, missionary professors at the Makumira Lutheran Seminary, James and Judy Bangsund, filled me in on aspects of Gabriel Kimirei's ministry that he was too modest to mention. By their account, he weathered many a storm in dealing with clergy misconduct in high places, including shady money handling and dereliction of duty in administrative responsibilities. It was Kimirei who held things together and made things work in those days, they said. In my brief visits with him, brief though they were, I could sense the qualities in him of which they spoke.

In my second meeting for conversation with Kimirei, I felt there was enough fraternal trust between us to open up a question that increasingly vexes the relationship between African and American Christians of the mainline denominations, the ministry to and with homosexual persons. I put the matter before him not as an abstract theological issue but in the form of an actual pastoral situation in my ministry some years ago. A man came to see me in my study who introduced himself to me as one who has been quietly visiting Grace Church for some years, listening carefully not only to what was said in sermons but how it was said and to what end it was stated. He said that he is a gay man who has experienced two painful extremes in his life as an adult. The first is outright rejection in a congregation and denomination to which he formerly belonged, a wounding experience that drove him from attending any place of worship at all. It also set him on a path of anonymous sexual encounters in gay bars and other modes of cruising. This also was a way of life that has left him wounded and empty, and he did not need me to tell him its emptiness and futility. He then asked me directly: can he be accepted here? If not, why not? If so, how so? He made it clear that he sought no special terms apart from the Law and Gospel of God. He asked if he would be received as a homosexual person with no prospect for change in his sexual orientation, but also as one whose desire to live the Christian life is sincere. I told Kimirei my response: "welcome to the family of forgiven sinners, where God takes us where we are but doesn't leave us there." I then asked Kimirei what his would be.

He began by acknowledging the distinction between sexual orientation and sexual behavior. Why some of the same sex are attracted to each other is not known; the Bible doesn't clearly speak of this condition. What the Scriptures do address clearly is our behavior, and both heterosexual and homosexual promiscuity comes under Divine judgment. So far, agreement between us. What he named as the African problem is burying the whole matter under secrecy and taboo. Without acknowledging the presence of vast numbers of homosexual men and women throughout Tanzania and well beyond, the American problem, on the other hand, was to meet in church conferences called on this subject, clash violently, and then go ahead with unilateral pronouncements and sanctions of homosexual behavior regardless of the impact on other Christian communities in other lands, Africa in particular.

He then made a truly wise statement not often heard in discussions on controversial subjects. "Before you can understand the culture and context from which I come, you must come and live among us—only listening and not talking—for as long as it takes for you to learn how we think and understand what we say or don't say. And I must do the same with you." He noted that the western way to deal with such matters is to write books, publish articles, and absorb what others say on the subject, but not to actually take one's place in the location of the other. In Africa it is different. Two things are happening regarding homosexuality. The first is a real and deep hostility, even hatred, for homosexual persons. The second is that there is no inclination to ban such persons from the community. Furthermore, he explained, the traditional African way to deal with the homosexual person, still part of the community, is that the elders of the tribe instruct him to go to a sorcerer or witch doctor. There he must make sacrifices to the spirits, so that he can be released from the curse that is responsible for his condition. I asked what if he does all that, but is still unchanged in his condition? With a shrug of his shoulders he answered: "Then the next thing that will happen is that he will be beaten severely." This, he added, is the hard thing about African culture that outsiders find so difficult to understand. He did not defend the culture he described, but cited how deeply it is embedded as the culture in which the church lives and works. It was time for our conversation to conclude, since ambulatory patients and their families were forming a lengthening line outside his office door waiting to bring him their needs and receive the ministry he brings. We parted with prayer, a warm embrace, and the agreement that continued contact by email would be mutually worthwhile.

A follow up conversation with Dr. Mark Jacobson took place a week after my hospital visit. He described plans for an ambitious new seven million dollar hospital addition soon to start on land donated by the ELCT and funded mainly by Lutheran congregations (I was surprised to learn that a few have Tanzanian members who are millionaires), Rotary International, and other philanthropic organizations. In this connection he pointed out a positive aspect of Tanzanian culture. When someone rises economically the expectation is that increased support will go toward a hospital like Selian as part of the obligation to take care of the immediate and extended family. In response to my inquiry how Wheat Ridge Ministries in the United States might help he spoke not of funds for the new hospital but support for extending Selian's network of medical care to outlying areas where marginalized people lack such resources. His image for the holistic mission of the hospital was an African three legged stool—good medical care, culturally relevant health education, and sound theological motivation uniting all three. Life and health in Africa are understood in terms of relationships, a cultural trait that stands out in contrast to western individualism. Without missing a beat he quoted II Corinthians 5:19 from memory as basic to what Selian Hospital is about— "God was in Christ reconciling the world to himself, not counting their trespasses against them, and entrusting to us the message of reconciliation." He followed the quote with this remarkable story.

A young Maasai herdsman, in his early 20's, was tending cattle with two others in the Serengheti plains area, several hundred miles west of Arusha. At nightfall they surrounded themselves with a protective thorn encampment and went to sleep. Sometime in the middle of the night three lionesses jumped the corral for the cattle. The three arose and chased two of them away. But the third turned on one of the men, caught him first by the shoulder and with one swipe of her paw tore away part of it. Then,

Donors

Cong

Family

having pinned him down she went for his head, encasing it in her lethal grip—with the teeth of her upper jaw penetrating his skull, within an instant of killing him. Drawing on generations of hunting, the other two managed to kill the lioness before she could finish off their companion. They then fashioned a sling in which to carry the half dead herdsman through the night to the nearest main road. There they hailed a lorry carrying charcoal. They piled him onto the open truck bed and began the fifteen hour ride to Arusha, comforting their wounded friend as best they could as the lorry bumped along the road. As the lorry came near the hospital entrance it broke down. They borrowed a wheelbarrow to wheel the exhausted, nearly dead herdsman through the Selian campus gates and into the emergency room. Then the emergency medical team went to work immediately. Three weeks later, Jacobson went into his room to tell the young fellow he was ready for release. He then told me this: "Every day I've been here getting the care that saved my life, I've looked at the cross on the wall in front of me and wondered what it means? Can you tell me more about this Jesus of the cross?" Jacobson assured him that he could. He left Salien Hospital a baptized man with not only a healed body but a new life through the good news of II Corinthians 5:19. "That's what we're about," he said in conclusion.

On the subject of AIDS, Jacobson thought that the disease may be reaching the crest of its wave in the region. There are parts of Tanzania where it is leveling off and other parts where this is not so. He was grateful that the ELCT had moved beyond its earlier condemnation to the point that now every congregation connected with Selian is a caring congregation. As this continues, he mentioned that 300 of the 600 pastors of the Arusha diocese of the ELCT have been trained to welcome persons with AIDS with love and compassion and to make the local congregation the focal point for the surrounding community to gain accurate knowledge of prevention and modes of care. Such instruction is now part of what confirmands learn in their classes. Jacobson cited AIDS as *the* issue of this generation, medically as well as spiritually, and if the church loses it calling here it misses its prophetic calling altogether. He spoke of the daily tension he feels when confronting the endless array of human problems in an environment that courts despair and he acknowledged his frustrated reaction to conditions that need not be as they are. The hapless disarray continues because there is insufficient will to change it.

The other side of what he feels daily is that Tanzanians are so accepting of foreigners like himself, whom he described as "a Type A personality in a Type B culture." It is the durable patience of Tanzanians around him that keep him going when fatigued and lifts him beyond anger when it threatens to take over his emotions. As a veteran of twenty years of medical practice in Tanzania he has come to accept his role as a "native foreigner" as he put it, sometimes ripped apart by being in two worlds and other times encouraged by creative bridge-building that occurs unexpectedly. A recent example: he spent a two day seminar with pastors on thinking outside the box, in this case, introducing the concept of hospice. "Every pastor got it in a matter of minutes" he said with admiration for the ways in which the Gospel leads to more immediate application in a culture formed by a priority on mutual care than one driven by a market economy. This gives him joy in the work and enables him to draw upon that instinct that led him to switch from law to medicine years ago at Harvard, the hands-on opportunity to make a difference daily in those he serves.

He pulled a photograph out of his billfold as a visual sign of hope in his vocation. It showed seventeen young fellows, all AIDS patients surviving on medication, smiling, and looking fit. He made it clear that Selian is open to short term volunteer doctors, especially retired physicians who have more time and means to come over for varying lengths of service in their medical specialty. He said how much he wants to tap into that reservoir of doctors in America who are unfulfilled professionally and looking for something more. Next week a plastic surgeon was coming who would be busy for a week with cleft pallet cases. Others come for a month or a year. And some, who come in good faith but unprepared for the incidence of two to three children dying each week, find that they must return.

What sustains Mark Jacobson, by his own words, is the providence of God that is over him daily through his wife, Linda, and their three daughters. The morning prayers with the hospital staff provide daily bread for his soul and the team spirit of there is the fruit of those prayers. I gladly add this footnote on the outcome of the coffee shop conversation in Arusha; Wheat Ridge Ministries has responded with a major grant to Jacobson's proposal for extending medical care to rural villages in Tanzania. Epidemics that threaten children come in all forms throughout Africa, including that of teachers worn down by oversize classes, wretched facilities, and inadequate salaries which can drive them to give up, or come to school drunk if they come at all. Against that dark reality are faithful teachers, with heroic commitment and solid pedagogical skills, who are devoted to the daily good of their students year in and year out. They carry out their calling minus the educational amenities that their western counterparts take for granted.

Joyce Lwakatare personifies such excellence in Tanzania where she has been the teaching principal at Kibeta English Medium School of the ELCT in Bukoba, a town on the western shore of Lake Victoria. She is in her early fifties, slender, with closely cropped hair framing a face that seems bland at first but turns warm with animation when she speaks of her 275 students. She made time for me during a morning break in classes, joined by two American teachers, Beth Hinsch and Gayle Kliever, who came to the Kibeta faculty on a two year teaching program via the Evangelical Lutheran Church in America. Joyce, now in her twenty-fifth year of teaching, with fifteen of them at Kibeta, was particularly keen on showing me the computer lab in one of the classrooms, a rarity in the area where internet cafes are scarce. She knows that such skills are essential for African students who must compete in the cyber-world that connects everybody everywhere, having experienced that wider world through five years spent abroad. She and her Tanzanian Lutheran pastor husband, Phineas, lived in Germany where he served as a pastor in a partner parish program with the Lutheran church in Germany. At the time of our meeting she spoke eagerly of her plans to visit schools and congregations in New York City through arrangements Stephan Bouman, the ELCA bishop of New York City, whose son, Timothy Bouman and his wife, Erin, had taught at Kibeta for four years. Her enthusiasm about coming reflected her primary and passionate interest, good education for Tanzanian youth.

The conversation inevitably turned to AIDS and how schools and congregations of the ELCT are facing this massive threat to the entire population of the continent. She was straightforward about the responsibility of Kibeta to educate students, parents, and the community on how the disease is contracted and prevented, including the use of condoms. The policy of the school is to urge abstinence until marriage, and the growing awareness of AIDS is an influence to wait. For students who do not, she said, the church cannot be the arbiter of every moral decision. She expressed concern about the growing influence of Muslim business people in Bukoba who are aggressive in using their money and status to spread Islam. Her best response is to let the story of her own Christian roots speak for itself in her leadership role in the school. Her father was a pastor, the first Christian in his family, whose baptism of his own father was an event Joyce remembered from her childhood. It took place outside, under a large tree that was believed to shelter ancestral spirits who required food, money, and beads, to be offered there as a sign of respect. As she recalled, her father believed none of this, but chose the location as a witness to the ancestors of the new life that the Lord Jesus brings. As I listened to her account of that turning point in the line of her ancestors, I sensed how generously the strength of her father's faith flowed down to Joyce and through her to the many young lives she influences.

Our walking tour of the school included a visit with Sister Fraisca Kweyenga, a Lutheran deaconess whose previous years of congregation work with women and youth serves her well in her present Kibeta School assignment of teaching and care for the youngest students, some of whom were orphaned by AIDS. Deaconesses have long been a staple in Lutheran church life and mission in Tanzania from the late 19th century arrival of German missionaries who brought the diaconal tradition with them. Though their numbers have diminished since women have been ordained into the pastoral ministry of the ELCT, they are still valued for their spirit of service as well as known by their gray and white attire, much like their German counterparts, to this day. Thus when Fraisca welcomed us warmly at her door, she was in the gray and white dress of her calling and ready to tell me about her principal work at Kibeta, caring for twenty-five

Fraisca Kweyenga and child

61

Sacrified *mission* *Aids*
grief
Suffering
Ugh!

of the youngest children of the school who have lost their parents to AIDS. Her credentials for teaching about the disease reach far deeper than her academic preparation, which included a year and a half of education and English language study in neighboring Uganda. When I asked about her family and early schooling, she made brief mention of her parents and upbringing, then moved directly to the calamitous series of events compressed into the last ten years of her life. He sister died of AIDS at age 35, leaving four children. Within a year of her sister's death, her husband died of AIDS. Then Fraisca's brother died of AIDS two years later, followed by the death of his wife from AIDS, leaving their young son without parents or house to live in. In less than a year after the death of his daughter and son and their spouses, Fraisca's widower father succumbed to AIDS. In just over five years Fraisca lost all the members of her immediate family and took on the care of the five young children left in her charge. She told me these things with a steady. soft-spoken voice, in sentences unbroken by the staggering emotional toll of what she was describing. I was speechless as well as humbly awed by her strength in mothering five of her siblings' orphaned children in the few years that five of her closest family died. *The Unfinished Task (movie)*

I could understand Fraisca's words but not the layers of shock, loss, grief and dismay that lay beneath them. The abstraction of AIDS deaths, estimated at twenty-five million new cases annually in Africa alone, became human and immediate in the person of the deaconess in front of me, telling her story. She embodies that vast, anonymous company of those who care for and mend the broken families riddled by pandemic death on a scale comparable to the Black Plague that wiped out a third of the population medieval Europe. How does she do it? I asked. Again, in measured, even sentences without overstatement, she told of her dying sister's plea to care of her children and her promise to do so. When she made that promise, Fraisca continued, she had no idea of how she would keep it, nor could she know of the other child added to her care when her brother and his wife died. As she put it, her promise rested on another promise. With a clarity both beautiful and profound in its simplicity she spoke her trust in God's promises which are all Yes and Amen in Jesus, as she learned from the Scriptures and finds it confirmed in her experience.

She was eager for me to meet two of her nieces who were waiting outside, the two whose school fees at Kibeta were being covered by an American pastor in New York. In they came for handshakes and words of welcome in English, soon followed by a troop of other laughing, smiling students who shook hands, giggled, and were happy to pose for a picture—followed by more hoots of delight when each saw herself on the camera replay screen. What were her chief satisfactions? I asked. She answered—the joys found in loving her kids and offering hands-on hope to students at Kibeta who need somebody to exemplify what it takes to live through the monstrous heartache they've already felt. Her chief problems? Poverty all around and the woeful lack of means needed to help the youngest and most vulnerable. But ultimately, Sister Fraisca is an heiress with more to give than material wealth. It was upon faithful ones like her that Jesus pronounced the beatitude: "Blessed are the meek for they shall inherit the earth" (Matthew 5:5). And what do the indomitable meek like Fraisco do with the earth they inherit? They care for it, tenderly, and against all odds, persevere.

A light rain was starting when the American teachers, Beth Hinsch and Gayle Kliver picked me early for a Sunday at a congregation a half hour beyond Bukoba on a lumpy, red dirt road beginning to get slippery as we stopped along the way to give a lift to some parishioners walking to Ntomah Church. It was the Sunday before Ascension according to the church calendar. Five months had passed since Chistmas. Nevertheless the strains of Silent Night played over the tape player turned up loud enough to greet us as we disembarked and were greeted by Pastor Elmerick Kigembe, who promptly handed me a white alb (which fit me surprisingly well) as the guest preacher for the joint service with three surrounding congregations and their pastors participating. Worship began at 10 a.m. sharp as an elder delivered three loud sounds on the ceremonial drum placed on the veranda just outside the entrance doors. As we clergy processed down the aisle the nave, which seated some 350 or more on wooden benches, was about three quarters filled. The first four rows were occupied by youngsters and guest youth choirs, with all present singing the familiar Praise To The Lord with not quite the gusto I heard later in the hymns of African origin. There was no organ or keyboard to accompany the hymns or the liturgy which was beautifully chanted by Pastor Kigembe, who, I was surprised to learn, had been ordained just three months earlier. I was flanked on either side by pastoral colleagues who were careful to see to it that I had a copy of the Swahili hymnbook which I could not understand, to be sure, but filled with a sprinkling of venerable Lutheran chorales, side by side with hymnody of African origins. I was introduced to the congregation; the epistle and gospel for the day were read by lay readers, interspersed with singing from both guest choirs and announcements that went on at some length. I was told why: detailed financial reports were given that reflected the stewardship of each congregation so as to increase a competitive spirit for the prize awarded to the congregation with the highest contributions. The prize was awarded on the spot. It was a drum which the winning congregation kept for a year. Three successive years of being first in stewardship meant that that congregation could keep the drum, an arrangement which I found intriguing and well suited to its African context. By this time the first hour of worship had passed and all seemed enthusiastically engaged in the stewardship theme which was featured on this Sunday. The Bukoba area congregations, I was told, is well known for its stewardship which is good news to an ELCT perennially strapped for funds.

The sermon text I chose was the first three verses of Psalm 100 with its call for all of God's people of all the earth to sing in praise of his mercy which makes us his own. As Kigembe translated me into Swahili it struck me that my textual choice was one that resonated well with these Tanzanian Lutherans for whom singing comes as naturally as breathing. They are Africans, after all, and sing with gusto, rhythmic swaying, in beautifully harmonized voices, without instrumental accompaniment and mostly by memory as far as I could tell. The worship of God is always enriched by someone from outside, in this case from far outside, and the hearty response to my words made me think that a preacher from an ocean and a continent away was not an every Sunday event here. The Eucharist was celebrated, with the four pastors serving and the fact that the people received by intinction (the wafer dipped in the wine) not hard to understand.

Following the benediction the congregation gathered outside where pineapple, corn, sugar cane, and various home grown vegetables were auctioned off by several of the men who were good in keeping the bidding lively and in good humor. This was another example of stewardship with a creative flair, and throughout the forty five minutes of auctioning each purchase was carefully noted in a ledger book. During that time, various youth confirmands gave their pastors (all four of us seated in prominent view) their confirmation record books to record their presence. Everyone enjoyed the occasion as men chatted with men and women with women (who outnumbered the men by three to one) and deaconesses stood by in their neat gray dresses set off by a white collar and cap. It was a memorable sight and another reminder of how natural it is for Africans to gather and enjoy the sheer fact of being together.

Two Tanzanian women, within a half hour of each other in the Bukoba region, exemplify ways in which the church finds its distinctive calling in serving people with AIDS, the pandemic threat to Africans wherever they are on the continent. They are presented here side by side, one as a director of an orphanage serving abandoned infants and the other as a leader in a church-wide program of congregation-based education toward prevention of the disease.

Within a short walk from Ntoma Church is a cluster of single story buildings on well kept grounds. The first thing to catch one's eye are the clotheslines off to one side from which several hundred cloth baby diapers were flapping in the breeze like banners heralding the important work done inside the buildings. The Ntomah Orphanage is an independent but ELCT-connected haven for thirty infants who have been placed here by single mothers who cannot care for them. Presiding over their care is a force of nature, Evangelina Kamazima Mahamba. She is a woman in her fifties, short in stature, dressed in a white skirt and navy t-shirt, and blessed with an engaging, outgoing manner. She knows about troubled beginnings personally. Her mother was a Christian, her father a tyrannical man who tried to sell Evangelina for

Evangelina Kamazima Mahamba and infant

65

marriage at age nine. She ran away from the home (from which her mother had already fled) and was sheltered in the family of a pastor in Bukoba. While in her high school years she began working under the tutelage of the German deaconesses who had founded this orphanage earlier. They were instrumental in sending her to The Bielefed Mission House in Germany from 1968–1972 where she earned her degree in pediatric nursing, after which she returned to Ntomah where she has served since.

She told us her story as she was taking us from room to room, stopping from time to time at a crib to explain that this infant had been found in a sack along the roadside, that one had been brought in by the police. When I asked her for a profile of a typical mother and what brings a woman to the point of abandoning her newborn, her answer was straightforward and non-judgmental: most mothers are students in their teens, abandoned by their boyfriends, rejected by their families, without job or means of support. Evangelina described her own son who had fathered a child out of wedlock during his medical student days, and after two years of makeshift arrangements for the care of the child asked the orphanage to take over— which Evangelina did without hesitation. This story had a happier ending than most. The child is now back in the household. Her son is a doctor, and things are going well.

When an infant arrives with some family connection, an agreement is signed requiring a family member to visit at least once a month. Evangelina added that after three months the family visitations usually begin to drop off, then eventually stop entirely. She and her staff of two nurses, assisted by ten workers, tend to the thirty infants at Ntomah until the baby reaches eighteen months. At that time Evangelina visits the child's family herself, if the family is known, to inform them that it is now time for them to take over. If that does not follow, she then makes arrangements for adoption, sometimes to an overseas family that meets the government standards. The ELCT cannot provide support for this remote Lutheran oasis of care. For years Evangelina has sustained the support of the orphanage herself, primarily through continuing ties with European sources, particularly from Germany whence the founding deaconesses came. She took pride in showing me the vegetable gardens and fruit trees on the orphanage grounds which help put food on the table for the staff. and took time to explain in detail the Rube Goldberg-like setup of storage tank and connecting pipes which turn cow manure into bio-gas as a fuel supplement for the cooking stoves in the orphanage kitchen. Evangelina Mahamba is a woman whose early life experiences prepared her to turn crisis into opportunity in the face of daunting odds. Toward the end of our afternoon visit she introduced me to her husband who, as a retiree, keeps busy in maintenance chores on the compound. She spoke of their three children, one a doctor, another a nurse and the third a midwife, as signs of Divine grace in her own remarkable life journey and symbols of the hope she has for every newborn in her care.

Judith Bukama represents a wider scope of ministry that picks up where Evangeline's orphan ministry concludes. She is an assistant director in an ELCT program that coordinates ecumenically with other church groups in equipping congregations as major care providers for children orphaned by AIDS. When I walked into her second floor office Bukoba she rose from her desk and welcomed me with a giant bear hug, then settled into a well prepared account of how essential the ELCT is to the nation at large: 45% of the health centers in Tanzania are under the auspices of the church, in previous decades nearly all of the elementary schools were under church direction, and the church has been in the front line of social work in establishing institutions for the mentally and physically handicapped, the deaf, the blind, and orphanages well before the AIDS pandemic. The distinctive mark of Christian work is Christ's unconditional love as motive, as indicated by the fact that 70% of the orphans served by the ELCT nationwide are not Lutherans.

I had to talk fast to steer Judith from the statistics she had in hand to her personal story. She paused long enough to shift gears to her childhood in a troubled household where she was traumatized by witnessing her father's attempt to kill her mother. She managed to escape to the safety of a relatives' family, but had to struggle to put the chaos of her early life sufficiently behind her to be able to concentrate on her studies. Her perseverance was rewarded. She completed her training as a teacher and later became the headmistress of a special school for girls needing an educational bridge from poor schools in poor areas to higher levels of educational opportunity. She pioneered a new curriculum which gave girls a vision of acquiring skills to become nurses, social workers, or the altogether new opportunity of being self-employed as business entrepeneurs. She beamed when telling me that she keeps up with many of the 600 graduates who are now living productive lives throughout Tanzania, and mentioned two in particular.

One came from a pastor's family where she was never allowed to smile. Judith sensed the loveless beginnings from which she had come and in talking with her was alarmed by her readiness to commit suicide. She conferred with her teaching staff for a student best suited to befriending this girl by sitting with her for the daily morning and evening prayers at school. After three years of patient friendship offered by Leonida, the more mature student asked to mentor the troubled student, she began to open up, smile, and participate—in Judith's words—"not as a zombie." She then pointed to a decoration on her office wall, a gift from the girl brought back from the brink who told Judith of her thanks for rescuing her from destroying herself. As she recalled the memory of that student and how things turned out she smiled broadly and said that every telling of that story brings goose bumps, this time included.

One story led to others that she was glad to recall, appreciating the novelty of this kind of interview that set her to thinking again of girls become women of whom she is proud and who give her hope for her church and nation. She spoke of pastors who had make a difference in her life, those who take time to visit homes, not only of Lutherans, but of all who need them and welcome their prayers and encouragement. She spoke critically of pastors and workers in the church who narrow Christ's unconditional love to Lutherans alone, neglecting them as well if they bring little besides their troubles to the congregation. Judith said that her leadership in the agency means exhorting her support staff of thirteen who, in turn, reach out to 200 field workers, to keep Christ-given love uppermost as they reach some 17,000 households a year who are in some way involved with families riddled by AIDS. Most of the field workers are volunteers, among whom are many who are alumni of Judith's care program. Her agency is known among the 1.2 million population of the region as HUYAWA, but the best identity is not in the name but in the reports outside evaluators bring back from their contacts with those served: "they visited us, not to demand, not to criticize, but to listen, to care, sometimes just to notice us and say hello." As our conversation was concluding, she rose to tell me of a Tanzania way of seeing guests off properly. She put her arm around my waist and mine around hers, and off we went, up the path to the to the gate, talking as though we had known each other for years.

Missionaries from overseas are still needed, not only as witnesses to the fullness of Christ's body, the church, but as those who see with the eyes of cultural outsiders what those within the culture can miss. This is an art which does not come simply by being an outsider; it comes from years of listening, learning, and loving people enough to speak the truth in love. James and Judy Bangson have earned the right to do so through their twenty seven years as missionary educators on the faculty of the Lutheran seminary in the town of Marumira, not far from Arusha. He teaches Old Testament. Before they were called to Africa, she was a nurse and musician as well as ordained to teach homiletics and serve as student chaplain.

This congenial couple invited me to their table for food and candid conversation on the ups and downs of their calling. Among the ups: the promising young faculty members contributing their vitality of mind and spirit to students who will soon lead congregations throughout the church. These younger faculty colleagues are signs of hope, and no small reason why the Bangsunds want to return to Tanzania after their several months on home leave in the USA, to begin in several days. The downs: concerns about motivation for ministry that makes it a stepping stone to status and the petty, divisive jealousies that inevitably result, instead of the willing spirit of service which unifies and brings joy in the work. Another concern had to do with quirky efforts to develop a whole African theology around ancestor reverence that too easily becomes ancestor worship, and the folly of Lutheran luminaries abroad who are overly sensitive to cultural context and under-equipped in sound theology. The example he cited came from a recent campus brouhaha. Before preaching a sermon proclaiming Christ's grace as sufficient to deliver from the fear of punishment by ancestors, he purposely wrote it out and made it available to the campus community because he knew his vulnerability to accusation of being an outsider who doesn't understand. The sermon did indeed cause an uproar among some students who took up a petition to have him expelled. The effort failed. Hearing his recall of the incident provided a reference point for seeing how missionaries as outsiders to a culture bring needed prophetic critique from the Scriptures, an often thankless ministry without which the church, wherever it is in the world, compromises its calling to be the conscience rather than the captive of its cultural surroundings.

Is there a Tanzanian version of the traditional-contemporary challenge in liturgy and hymnody? According to Bridget Kijogo the answer is yes, based on her awareness of church-wide trends as principal of the Ruhija School of Music, where students from ELCT congregations come for a three year course in church music. She made a three hour trip by bus to meet with me at the Bukoba headquarters building of the Northwest District and began the conversation with the story of her background. She was born in Bukoba, one of eleven children in the household of her father who was a pastor with special music gifts of his own. She trained as a midwife after high school, but encouraged by memories of her father playing hymns on the harmonium at home, enrolled at Ruhija, took her diploma there, went to the Philippines for three years to study Asian church music as well as major in composition and choir conducting. It was not an easy task to relate Asian rhythms and instruments to her African musical heritage, yet she valued the experience which both broadened her knowledge of other worship traditions and sharpened her awareness of the power of her African music roots.

After returning to Ruhija in 1998 she became the principal of the school and settled into her vocation of writing more hymns that carry an African feel as well as introducing standards that foster good music in the church. The ELCT hymnal, already six years in use, has some African hymns but not enough, according to her preferences. She took a dim view of some contemporary church music from outside Africa that she regarded as shallow textually and musically anemic. She sang one to demonstrate, explaining that the heavy repetition of the phrase "Jesus is coming, Jesus is coming" lacks any witness to why his coming is needed and the salvation hope his coming brings. In her view, electric guitars are unsuitable in congregations. Better to let African drums carry the beat that touches African souls. She is glad for the mostly positive reception given her students in congregations where they serve after graduation, especially among youth who continue the unique practice of choir competition on Sunday afternoons several times a year. Kijogo spoke of the attraction of these events in areas well populated with Muslims. Christians are unique, she said, in coming together to sing of the lordship of Jesus that means more than winning a ribbon in a choir contest. She cited an experience of noticing a Muslim girl who stood outside the church door, too shy to come in. But over time she moved from being an outside listener to a believer who professed Christ and took her place within the choir of the congregation. Music was the medium through which that conversion occurred. She also spoke of what singing the comfort of the Gospel means to people surrounded by poverty and disease. It is natural for Africans to sing at home, outside, at work, at school, wherever— but for such singing to be more than a palliative that numbs the spirit there must be truth that nerves the soul for active discipleship. What puts a song in her own heart, she said, was not only the music she sings and writes but also the students, ranging in age from 22 to 40, who are preparing to serve congregations where singing the faith outlasts the silence of despair and suffering all around. As we parted she gave me the latest CD from Ruhija School of Music as a reminder of a conversation with a gifted musician who helps keep the church singing.

How to reach the growing number of youth in Tanzania who are caught between the times of their grandfathers who once tilled soil as landowners and the present when their grandsons who cannot make a living on the overworked land leave for the city where unemployment rates exceed 50%? That scenario was not an abstraction but the life situation for so many youth who are the concern of Jackson Mushendwa, the Coordinator For Youth And Student Ministry of the ELCT. He's 40, pastorally experienced, and street smart through close contacts with youth in his region. He explained that the word youth applies to those between 18 and 35 in Tanzania, but more important than chronological age is the vitality he finds in their singing, dancing, and lively participation in congregations where his ministry takes him. He spoke of the increasing influence of Pentecostal ways on Lutheran youth, making them question if they are truly Christians unless they can

71

speak in tongues, work miracles of healing, or outshout each other in prayer. He smiled at my telling him of my bewilderment when once sitting amidst such a cacophony of praying voices and suggested that I not take that as the standard among Lutherans who were taught to pray by German and Scandanavian missionaries disinclined to shouting to get God's ear. In Mushendwa's view, the emphasis on the Gospel message rather than exotic ways of expressing it is what Lutherans have to contribute to the wider good of African Christianity. Let African Lutherans be African, however, he emphasized, and "don't expect us to stand still when we sing or pray in liturgical sentences crafted in Stockholm or Wittenberg or some Lutheran seminary in Iowa" he added with a wry smile.

How, then, does he connect Lutheran theology with ministry to youth? His first reference was to baptism and, as he put it, "the full Jesus who comes in the Holy Spirit's working through this sacrament." Then he followed with the point he often makes, that the Spirit's gifts through baptismal grace differ, as the New Testament teaches. He helps youth understand that those varied gifts may include speaking in tongues, driving out evil spirits, and healing, but that each comes from and points to the foremost gift of the Spirit, which is Christ's cross as the power for a new life with other believers. He illustrated this by a story about a troubled girl who came to him for counsel. Her mother had died years ago and her father remarried. In her sleep she kept dreaming of her stepmother coming to kill her, till the problem became so severe that she left home to live elsewhere. In ministering to her, he said, tongues and clamorous praying only distract from the consoling mercies of Christ she needed. Mushenbwa arranged for other youth in a Bukoba congregation he had previously served to include her in their circle of payer and friendship. That association proved healing over time, bringing gain to the troubled girl as well as he supportive friends.

This experience prompted him to expand this pastoral experience into a paper he was now writing on the Gospel core of the gifts of the Holy Spirit. As further preparation he contacted Pentecostal and Roman Catholic, Baptist, and Anglican pastors in the area, inviting them to come together informally for shared experiences in outreach to youth. He learned the necessity of building trust with each before a group could be formed, and though it was taking time he counted it worth the effort it took as a pioneering venture of contact between otherwise isolated clergy. An unexpected invitation by the Pentecostal pastor to address a meeting of forty Pentecostal ministers was a sign of promise for his cause. He had met with them for a day filled with many questions but one that ended positively with more agreement on basics than loose ends on differing ways of applying basics. It was gratifying, he said, to know that in this bridge building experience he could hear them say, among other things, "Maybe you Lutherans, too, are believers!"

Such a turn in our conversation had more than anecdotal interest. It indicated how the action in one local setting speaks to the broader calling for Lutherans in Tanzania, and well beyond, to be more and more of a confessional movement within the Body of Christ, not emphasizing denominational separation, but faithful engagement with fellow Christians to help each other grow in mutual spiritual nurture and common participation in God's mission into the world. It is local initiative, of the sort Kushenbwa was describing, that is urgent.

Regarding the focus of his mission, he named jobless youth as a primary concern. Bukoba, in the Kugera region of western Tanzania, is largely agrarian, like so much of Africa. But with overpopulation on overworked land, youth face a future already marked by 60% unemployment in many cities. Two years ago the ELCT initiated a program borrowed from the Church of Sweden whereby youth contribute to a common pool of funds available for loans for vocational education and small business startups. Soon, Kushenbwa noted, thirty-six leaders were to meet in Bukoba to strategize on efficient loan administration. This sense of mission also requires coordination with government oversight, a task growing more and more complicated by the fact that when Tanzania became independent in 1967 there was one political party. Now there are sixteen. Political differences affect decision making in congregations where youth are now encouraged to speak up instead of remaining passive before their elders. Kushenbwa himself has gone to congregations to appeal to elders to open up to their youth. Doing this, he added, has required a thick skin and ready supply of jokes to get ease tensions and make headway.

Such a conversation with one overseeing youth ministries cannot omit AIDS, a subject about which he had these things to say. In contrast to the decades of the 1980's and '90's when denial and reticence were disastrous choices of ELCT congregations, the disease is now openly addressed and education programs are in place throughout the church. Because of economic problems, youth are marrying later and therefore must come to terms earlier with their sexuality as a part of life. Regarding sexual intimacy before marriage, older clergy teach that is sinful if practiced before matrimony, with the result that most young people do not talk with them about it. With pastors who are more open to what goes on, youth do seek out pastoral guidance which can be effective, if pastors will do as much listening as talking. While abstinence until marriage is preferred, when it is not followed then the next best counsel is to be faithful to one person. "As pastors we need to educate young people more thoroughly in the faith which is centered in Christ's transforming love and help them learn to truly enjoy life under God's grace." That was his summary of what builds moral behavior. Rules alone won't do it.

Before leaving Bukoba, I had the benefit of time with Bishop Elisa Bubewa and several of his assistants as they welcomed me in the church office building only a few minutes from the shores of Lake Victoria. The principal subject was what fostered the remarkable growth of the ELCT. Bubewa offered these reasons, again listed here as he spoke in brief sentences—each one of which could be the subject of extended comment. 1) African people have always been religious in some form, open to the world of the soul and spirit, thus providing fertile ground for the Gospel here. 2) African society is rich in family ties which can be of positive when one member embraces the faith and others in the family follow. Conversely, as in eastern Tanzania where Islam is strong, one member converts to Christ but is rejected by the family and becomes isolated from further opportunity to witness the new life that the Gospel brings. 3) Africans have an innate sense of community whereby the individual becomes significant because of membership in the community. Thus, in Bubewa's own life experience, the strength of Christian community was real to him as he grew up in a Christian family, became a teacher, then a pastor in a congregation. His calling was enhanced by three years of further study at Wartburg Seminary in America, which served him well when he took up his duties as a bishop. At each step of the way he felt the support of the surrounding faith community, so that numerical increase in numbers is not an end in itself but a means toward a deeper belonging with others in readiness to witness and serve.

What do Lutherans offer? Again, his comments were succinct: Jesus, crucified and risen for our salvation, the Bible centered in the Gospel, preaching and teaching a gospel centered theology that builds a bridge to cooperative work with other Christians, a heritage of educating laity in congregations and schools of the church. What do Lutherans have to learn from other believers? From Roman Catholics, he said, "we admire their way of incorporating obedience to the Lord into an orderly life in the church, illustrated by the greater frequency in church attendance than Lutherans." From Pentecostal Christians, Lutherans can learn more about the person and work of the Holy Spirit.

His final point was more than the last on a list of subjects he had jotted down in anticipation of my visit. It had to do with the way we—all of us who belong to Christ's body and therefore to each other—can work together. It was not about what others can do for us, but what we can do together. He paused for a moment to search for a single word to sum up his key point, then smiled as he added: "For you whose language comes from Latin roots, the key word would be something like 'interdependence'. For us who are at home with language taken from life as we live it, it would be this." He rose from his chair, not to speak, but to show me an African way of greeting, first thumb wrapped around thumb, then little finger around little finger, then a handshake, then an embrace. I had seen it done as friends met along pathways or at bus stops. It was a surprise for me to receive it from a bishop, but this was Africa. It fit the moment well. It was felt, not just heard. It brought together in a single gesture the wealth of all that had been given me during my African days, in a way of greeting and departing that every African could understand.

Where else in the world can one walk into a Lutheran church at 6:15 on a Sunday morning and find it already filled to the doors with 3,500 people—and more hurrying in to find a seat before the Service began at 6:30? It happened in Antananarivo, the capitol city of Madagascar, that thousand mile long island off the south-west coast of Africa.

MADAGASCAR

W e were hardly prepared for this sight that greeted us as we approached 67ha Lutheran Church (oddly named by its real estate lot designation in downtown Antananarivo). Cars and pedicabs filled the surrounding streets and sidewalks, and vendors were out early hawking their wares as streams of neatly dressed parishioners, many with children in hand, made their way to the church. The building was sizeable but was architecturally unremarkable with its gray concrete sides supporting a squat tower topped off with a cross painted bright blue. We entered to find the vast sanctuary filled to the doors, fifteen minutes before the 6:30 a.m. service began.

It was Pentecost Sunday morning. We were seated in the front row before a wide chancel area, with the altar dressed in red colors for this festival day. Above it were the words in Malagasy from Ephesians 2:20—"Christ Jesus himself the cornerstone" a reminder of the truth more important than the exterior architectural style. The service began with four clergy, robed in white albs with Pentecost red stoles, processing down the main aisle, while the 100 members of the choir were already in their places aside the chancel, joining with the organist in leading the congregation in the opening hymn.

The liturgy was familiar in its form and made us feel at home despite the language difference. The preaching was soundly textual. The pastor's wife sat next to me, and translated sermon highlights on the fly, enough to provide the main theme of the varied gifts of the Holy Spirit, all centered in the crucified and risen Jesus as the power for faithful living through hard times.

Following the sermon, lines of worshipers came forward to the chancel from various sections of the nave to place their offerings in one of four large receptacles, blue for local needs, red for special causes. After prayers and the liturgy of the Eucharist, a second series of processional lines brought nearly four thousand worshippers to the altar area to kneel for communion. Both actions combined took over an hour of the three hour Service. As these took place the choir sang anthems ranging from Bach to the traditional Malagasy hymns in which the congregation joined in strong voices, many singing from memory as they waited their turn in the processional line. Following the benediction, a spirited singing of Handel's Hallelujah Chorus by the choir concluded the service.

I met afterward with the senior pastor, Peri Raisolandraibe, and asked first whether Pentecost Sunday accounted for the packed sanctuary, the full choir, plus two more services scheduled for the day, one at 11 a.m. and the other at 3 p.m. No, he answered, this was not unique, but typical of the Sundays throughout the year. He added, however, that tomorrow would be unusual. Pausing momentarily to make sure of his statistics, he told me that on Pentecost Monday, 128 would be baptized, 48 confirmed, and 20 weddings would be performed—information I received with no small amazement and wished for more time to learn how 67ha Lutheran Church does it and where it fits into the larger picture of the astonishing work of the Holy Spirit among the seventeen million population of Madagascar, the ninth poorest nation in the world.

The day before I had begun to learn of extraordinary things, both blessings and burdens, in the larger scope of Malagasy church life when listening to Dr. Endor Modeste Rakoto, the president of The Evangelical Lutheran Church of Madagascar, the sole Lutheran church in Madagascar. He welcomed me in his office of the headquarters building in Antananarivo and began our conversation with a sketch of his own family background which he described as typical of many of his generation. His grandparents were the first Christians in the family. They came from the south of Madagascar where most Lutherans live. His mother grew up a Roman Catholic, the largest among the churches of the land, but joined with her husband in the Lutheran Church after her marriage. Modeste grew up under her strong influence, evident in her persuading him to begin teaching Sunday School when he was seventeen and continuing into his twenties. His first inkling of a pastoral calling came through an event that made him chuckle as he recalled his

Dean Lueking and Endor Modeste Rakoto

teenage overconfidence in judging sermons. He attended a special service that drew thousands from all around his home congregation, but was so irked by the poor preaching that he was sure he could do better. Prompted initially by impatience he later grew into a more seriously inquiry into what it meant to become a pastor, much to his father's displeasure who had plans for his son's more lucrative career through a university course in which he had already been accepted. The fact that the Lutheran seminary delayed overlong before sending any response put him in an increasing quandary, so that after months in limbo, he packed his belongings to go to the university and please his father. It was when he was literally walking out the door of his house that the letter arrived with word of his acceptance into the seminary student body. He saw the timing as a test and a sign of God's call. After four years of theological study he received a scholarship for a master's degree at Luther Seminary in St. Paul, Minnesota. He returned home for four years of teaching at the national Lutheran seminary, then went again to America to earn a doctoral degree at the Lutheran School of Theology in Chicago.

I asked him how many Lutherans there are in Madagascar. His answer was surprisingly candid: "I don't know—somewhere between two and three million." He went on to explain that accurate statistics are not easy to come by in a church body where many of the 1,200 pastors serve multiple parishes and mission outstations, sometimes as many as nineteen in rural areas where membership statistics are imprecise. He acknowledged the importance of a church wide census, but counted it more urgent to find and train more candidates for theological study in the six regional seminaries and one national Lutheran seminary. His attention was clearly on quality rather than quantity in the pastoral ranks. A major problem he cited was the attraction of Pentecostalism with its appeal of spectacular signs and miracles to win convert, but without solid spiritual anchor to hold believers in a well grounded faith. Given this context, he named sound theological education as the best contribution Lutherans are making to the ecumenical church in Madagascar, with soundness defined as the Christ's grace for sinners as the centering truth of all that the Bible reveals and the key to interpreting the Scriptures in the church. This, he said, is how the church today continues the faith and doctrine brought by the first Lutheran missionaries from Norway in the 1860's, followed by Lutherans from America in 1888 and thereafter, who laid the foundations for the national church body.

Modeste spoke openly about problems in the church, including those imported by tensions among Lutherans in Europe and the United States. Having recently returned from meeting in Sweden with Lutheran leaders from around the world, he expressed dismay over an agenda overloaded by sexual ethics, homosexuality specifically, but short on attention to the mission to the impoverished and war-ravaged peoples in Africa and elsewhere. He reduced the vexing complexity of what he had heard in Sweden to a one sentence summary of how it is in Madagascar: "Here we know that homosexuality exists as a condition some people have, but we forbid communion to those who act immorally in ways forbidden by the Bible." It was a telling and oversimplified summary, indicating the gulf between Lutherans south and north of the equator. It brought to mind similar conversations I had heard in Africa. Modeste agreed that the need is urgent for Lutherans to be mutually teachable as well as unequivocally faithful to Christ's lordship over the whole church and the whole lives of believers. How to accomplish that? In his view, he said, large gatherings of bishops and church presidents have limited value. He had no immediate suggestions for how to resolve the North-South tensions he knows exist, but was determined to keep trying to find solutions without schism. An awkward pause followed in our conversation, making each of us aware that prospects for such solutions are not at hand.

My host was eager to move the conversation from North/South tensions to the subject closest to his heart, his definition of a Lutheran "as one who is a missionary." It was more than a cliché when he used it in describing the ministry of the laity in the Lutheran Church of Madagascar. He spoke of the lay "shepherds," a term with specific meaning here, referring to laity who undergo extensive training in order to carry out their key role in virtually every Lutheran congregation. The movement began in the early 20th century, led by laity, especially by women who comprise 75% of the 50,000 shepherds now serving in Lutheran Church of Madagascar (that does not yet ordain women to the pastoral ministry). Women and men serve without pay. They train for two years of congregation-based instruction under local pastors, offered on Saturdays, and centered in three areas: the Bible, the ministry of healing prayer for the sick, and the care of the poor and marginalized through casting out evil spirits. This triad of priorities says much about Malagasy Lutheranism and its conscientious response to the work of the Holy Spirit through the *laos*, the people of God.

Modeste emphasized one more unique facet of the active ministry of Malagasy Lutherans, the role of a woman born in 1921 and baptized in a village congregation on the southeast corner of Madagascar, Germaine Baolava, though raised in the humblest of circumstances, at the age of 10 began to tell her parents of mystical dreams, visions, and voices—things which make Lutherans in the western world nervous, but are more readily accepted in the religious culture of Madagascar. These visitations continued through her teen years as she grew to be unusually tall (6'2"), causing later detractors to nickname her Ninelava, "the tall mother." In May, 1941, she experienced a vision so vivid that she saw Jesus taking her into his heavenly presence, teaching her various tongues and making himself known to her in three languages. Her parents feared for her sanity and sought to solve what they perceived to be her abnormality by arranging her marriage to an older widower, a catechist with many children, He died when she was 29. She did not remarry but grew in her conviction that, notwithstanding her plight as a young widow unable to read or write, and with step-children to care for, Jesus was calling her to deepen and expand the ministry of the laity in Madagascar.

Not surprisingly she met opposition both within and outside the Lutheran Church. But because she consistently disavowed any desire to challenge pastoral authority or lead the lay movement out of the church, she was finally and formally accepted by the Lutheran Church in 1953. By that time her nickname, Ninelava, had become a title revered by vast numbers within and beyond Lutherans in Madagascar. As early as 1938 her unique gifts were recognized through a Norwegian Lutheran missionary who saw in her the essentials of deep devotion to Scripture, the charism of healing, care for the lowliest, and gifts for evangelizing and mobilizing converts for service without ruffling the feathers of the Lutheran hierarchy. After being taken into the Lutheran fold (instead of going to other denominations eager to welcome her) she expanded the lay ministry of shepherds by establishing a series of camps to train shepherds in specialized care for people afflicted with severe physical, mental, and spiritual needs. Now there are thirty nine such centers around the country. Until her death in 1998 she was consistent in her primary aim of leading people to Jesus, caring for the lowliest through healing prayer and casting out demons. When she died she had become a spiritual leader honored by both the church and the government. "Jesus is Lord" (I Corinthians 12:3) remained her watchword, and her warning was that if this confession is displaced by dependence on miracles and varieties of visions, the shepherd movement will perish. Holding fast to the confession will mean deliverance from worries about its continuance. As to her place in that continuity, her counsel was simple: "If you want to call me Mama, love Jesus."

What can be learned from Malagasy Christians came through in a conversation with Pastor Peri Raisolandraibe of 67ha congregation in Antananaivo where 600 (!) shepherds serve among the 8,600 members. During an earlier time in America as a guest professor at Luther Seminary in St. Paul, Minnesota, he was contacted by a local pastor and asked to minister to a parishioner diagnosed as demon-possessed. Pastor Raisolandraibe refused, preferring instead to teach the pastor to carry out this ministry himself. The pastor demurred, acknowledging his fears of entering into a whole new area of pastoral care. Raisolandraibe helped the American pastor understand that his fears were not misplaced, since according to our Lord's teaching (in Mark 5:1-13, the healing of the demonized Gerasene), expelled demons don't simply evaporate but seek others in whom to do their evil. Against that fear, the Gospel brings Christ's resurrection as victory over the demonic powers that strut and threaten. Armed with such a conviction the American pastor took up the full armor of God and grew in his pastoral calling, much helped by a fellow pastor from afar.

Meetings other shepherds in and around Antananarivo broadened my awareness of this unique lay movement that has yet to be taken seriously by Lutherans outside of Madagascar. The following are examples.

Mary Noro is 49, a high school teacher of French, German, and English, is a single mother whose husband left her when she announced her intention to become a shepherd. Her ministry takes her on jail visits each Saturday and Sunday morning, often taking used clothing she has collected during the week. She teaches Scripture and finds ample opportunity for the ministry of casting out demons among prisoners whose rap sheets range from murder to illegal squatting on government land. Hers is not an easy life as she is raising her daughter, now 13, alone and on the meager salary earned by teachers. I was touched by the effort she made to come a long distance after school via public transportation. My thanks was to send her home in a cab as night was falling, after praying with her that the Good Shepherd keep her in his sure care

Another shepherd is a church vehicle driver, Hasina (whose family name I failed to learn), who drove us everywhere in Antananarivo during our visit. He is in his late twenties and was glad to get a job after struggling through his late teens with drinking and drug problems. He's good at sports and uses that interest as common ground for connecting with kids. His mother was saintly in her patience and prayers for him. Through her influence he turned his life around before it was destroyed. He corresponded with Ninelava about becoming a shepherd. She wrote back that because of his youth he should take four years instead of two for the preparation course. He went every Saturday and Sunday afternoon for study while supporting himself as an auto mechanic. On the day of his commissioning in the late summer of 1999, ten thousand people came to the service in which he was one of 480 shepherds received into lay ministry. He and his wife are now parents of a two year old daughter. There are 110 shepherds and two pastors in the congregation of 2000 where he serves. Each second and fourth Sunday, following the benediction, he and other shepherds come forward, after donning their white robes ("devils don't like white" he told me), to pray over those who are sick and troubled with evil spirits. Hasina remarked that many do not recognize their spiritual enemy within, but the symptom that always identifies the evil spirit is fear. Sometimes this ministry occurs quietly. At other times, when people wail loudly and fall into violent fits of shaking so as to hurt themselves, other shepherds join in holding the suppliants from physical hurt as they await the cleansing which brings peace.

Germain Radesa, 49, is married, and has been a teacher for the past eight years. He was a Roman Catholic when he heard about Ninelava and attended a camp to see the famous woman's ministry in action. The experience was so powerful that, in his words, he asked himself "Why not me?" and began to inquire into Lutheran doctrine and practice. The first pastor he consulted had no interest in the lay revival movement, but his second try was more successful, and he entered that congregation to take the two year course to become a shepherd. He explained that Roman Catholic laity can and do train as shepherds in Lutheran congregations without giving up their membership and ministry in Catholic parishes. In his case he felt called to join the Lutherans who trained him. He plays a guitar when evangelizing among young people who often come, he said, but do not always follow up. He described two visits to France for outreach organized by Malagasy Lutherans who emigrated there, but he found virtually no response from French youth who liked the music but not the message calling for repentance and faith in a Lord who unites the nations. His said his zeal for evangelism remains strong, however. He brought Julia Raharinirina with him, a woman he had not met until this day. He had dialed a wrong number in making a phone call and reached her by mistake, but instead of hanging up he began a conversation that included his witness to Christ and an invitation to join us, the Americans from Chicago. It made me think about being ready to speak of the hope that is within the Christian heart, even when the opening comes via a wrong number dialed.

Though not a shepherd, Helene Ralivo is a woman leader in the church here. She is the director of the Malagasy Lutheran Church Women organization and founded the Women's Center on the outskirts of Antananarivo in the mid-1990's. Now, sixty women are enrolled in a program to provide practical skills for women at the bottom of the economic and social ladder. The center is equipped with sewing machines and clothing templates in a neatly kept building with wide windows and ample fresh air for those at work. Helene and her husband, Pastor Rene Ralivao hosted us for a Sunday dinner during our stay. At the table were Lutheran missionary Douglas Cox and his wife, Monica; he is on special assignment in the northern Madagascar, where the Muslim population is concentrated. We were impressed with the high commitment and competence evident in both families. The Cox couple were at ease in Malagasy, a reminder of the labor of love required of the many missionaries who have invested months and years in language study. The Cox word on the matter was that it is hard work but essential in becoming servants rather than strangers in a foreign land.

Honorine Razofindravao is not a shepherd, either, but everything about her calling as cook and keeper of the Lutheran Church House in Antananarivo shows her shepherding heart. For nearly thirty years she has done laundry, shopped for food, cooked, cared for children, and made visitors from all over the world feel welcome and well cared for. She told us a story from her childhood. When she was six, times were hard for her family. Her father had to search near and far just to find food enough for the family to survive. On one occasion he returned from hours of doing any kind of work, soaked to the skin from the rain, with but one small bag of rice for his family. Her father's plight moved her to pray that God would help her grow up so that she might help support her family. She came to Antananairivo at age 20, found work in the church house, and counts it a joy not only to support herself but to provide for her parents—now in their seventies. She smiled often while telling us her story, a sign that her life is a testimony to the grace that puts a song in the heart. In her own gracious, hospitable way, Honorine exemplified to us President Modeste's word that "to be a Lutheran is to be a missionary."

Madagascar is known for its lemur monkey, found only in this Island nation. More unique by far, so it seemed to us, are the Malagasy Lutherans, who, amidst poverty and all its attending woes, teach much about the power of the gospel to enliven the church with laity who are deep into the Scriptures, who know the power of healing prayer, and who care for the poor.

PART 3

INTRODUCING
EASTERN EUROPE

Russia, Lithuania, and Slovakia are featured in this section. In each country, Lutherans have endured, with all Christians, Jews, and Muslims, the oppression of forty years of Communist domination following World War II (and in Russia, in the decades following World War I as well). As their testimonies indicate, the degree of their suffering has varied both within and between nations. In Russia, where Lutherans have been for five centuries as a largely ethnic German presence, the pressure of persecution tightened after the Soviet regime and the German Reich became enemies instead of allies. The result was mass expulsion of German Russians and the drastic reduction of the Lutheran Church of Russia to a shell of what it once was. In Slovakia and Lithuania, where Lutherans were native Slavs since Reformation times onward, Lutherans had nowhere to escape. They managed to survive, some by compromise, others by defiance, with the penalties of disrepute and imprisonment that went with it. An authoritative history of the Lutheran churches through this dark era remains to be written. When I asked one churchman who experienced it why that had not yet been done, his answer was a grimace and the dour comment: "it is still too painful to write about ourselves and our colleagues." There is, however, a strand of that history marked by stories of faith and endurance among clergy and laity that needs telling for their lessons of courage and hope. Hints of these appear in the chapters following, especially from the younger generation who remember what their forbears went through, and now confront the challenge of new problems in new times. The main theme unfolding here is the task of congregations and schools of the church to forge new ministries soundly based in the Gospel and ready to bring the hard-earned witness of persevering through totalitarianism to the wider church in its global mission. The prospects for that are hopeful, as the voices of a new generation of eastern and middle European Lutherans are heard in this chapter.

Lena Bondarenko is a capable, quiet-mannered young Russian whose fluency in English and German, plus her doctorate in linguistics, make her a valued faculty member of the Lutheran Seminary in Novosaratovka, a suburb of St. Petersburg. Her second degree is in theology which qualifies her to teach introductory courses in Biblical subjects. She lived down the hall from the room Beverly and I occupied in the school dormitory (an imaginatively converted former church building built over a century ago by Russian Lutherans of German descent) and often joined us for late afternoon tea and conversation. Among the stories she told was one heard in her childhood from a ninety year old woman of her Lutheran congregation in Samara, a city on the Volga River in south central Russia. On a January Sunday in 1930 the police stormed the church, drove the members out into the bitter cold, locked the doors, and took the pastor and elders off to a Siberian prison camp from which they never returned. It was the beginning of the Stalinist reign of terror followed by six decades of persecution of Russians of all religious traditions, ending finally in 1989 with the collapse of Communism. That story and others like it helped us understand how lasting are the scars remaining from that dark time, and how resilient are the faithful who have endured to forge new beginnings for the church.

Lena Bondarenko and Dean Lueking

RUSSIA

Lena Bondarenko represents the present hinge generation among Russian Lutherans. Behind her is a family lineage of mixed Russian, German, and Polish ancestry, Lutheran for over a century. Most of her fellow Lutherans throughout Russia share a similar family background of mixed ethnic ancestry. Ahead of her is a future in a church less ethnically diverse, more Russian in its identity, and increasingly open to the full participation of such gifted women as Bondarenko. Another factor in understanding the present situation of some 75,000 members of the Evangelical Lutheran Church of Russia and Other States (ELCROS) is the geographic isolation of its 406 congregations. Their range, all across Russia's vast distances of twelve time zones from St. Petersburg to Vladivostok, reflects the widely separated settlements among German Lutheran migrants who first came to Russia as farmers and craftsmen as early as the 1530's. In the 1760's Catherine the Great, herself German-born, welcomed thousands of her countrymen as settlers, especially along the Volga River in central Russia, swelling the numbers of German Lutheran Russians to more than one million by World War I. After the 1917 Bolshevik Revolution and especially during the Stalin reign of terror in the 1930's, tens of thousands of Russian Lutherans of German ancestry were forcibly deported back to Germany as World War II came on. Those who remained became part of the "babushka generation" in which grandmothers were often in charge of handing down the faith to younger family members in secretive house church gatherings for prayer and worship. That generation, in turn, was diminished by another major exodus of Russian Germans who chose to return to their ancestral homes in Germany after the 1989 collapse of Communism.

This tumultuous, zigzag history is essential in understanding how a once flourishing Lutheran population in Russia has bequeathed a mixed heritage to its present heirs. Contemporary Russian Lutherans, while spiritually rooted in the Bible and Luther's Catechism, are still perceived by many of their fellow Russians as more German than Russian. In their heyday before World War I, Russian Lutherans built magnificent churches resembling the ones they left behind in their ancestral German towns and cities. Now these buildings are sparsely attended by a remnant of the faithful who are hard pressed to repair and maintain them without substantial outside help, primarily from the church in Germany. Russian Lutherans are a slender but plucky minority today, facing new and daunting challenges in a nation of 145 million Russians whose spiritual heritage as a nation is inextricably interwoven with the thousand year history of the Russian Orthodox Church dating from 987 A.D.

ELCROS was formed in 1998. It is recognized by the government and Russian Orthodox Church because of its four century history in Russia as the spiritual home of German Russians who have known the tears of suffering as well as the joys of service as part of God's Russian family of believers. It is also accepted by the Russian Orthodox Church as a bona fide partner in ecumenical relationships because Lutherans disavow the aggressive proselytism of Russian Orthodox believers by more recent sectarian religions from the west. What is noteworthy about its new beginning as ELCROS is its growing constituency of gifted young Russians such as Lena Bondarenko whose faith is Gospel-centered and whose thinking, speaking, feeling, and sense of cultural identity is thoroughly Russian.

When I questioned laity and clergy about priorities they saw for ELCROS their answers most frequently began with financial solvency and training more pastors, but then often moved toward the church becoming more Russian, a church in which all Russians can find a spiritual home. This emphasis was not surprising when heard from students and faculty on the seminary campus. It was confirmed, as well, by most of the lay and pastoral delegate whom I could reach for conversation and comment during a national ELCROS convention in St. Petersburg that brought together several hundred delegates from every region of Russia, Kazakhstan, Uzbekistan, Georgia, and the Urkaine. One promising sign of such indigenization at a key level is the appointment of Anton Tikhomirov as the first Russian born Lutheran to become the president and professor of theology at the Novosaratovka seminary. He is an answer to many prayers for indigenous leadership in guiding the training of the coming generation of pastors and lay workers who will lead ELCROS into the future.

Even greater signs for the continuing trend of indigenization of ELCROS in Russia are the current seminarians. Twenty-four are in residence on the seminary campus and eight others are away for their year of internship in congregations. It was our good fortune as a couple to become well acquainted with students of the four year program by living alongside them in the seminary dormitory during my short term as an ELCA sponsored guest professor, teaching a course on the pastoral role in marriage preparation and family life. Here are sketches of four seminarians, each with singular gifts, who together form a profile of the regional diversity of Lutheran congregations in Russia.

Vladimir Tatarnikov, 21, is from the city of Vitebsk (the birthplace of the celebrated artist, Marc Chagall) in Belarus, the landlocked country on the southwest border of Russia where four Lutheran congregations are struggling to revive their life and mission. Two of them are led by laity; the other two are served by a Lutheran pastor who was formerly an Orthodox priest. These four congregations came together in a common effort to send Tatarnikov to the seminary in Novosaratovka, intendng for him to return with pioneering zeal, sound theological training, and the courage of faith needed to unify and provide pastoral oversight in reviving a once flourishing Belarusian Lutheran church. Like most of his seminarians he cannot assume that a call with an offer of full support awaits him since the circumstances of his future pastoral calling in his homeland are uncertain at best. Added to the challenge ahead are political realities Tatarnikov faces when returning to a Belarus where religious freedom is restricted by an authoritarian president and his policies in an isolated nation of nearly ten million population. All this notwithstanding, Tatarnikov maintains an overall mien best described as a combination of holy naivete, academic seriousness, and an engaging love for people—all qualities that made him a standout student in class and lively participant in our late afternoon dormitory conversations. We learned more about his ambition and capabilities when he applied for a scholarship offered by the Evangelical Lutheran Church in America and came to the USA for a broadening experience as a summer youth camp counselor and a visit with us in our home. How he will be able to muster the necessary ways and means to build ministry among a scattered handful of believers in his homeland will be a bold venture of faith that will require networking with every possible ELCROS resource plus connections abroad. Now in his early twenties, with a daunting future beckoning, with Belarussian Lutherans counting on him, he has the grit, smarts, and above all the trust in God to equip him for what lies ahead.

Natalia Zaripova, in her early twenties, is a native of St. Petersburg where she is spending her intern year in a congregation averaging about one hundred present for Sunday worship in a church building restored a dozen years ago after its use under Communism as a maritime office. Payment for the restoration came from various sources, she explained, including the voluntary work done by members with construction skills. Her congregation, like many, was founded by Germans in 1850 but was closed in 1933 by Stalin's orders. To gather a congregation long scattered and decimated by sixty years of political repression and the unspeakable suffering of the population of St. Petersburg—called Leningrad during World War II—is a missionary calling that tests the dedication of the most seasoned pastor. She spoke well of her supervisory pastor and his varied gifts, including his musical talent as a means of ministry among Russians who are music lovers. She is learning pastoral ministry in a major Russian city through a full round of duties which include prayer meetings twice a week, home visits, preparing materials for neighborhood outreach, leading worship, and preaching twice a month.

Dmitri Tschisch is native Ukrainian who joined us for a dorm room conversation. He is 23, handsome, solidly built, and blessed with a deep baritone voice well suited to chanting the liturgy as Russians can do it in a manner not soon forgotten. On this occasion he joined us for conversation together with Natalia Zaripova, maintaining a discreet silence in her presence about his opposition to women's ordination. His Lutheran Church in the Ukraine does not follow the general ELCROS practice of ordaining women; thus on this question he reflected the policy of the church in which he grew up. He is interning under a pastor serving two congregations in Dnepropetrovsk, one numbering 150 and the second 40. The larger congregation has reclaimed its church building which had been used as a gym from the 1930's till 1990; the second, smaller congregation has received back its building which the Communists had turned into a museum promoting atheism. The Evangelical Lutheran Church in Germany has been of major help in funding restoration costs in both congregations, as well as providing a substantial share of the ELCROS budget. The Evangelical Lutheran Church in America provides a lesser amount for seminary staffing. Dimitri wore his clerical collar and spoke of how much his opportunities to lead liturgical worship mean in his internship experience. It was an indication of his appreciation as a Lutheran of the sustaining spiritual power of the liturgy that has been the strength of Russian Orthodoxy for a millennium, and his awareness of what Russian Lutherans can learn from that tradition.

The fourth seminarian in the conversation, Manzer Ismailova, is in her mid-30's, a striking woman with jet black hair and flashing eyes, from Azerbaijan on the southern border of Russia. Her conversion to the Christian faith from Islam occurred through the witness of a Norwegian family living in her home town of Sheki, where the husband in the household was stationed by a Norwegian agency for environmental development in the area. His wife met Manzer, and after learning of her devotion to children and hired her as a nanny. Following a lengthy period of living with the family, and with great courage, Manzer began inquiring into what lay behind the love she saw at work in the daily relationships in the household as well as in their hospitable acceptance of her as one of the family. Their response to her inquiries into the Christian faith was sensitive to the personal problems she faced if her inquiry became known. The result was not only Manzer's conversion but her own family's acceptance of her baptism and their eventual embrace of Christ's Way as their truth and life in a country with a 93% Muslim population. In time she found her way to the seminary in Novosaratovka and became a mature and endearing influence among the mostly younger students. I heard her preach in a matins service in the seminary chapel one morning, and when reading the English translation understood why her sermon made a powerful impression on her fellow students. In English translation, here are excerpts from her homily based on Jesus' call to leave all for the gospel's sake (Mark 10:29-31):

> *It is difficult to understand that when following Christ's call, others shun us. When I came to believe, the neighbors who lived in the same yard with me (and we had everything in common) shunned me, thinking that my family and I had destroyed our own home and lives. Even till now the doors of these families are closed to me and my family. This is very painful. Once I was afraid that I remained alone because there were no Christians around me, but now in my home town my family and some friends came to believe! Together with our growth our problems grow, too. But Jesus never suggested a simple way. He always taught that the price to be a Christian is very high. Nor did Jesus ever try to blackmail his followers. He challenged them to be ready for risks and to follow not because of rewards but because it is He that calls. Brothers and sisters, when we graduate from the seminary nobody knows in which congregation we will serve or whether we will even have the chance to preach the good news or whether people will accept it when we do. We simply must be ready to leave everything and follow Jesus for his sake. The Lord has promised his rewards in his own way and time. I know that, dear seminarians, because studying here at the seminary with you is itself a reward I never dreamed*

could come. So, let us be strong in Jesus and not worry about a career and power. We are not striving to become pastors who stand at the door after a worship service and people kiss their hands. Give yourselves to God's hands Do it simply and sincerely. Then we will know what he meant when saying that the first shall be last and the last shall be first. As a child trusts its mother, let us trust God for everything.

In a recent communication from Manzer Ismailova we learned that she is practicing what she preaches. "I'm not certain that this is my permanent calling but I really love this work and am content with it for now." She described her service in a program to help abandoned Azerbaijani children find placement in families, including in some cases a return to rehabilitated parents who had given up hope of ever being able to support their own.

Those who since the early 1990's have come to Russia from the Lutheran Church in Germany as missionary pastors and theological educators merit tribute as pioneers whose sacrificial commitment has been a sign of Christ's Spirit at work in meeting the challenges of this new era in post-Communist Russia. The first of these was the now retired Georg Kretschmar, who came to Russia in the 1990's after serving congregations of Russian Lutherans in Germany. In that chaotic time when a new Russia was struggling to emerge from what had been the Soviet Union, he was immersed in the complexities of threading his way through the Russian governmental maze to secure legal status for ELCROS as a loosely knit umbrella church organization of congregations in Russia and the former Soviet states. He was also initiated important ecumenical relations with the Orthodox Church; his title as the Lutheran archbishop (rare among Lutherans; only the Lutheran Church of Sweden has a similar office) of ELCROS was an asset in that endeavor with the Orthodox who take such nomenclature seriously. What he lacked, some said, was an adequate oversight of administrative and financial systems of the new church with the result that instances of inefficiency and irregularities were defects beyond his control to prevent. My first meeting with him was in his office in the imposing Lutheran Cathedral of St. Peter and St Paul on land deeded to Lutherans by Czar Peter the Great over three centuries ago. It is a prime location on Nevsky

Prospekt, St. Petersburg's grandest boulevard and a short walk from the world famous Hermitage Art Museum. He was understandably proud to show how the sanctuary, severely damaged during the horrific siege of Leningrad in 1943 by the Nazis, then turned into a swimming pool during the Communist decades, had finally been skillfully restored to multiple use for worship and various church assemblies as a sign of new resolve by Lutherans in a new era. He added with a touch of ironic humor that the chlorine odor still lingering in his office where we spoke was a carry over from its location as part of a former swimming pool. Kretschmar retired as archbishop of ELCROS leadership in 2005, after pioneering the years of its re-formation in 1998 as a network of Russian Lutheran congregations of German ethnicity scattered across ten thousand miles from Russia's east to west.

His successor, Edmund Ratz, was elected archbishop in 2005 after serving for five years as bishop of the German Evangelical Lutheran Church in Ukraine. He was born in Bavaria and studied law in Germany before turning to theology and became a Lutheran pastor in Germany. Among the prior posts he held was an eight year term of international ecumenical experience as head of the Lutheran Council of Great Britain. We sat down together early one morning in the seminary dormitory commons room for a breakfast conversation in which he commented on his hopes for varied styles of witness and congregational life to emerge in the ELCROS mission to a new Russia with vast numbers without any means of hearing the Gospel or belonging in a congregation. In reaching such Russians, Ratz emphasized, Lutherans will continue to avoid proselytism. To that end he spoke of a recent visit with the Russian Orthodox Church's Metropolitan Kirill in Moscow to strengthen a long-standing and close ecumenical fellowship and to clarify procedures whereby each church respects the other in mission polity. For this to go forward, he stressed, his priority is to consolidate the geographically widespread, isolated congregations into regional clusters for greater mutual cooperation and effectiveness in mission as well as organizing on site continuing pastoral education opportunities for pastors distant from the seminary. Ratz, who had earlier studied theology in the United States, and drew upon that experience to help me understand what isolation means in Russia: an ELCROS pastor in Vladivostok is as far from the St. Petersburg suburban seminary campus in which we were talking as twice the distance from New York to San Francisco. His vision of the Lutheran presence in Russia held another important insight: "the Lutheran church in Russia is an international church and should remain so." As one German-born, his wisdom in cautioning against the Russian Lutheran church becoming overly identified with being Russian reflected what he learned from a Lutheranism over-identified with being German during the Nazi era, the loss of its prophetic role in denouncing nationalism gone amok. Ratz is a churchman in his early seventies who intends his term as archbishop to be short, an interim step of transition toward Russian Lutheran leadership.

Numbers of American professors of the ELCA have joined with Germans in shaping the first decade of seminary education at Novosaratovka. Bradn Buerkle is one of them. He came to Russia initially as an exchange student from St. Olaf College where he studied Russian language and literature. During that exchange year he met his future wife, Natasha, from the Black Sea city of Rostov on Don. After completing his college and seminary education in the United States, he returned to Russia in 2003 as a seminary faculty professor of church history. One evening during our brief stay we were guests of the Buerkle's in their apartment of the Katie Luther faculty residence building across the walk from the student dormitory. During a dinner of Russian cuisine, served home style, we learned much from him about the Lutheran presence in Russia, past and present. Buerkle's fluent Russian is not only an essential asset in his daily classroom teaching of seminarians but also serves him well as he travels often to Moscow, Saratov, Odessa, and other places for on-site seminars with pastors and laity. He spoke candidly of ELCROS problems: reducing financial dependence on German and American church support, limited prospects for call and placement for seminary graduates, the history of distrust between laity-led congregations and the seminary which prepares professionally trained graduates, the necessity for ELCROS clergy to relate more positively to Russian Orthodoxy through shared social ministry, and—as he put it metaphorically—helping the Lutheran church to wear its Russian dress without losing its Lutheran soul. He also gave us an overview of the history of Finnish Lutherans at work in western Russia, useful for a visit several days later to the campus of the seminary of the Ingria Lutheran Church located in a suburb on the opposite side of St.Petersburg. Buerkle did not miss the irony of the fact that the only two Lutheran seminaries in all of Russia's six and one half million square mile land mass are an hour from each other. Their interaction is cordial but infrequent, due in part to the more conservative theology of the Ingria Lutheran Church but also due to the respective Finnish and German cultural affinities that mark the different histories of both seminaries and Lutheran churches.

Buerkle is a modest, thoughtful young church historian who brings a background from the broad plains of his native Montana to his love for Russia with its vast steppes, rich literary tradition, and above all, to its people with whom he is joined by marriage to his Russian wife. As an outsider/insider he is well positioned to be a loving critic of the Lutheran church and its four century Russian history. As a young seminary faculty member he is able to contribute even more to the future of the Lutheran presence in Russia by continuing its international character while furthering its calling as a leaven of Gospel-centered theology in the Russian context of its mission. He concluded our conversation with words of quiet hope mixed with cautious realism about his vision for ELCROS and its future. His appeal for patience and understanding, restraint and respect, have the ring of sincerity. In his own person and calling he is demonstrating those very qualities he appeals for others to appreciate, including people like us who came for a short time to see what Russian eyes of faith see and to tell their story that deserves an empathetic hearing.

In late November, 1989, eastern Europe was on the brink of momentous change as communism was collapsing throughout the region. Among the many participants in that drama was Adrian Kacian, then a nineteen year old student in his second year at Comenius University in Bratislava, Slovakia. Just before the collapse, when political agitation was dangerous because outcomes were unclear, he was among the university students who distributed flyers (typed by students working in shifts of fifty through the night) throughout the city. On one bitterly cold November night he and other students stayed out in the streets till 4 a.m. when a police car spotted them with their subversive pamphlets in hand. The police knew well enough what they were doing, but when the officers offered to give Kacian and others a ride back to their dormitory instead of to jail for interrogation or worse, they knew that a tipping point had been reached. It was one small but potent sign of the reality of the change that the wider world would see a few days later in the iconic pictures of the dismantling of the Berlin Wall in East Berlin.

Adrian Kacian and Bohdan Hroban

SLOVAKIA

Adrian Kacian recalled this moment ten years earlier in his life as not only decisive for himself but representative of what many more like him experienced who had grown up in communist eastern Europe from the late 1940's until 1989. He was a son in a typical Slovakian family. His father was a machinery engineer and onetime member of the Communist Party who had mastered the art of getting along by going along. His mother, a chemist, was Roman Catholic, with only vague connections to her baptismal roots. His schooling in the eastern Slovakia town of Tisovec, population 5,000, was representative of the ideology that shaped him, more of a subtle brain washing rather than a direct assault on his mind. It was centered in the socialist concept of the primacy of the collective. Whatever values existed came from a person-centered way of thinking; an irony, he noted with a wry smile, since it was an ideology bent on erasing human individuality by immersing lives in collective enclaves. There was occasional mention of "fate" out there somewhere, but that was always kept in the background and teachers told Adrian and students like him to forget about it. "You are the architect of your own life and from Marxism comes world peace and your place in it" was the core theme of the propaganda that dominated his schooling, with little counteracting influence from his home life. To be honest, he added, his teenage world was more involved in soccer than aspirations toward the socialist ideal of manhood. He made good grades, but the academic standards were minimal. He admitted, in fact, that he had become expert in cheating on the exams that got him into university studies. His body was fit from soccer. His soul was a spiritual vacuum. His mind was empty of any clear purpose for his future.

To his surprise, this would soon change. One factor bringing it about was the onset of a debilitating disease that weakened him for two years and brought him face to face with his hollowness within. Soccer was no help, nor was increased medication his doctors prescribed before finally telling him they could do nothing more. In desperation he turned to yoga and diet change, which made no difference. What did begin to shake him loose from a gathering despondency was joining other students in the growing activist confrontation with the foundering communist regime, spurred on by the closely watched public uprisings in nearby Prague. The adrenalin of high risk participation in student-led strikes and forays into the city and countryside as "truth tellers" to crowds brave enough to assemble gave him a lift. He was discovering his capacity for commitment to a cause, something unknown before, and although he was far from a polished agent of revolution, he reached the point where he could address a crowd of 500 high school students (the faculty had fled the building rather than risk staying to listen) with convincing brashness, responding to their tougher questions with answers he made up on the fly. These experiences, especially the early morning showdown moment with the police, showed him signs of an inner transformation developing through external acts of courage. Without any set plan, and apart from any clearly formed prior motivation, together with thousands of others like him, he was swept up into the forefront of the Velvet Revolution which brought down an iron-fisted communism in Slovakia, the Czech Republic, and beyond in late 1989.

Kacian met another student activist who would have an even deeper impact upon his life beyond the political cause for which he risked his neck. Bohdan Hrobon was a fellow university student, two years his senior, who became a friend, mentor (and later his baptismal godfather) of life-changing importance. Hrobon's family background could not have been more different. Preceding him were six generations of Lutheran pastors dating back 200 years. His father, Jan Hrobon, was a legendary pastor and outspoken critic of the Communist regime who became so widely known for his uncompromising stance that even the Slovak version of the KGB quietly put up with him rather than deal with the uproar silencing him would have created. Bohdan was the third and youngest son in the family, who, with Hrobonesque singularity of purpose, broke the mold of Hrobons as pastors to seek instead the teaching ministry. To become an openly Christian teacher in the Slovakia of the early 1980's was something of an oxymoron (even though Lutheran pastors and Catholic priests taught religion in the public schools of Slovakia under severe restrictions and with pittance salaries throughout the four decades of Communism—a compromise intended to slowly suffocate Christianity instead of strangling it outright, Stalin style). Facing facts, he switched his university major from education to a computer science major. That decision, however, did not dispel his increasing disillusionment with the academic hypocrisy he encountered in the university and especially the propaganda, mixed with the pornography served up to him during his year of required military service. In Kacian he found a kindred spirit. Their friendship deepened after their university days when the full scope of the challenges of post-communist life emerged following the euphoria of the regime's collapse.

Hrobon learned of a teaching opening in one of the Lutheran high schools re-opened after 1989. With no better options at hand, he applied. The teaching staff was a hodge-podge of applicants, so haphazardly thrown together that Hroban was put off by the prospect of teaching English and catechism in a school of minimal promise. The principal, a woman with educational expertise but without Christian faith experience (he later had to teach her the Lord's Prayer and outline the rudiments of the faith), made one effective move, however, in persuading him to get beyond his initial reluctance to teach. She took him into a classroom to let him see the students' faces and hear their words of aspiration for learning English. It worked. The dilemma of youth struggling to learn something in a school of meager resources moved him to accept. He plunged into his classroom challenge with every innovative method he could devise, including informal evenings open to the students to talk about anything on their minds. Meanwhile his friend and soulmate, Adrian Kacian, had joined the staff as a teacher of math and physics. The two of them became popular with the students as the young Turks whose classes were lively and demanding, while the school's governing board grew increasingly nervous about their pace of educational innovation and appeal for spiritual integrity that Hroban and Kacian pressed upon the entire faculty. Kacian, for example, had been baptized secretly in his infancy but had never been taught the faith. Yet he was expected to began each classroom day with prayer, something he refused to do as a baptized agnostic. Instead, he enlisted students who professed the faith to pray. Those student prayers began to bring answers that affected him personally, beyond anything he expected.

Nearby the school in Tisovec was a camping site to which Kacian and Hrobon would take students on outings. On one of these occasions, a three day outing, Kacian became more and more taken with the sincerity of faith he saw in his students as they studied Scripture, sang hymns, and talked openly of their convictions and doubts alike. On the third and final evening, his inner stirrings led to a breakthrough of faith. He remembered seeing a shooting star in the heavens and took it as a sign of Christ, the Light of the world, reaching for him. It was his "I met him" moment, a turning point of encounter with the living Christ. He shared the experience with Bohdan Hrobon, who helped him place the moment into the larger mystery of the ways of the Spirit of God, all leading finally to the good news that God is gracious to sinners through his crucified and risen Son, Jesus Christ. Oddly enough, his deepened zeal through conversion now applied to his dedication to innovative teaching, only made his superiors the more uncomfortable with his confrontation with educational incompetence and spiritual disarray. Side by side with him in this increasingly unsettling circumstance was his spiritual mentor and teaching colleague, Bohdan Hrobon. Another problem was the arrival of American teachers of English and religion, among whom were some who brought a Lutheranism that was narrow doctrinally, culturally uninformed, and ignorant of the Slovak language. The newcomers were well intentioned but ill equipped, especially when teaching the faith in a language least familiar to the students who found themselves frustrated by being unable to express their real thoughts and questions.

Both Kacian and Hrobon were eventually fired, to the surprise of neither. Adrian Kacian decided that his next best step was to pursue his doctorate in mathematics at Comenius University in Bratislava, plus enroll for further work toward his degree at the Institute for Mathematics of the Slovak Academy of Science. To complete his academic triple play he also enrolled at the theological faculty of Comenius University where the Evangelical Church of the Augsburg Confession, aka the Lutheran Church of Slovakia, trained its clergy. While he was studying theology he met an American guest professor on the faculty whose theology was solidly Lutheran and intellectual standards were rigorous. Paul Hinlicky, a visiting professor from Roanoke College in Virginia, was influential as an academic mentor who encouraged him to complete his doctorate in mathematics, continue on with his theological studies at the same time, and, not the least, to put Kacian through a disciplined learning of English that lifted him to a level of competence needed in his future studies abroad. His close friend, Bohdan Hroban, was instrumental in encouraging him to apply for a scholarship to Wheaton College in suburban Chicago as a supplement to his seminary work in Bratislava. He studied there for a year and a half, then returned to make his oral defense of his doctoral thesis early in 2000. As the enormously eventful decade of the 1990's in Slovakia was drawing to a close, Adrian Kacian and other young Slovaks were being prepared for vocations of service in the church which they could not foresee, but nevertheless became the groundwork for their unique ministries to the hearts and minds of Slovak laity who had never had an opportunity to receive much instruction in the faith.

Bohdan Hrobon, meanwhile, lost no time in picking himself up from being an ex-teacher in a struggling high school to work the angles necessary to qualify as a youth camp counselor in Bemidji, Minnesota. He saved $200 from the amount his pastor-father gave him for air travel, using it to extend his visa and adopt a bohemian lifestyle (pierced ears, ponytail, $5 in his pocket) as part of his ongoing education. His hippie era introduced him to people all across the human spectrum, from the fundamentalist Lutherans he met at a Bible School where he took some courses, to the gay man who was the most helpful individual he had met so far in his USA odyssey. He held off hunger by doing odd jobs at the Bible School and attended to his intellectual appetite by frequent visits to the library of the Bible School he attended briefly in Minneapolis. On one occasion a student did take notice that he was reading Hebrew and asked what it was. When telling her that he was reading the Old Testament in Hebrew she dismissed the idea. Her "I have Jesus—that's enough" comment was his introduction to one aspect of American fundamentalism. His view broadened, however, when he met Peter Burton of the Bible School faculty, who taught Hebrew in the school and became Hrobon's private tutor and inspiration for an eventual doctoral study at Oxford University in England.

His continuing American odyssey took him from the Bible School in Minneapolis to Wheaton College in Illinois for a year, a return to Slovakia and a lucrative job offer with a German firm (car, office, good salary, perks, etc) which he turned down. Two days thereafter he had a letter from a Minnesota family offering him support for a return to study at Wheaton, where he then spent the next three years, with short trips to Israel and Brazil for insight visits. He and Adrian Kacian continued to correspond, comparing notes on their respective experiences and searching together for what purposes God might unfold through their many-faceted experiences since their student days of risking their necks to release their homeland from the hammerlock of hard line communism.

In their relationship to the Evangelical Church of the Augsburg Confession, as Slovak Lutherans have named themselves since their origins in the 1530's, Hrobon and Kacian were obedient rebels. Their obedience to the Gospel plunged them into an unsought role as faithful rebels against the paralysis resulting from the oppressive communist decades. Some pastors, few in number, had openly defied the regime. Others, for reasons of their own, did not. The majority, clergy and lay alike, kept their heads down and made few waves. Slovaks as a people, the late Slovak American theologian, Jaroslav Pelikan noted, have long had to master the art of compromise as a means of survival as a small central European nation caught between the

East and the West. As a body of Lutheran Christians, Slovaks developed a parallel *modus vivendi* as a minority of some 400,000 believers among the predominantly Catholic Slovak population of 5.5 million. Under the Austrian Hapsburg Empire they endured two centuries of oppression, forbidden to build churches with entrances on main thoroughfares, without steeples or crosses, no nails allowed, and construction completed within a one year time span. All faiths, of course, suffered under socialism, but Lutherans know a longer history that needs understanding when assessing their condition by the end of the 1990's. Bohdan Hrobon and Adrian Kacian were not unaware of this history. But neither were they unaware of the paralysis lingering in the church as the Velvet Revolution ushered in a new era as filled with peril as with promise.

Both were educators, having learned a new pedagogy on the streets of Bratislava more than in the university classrooms. Their passion was to address the vacuum of a whole generation of laity largely lost to the church during communism. Those who been force-fed on atheist doctrine had either regurgitated it and resorted to cynicism or kept its toxic poison within. Those faithful ones, often the mothers and grandmothers who had, sometimes in secret and other times openly, passed the Biblical faith on to their children and grandchildren, were now in need of some new means of reclaiming those of a lost generation who were ready for new beginnings. There were pastors, too, who saw the need for some agency beyond their own ministries to begin something never before systematically thought through or put into church institutional form—an intentionally trained laity. The seminary of the church in Bratislava was too swamped with forming a new faculty and finding even marginal classroom facilities to meet a surge of new students. More to the point, its older faculty was without time, vision, and energy, to equip pastors to train laity for congregational leadership in teaching Scripture, youth work, liturgy, administration, and stewardship. The presiding bishop at this new time, Julius Filo, had more than enough to engage his considerable talents and energies as a pastor to struggling pastors, a full time professor of preaching at the seminary, and frequent traveler to Geneva as a vice-president of the Lutheran World Federation. The most important thing for an outsider to grasp about the Slovakian churches, Catholic, Lutheran, Brethren, and a few other

Protestant bodies alike, was that centuries of traditional ways had a two-fold effect as Christians entered the 21st millennium. The power of tradition had seen them through times of severe testing. The down drag of traditionalism also held them within the stultifying narrowness of a "We've never done it that way before" mentality.

Hrobon and Kacian were young veterans of revolutionary activism in the national political struggle. They had also gone to the United States and learned from American church life, enough of it at its least to make them wary, but also enough of it at its best to widen their vision. This applied especially to their passion to educate a new generation of lay leaders in congregations of the Evangelical Church of the Augsburg Confession. They were smart enough to realize they could not win over the establishment of the Slovak Lutheran Church to support their goal and lost no time and energy in trying. They were gutsy enough to stand their ground against direct official opposition, knowing that their vision would be misperceived as competition with the seminary rather than partnership for a larger ministry of the laity in the congregations. Both had faced down far more ominous opposition in the streets of Bratisalva a decade earlier. They were savvy enough, and prayerful as well, to realize that an enormous potential of theological soundness, practical know-how in the training of laity, and financial support lay across the Atlantic, especially in the American heartland where both had studied, worshiped, and celebrated (Slovaks know how to party) the joyful abundance of God's grace promised for every new beginning in his name.

In conversation with me about these beginnings, Hrobon and Kacian spoke of factors behind their decision to start a Bible school for laity in the north central Slovakian city of Martin, where the modern Slovak literary tradition began and where Jan Hrobon's significant pastorate had been an inspiration for fresh beginnings in the church. One factor, as they put it bluntly, was that too many pastors saw themselves as a one man show and for that reason stifled the development of lay leadership in their congregations. The second stemmed from what they had learned when teaching at the high school in Tisovec, the determination to turn negatives into positives—and to persevere even when they were fired for their efforts.

By the fall of 1998 they were underway with their first effort of what would become a Bible school, later renamed The Center for Christian Education. They had sent out invitations to congregations and clergy of the church, hoping for perhaps two dozen to form the first class. Eighty signed on. They came on Saturdays, some traveling three hours to be present for the 8 a.m. beginning, and returning home by 8 p.m. at the end of a full day of Scripture, theological basics, teaching methods, and an overview of church history. It was a substantial curriculum from the outset, with a heartening balance of men and women of varying age making the commitment to come each Saturday during fall and spring semesters. The facilities were the renovated rooms of the parish house and school of the Lutheran congregation in Martin, within sight of the scenic Tatra Mountains of north central Slovakia. The faculty consisted of gifted pastors Jan Hrobon and Magda Forgacova, a renowned historian, Milos Kovacka, and Peter Gazik from the Bratislava seminary whose presence insured the fledgling school its academic standing within the university system of Slovakia. Generous financial help from various USA congregations was essential from the beginning, coupled with the fact that the plucky staff of teachers and administration worked for minimal salaries. Hrobon became the director of the school. Kacian the academic dean, his credentials having been established already through his university doctorate in mathematics. Hrobon has completed his doctoral degree at Oxford University in Old Testament studies.

Both men were skilled in finding gifted graduates from the Bratislava seminary with sufficient commitment of faith and a pioneering spirit to join the staff from its first years onward. Michal Valco and Tomas Gulan are examples of stellar theological talent; both married spouses with similar aptitude for teaching, as did Adrian Kacian. By the end of its first decade in 2008, the school has achieved remarkably. It serves a total student body of 304, some of whom are housed in a newly built student dormitory. Classes are conducted in a renovated classroom building that includes a sizeable assembly hall suitable for worship and other special occasions, plus an expanding library. The curriculum includes a program of social studies fully accredited with the nearby University of Zilina, a Lutheran Academy serving youth from kindergarten through high school, a teacher training program preparing candidates for teaching religion in Slovakian schools, a bachelors degree program for training of congregation leaders in evangelism, youth work, and parish education, and an annual budget of 1.2 million USD, of which 72% comes from Slovakian sources.

What I found most notable in my association as a sometime visiting instructor during its first decade is the spirit that animates the Bible School faculty and students. These young men and women people clearly want to be doing what they are doing, and they clearly enjoy being together. Their sense of calling is strong, durable enough to withstand the inevitable tensions or letdowns that are part of the Martin experience. Their spirit of mutual support and venturesome readiness to take on new challenges comes directly from the unity derived from their dependence on each other as people called by God to do something heretofore unknown in the nearly 500 years of Lutheranism in Slovakia—train lay Christians to live out their baptismal calling in their congregations and in their many faceted aspects of daily life. They suffer few illusions about the risk that has marked every step of development since the Bible School began, and the size of the challenge of changing the average Slovak Lutheran lay person's perception of what their role in the congregation is. This was evident in a research project in 2007 by Slavka Gulanova (wife of faculty member Tomas Gulan and partner with him in theological research) among several hundred Slovak Lutherans in over a dozen congregations in varied locations in Slovakia. The scope of the survey touched upon Lutheran identity, worship, congregation life and education, and the hopes and anxieties of the laity. Her research showed how deeply the past decades of Communist suppression and the present era of rising economic prosperity in Slovakia have worked a double burden on lay Lutherans: family prayer is reported in 12% of the respondents, 5% regarded the Reformation touchstone of "grace alone, faith alone, Scripture alone" as faith's center, 7% regarded liturgy as meaningful, 10% knew some form of lay participation in the congregation, with less than 6% serving according to their gifts. In 11 of the 14 congregations studied, the pastor led whatever youth activities there were. The project revealed two things: the courage to search out facts on the ground concerning the need for serious lay training and the zeal to meet those needs with as thorough a Lutheran educational program for laity as I have seen anywhere in global Lutheranism.

The challenges they face are significant. Now that their first decade shows that their place is promising in Slovak Lutheranism, their task is to gain the support and participation of wider numbers of pastors who are still the gatekeepers of what goes on in congregational life. With that wider acceptance will come a more enlightened laity in a church that has lost an entire generation to an atheist ideology and now faces new obstacles of the consumerism that comes with cultural globalization. The increasing economic prosperity in Slovakia poses the challenge of greater financial support from faithful Slovaks. Although the leadership has clearly defined its purpose of training laity rather than candidates for pastoral ministry, the time will come when the sheer quality of its overall service to the church may well mean that the question of a new vision of pastoral education must be faced. The school has already made tentative contacts with other Lutherans in the Ukraine, in Russia, and elsewhere in central Europe. Expanding those contacts can mean widening the service to regions where Lutherans and other Christians will be increasingly interested in adapting the model in Martin, Slovakia. Above all, the challenge will be to maintain what St. Paul celebrates as the unity of the Spirit in the bond of peace (Ephesians 4:23) that blesses the current staff and students. That gift, so convincingly present now, will surely be a prime target for dark forces never far from the church's most promising vanguard.

Mindaugas Sabutis was 30 when elected bishop of the Evangelical Lutheran Church of Lithuania in 2005, which made him the youngest Lutheran bishop in the world at that time. Mindful of the customary image of a bishop as one twice his age, he began his consecration sermon with the promise "to grow old as soon as possible." The tongue-in-cheek quote led to more important subjects as we talked together in his office in Vilnius, the nation's capitol. He explained that his unusual age as a leader reflected circumstances in Lithuanian Lutheranism at the time of the collapse of Communism in 1990. There were only six older Lutheran pastors left to serve the twenty congregations that had survived a half century of war and oppression. But by 2005 a new generation of younger clergy had joined the ranks of those serving more than double the number of congregations starting again. He was a young bishop elected by young pastors in a Lutheran Church facing new challenges after one of the darkest eras in its nearly five hundred year history in Lithuania.

Minaugas and Vilma Sabutis

LITHUANIA

Bishop Minaugas Sabutis cited his own family history as a mirror of the heartbreak and heroism that marked the lives of so many Lithuanians during the latter half of the 20th century. As a boy his father had eluded the worst of the German army occupation in the early 1940's by fleeing into the woods, sometimes surviving on wild roots and water. When the Russians came he was drafted into the army of the Soviets and served as an officer. His mother, a nurse, came from a Lutheran family in which her father was killed by a drunken Nazi officer early in World War II. Later on, when the Russians invaded, her mother and remaining family were among the first deported to Siberia as punishment for their status as prosperous landholders. The chaotic disruption of the family at that time meant that his grandmother had to leave her children behind when migrating to

Uruguay via the United States. She died of a broken heart, he said, for never having had the opportunity to reunite her family. Mindaugas remembered his own mother as a strong woman who saw to his baptism and became the mainstay of his growing up years by teaching him Bible stories, prayers, and an evening hymn that, in his words "still puts me to sleep every night." She did this despite the battering the Nazis and Communists gave the Lutheran Church of her family had known, shrinking it from a quarter million in 1940 to twenty thousand in 1990. Many of the congregations had simply disappeared with no records left of their existence. Those who did survive suffered the after effects of long simmering internal conflicts between church members with German or Lithuanian nationalist leanings, sometimes boiling over into fist fights and worse.

Such were the realities that he and his classmates faced when finishing seminary in Klaipeda, on the Baltic Sea coast. But within embattled congregations, he was quick to add, there were also those who often had to make a choice between two directions during the Communist decades. One was to get along by going along with the regime, confining the faith to Sunday ritual. The other was to hear the Word on Sundays and take the consequences of practicing it during the week. Those who took the latter course found ways to get around the consequences which in some cases meant their church was closed to become a gym or storage barn. They would meet in cemeteries on days set aside to visit family grave sites, a long standing tradition in Lithuania that was too deep rooted to change. The faithful would do more than place flowers and candles at the grave. They added to a venerable custom by holding a worship service in the cemetery. If the police caught on, they would move to another cemetery, always watching for the black car of some *apparatchik* trying to track them down. His parents were among such believers and he was proud of the stories his father told him of playing trumpet in the brass choir in defiance of snoopers. Bolstered by such witness of a faithful remnant, Sabutis began his ministry by serving three congregations in western Lithuanians scattered over an area which meant traveling 150 kilometers every Sunday. It was hard work, he remembered, especially among the teenagers who were still brainwashed from their dedication at seven years as Communist Pioneers ("Lenin's grandchildren") and again at fifteen through the more intentional indoctrination by the

Communist Youth Organization. Lingering tensions from earlier times between Catholics and Lutherans were another problem. Yet his overall summary of his first years of ministry was that it was a good immersion into realities of church and national life in Lithuania and a continuing education in things the seminary could not teach. He understood the ministry of Jesus better through deeper absorption into the Bible than during his student days when he read the works of philosophers Martin Heidegger and Soeren Kierkegaard. But when finding himself face to face with people whose lives and questions had little to do with such thinkers, he learned that "being a pastor was not like being a movie star, because ministering God's truth to rowdy believers never makes pastors popular."

Something else buoyed him in those first years. At the seminary he had met a church music student who sometimes accompanied him as an organist and Sunday School teacher on his Sunday rounds. Her bright, vivacious spirit not only drew people of all ages to her, but drew his heart as well. They fell in love and were married three years after Mindaugas' ordination. Vilma Sabutis joined us later in our conversation, and was interested in exchanging stories familiar to pastors' wives. Beverly brought up the subject of how our home congregation had received its first ordained woman a decade earlier and the enrichment her ministry meant in the congregation. Vilma thought that the church in Lithuania was at a different place, meaning that although women are not ordained she was not hampered in her own ministry as organist, choir director, and teacher of youth. She spoke gratefully of the strong spiritual foundation she had received from her family whose faith had been tested by Communist suppression of religion. The adults in family gatherings would include her in serious conversations about standing up as Christians when it was not easy. She remembered one time when she was quite young that her surprisingly mature words made an uncle say that "if you were a boy you would be a pastor." The response did not bother her, given the context of the times. The church was struggling to survive and women's ordination was no one's concern. Now, as an adult woman in the church she did not feel she had missed her calling. She is using her gifts to the fullest as she joins with her husband in serving wherever she can. Women's ordination might well be a subject taken up in the future, she guessed, but there was little advocacy for it now, nor were there women students at Klaipeda seeking ordination.

She added another reason for the status quo on women's ordination. Pastors are poorly paid in Lithuania, receiving salaries less than some who are on unemployment assistance. Another reason came to her mind as she warmed to the subject. Lithuanians, who watch trends in the Church of Sweden where women have been ordained for some time, are wary of what they see. She referred in particular to recent actions taken by the Swedish Church in blessing same sex unions, a decision she felt Lithuanian Lutherans would not favor. While she did not wish to imply that ordaining women would have a domino effect leading directly to church sanction for homosexual couples, she recognized differing hermeneutical principles between the two churches. It was impressive that she addressed the issue at that level. When she turned the topic over to her husband for further comment, he said that she had covered the matter well and left it at that. He turned instead to the benefits of generally positive relations with the Lutheran churches of Latvia and Estonia, both with larger Lutheran populations which were organized along somewhat different lines. He also spoke of ongoing exchange visits with Lutherans in the United States from the Missouri Synod and Evangelical Lutheran Church of America. My friendship with Bishop Hans Dumpys, who has served the Lithuanian Lutheran Church of the Diaspora in America, had made me aware of another significant aspect of international relationships between the church in Lithuania and its widely spread refugee and immigrant membership in the United States and Canada. Mindaugas also spoke of deepened ties brought about by the Missouri Synod Lutherans offering scholarships to Lithuanian students for theological study at their two seminaries in the United States. What that implied for the Evangelical Lutheran Church of Lithuania in its broader relationships as a member of the Lutheran World Federation (which the LCMS has chosen not to join for doctrinal reasons) was a subject he did not take up.

I asked him about joys in his work. His response was forthright—"to see the grace of God at work in people who have been through so much." He applied that especially to the older ones who had not been embittered by war, suppression of freedom, or the corrosive inroads of atheist ideology. Every baptism, he said, is a new affirmation of that same grace at work in the present generation. As to burdens, they "like the poor are always with us."

The hours of the day are too few for all he wants to accomplish as bishop. His total church staff of three is hardly enough. Speaking of another problem, he cited a recent government action of assessing a 1% fee on the market value of a church building whether it is used or not, a measure that struck him as stupid and unnecessary. He summed up the most important burden he carries as the one inseparable from his calling as a bishop, being available to pastors and people of the church in their time of need. He is young and has much to learn, he acknowledged, knowing that he cannot "grow old as soon as possible."

It was 7:45 and time to go to supper. We walked around the corner to a restaurant for Lithuanian food, more conversation about families, highlights of our recent global journeys, and enjoyment of the particularly lively table of Polish tourists next to ours. They were well into a rollicking night of eating, drinking, singing and their invitation to join in toasting each other was irresistible. A trio of two violins and flute came by to get everybody in the room singing, clapping hands, and stomping feet to the rhythm. It was late when we left, happy to cap off a day of attention to serious matters, past and present, with a taste of how well Lithuanians and their Polish neighbors know how to party.

Janine Galkauskaite, a middle aged woman smartly dressed in slacks and a warm sweater, was initially shy about being interviewed. Her disclaimer ("I'm not an important person, you know") was more about her modesty than her significance as one who indeed had much to offer. She was among those with memories of meeting in cemeteries for worship and she recalled them as scary and exciting. Her family of devout believers joined with crowds of people from all over who stood together for prayer, Scripture, and hymns that reminded them they were not the first to endure persecution. Janine's family had no church building in which to worship in their town of Taurengi (it was closed to become a cinema) and while the cemetery gatherings frightened her as a child, she also remembered the fun of playing with other children in a forest nearby. As she approached her teens, her mother knew of a pastoral couple in a town an hour away who agreed to prepare her for confirmation. She went by bus, usually once a week but sometimes less frequently, to learn more of the faith she saw practiced by her parents in their collective farm household. There were fifty in her confirmation class taught most often by the pastor's wife who had to be strict in order to hold that many youth together. She characterized her experience as fairly typical of what the church faced before Communism collapsed in the early 1990's. Though police knew of youth being confirmed, the Don't Ask-Don't Tell policy meant they were not officially forbidden. Subtle pressures were always at hand, however, and could surface when it was time to file applications for university enrollment. If no record of participation in Communist Youth organizations appeared, complications could follow. Janina's excellent academic record in high school was enough to get her by that barrier for five years of study in physics at the University of Vilnius. Thereafter she taught an overloaded schedule of science classes in a rural high school that left her exhausted after three years. She returned to Vilnius to complete another degree, this time in computer programming. Her fluency in Russian gave her an edge for a teaching job in a school that included many Soviet citizens then living and working in Lithuania. How was that relationship? She answered that in her case it was satisfactory but not always elsewhere as circumstances varied widely depending on the place. Her brief response was enough to hint at her gifts of spanning prejudices against Russians who were stigmatized as workers on assignment under an unpopular occupying army.

Her memory of March 11, 1990, was one she wanted to describe in detail. That was the date of The Change, as she spelled out the words with capitals. The collapse of Communism in Lithuania was imminent as signs of its loosening grip became increasingly evident. At sundown on March 11 a huge crowd gathered around the parliament building in Vilnius. Janina was living with her mother at the time and helped prepare sandwiches and coffee for the protestors. The Russian army of occupation continued its threatening presence throughout the night. They had killed thirteen Lithuanians trying to take over the television tower during the day. More were shot as the night progressed, some were youth barely in their teens and others were grandfathers whose lives had been severely altered under Stalin-style Marxism. Then, suddenly, it was over. An almost eerie atmosphere of euphoria mixed with confusion followed, she said. Janina's immediate thought was that her church, earlier gutted and turned into a basketball court, could now be restored. By the time the Queen of Sweden visited in 1992 the sanctuary was back in use, an accomplishment for which many had worked hard every night after work for seven years. Her current schedule of full time work in the computer lab of the university limited her time to work in the church office. Was she paid? Pay was whatever was available. But that didn't matter since money was not her motive—said in a tone that made further inquiry inappropriate. She turned to the subject of the Lydia Project, and her enthusiasm for this ecumenical program in eastern Europe to help women lift themselves out of poverty and the ills it begets. Her contribution was grant-writing for new projects and she spoke of the satisfaction of her recent trip to Prague for three weeks of teaching computer skills to women who, in turn, would teach other women seeking a new and better life.

Beverly asked Janina to describe her hopes for the church in Lithuania. 'It would look like a family" she answered, "where people don't just say hello and leave, but care for each other in practical ways." By this she meant no criticism of the priests (aka pastors) in Lithuania who are too few and overworked—she mentioned one serving five congregations. Her point was that church is too often limited to Sunday worship on a formal level. It was through her memories of close knit ties formed during her childhood days of cemetery worship and more recent times of helping rebuild the church that she gained a sense of church as family that she wanted for the coming generation. As she told us her hopes she wondered aloud if her life as a single person colored her vision of the church as family. After listening to her insights from an eventful past and fully engaged present, we said that her aspirations spoke to universal needs in the church everywhere and that she was hardly the unimportant person she announced herself to be as our conversation began.

Meeting with Alfredas Reikertas gave us another facet of the many sided makeup of the church in Lithuania. He, too, had volunteered hours, if not days, of expertise in directing the overall plan for the rebuilding the several structures on the church headquarters compound. He told us that as a youth he had little interest in school but was good at building things. When he began to realize what an opportunity an education was, he got serious about schooling and after five years completed a degree in construction engineering, much of it in night school classes after working all day pouring cement, wiring electrical circuits, or pounding nails as a carpenter. He spent a year of building houses and barns on collective farms in the 1970's which gave him a view of Communist theory as well as its limits of realization in practice. He had been raised in a Christian family in which his mother's strong convictions steered him away from becoming a "Lenin's grandchild" or participant in other Communist youth programs. He never knew his father. But the step-father who raised him was all that a father could be in making him the man that he is. He married in 1976 when he was older; he and his wife have a son and daughter in their teens. All are active in the Vilnius congregation where he led in restoring the building beginning in 1992 (the regime had turned it into a first floor storehouse and basketball court on the floor above) and will be completed as soon as a pipe organ is installed. "The organ coming will be the best in the country and make our church a place where sacred music will be played that hasn't been heard for sixty years" he said with pride in his voice.

Alfredas Reikartas impressed us not only as an expert construction engineer but as a sign of the strength of lay leadership among Lithuanian Lutherans. He is chairman of the church council comprised of five men and five women who meet once a month with Bishop Sabutis to administer the work of the congregation. His administrative experience serves him well in his leadership on the church council with its duties ranging the Sunday School to youth work to overseeing worship to switching the church heating system over to natural gas. Another responsibility is the management of newly constructed apartments in an older part of the church compound, half of which provide rental income and the other half designated for aged members who pay as they are able. What were his hopes for the church? His answer was as interesting as it was unusual. "You know why I get along with just about everybody I meet—Catholics or Jews, Russians or Poles?" he began. "It's because I hear good preaching from sermon texts that are two thousand years old that still apply today. That's my hope for the church, that people will trust God who doesn't change even though things change all the time." He wanted to add something about the American pastors who have come to serve from time to time, but his time and ours was up. We thanked him, shook hands, and were on our respective ways.

Not once did Saida Ronkiene allow herself to smile as we talked with her on a grey, chilly day in the church headquarters office. It was not that her expression was dour or blank as much as unstintingly serious as she told us of what it meant to be a young adult in the church and nation. She was born in the southwestern tip of Lithuania several miles from the border with Kaliningrad (a postage stamp-size patch of land between Lithuania and Poland administered by Russia). She said that the spiritual life of her parents had been much diluted by Communism, which made her typical of a generation in which grandmothers were the main keepers and transmitters of the faith. Saida recalled her own grandmother's custom on Saturday evening of reading Scripture and praying—allowing for no frivolous play in the household—as she prepared for communion and strict Sabbath keeping on Sundays. She admired her grandmother for passing on to her a conviction that God made people strong through keeping the Ten Commandments when others flouted them outright or compromised them by hiding their obedience for fear of being reported to the police. Her grandmother's influence was the reason she was confirmed at fourteen. She did well academically in high school but was beginning to have more questions than answers about God as she entered university in the early 1990's. That spiritual restlessness was behind her switch to the theological curriculum at Klaipeda where she took courses (Mindaugas Sabutis was among her classmates), seeking to know God more deeply and discern what that meant for life in the post-Communist Lithuanian world. That quest, she told me, went largely unresolved in the academic atmosphere of the seminary.

While at Klaipeda, however, she met an American guest instructor in clinical pastoral care, Fred Schmucker, whose courses in pastoral counseling and other methods of applied theology related directly to such real life problems as drug abuse and alcoholism. When he urged her to consider studying in the United States her initial reaction was that her lack of English and absence of any scholarship prospects made it pointless to try. But then the thought of her grandmother's courage in the face of far more daunting problems motivated her to accept Schmucker's help and she traveled to America "by faith rather than by sight." She outlasted culture shock and found her mind stretched by a year of study at Eden Seminary in St. Louis, then returned home and two years later went to Denmark for a half year of diaconal studies. While there she received, quite unexpectedly, a generous offer from St. Louis congregations to sponsor her for two years in New Testament studies at Eden Seminary where she earned her degree.

She wrote her thesis on the role of women in the church, and although it was based on the pastoral epistles of the New Testament, her subject did not make her a sought-after scholar when she returned to the Evangelical Lutheran Church in Lithuania. In response to my question about whether her frequent international moves and diverse menu of studies had brought answers to her earlier quest to know God and discern his work in the world, she answered "Yes, but I was all dressed up theologically with no place to go in Lithuania." Her grandmother's example of strength of faith served her once again as she found work teaching religion in a public high school (European church-state relations differ from the USA), occasional translating, Sunday School teaching, training Catholic youth camp leaders, and major involvement with the Scripture Union.

Her mention of Scripture Union, an ecumenical Scriptural study program begun by British evangelicals and widely known in Europe, made me curious about what she learned as she traveled among Lutherans to advocate its use. "Lutherans in Lithuania don't read the Bible much, given what they've been through" she said, then added "but get interested when they get into small groups and read it together." She explained that as the goal of the Scripture Union method and materials. Since the movement was ecumenical, wherever it was received it brought Lutherans together with Catholic and Reformed Christians in ways new to people from each tradition. Initially it was suspect by clergy who were not used to lay leadership in ecumenical study groups, but when young people came back home from youth camps with enthusiasm for what they had discovered, parents and pastors began to take notice. Since many households have no Bible, or have left it long unused, Saida counts her efforts to change that circumstance as a chief satisfaction. She welcomes it after a zigzag path of half dozen years of international theological study. Her work is voluntary at the moment. She did not go into details of her means of support. She sees herself as a bridge-builder seeking to apply the best she has gained from her past to new challenges in the Lithuanian Lutheran church she has no intentions of leaving. Though her dream of seminary professors in Klaipeda connecting with their ("far too liberal") counterparts at Eden in St. Louis was fanciful, she hoped for the day when the role of women in the Lutheran Church in Lithuania would not be determined by gender but by God's calling. Women presently outnumber men among active Lutherans, she added as a footnote, but held little hope that statistics alone would change minds in a church that had never supported her studies abroad. She discusses these things with Bishop Mindaugas and understands his pragmatic view that the time is not right for women's ordination. In her closing thoughts she emphasized that she did not presume to speak for the majority opinion in the church, then added that neither did her grandmother in her time. That was enough to keep her confident that what she was doing had promise.

Kestutis Pulokas met us later in the day. Smiling comes easily to this genial man with his round, ruddy cheeked face set off by thick black hair, matching mustache and goatee. Like Saida, he is in his thirties, speaks fluent English, has been to the USA several times, studied theology in St. Louis (a summer course at Concordia, the Missouri Synod seminary), is single, active in youth work and lives in Vilnius. Unlike Saida, his visit was short but informative on comparative statistics he brought along. Roman Catholics make up 79% of the Lithuanian population of 3.6 million. His information was that 15% are actively involved. Because Lutherans are a minority of just over 20,000, he said, a higher percentage participate. Sunday attendance in Vilnius is comparatively good—better than in the country-side. It was an insight that surprised us, given the secularizing trends of urban life elsewhere in the world. We mentioned the Thomas Mass in Helsinki and our high regard for it as an effective new form of urban mission. He had attended one in Helsinki also and agreed, adding the hope that it would be well received in Lithuania if well prepared beforehand by competent leaders. He gave us a half dozen web sites on Lutheranism in Lithuania, Latvia and Estonia (both of the latter have larger constituencies) and suggested that we talk further over supper about his work as a journalist, translator, and leader of a Scripture Union group.

Listening to a representative group of Lithuanian Lutherans left as with these impressions. They are one more example in the long history of the church of how suffering for the Gospel produces new seeds of purified faith. The faith survived largely through the heritage of pietism in which lay preachers would gather people in homes for song, prayer, and preaching. Thus was the Gospel handed down from one generation to the next through the decades of war and totalitarian oppression from the 1940's until the 1990's to form the faith in those with whom we spoke. They told us of the renewal they experienced in reclaiming church buildings desecrated during the Communist years in a church reborn under younger clergy led by a young bishop. Tensions carried over from a totalitarian culture of mistrust and accusation still linger, as do rifts aggravated by centuries of strife between a Lutheran minority in a Catholic majority. The Lithuanian Lutherans with whom we spoke prize learning and sacrificed much to gain it. Those who gave us their time were generously candid in their views of the ups and downs in the church, sometimes wary of unexamined change to mimic others, sometimes stubbornly resistant to change initiated by the Holy Spirit. And this impression is lasting: they are people of a small country who showed a large hospitality to strangers like us who came to learn and listen.

PART 4

INTRODUCING
WESTERN EUROPE

A common report from tourists returning home from Europe is that the churches they saw were magnificent. And empty. Thoughtful European Christians, including those of the established Lutheran churches, know this painful reality better than tourists. But they would also have those interested in more than surface impressions know what they are doing amidst an increasingly secularized culture that contains elements as pagan as any the world over. In Sweden, as the chapter below indicates, Lutherans are gradually moving away from state church status into a new relationship with the national government in order to permeate Swedish life in ways beyond Sunday morning church attendance. New methods of mission are also evident in Germany, where, as in the former East Berlin, the outreach is to a generation lost to Marxist ideology, and in the western German area of Darmstadt, where laity and clergy employ ingenious ways of mission outreach from the town fire station. The Finns (who would rather not be lumped with their Scandinavian neighbors to the west) also bear witness to new beginnings, as exemplified in the Thomas Mass, a venture in urban mission that combines traditional liturgical form with innovative methods in reaching those adrift from the faith with a taste of what they are missing. Lutherans in Norway present notable examples of the current mode of "acting locally, thinking globally" and in Denmark the witness of clergy and laity to the Gospel comes with typical Danish restraint and understatement. The theme imparted throughout this chapter centers around western Europe as mission territory, where the church is extricating itself from museum status by starting afresh in creative ministries without abandoning the treasure of more than a millennium of Christian tradition.

Dressed in white Docker slacks, blue shirt and sporty mocs, his tousled blonde hair falling loosely around his shoulders, Alexander Garth does not fit the stereotype of a typical German Lutheran pastor. Nor does his ministry in a gritty neighborhood of what was formerly East Berlin. "Ours is a church for atheists" he said, describing the spiritual wasteland of the urban, post-Communist generation he is called to reach. We met on the fifth floor of a commercial office building where his congregation of new believers meet for worship and friendship. It is a spacious area imaginatively renovated with red leather easy chairs, a coffee bar, and square top stands for conversation in the entrance area. Doors open up to a larger space used for worship and other gatherings, brightened with generous splashes of color visible in the banners from the ceiling, posters around the walls, and wooden benches painted bright red. Sunday worship is at 6 p.m. to accommodate people who are busy or sleeping on Sunday mornings. Everything about this congregation of the Evangelical Church of Germany (EKID) is intended to engage people with no concept of the church or who want nothing to do with the traditional church as they have experienced it.

Alexander Garth

GERMANY

"Want some coffee?" Alexander Garth asked in American-accented English as we began our conversation. Before I could answer he added "in Germany, you know, we have real coffee instead of your colored water in the USA." His casual jokiness was not off-putting but helpful in setting a tone for understanding his unconventional approach to urban mission in Germany today. As he served what was indeed stronger than colored water, he described himself as a church planter, which in his case meant "one too restless to stay in one place very long." During the past year and a half he has learned to stay put in an underclass neighborhood where he and his wife meet people of all kinds on the street, in shops, and wherever possible. "What happens when people show interest?" Beverly asked. His answer came with a typical German orderliness of thinking that belied his untypical appearance: "This is our method. We invite them into our home. Everything starts when strangers feel at home in our living room. Music helps. And something to eat, as well. People come not because of interest in God or religion. They come because they are curious or lonely. In a year's time around fifty have formed the core group. They show real interest in what Jesus Christ means for life. They are the Wednesday evening regulars who are ready for the Eucharist and deeper discipleship. The Sunday evening service has 'a little louder music.' It's for those still at some stage of getting started." His reference to Wednesday regulars and Sunday seekers reflected what he had brought back from an earlier visit to the internationally influential Willow Creek mega-church in suburban Chicago. He made other stops in the Bible Belt of the American south to witness Pentecostal revivals which were like nothing he had ever seen before. "People of all kinds—a former helicopter pilot, a wealthy banker, a school dropout, a homeless woman—came forward to kneel, shout, and cry as they confessed their sins to Jesus." He said he needed time to digest his American experience and adapt what he could to people in the Berlin neighborhood he now serves. He has not worked alone in that process but has joined with others in what is called *Junge Kirche Berlin,* the Young Church In Berlin.

His reference was to a network of twenty urban mission congregations under the auspices of the Berlin City Mission, which in turn is part of the EKID, the acronym for the *Evangelische Kirche in Deutschland* or Evangelical (aka Lutheran) Church in Germany. He offered this example of how his work fits in. On the first Sunday of the month his core group of new believers, people mainly in their twenties, attend a small Lutheran congregation nearby to join with those twice their age for friendship and worship in a traditional church building with an organ, stain glass windows, and so forth. The experience has proven mutually beneficial as people of differing age and background begin to discover that belonging to Christ means belonging to others unlike themselves. Garth has been surprised by the positive influence of his younger core group who have not experienced the deep disillusionment of a failed Communism on the older ones of the nearby congregation who have. He broadened the reference to include many older people of the former East Germany who are still bitter over all they lost to an ideology they never accepted, or are bitter because the

Communism they still believe in is gone. That makes him wonder, he said, whether some in that older generation of the *Deutsche Demokratische Republik,* as the Communist regime was known from 1946–1989, can ever believe in God. He spoke from experience as one who grew up with the generation he was describing.

He was born in 1958 in what was then the East German state of Saxony, one of four children in a household where churchgoing meant "the big four and no more"—Christmas, Good Friday, Easter, and Pentecost. His spiritual care came mostly from his mother who made sure he was baptized in his infancy and who taught him the Lord's Prayer and Bible stories in his early youth. His father, a businessman who was elected the mayor in his town, opposed the Communist takeover in the late 1940's at the cost of both his business and his health. Alexander had only vague ideas of what the Christian faith meant as a youth growing up in the atheist ideology promulgated in the elementary and high schools he attended. That changed when he met youth of the Jesus People movement who helped him "find the Jesus who had found him in baptism" he said with an interesting theological point implied in his words. When I asked him about it he replied that his Lutheran convictions had always stood on the pillar of the Gospel, the Bible, and sacraments of Communion and baptism, but the Jesus People awakened his sleepy soul when he was searching as a seventeen year old. "Jesus was alive. The Holy Spirit had power. The songs, sermons, and prayers in the weekly Jesus People meetings were like nothing I had ever experienced as a Lutheran" he said with animation. What impressed him as well was their refusal to be intimidated by the Stasi (secret police of the East German state) who infiltrated their meetings.

He spoke of these events as his conversion, followed by times of prayer in a small chapel that became his place of refuge as he sought God's direction for his future, and then found it in what he accepted as a clear message from God that he should become a preacher of the Gospel. He studied theology for four years theology at the University of Leipzig under a faculty that he found more boring than helpful in his intention to keep faith with his call to ministry. Following his graduation, his regional Lutheran church (still functioning though restricted by the Communist state) assigned him to a pre-ordination year of practical experience in a

Leipzig congregation. The year was 1988. His supervising pastor and congregation joined with church and wider forces working to bring down a Communism beginning to collapse throughout eastern Europe. He co-edited an underground newspaper and joined the Monday night candle processions that drew thousands in procession through the streets of Leipzig despite threats from the Stasi. The attempts of the state police to arrest and imprison him and other activists were deflected by church and Human Rights groups who acted as a powerful buffer. Finally, late in 1988 his activism led to his expulsion from East Germany and landed him in a West Germany critical of East Germans in general, and in a Lutheran Church with no place for him to serve. He taught school for a year in Munich where he also began a new congregation supported by German Pentecostals, an experience that became an encouraging sign of his church planting gifts. The EKID then took him on and assigned him to a town in southern Germany near the border of the former East Germany where many had come to find housing and work. In the seven years he was there the congregation grew from zero to five hundred people—the more important statistic was that attendance in worship averaged four hundred on Sundays. This brought him and his church planting skills to the attention of the Berlin City Mission leadership and through that mission arm of the EKID to his present work in Berlin.

Before leaving him I asked what he might like to say to us in the west. He welcomed the invitation and began by saying that for him the west begins across the Elbe River in western Germany and then stretches across the Atlantic to America. He wants the church to be more creative in mission, less content with ministry that leaves too many stuck in the "Four More and No More" mockery of serious discipleship. As for the faithful in America—"What can I say other than to love God and Jesus who binds us together in his love. Love people adrift in your cities. Don't love money. Love your environment. You waste too much." He was ready to go on with statistics on American profligacy in causing global warming, but then caught himself, thanked us for coming and sent us on our way. We left Alexander Garth convinced that he and those with his creative gifts for finding those long unloved by the church are needed on both sides of the Atlantic and well beyond.

It was but a twenty minute city train ride to the *Stadtmission Berlin,* the City Mission of Berlin, located nearby the Central Rail Station in the heart of the city. Recently built, it is an attractive four story building that houses City Mission offices and meeting rooms, a restaurant, and guest rooms with accommodations for up to three hundred guests (at the bargain rate of $100 per night), each with a balcony overlooking well landscaped grounds to form an oasis of greenery amidst big city sprawl. The strategic location has an interesting background story. After the main railroad terminal was rebuilt following World War II, it was meant to showcase the new city arising from the total destruction of war. Despite the heady economic boom of the post-war years, however, the government and national railroad ministry officials did not take kindly to the increasing numbers of "riff-raff and homeless bums" loitering at all hours in the resplendent new railroad terminal. The government sought some agency that could remedy what it saw as a blotch on its carefully polished image of the main terminal as symbolic of the newly prosperous Germany. The City Mission had to struggle to pay for the prime land offered (at $20 million USD) in a win-win negotiation in which the homeless poor found shelter in the City Mission and the City Mission found a place for its calling to those never treated as riff-raff.

The *Stadtmission* has a 130 year history in Berlin. Its staff of six hundred is spread among forty social ministry facilities serving senior citizens, disabled persons, prisoners, prostitutes, and the numbers of homeless people of all ages coming to the city for work and finding none. I had learned of the SM from Alexander Garth whose church planting ministry is one among twenty congregations of the *Junge Kirche Berlin* network it sponsors. We found the director, Hans-Jeorg Felker, in a large meeting room as he was about to begin morning worship with the staff of eighty, gathered in a circle, a lighted candle in the center as an invitation to silence before worship. We took our places to hear the director's meditation from the Joseph story in Genesis 38 on readiness for the surprises that Divine providence can bring on any given day. We heard him lead in prayer that God would prepare us all for the surprises at hand on this day. Then he was up and on his way for what was assuredly a full schedule. Since my prior request for time to meet with him had failed to reach him—his abrupt departure made that clear—I dismissed my hope of becoming the first surprise of his day and looked around for another who might take time to inform us on the Berlin City Mission.

Sabine Jaeckel-Engler was that person. She spotted us with her attentive eye as strangers without a prior appointment, eager to make an impromptu visit count, with no way to make that happen, who suddenly show up as Genesis 38 surprises on the spot. She introduced herself in English so fluent I thought she was an American, then filled the next hour with information on the range and depth of the SM that was precisely what we needed. She explained how this arm of the EKID was associated with similar partner agencies throughout the world, including the American Gospel Rescue Mission with branches in America, one of them well known as the Pacific Garden Mission in Chicago. Instead of dwelling on statistics, she told the story of the creative imagination at work in the mission's purchase of five hotels in Berlin and eleven more resort hotels along the North Sea to provide a major source of income. Donations help fill up the balance. No less important than money, she said, are the volunteers who give time and talent in services ranging from building maintenance to directing people in need to the Mission. Her most recent example was one more surprise in keeping with the text of the day. A member of the German parliament (the *Bundestag* is only minutes away) who often passes by en route to his office had noticed the high numbers of guests leaving the dormitory for homeless men and women and stopped to say "we had a lot of guests last night." She told why that comment meant much: "the Berlin city government is broke, anti-church, and pays little attention to us. But it helps when someone from the national parliament has a good word for what we're doing. They ought to—without us they'd be sunk!"

Her story of how it happened that she joined the staff as Felker's assistant was interesting as one more commentary on the theme of daily surprises. She had been a journalist in another city but grew restless with her work and sought something more meaningful. The contract on her studio apartment had expired, and when the new one she signed was unexpectedly cancelled she mentioned her situation to her pastor. He steered her to a position just opening in the Berlin Mission. She came, interviewed, and immediately signed on. The meaning she finds in her work came through in her description of a homeless man—"a real grump" as she put it, had taken a room in the Mission dormitory in exchange for housekeeping and yard work. Morning after morning she would greet him when she arrived, always without response. Then, to her astonishment, one morning he did greet her and the fact that he had shaved off his scraggly beard was another sign that he was coming out of whatever shell encased his life. Recently she met him by chance at a subway station and when he saw her he exclaimed "I've got a job!" Such moments bring her glimpses of her part in the vast mission of the agency, and she emphasized that these are the reasons why her work continues to be fulfilling. When asked by Beverly about what the next ten years might hold, she said that she is a licensed pilot and hopes to build her own plane. Or she might run for political office. And, since her husband is a pastor in one of the *Junge Kirche Berlin* congregations, they might take on a new challenge of starting a congregation in an office building—like one of his colleagues in the network has done. When thinking of all that this bright, committed, beautiful young woman gave us in an unscheduled hour of her time, I wished for the opportunity to tell Director Felker that his homily on surprises carried more immediate application than ever he might have imagined, right under his nose.

Hermannsburg, a town in north central Germany, is an idyllic place of houses and shops notable for their striking white plaster walls and darkened cross-beam exterior, in the Lueneburger Heide (an open heathland) celebrated in German poetry and song. In 1849 its most remembered citizen, Ludwig Harms, the pastor of local Lutheran congregation, founded a missionary society and training school which has sent hundreds of missionaries to Africa and other overseas lands. I wanted to visit the Hermannsburg Mission Seminary, which continues now as part of the EKID, because of my interest in its unique place as the only integrated mission education and practice school left in German Lutheranism. I had met some of its alumni who teach at the Lutheran seminary in St. Petersburg, Russia, and have long admired the school for its role as a voice for the global mission of the Gospel in a church body that needs it. This was a first visit to the seminary campus where Director Henning Wrogemann welcomed us hospitably and arranged for several days of visits with faculty and students. He earned his PhD in Islamic studies at Heidelberg University and, as is the case with all Hermannsburg faculty members, has had missionary experience outside of Germany.

As we talked together he placed the Hermannsburg mission tradition in the context of recent trends. In the 1960's there were six other German mission societies within the EKID. Today Hermamennsburg continues alone; the others have been integrated into their regional church branches or into the World Council of Churches. He regretted this trend as a loss of the spiritual vision necessary at the core of the church's life in response to Jesus' command to bring his good news to all the nations. Financial support for global mission has shrunk. Moreover, the wider numbers of members in congregations in Germany who once identified personally with missionaries can no longer do so. Only in Hermannsburg does this still happen. This trend is part of a larger decline in mission awareness among Lutherans in Germany, as the statistics he cited indicate. In 1999 there were 1,500 missionaries in cross-culture ministries sent out by the EKID. Ten years later the number was 700. Of these, 120 are long term overseas missionaries sent from Hermannsburg which is the only place remaining in Germany where candidates are trained in a curriculum that integrates mission with pastoral theology. I asked him if this had any bearing on the perception of this school as less prestigious than the theological education offered at Heidelberg, Tuebingen, Hamburg and other universities, a view I had picked up when listening to clergy in Germany. He acknowledged the perception as widespread but made no apology for the 150 year old Hermannsburg tradition which is needed more than ever in today's Germany. While national statistics cite the nation's population of 82 million as 65% Christian (27 million Roman Catholic, 26 million Lutheran), the more revealing data comes from a city like Dresden where 2% of the population identify themselves as Christian, or Chemnitz, with 5%. Both cities were formerly under East German Communism, but Wroggeman's view was that West German materialism is no less a challenge to the faith as it spreads throughout the nation. Academic theology in prestigious universities must change to meet new realities, he said, and Hermannsburg's less-than-elite reputation may be more relevant in enabling that change than is recognized.

He described his own background as a paradigm for what is needed on a large scale. He was born in Hermannsburg and raised in the *Grosskirche*, the local congregation which has played a central role in the century and a half history of the mission school. His early interest was in environmental engineering, but as a university student he was moved when attending a mission festival (2000 people gathered for a day of preaching and mission-centered worship) in which he sensed a call to ministry. He switched to theological study under the Hermannsburg faculty and was further enriched for his vocation by participation in fellowship groups of youth who met for prayer, retreats, Scriptural study, and sharing faith with others. He explained that such groups have spread elsewhere in Germany and expressed the hope that others can experience the benefits he found in the solid spiritual influence of his fellowship group throughout his time of university study. That basis also prepared him well for his two years of required military service, followed by his doctoral studies at the at the university in Heidelberg. As a freshly minted PhD in Islamic studies, he kept the Hermannsburg tradition of overseas ministry, in his case a term of several years as a missionary in Africa. What followed his time abroad was a six year pastorate in a congregation in Hannover. As he filled out this picture of the past two decades of his life, I could not miss the strong undercurrent of devotion to formal education from the early teens through graduate school, matched by the equally strong effort to form the life of the soul together with the life of the intellect that comes through in the Hermannsburg tradition. In a lighter vein he told me that his life has been happily broadened by his marriage to his American wife (born in Chicago) and by their three young children who tease him about his funny English and their mother about her funny German.

Our days on campus put us in touch with some of the forty students currently in residence who talked with us about the rigors of the six year program for a degree. After their third year they receive a bachelor of arts degree awarded in conjunction with the University of Birmingham in England. Then comes an internship somewhere abroad, and after returning, students continue on three more years for a master's degree awarded in conjunction with the Norwegian Mission Society in Stavanger. It was another indication of the unique Hermannsburg intention of immersing students in a continuing awareness of the global mission of the Christian faith as it also grounds them as a leaven of mission influence within the EKID. How does that leaven work? I asked. Wroggeman described the coming plan to bring students from other theological faculties in German universities for a semester of missiological study at Hermannsburg, followed the next year by a two month internship overseas and a final requirement of a one hundred page thesis reflecting the impact of their experience. He was pleased to describe these plans for widening the range of mission studies and spoke appreciatively of the willingness of the faculty of nine (equivalent to the faculty positions of integrated missiology in all the other German universities combined) to take on the challenge of added duties. "We're still far behind Fuller Seminary in California with its forty professors in this field" he added, with the further note that declining financial support from his own regional Lutheran Church of Lower Saxony makes it all the more challenging for Hermannsburg to continue its traditional role as leaven for mission within German Lutheranism. He used an interesting metaphor to describe it. "We're like the medieval court jester who alone had the place of questioning, mocking, criticizing the king. The overseas missionary is that person in today's global church, asking key questions from the outside while demonstrating dedicated ministry from the inside." Several days of conversations with students and faculty confirmed our impression of the importance of their asking critical questions of the church and demonstrating answers through faithful mission lived out at home and abroad. At the Hermannsburg campus and during our previous days in Berlin we heard frequent concern expressed over the decline of the church, evident in the shrinking numbers of people who gather for worship and disperse for witness. We were ready to test those assertions in different settings among people with other experiences. That opportunity came in the southwest German city of Darmstadt and its environs, less than an hour on the autobahn from the Frankfurt International Airport.

Rolf Diepen, a retired dentist in his seventies with bushy white hair and beard to match, is a warm-hearted, outgoing man who chauffeured us to various people in and around Darmstardt whose stories we wanted to hear. While doing so he told us about himself, beginning with the circumstances he faced when graduating from dental school in 1947. World War II had ended only two years before and there were few openings for him to begin is practice or even find a building still standing in Darmstadt for an office. More importantly, it was a time when he felt that he as a German should make some positive contribution to the world. This became possible when he went to Papua New Guinea as a member of the medical mission team of the American Lutheran Church to serve people much in need of health care. He said he relished the work through five years without furlough, but had to return to Germany because of health problems his young wife encountered. He has been an active member of his congregation during the thirty two years since, and now in his retirement serves as a volunteer welcoming new residents in the area—including Muslim families from Turkey and elsewhere in the Middle East. His matter-of-fact manner in describing his lay ministry made me wonder if he was exceptional because of his earlier international experience and lengthy years of congregation participation. "I don't think so" he answered, "there are more of us than you realize." I wanted to hear more but we arrived at his home where his wife, Ine, shared her five course birthday (her seventieth) dinner with us as guests around the Diepen table. It was memorable not only for the splendid cuisine but as another opportunity to sit in the home of a family to hear stories that reflect the faith they live.

Ine told of her close friendship with Sister Josefa, the abbess of the *Marienschwestern,* the Sisters of Mary, which is a Lutheran nunnery in Darmstadt situated on spacious grounds where many go to pray, think, or simply be. Ine mentioned that Josefa is the name Klara Schlink took when joining the Lutheran order of nuns, and that she is the sister of the late Edmund Schlink. He was an internationally known theologian and churchman whose writings I had read at the seminary and later in my ministry. By coincidence he was associated with a memorable event in my life. It happened on a Sunday in August, 1954, the occasion of my first sermon preached after being ordained and installed as an assistant pastor at Grace Lutheran Church in the Chicago suburb of River Forest. I remember greeting people in the narthex after the service, and when shaking the hand of a distinguished looking man with a German accent heard him say that his name was Edmund Schlink. I was more flummoxed than flattered when realizing who he was, but I did catch the wry humor of the one complimentary comment he could offer—"splendid music!" He had come to Chicago as a delegate to the World Council of Churches which began in nearby Evanston the next day. When hearing the story the Diepens insisted on taking us to meet Sister Josefa—Klara Schlink—the following day. We did so, much to her delight when hearing my story about her brother, and to our benefit when learning more about the ministries of the nuns, and walking the well kept grounds to admire the magnificently wrought bronze depictions of Jesus' passion and resurrection.

Two more regional church leaders in the Darmstadt area told us of their work and significance for the larger picture of church life. Arno Ahlmann, 50, has the oversight of clergy and congregations of the EKID in the Darmstadt area which reaches 54,000 people who are registered as Lutherans. He came up in the tradition of university theological education, and studied under Juergen Moltmann and other notable theologians at Tuebingen in the 1970's when universities in Germany were experiencing the convulsive changes that shook campuses throughout Europe and America. He said that during his practical year as a vicar in a Darmstadt congregation he discovered his calling to ministry. He also learned the valuable lesson that "the pastor must prove himself as someone more than an authority figure in a black clergy gown." He words implied the challenge of more time and improved efforts to reach the non-traditional German population, especially Muslims (12-15% of the current population) who migrate to Darmstadt for jobs in the chemical industries headquartered there. He said there was no shortage of pastors to serve congregations; the need was for continued practical education of existing clergy to meet new demands for which their highly academic university years of theology did not prepare them. This is the challenge of his work as superintendent of a region, to develop materials that can give traditionally trained pastors in traditionally Lutheran congregations a clearer vision and better methods for their vocation in the complex, rapidly changing urban life of modern Germany. Any examples? I asked. He mentioned clergy who network in collegial groups to learn from each other's practice of specialized ministries. He described the Open Doors program, already three years underway, in which church doors are intentionally kept open and trained people stationed inside to receive those with myriad needs who have nowhere else to turn for help. He spoke of the effectiveness of the Taize Liturgy offered in various congregations on Friday evenings. It is a way of worship imported from France that emphasizes short passages of Scripture, readily singable songs composed with artful simplicity, and broad spaces of silence for prayer and meditation in a sanctuary illuminated by candles. What keeps him fresh for his work? was my other question. "I am a friend of Italy and Florence" was all he needed to say in referring to his annual vacation visits.

Helmut Spengler, the retired president of the Hessen-Nassau regional church of the EKID, received us in the living room of his amply-furnished flat. He looks the part of a leader—a tall man, dignified, and an easy manner in making strangers know they are welcome. Rolf Diepen had given Spengler a briefing on our purpose, and after introducing us offered to be the interpreter if needed. That the two men were longtime friends showed when Spengler kidded Diepen that his English was twice as fluent as Diepen's. He then moved directly into a subject of interest to me, one that I had not yet heard addressed by older Germans who lived through the rise of the Nazi movement in the 1930's and the disastrous years of World War II. Spengler, first cautioning that his was but one of many with such stories, offered it nonetheless as a reflection of what many carry into the present from those dark times. His parents were among those ousted from Silesia, a former German territory until 1918 when post-World War I arrangements redesigned eastern Europe, and had fled as refugees to the Marburg region of central Germany. There they started a new life by working hard through the harsh economic times of the 1920's without succumbing to Hitler's seductive ideology of strident nationalism that swept him and the Nazi Party into power in 1933. In contrast to many Germans of the time who resented their nation's post World War I humiliation, they could recognize in Nazism the poisonous intrusion into the Lutheran church that it came to be. Early on they opposed the "Deutsche Christen" movement whereby church leaders handpicked by Hitler became feckless puppets of a compromised faith. His father, a layman who had worked variously as a teacher, furnace installer, and choir director (regularly harassed by Nazi stooges in his village), showed courage by circulating the banned writings of Martin Niemoeller, the famed U-boat captain-turned-pastor whom he knew. Growing up in a such a household, Spengler was attracted to meetings of a Christian Student group led by an influential pastor. He took his guitar along as he joined others going from village to village to lead small gatherings in homes for prayer and Scripture, often hosted by simple farm people whose piety and hospitality moved him deeply. His theological education began at the conservative Bethel seminary in Bielefeld and continued at the University of Marbug under the widely known New Testament scholar, Rudolf Bultmann ("I thought more of him when I learned he attended church on Sundays and made pastoral calls on patients in a sanitarium"). He skipped over much in his years as a pastor and regional church president, preferring instead to describe such subjects as the theological tensions between the Reformed and Lutheran traditions in his branch of the EKID, his study of Jungian psychology to become a better pastoral counselor, his advocacy of women's ordination when that issue arose, and the more current challenge of a growing immigrant Muslim population. He used a term new to me, *Evangelikal,* to describe Lutherans who reflect earlier pietist movements and still emphasize the necessity of personal relationship with Christ, the inerrancy of the verbally inspired Scriptures, and non-acceptance of homosexuals in the church. It was one among numerous themes that could have been aired further, but Rolf Diepen was looking at his watch as a sign to leave for the next stop. After expressing our thanks to Helmut Spengler for his time and insights, we were on our way. Two German clergy had given us their thoughts on the life of the church in Germany. It was time to listen to laity on the same subject.

Iver and Barbara Brackert can hardly be described as typical German lay Lutherans. He is a retired university professor. She is an accomplished artist. Nor can their household be described as typical of what one would find commonly throughout Germany. Their living room is spacious, tastefully furnished, with a grand piano at one side. On one wall Barbara's framed art work is displayed. On the opposite wall are shelves lined with books reflecting Iver's lifelong academic career. But their hospitality can be described as typical of the welcome we received from hosts all

Beverly Lueking, Iver and Barbara Brackert

along the way. As was their impeccable English. And this as well: the coffee and cake served at the late afternoon hour of our arrival. The vegetarian supper served later on was not typical, the Brackerts explained, when we enjoyed it at their table. By that time our early impressions were well formed that we were in the company of people whose welcome was warmly genuine, offered with German reserve and mannered propriety. If that made the Brackerts seem somewhat distant, not by intention but by circumstance, any perceived barrier was removed by the remarkable openness with which they revealed themselves in the hours ahead. They were not politely aloof but forthcoming in ways we would not forget.

That openness began during a walk through the woods nearby. They brought up a matter they had in common from their family backgrounds having to do with their fathers as the reason for their alienation from the church from their early years on. Barbara's father was a U-boat captain in German Navy who, before losing his life in World War II, made his career his religion and thus his family had no spiritual support from him in their time of need. Iver's father was a pastor who pressed upon his son—and everybody else—a joyless Lutheranism darkened by incessant reminders of sin and human unworthiness. Furthermore, he said, his father's stern temperament could only be described as a psychopathic meanness deeply lodged in him. He recalled the bizarre circumstances of growing up in a family where "Every night at six o'clock, as regular as clockwork, my father would blow up in anger at me—repeating what he had experienced from his father in his childhood!" Years of that nightly abuse made him eager to escape the nightmare of living at home by leaving it for study at a university. The emotional scars of his upbringing did not leave him, however. He carried them through his graduate studies, his first marriage, and his early years as a young faculty member in the early 1970's. His world collapsed when he broke down under the pressures that trapped him in the crossfire between the radical and reactionary factions of his university. His marriage failed, and he said it took six years of psychoanalysis to peel back the layers to the core problem—the damage done by his psychotic father and the meanness of his ersatz religion. As he spoke of these personal traumas with a disarming candor we came to the end of our walk and were back at the Brackert door, ready for the veggie dinner and lighter conversation about family, travels, and the virtues of good German wine.

The next afternoon Barbara picked up the conversation where Iver had left it. She, too, had been divorced and had no place to turn during that bleak time except to a friend who introduced her to yoga. She called it a stepping stone toward regaining much need self-esteem. What blessed them both in the most healing and lasting way was finding each other, falling in love, and beginning a new life together that had promise in every way except for a shared spiritual grounding with opportunities for meaningful fellowship in the faith. A close friend of Barbara's sensed that vacuum and was bold enough to suggest to them both that her experience in an ashram in India could be the transforming experience for the Brackerts that it had been for her. Iver dismissed it out of hand. Barbara mimicked his mocking response as she quoted his rebuke: "Picture this, two German intellectuals going off to India to absorb in a week what took a millennium of Hinduism to develop!" But Barbara was not dismissive of the idea and continued turning it over in her mind. As she did so she was startled on one occasion—it was during a yoga exercise—when she had a sudden vision of a mystical light of blinding whiteness. It did not send her off to India but instead to the library to read up on Indian mysticism. "We're Germans, you know" she said, with humor for the German tendency to analyze the mystery out of everything. After that, Iver began to show signs of interest in the ashram idea and joined Barbara in discussing her findings. Then came the day when, to her surprise, he announced "We're ready, let's go" and they were off to Puttapotty, the town in India recommended by Barbara's friend. What they found there captured them absolutely, Iver said, and their lingering skepticism quickly dissipated. He named it as the unconditional love which they felt from the moment of their arrival as the *dashan,* the Indian guru, went among the hundreds of people gathered not with a formal outline of daily schedules and required activities, but with simple words of welcome and gestures of caring attention for each. The ashram was held in a large building, surrounded by small tents for sleeping. Both recalled how they felt something utterly new to them as the days unfolded. It was an acceptance and freedom in daily meeting with people of different traditions who were open to each other, without aggressiveness or judgment, sometimes confessing long held hurts, other times listening to the same from others. The time was just before Christmas in 1992 ("blistering hot weather for us who had left Germany in the coldest December in decades"), when the guru invited the Christians present to celebrate the birth of Jesus. A cantor from Hamburg gathered a choir, and when singing O Come All Ye Faithful and the Hallelujah chorus from Haendel's Messiah, Iver said that for the first time in his life he experienced the joy in the Christian message that he and his father had missed all their lives. They stayed at the ashram for three weeks. Barbara's bout with Indian food caused their return home, but not before the Indian guru had urged them to find their Christian roots back in Germany and count the India experience as a prelude to knowing God as Christians who could sing with joy because their hearts were flooded with God's love.

"We took his advice" Iver said, "but when returning home to tell our families of going to India with skeptical curiosity about Hinduism and coming home with an appeal to rediscover our Christian roots, things took an unexpected twist. Our relatives disapproved of the ashram journey altogether." One of them, he added, even sent Barbara a book warning her about the bad influence of Hinduism. Barbara interjected to say how sad it was that her family could not be open to the possibility that an Indian Hindu could lead them into a joyful embrace of God's love as Christians—something the relatives themselves have yet to experience. Iver then told of a post-ashram event that came as a gift he thought could never happen in his lifetime. It was the healing of memories still festering from his disastrous relationships with his late father. The way it occurred was through a therapeutic process he called *Familie Austellung*, (literally "Family Exhibit" or, in less awkward English, family re-imagining) a term from German psychological vocabulary meaning the reconstituting of a dysfunctional family. He described it in considerable detail as a group process led by a psychologist in which participants reconstruct the trauma of failed family relationships. They take roles, face conflicts, probe causes, examine reactions, expose denials, enact forgiveness, strategize for ongoing reconciliation, make timetables for accountability, and thus help each move toward healing. The depth of what *Familie Ausstellung* meant to him came through as Iver wept openly in our presence when retelling the profound emotions he felt and the flood of tears he could not hold back when his turn came to confront the unhealed memories of his father's ranting. In such moments, shared with us in trust and without a hint of embarrassment, we were allowed entrance into a sacred inner space in the hearts of our hosts. Stereotypes fell away. They gave us something we could not have anticipated the day before while sipping coffee and enjoying the formalities of a nascent acquaintanceship.

Brackert remembered to add an important word about how the psychologist chose to conclude the therapy. "We cannot heal our broken families without God laying his peace upon us" he said, and then explained how he asked one person in the group to symbolize God's act of peacegiving by going among the participants, placing a hand on the head of each, and speaking a benediction. That was more than a symbolic gesture for the Brackerts. It was a stepping stone that led them to do as the Indian guru had urged. They joined a congregation.

Andreas Klein, the pastor of the Lutheran congregation in the Darmstadt suburb of Traise, took the Brackerts under his wing as one well equipped to minister them. We met him on a Saturday afternoon in the parsonage where he, his wife, Johanna, and their three young sons live. He is personable, bright, and well positioned to understand my interest in gaining his perspective on church life in today's Germany. He began our conversation by sketching three concentric circles on a page, with the outer circle representing the roughly equal numbers of Catholics and Lutherans that make up the main body of Christians in the land. The next circle in represents the Evangelical Church of Germany (aka EKID, or Lutheran) with its conservative wing (conservative here means

Andreas and Johanna Klein

a closer adherence to the 16th century documents growing out of the Lutheran reformation) and a liberal wing still well represented in theological faculties of certain universities. The third circle signified a somewhat newer "evangelical" wing in the EKID—evangelical in the sense of connection with the American mega-church and Billy Graham associations. "If this can help you place me among these circles I've described, I am a left wing evangelical" he said in an interesting phrase that gave focus to our conversation. What would a right wing evangelical be? I asked.

His answer turned to the free churches that were ultra-conservative Lutherans, never within the EKID. The German Baptists were examples. As a left wing evangelical, he went on to say, he was something of a theological hybrid. He was raised by devout parents who sent him to middle and high schools where he learned Latin and Greek for a future in pastoral ministry that he had envisioned in his youth. He chose voluntary work in a community instead of the mandatory two years of military service, then studied theology under well known New Testament scholars at the University of Tuebingen. In 1990 he married Johanna and switched his studies to the more conservative Lutheran faculty in Erlangen to complete his formal university training for ordination. Following that, he spent two years as a *vikar* under a capable pastor who mentored him in ministering to people represented in the three circles he had described. "I had no problem with any of them and in fact gained from the experience" he said. As I listened to his recitation of the academic demands of the decade of his educational journey from high school through university through post-ordination continuing studies I was struck by the two things about German clergy. They study intensely. And this German clergyman, at least, made that clear in his facile English. I asked him if the intensity of German theological education makes for better parish pastors, and, as a footnote, inquired where he learned English so well. The footnote was easy, he said, with brief mention of a sabbatical in the United States. The other question about being a better pastor was answered in this thoughtful comment: "A good pastor is measured by how well the laity do their daily ministry in the world." It was more than a cliché. He showed me a forty five page document he had authored on ways of equipping baptized Christians to be the front line of where the church meets the world. It summarized his three month sabbatical leave spent in Germany (at an institute for church development in Greifswald) and the United States (among Lutheran congregations in Minnesota) for the purpose of deepening his personal spiritual life, engaging with leaders of widely varied church ministries, and learning from those adept in fostering lay ministry. The sabbatical, coming after ten years of pastoral ministry, confirmed his determination to offset the long-standing tradition of the pastor-centered congregation. It furthered his vision of pastoral ministry as focused on preparing an enlightened laity who understand themselves as *being* the church in full partnership with the pastor who serves them. He cited examples from his work: small groups of married couples meeting for Bible study on family life, lay visitors to the homes of the elderly (who are sometimes asked why the pastor is not doing this), and in connection with a first-time event scheduled for the next day, working with lay leaders in preparation for a Sunday service in the local fire station.

The fire station setting for a service had a mission purpose, Klein explained, to attract people of the town as well as provide a unique live television connection to missionaries in West Africa and Central Russia. We arrived at the Sunday morning fire station site early enough to see pastor and people working together. Some were getting the impromptu altar in place with a sizeable television monitor screen alongside, testing the setup to make sure the overseas transmission was working. Others were busy filling up the space normally occupied by two large fire trucks with chairs for congregational seating. Outside the station a merry-go-round had a waiting line of kids to get on. Another group was serving bratwurst and soft drinks to adults and more children, the latter coaxed away from climbing on the parked fire trucks by the prospect of a hot dog at their parents' behest, then a quick run back for more play on real life fire engines. The obligatory brass band (four trumpets, two trombones, a French horn) was warming up, ready to accompany the congregation of over a hundred congregants, nicely mixed in age, in the hymns for the morning service about to begin. The televised connections with the overseas missionaries went without a hitch, a tribute to German technological know-how I thought, admiringly, and their reports fit well with Klein's homily on the global reach of the Gospel. He asked me to add my words to the theme of the day, which I did with examples of the exponential growth of the church south of the equator and the lessons that holds for us in the global north. I also took the opportunity as an outsider to witness to the work of the Spirit we had seen in Germany in recent days. As I did so my eye fell on Iver and Barbara Brackert sitting in the congregation. They were smiling.

As pastors everywhere are given to doing after Sunday worship, we enjoyed a post-mortem while seated on a porch with a view of the town of

3,000 around us. Klein told us that about 1,700 are registered by law as members of the *Evangelische Gemeinde Traise*—the Lutheran Congregation in Traise. Sunday worship attendance averages between seventy to one hundred, a favorable number in Germany. Catholics sometimes attend and commune, a sign of good ecumenical relationships with the neighboring priest. Johanna spoke of her place in the ministry and the pleasure she finds in working with youth. She and twelve other women team up to guide the fifteen to seventeen year old boys and girls who take turns in leading a youth service each Sunday morning between ten and eleven, with many parents attending. She said that the teens themselves are the most effective influence in attracting and holding the younger children up to twelve. Among the satisfactions of ministry Andreas mentioned was one I have not often heard from clergy—preparing teen age youth for confirmation. He described a program that has now grown to thirty in number as he has continued to fine tune it over the past ten years. In keeping with his emphasis on pastor-laity partnership, he has formed a team of five mothers and several older teens to join him in instruction. He teaches the basics of the faith. The mothers and older youth help apply them to the home and school life that is the daily milieu of the confirmands Their preparation begins at age ten and continues through fourteen in segments of eight weeks with breaks for retreats along the way. His creativity in engaging laity to enrich their common ministry to youth was another sign of the a willingness to innovate for the sake of mission so wonderfully evident in the fire station service.

As we sat together on the parsonage balcony talking further of the ups and downs of ministry in Traise and beyond, Klein was quiet for a moment. Then, looking in the direction of the Alpha and Omega Greek letters displayed across its white stucco exterior, he said: "Those two letters say it all. Christ is our Alpha and Omega. In his name we keep trying to begin all over again here. And we count on him for the final outcome." His impromptu reflection was simple, unforced, and genuine. It came as a benediction on our day together, and our days with others in Germany who strive to live the Good News in this land where Luther's reformation began nearly five hundred years ago. They breathe a Spirit-given newness into a church not to be written off as a dying relic of a bygone age.

If one were to travel through Denmark today looking for signs of spiritual life among the 5.4 million Danes living on this peninsular flatland jutting out from Europe's northwest corner, a visit to the church in Bagsvaerd on the outskirts of Copenhagen would be a worthwhile stop. The building itself is an inspiration, especially in the use of natural light pouring in, seemingly whitewashed, as it reflects gently off the ceiling and walls to suffuse the entire sanctuary with an ethereal glow. The sense of expansiveness is enhanced by light refracted through the lattice wall of glass and wood behind the altar, providing a feeling of unbounded openness. The Danish architect, Joern Utzon (The Sydney Opera House, the Library in Alexandria, Egypt, etc.) and the parish community worked together for eleven years to overcome multiple obstacles before completing this worship space that is stunning in its uncluttered simplicity so typical of Danish style. Such is the impact of the architecture. What goes on when people gather inside?

DENMARK

Plenty goes on inside, said Charlotte Pedersen, the rector (*sognepraest,* the Danish term for senior pastor) of Bagsvaerd Church. As for the internationally famous building itself, she prizes it as an intentional departure from the romanticized ideal of the Danish village church with its red roof and stepped gables where little happens except a service on Sunday with few attending. At Bagsvaerd Church worship is well attended on Sundays since its dedication in 1976; also baptisms, weddings and funerals, afternoon confirmation classes for youth twice a week, concerts, classes, Bible study groups, The church is a framework for community, a place where people connect with one another. Bagsvaerd Church as well as all other Lutheran churches throughout Denmark also function as the repository for the records of births and deaths of all Danish citizens, church members or not. They are the conduit for the payment of the church tax which supports the construction and maintenance of church buildings, clergy salaries, and theological education of clergy. Since 1849 the Danish constitution grants freedom to other religious communities besides Lutherans to practice their beliefs; some eighty such communities exist today, including those made up of Jews, Muslims, Pentecostals,

Mormons and Jehovah's Witnesses. The parish council, an elected group between six to twelve in number, is responsible for the administration of local church affairs, has decisive influence in the appointment of pastors and bishops, hires church personnel, and sees to the upkeep of the church building and housing for the pastor. She added these statistics to round out my overview of the Evangelical Lutheran Church in Denmark: 2,500 clergy served 2,200 congregations, 1,000 of which are in towns with less than a thousand residents. In smaller communities 80% of the residents are registered as members. In Copenhagen that percentage drops to 60%, and in neighborhoods with a heavy migrant population the percentage is 30% or less. Women have been ordained to the pastoral office in the church since 1946.

A Sunday spent with our host in Denmark, Niels Henrik Olesen, the pastor of Simon Peter parish in Copenhagen, put names and faces to these statistics. He had met us at the airport the day before. He was recognizable by the Danish flag emblem on his coat lapel, and easy to converse with because of his fluent English and welcoming manner. Through Lutheran World Federation contacts in Chicago I had corresponded with him months earlier, introducing our purpose and asking his help in arranging contacts with laity and clergy during our short stay in Denmark. As in every place

Niels Henrik Olesen

during our global travels for this book, Olesen and people like him are essential. With cheerful efficiency he steered Beverly and me through the maze of airport arrival details and outside to board the public bus for the half hour ride to downtown Copenhagen. Before leaving us at our hotel, he gave us instructions on getting to church the next morning and was on his way home by public transportation. He doesn't need a car—a commentary on the adequacy of public transportation for getting anywhere in Copenhagen he needs to go; his bicycle serves him well for shorter errands in his parish neighborhood.

Simon Peter Lutheran Church (Lutheran is a redundant adjective in Denmark where 95% of the population is registered as Lutheran) is a brick building, just seventy years old and therefore regarded as still new in this land where King Harald the Bluetooth introduced Christianity in 960 A.D (and where King Christian III established the reforming movement of Martin Luther as the state church in 1536). On the Sunday morning of our visit there were 85 present in the church which seats 125. Olesen preached the sermon, conducted a baptism, and served Holy Communion vested in his black clergy gown and wearing the white pleated collar which looks like a beehive to an irreverent observer. The hymn tunes were ones we recognized. A man seated immediately in front of us handed us a hymn book opened to the right page as the liturgy began, a thoughtful gesture that communicated a wordless language of welcome. Following the service all went into the adjoining church hall for coffee and conversation. The first one to greet us was Rev. Tova Fergo, a member of the pastoral staff here for thirty-three years during which she also served a term as head of the Ministry of the National Church. Further conversation with her would have been invaluable but before she left for other duties of the day she introduced me to two others with stories to tell. Both were reminders of the truth that there is no such thing as "a simple lay person."

Niels Anton Dam, 67, began as a bricklayer, moved on to become a construction engineer, and on one occasion heard a returned missionary from India speak of the need there for volunteer workers with construction skills. That speech put him on a path that led to sixteen years of service in Bangledesh under the mission arm of the Danish church. I asked him a series of questions that were much more than he could condense into a coffee hour conversation. Rather than go on at length, he turned to his friend with the comment that here was one with whom I should speak. Ole de Voss, also 67, is married, the father of three, and grandfather of one. He was a teacher and later headmaster of a school in his native Copenhagen in which 90% of the enrollment were children of immigrant families from eighteen countries around the world. As is the case throughout Denmark, religion is part of the curriculum; de Voss said he had no problem when teaching religion, since many of the Muslim parents wanted religious instruction for their children and saw no difference between God and Allah in the classroom. He was preparing for his first trip to the United States and visits to New York and Washington with a group of Danish educators. Both men chimed in with observations on the national church in Denmark as they see it but the time was too short for them to do anything more than mention several mission movements at work in various segments of Danish society. These were impressive men, active in their retirement years, internationally experienced, and reminders of how important it is to look beyond statistics on church life in any given place and listen for the treasures hidden in stories from people who are rarely, if ever, asked to share them.

Later that afternoon Olesen told me more about his own ministry in response to my question about the family of the child baptized that morning. He knows them by name from his twenty year pastorate in the Simon Peter parish and spoke of pastoral care for various members of this family on other occasions, including some of the relatives who now live in England. He went on to explain that this is not as common as he wished, but it has to do with what it means to be a pastor in a parish. Parish does not mean congregation as the word is often understood in the United States, but refers to the geographic area in which the church is located, in this case to the 9,000 people live who are in the parish of Simon Peter Church. Most of them are registered as church members, but the 9,000 include some who are not Lutherans, but gather in what Nielsen termed as closed religious societies. The Danish government requires that as a congregation of the state, Simon Peter Church must register all births, marriages, and deaths of everyone living in the parish. I asked him if the family of the baptized child would be present again for worship anytime soon. He said that he hoped so, then added that it might be a dozen years hence when the child returns to prepare for confirmation, or not until another decade thereafter when it's time for a wedding, or perhaps not until the funeral at the time of death. I told him of my share in that same dilemma of cheapening grace by reducing it ceremonial visits to the church for baptism, wedding, and funeral. Some call it three wheel Christianity—wheeled to church when hatched, matched, and dispatched. He picked up on it immediately as a blight on Christ's church throughout western Christendom and agreed that here is a microscopic glimpse of why the church is in steep decline in Europe. Yet, he added, faithful ones like Niels Anton Dam, Ole deVoss, and all others they represent, are persons of hope who cannot be discounted. This moment, early as it was in the first day of our meeting each other, gave me a brief, fragmentary glimpse into the mind and heart of a Danish pastor who knows the complexities of ministry in a parish of 9,000 amidst a state church tradition that can be both a burden and blessing. He also knows how deeply he needs the gifts of the Spirit in stirring Danes who enjoy world class prosperity to find the true treasure of life in Christ's forgiveness of their sins and thus made free to worship God, build each other up, and share their faith in their daily calling in the world. We agreed that lifelong participation in a worshiping community is essential to hearing the Word of God and keeping it. For my part, I needed to guard against making my one Sunday visit at Simon Peter Church a basis for assessing the whole of Danish Christianity, since we Americans can too easily gauge the depth of Christian discipleship by counting noses on Sunday morning. That was on my mind as we took the public bus to the Lutheran Cathedral in downtown Copenhagen.

There we met Karsten Fidelius, a man whose hospitable greeting was necessarily brief on this day when his time for strangers was minimal. He is chairman of the Cathedral parish council and the head of DanChurchAid which was in the final hours of its annual Sunday of gathering money from the 2,200 congregations in Denmark on what is called "Silent Hunger Sunday"—the campaign name for the church's battle against hunger which, I was told by the materials at hand, claims the life of one child every six seconds around the world. He is a professor of history on the faculty of the University of Copenhagen, a man with a broad range of interests that include the use of the media and the mastery of Slavic languages. Though it was the end of a long and exhausting day for him as the one in charge of the total operation, he still had energy left over to show us around the DanChurchAid office on the second floor of a 200 year old building next to the Cathedral. The place was buzzing with staff people tallying contributions, preparing reports, and wrapping up details of a nationwide effort. Two of them took time from their duties to tell us what they were doing. Pastor Henrik Stubkjaer is the general secretary of DanChurchAid, his assistant is Mr. Mads Klaestrip Kristensen; both are in their early forties. DanChurchAid began in 1922 as an arm of the church and among its other responsibilities has conducted this national day of collection once every year since. This year some 19,000 volunteers took part throughout Denmark. The intake this time was estimated to be at the two million USD mark, less than hoped for. They guessed that the national flap over a recent cartoon caricature of the Prophet Mohammed in a Danish newspaper hurt the collection. It was not a failure, however; the fact that it happens is significant in itself. Besides the annual collection, DCA maintains 110 second hand shops around the country. The proceeds support the church's mission to ten focus countries outside of Denmark. It networks with congregations to present education programs on the global mission of the church and lobbies in the Danish parliament for humanitarian causes at home and abroad. As the two staffers returned to their unfinished work we enjoyed further conversation with other workers at the refreshment table, then went with Fidelius to the Cathedral for the closing moments of the Taize Service, a fitting conclusion to a full Sunday.

Further conversation with Niels Olesen the next day gave us a wider view of the man and his calling. He was born of pious parents in a household of the Holmens Parish in Copenhagen and baptized in the church there, one known from earlier times as the congregation of the Danish Navy. It now serves a heavily migrant population which has come in from eastern Europe and Africa. In the late 1960's he began his university studies as a physics and mathematics major, adding courses in theology as he sensed a call to ministry. For a time before his ordination he was a lay naval chaplain, serving on the naval base on the Faroe Islands, half way to Iceland the North Atlantic. He experienced his call to ministry as a gradual process well rooted in the Gospel-centered faith his parents lived in word and deed. He spoke of God as One who was transcendent beyond time and space and yet gracious in bestowing upon him a faith which was not forced but received as a gift. He was guided well by teachers in his Holmens Parish schooling where teacher taught him math and languages as well as engaging with him in with teachers in lively discussions of faith. He has kept in contact with those teachers and still benefits from the continuing exchanges on matters of faith through letters. In the theological faculty of the University of Copenhagen, where he studied theology, he chose to stay neutral in the face of any current theological trend at the time, nor did he choose a faculty favorite as his spiritual mentor. Language came easily to him; he read through the New Testament in Greek and the Old Testament in Hebrew. He resumed his study of Arabic that he had begun in high school. His interest in the Semitic languages and culture drew him to spend a year in Israel where he absorbed himself in the historical sites and supported himself as a tourist guide. All this took place during the time of student uprisings in the late 1960's; he found them too distracting as a student of the moderate wing of campus politics, more interested in what was offered inside the classrooms than demonstrating outside of them.

While advancing his study of Arabic in Tunisia, he met a fellow student from France, a Roman Catholic with whom he fell in love. They married; she retains her Catholic roots without difficulty as the wife of a Lutheran pastor in Copenhagen. They have two sons, one a Catholic, the other a Lutheran. After ordination and serving in urban parish ministry in Copenhagen, they both started doctoral programs in Islamics through a program offered by the Sorbonne in Paris. Both have finished their degrees. He was offered a teaching vocation at the Sorbonne but chose to stay in parish ministry in Copenhagen with its growing needs for service to refugees fleeing to Denmark for sanctuary from Middle East turmoil.

His recitation of the course of his life to date made it clear to me that Olesen was hardly the typical Danish Lutheran pastor. He demurred, however, suggesting that many more of his colleagues have equally unusual life journeys to relate. He has been at Simon Peter church for a dozen years. The greatest joys of his ministry are meeting people, engaging them in ways that make the Gospel of Jesus Christ real in their lives, and staying put long enough to see the fruits of faith in those he serves. It is that invisible realm of inner spiritual life that counts most, he said, in describing where the focus of his ministry lies. He sees the danger in the pastor becoming a religious functionary, useful and efficient in utilitarian duties, but at the expense of the church as the Lord's, not his. This humbles him because he knows that efficiency in routine expectations is necessary as part of what the tradition of centuries of Lutheranism in Denmark lays on him. But within this tradition he knows the freedom that comes from depending on Christ to be present among people. Thus he is freed from an authoritarian view of his pastoral office that makes him the one around whom ministry centers.

It is the baptized men and women, the royal priesthood of all believers, who are the church in their daily lives in family, work, and neighborhood. Reflection on that inner work of the Spirit is the main mark of ministry. Reflection is important to him as he lives the theological tradition of the church in Denmark, based in the Scripture, Creeds, Confessions and Catechism. The challenge grows to hand this reflective tradition on to Danes who have grown up distant from it, who are swallowed up by increasing secularism and the lure of creature comforts. Yet, he said with a shrug, the confounding thing about Danish society is that along with all its secular bent, Denmark still ranks first among the nations of the world when measured for honesty in daily life.

Beverly asked him about how the relation of church to state works in his daily ministry. His comment: all kinds of people in the parish come to him, including Muslims and those Danes who have opted out of the church. His required role of the pastor of the neighborhood parish makes those contacts inevitable. For example, within 48 hours of the birth of a baby, that information must be reported to the "kordegn"—a hard word to translate into English but its basic meaning is that of an administrator of the parish who keeps the records of births, marriages, and deaths. At Simon Peter on Sundays, this person is a woman appointed by the parish council. She participates in the liturgy, and although the pastor has responsibility for worship overall, the pastor is not comparable to a chief of staff. The oversight responsibility belongs to the parish council, making the parish system not pastorally hierarchical but decentralized. He went on to answer Beverly's question about finances by mentioning the church tax that is levied by the government through the parish. Currently, each registered member pays 1.84% of income, from 18 years on. As mentioned, pastoral contact occurs primarily at the life events of births, marriages, and burials. Some clergy refuse to serve those in the parish who are not registered with the congregation. Olesen does, hoping that the contact with unbelievers will create an opening for ministry.

"The Danish church is like a supertanker; it moves slowly and is hard to turn around." Thus Kaj Bollman, the general secretary of the Church Foundation for Development, began our conversation. Another term for his work is mission developer. I met with him in the church headquarters building in Copenhagen and appreciated his candor in describing the church's relationship to Danish history and culture. The bottom line:

Denmark is no longer the monolithic culture it once was. Then, instead of launching into a sociological commentary on what that meant, he chose to illustrate his thought by a recent experience in his work. A decision was in process about starting a new congregation near the Copenhagen airport on land which is church property. But the government is interested in the property as well since it is strategic for potential airport expansion. Political leaders are wary of claiming the right to take it over by legal action; there is a strong bishop on hand who would make that unwise. The local parish council, which has the ultimate say about the use of land within its area, lacks both experience and self-confidence in negotiating with the state, however. And so it has turned to Bollmann to help them chart their course. He cited this as a case study in how traditional church structure is both an asset and a liability. The liability is that the church is so strapped by rules, in this case those which govern real estate rights, that it blurs the vision of its mission. The asset is that it does own property and can use it for purposes of the larger good. Bollman is continuing to work with all sides involved, and expressed confidence that a new mission congregation will eventually emerge, the better for its challenge to mature by working through its responsibilities with spiritual integrity. He mentioned a recent conference on church-state relations in which he used this incident as a case study. Furthermore, he posted the issue on the internet and welcomed the feedback which favored freeing the congregation to get on with its mission sorely needed within a modern Denmark that is adrift from the meaning of the cross prominently denoted in the national flag of Denmark. As an commentary on what he was saying about secularized Denmark, on my way to this interview in downtown Copenhagen, my eye caught sight of a prominent billboard screaming the f-word in eight foot high English letters.

He spoke with gratitude for his beginnings in a family of solid Christian faith and practice in his home town near the German border. After some teenage experimentation in rebelling against parental piety, he surprised himself and them by taking up theological studies at the University of Aarhus. After graduation he met and married a young teacher from Copenhagen; together they plunged into the work of his first call in a tough neighborhood of Copenhagen, serving there for twelve years among people lost in addictions of every sort, immersed in a stridently anti-Christian culture.

Yet it was in that very setting that he found his lasting satisfaction in reaching people where they were and pointing them to The Way of Christ. He was the first pastor to speak in a meeting of the Labor Party of Denmark, a breakthrough experience that was a hundred years in coming. He learned the necessity of networking with every helping agency in sight, and in the process of those twelve years discovered the power of God's grace as that which kept him motivated. Now he uses that background in his present office which allows him to spread his influence throughout Denmark. I asked him for any word he would have for USA Christians. His response: "Denmark may be viewed as the most secular place in Europe but don't think of the church here as a lost cause; it is visible and working in a typically Danish way—modestly, without fanfare about itself."

Bente Clausen is a reporter for a major Copenhagen newspaper, assigned often to write on church and state relations. She was baptized and confirmed in the church but chose an interesting word to describe her present relationship as "relaxed." She said that during the week her work keeps her immersed in matters of church and religion. Sundays, she said with the hint of a smile, is her day off. She picked up on my question about what it meant for her to be a Lutheran in this Lutheran-saturated land and began her response by remarking on how much the presence of Muslims has changed things in Denmark over the past fifteen years. A reactionary mood of nationalism has arisen among some who are trying to make the church a bastion of Danishness against the rising tide of Islam at home and abroad. In her view Danes generally regard Islam as an aggressively intrusive minority who are here to stay and are increasingly wary of them as more militant than peaceful. Some church leaders she writes about see this development as a wake-up call for the church to do more than react, but recover its own work of mission. Others see the church as too distracted by internal divisions (in particular over issues of sexual orientation and even women's ordination—which began in 1947 but is still opposed by the ultra right wing Lutherans—who, she said with some irony, are called the left wing in Denmark) to be able to get out of itself and into serious engagement with increasing religious pluralism. Lest that sound too cynical, she added, the Evangelical Lutheran Church in Denmark does sponsor over 500 missionaries serving in thirty-five missionary societies at work in Africa, India,

Asia, South America and Europe. And it is still true that in a number of the world's major seaport cities the Danish Seamans Church continues a long standing tradition of serving sailors. Turning the subject back to tensions with Islam in Denmark, I asked her what the church should do toward more effective dialog. Without hesitation she answered: "Stop requiring Muslims and Jews to pay church taxes which support Lutheran clergy and churches." I asked her if she pays the church tax herself—which she does. With that, we shook hands and I was on my way to our last interview before leaving Denmark.

Gunhild Legaard is a modern example of a deep-running strand within Danish Lutheranism, the Home Mission movement. It began in the 19th century under the strong influence of Nikolai Grundvig (1783-1872), the pastor, poet, politician and prolific hymnwriter. Legaard is a lay counselor with the Federation Of Parish Charities, an organization of the church which unites various ministries centered on home care, hospice, prison chaplaincies, and service to the mentally disabled. We met her in her modest office in a multi-story frame building out from the downtown area of Copenhagen. She gave us an overview of her main work of training volunteers, some thirty of them were in residence at the time, for home care for those unable to manage alone. Many are affected by dementia and how to understand and serve them is an example of what her trainees learn. She brings in nurses, social workers and specialists in hospice-care to teach from their experiences. Legaard is in her mid-60's, and has an infectious, outgoing personality that inclines her to try to tell us too many things at once about what she is doing. She came to this work from an experience in her youth when a friend she knew from the Danish Red Cross asked her to help with a homebound person just for a day. That experience started her on a path of nursing education, followed by work with various home care organizations, hospice, and prison visitation programs. "To take care of people who can't get out—that's our calling," she said, and added that too often it's too easily overlooked as an essential and rewarding side of Danish church life. She has expanded her volunteer training program for home care into thirteen other centers in Denmark, each with a leader in place to train up to ten volunteers at a time for home visitation.

As we were about to leave, she gave me an illustrated book, which at first glance looked to be intended for children but was in fact written for adult members of families caring for someone suffering from dementia. She translated its Danish title (in English "Grampa Isn't Crazy") and paged through it briefly to give me an idea of something of practical use in homes where minds and memories aged members are fading. Though not able to read it, I could sense its effectiveness. In its own way it was a confirmation of an important comment I had heard earlier from mission developer, Kaj Bollman, about the Danish church working in a typically Danish way—"modestly and without fanfare about itself." In Gunhild Legaard and in Danish Lutherans like her that truth lives on, as Nikolai Grundvig expressed it in his most enduring hymn, Built On The Rock:

We are God's house of living stones, built for his own habitation;
He fills our hearts, his humble thrones, granting us life and salvation.
Were two or three to seek his face, he in their midst would show his grace,
Blessings upon them bestowing.

Kjell Magne Bondevik is a rarity. He is an ordained clergyman who has chosen to carry out his calling as a politician in the Norwegian government rather than pastoring a congregation in the Lutheran Church of Norway. At 26 he was the youngest person ever to be elected to the Norwegian Parliament. Twice he was elected Prime Minister of Norway. During his thirty-three years of public service he served as Minister of Foreign Affairs under four governments. After retiring from the Norwegian Parliament he was named by Kofi Anan, then the General Secretary of the United Stations, as special UN envoy in humanitarian affairs to the Horn of Africa. As a statesman he has conferred with leaders in Africa, Asia, South America and Europe, as well as with Jimmy Carter, Bill Clinton, and George W. Bush when each was in the White House. Martin Luther once advised parents to guide their most gifted sons either toward law and government service or toward theology and service in the church but could not have imagined that both could be combined in one person. Kjell Magne Bondevik has done so and now continues his unique calling as president of the Center for Peace and Human Rights, an international organization headquartered in Oslo which he founded in 2005.

Kjell Magne Bondevik

NORWAY

Bondevik was not hard to recognize as he walked briskly into the coffee shop of a downtown Oslo hotel. He has a presence, enhanced by years of being a media fixture as a public figure and much respected prime minister of Norway. What struck me, however, was not his interest in being noticed but his interest in locating us, two nobodies from America, who had communicated to his office months earlier asking for an hour of his time. We met. He greeted us warmly, ordered coffee, and sat down with us in the hotel lobby for nonstop conversation on the questions I had sent him about his calling as an ordained pastor who has spent the better part of his adult life as an elected political leader in Norway.

The first question he addressed concerned his background and how he came to his unique way of blending into one what are commonly regarded as two separate vocations. He condensed considerable detail into this: he comes from a family active in church and state. His teacher-father was a teacher and principal in an Oslo school who later became an elected member of Parliament, his cousin a bishop in the church, and there were other notables in his family line who were active in church and state. What he learned from them was the breadth of the meaning of calling, the heart of which is God's call to be his redeemed child and servant through Jesus Christ. From that center, the calling, or vocation, leads on to the particular way one lives out his gifts of mind and spirit in a chosen work. In his case, aptitude for theological study leading to ordination was joined with his aptitude for political office. His vocation as a Christian included both; he had seen that worked out in his father's life and it followed naturally into his own. There was more to that story, particularly how he recognized and negotiated the unusual passage from ordained Lutheran minister to elected political office at age 26. He skipped those details. Instead he proceeded to what he described as the three spiritual pillars which have supported him throughout his years and spoke of them with an ease that suggested how thoroughly he has integrated them into his life.

First was the safety he felt in the salvation won for him by Jesus Christ. "*Safety?*" I interrupted him to ask, since the word seemed an unusual choice. Yes, he answered, the safety of Christ's salvation as he has lived daily with the dangers of confusing rightful power with abusive power in the raw give and take of political decision making through the past third of a century of his life. Safety from that common pitfall is what he still needs; he defined it as the good news of the forgiveness of his sins through the cross and resurrection of Christ. I've heard that language before in pastoral conversation, but not in conversation with a twice elected Prime Minister of a sovereign nation.

The second pillar was the Scriptures. He spoke as one well formed in Lutheran doctrine when citing the Bible's center as the Gospel of the resurrected Christ as the true treasure of the Scripture given to the church to proclaim and teach. The Law, he continued, is that other word from God in Scripture which signifies God's action in ordering public life and curbing sinful human nature through the institutions of government by which God works for good in human affairs. It sounded like textbook Lutheran theology, which it was. He was speaking of it, however, as the daily reality continually calling him to use his brains for logical thinking, deciding what's best among imperfect solutions, and advocating morality in politics by balancing human self interest with the common good in a fallen world. The church is where the sacraments, prayer, fellowship prevail—all of which are Divine means to equip believers like himself to live the faith daily in family, community, and workplace. The government is a place where God rules not through the Gospel but through his Law and where people like Bondevik have responsibilities to seek justice and enact them in the laws of Norway. He cited Paragraph 11 of the Norwegian constitution as an expression of the challenge that poses for the nation to live up to its description as a Lutheran society. What that comment implied could have taken up the rest of our hour together, but Bondevik was not stopping for detours.

He moved on to the third pillar of support in his calling, the conviction that every human being is made in God's image and therefore has an innate dignity. That must make a difference in how people treat each other, as well as people treat the earth as stewards of creation. That pillar has guided him in dealing with the culture, outlook, and histories of people vastly different from himself, especially in international assignments through the United Nations in Africa and elsewhere—including White House discussions with President George Bush with whom he disagreed on matters such as the Iraq War but with whom he could still relate as one made in God's image. At this point he did slip in a short discourse on how much he appreciates America for its cultural diversity, how thoroughly he has enjoyed time spent in the United States, and how much monocultural Norway can learn from Americans. He returned to his orderly procedure in answering my questions as he took up two examples of how he has struggled with vexing problems as a statesman with a theologically informed conscience: abortion and poverty.

Regarding abortion, he said that his own deepest convictions do not allow him to compromise the life of an unborn child. But his convictions are not the only ones in play in political debate; thus his best action is to contend in the Norwegian parliament for that unborn child's right to birth and life without forgetting other realities that arise. Examples: when the mother's life is at risk or the provision for ongoing care of a child born with massive birth defects must be taken into account. He cannot mandate his own convictions; he must bring the best wisdom, persuasive skill, and political will in contending for them with his Party in the legislative body of Norway. The other matter he mentioned was the struggle for the poor and oppressed through government aid programs. He has fought year after year for increases in government funds to alleviate the conditions that underlie poverty and was proud that Norway's current one per cent of its national budget for that purpose is first in the world. The cost of leadership in such long term struggles is one he knows personally. He did not bring it up initially, but I had read of a time some years earlier when the assorted burdens of constant contending for wiser welfare, tax cuts, health, education, and the spending of the nation's vast oil reserves (Norway is the world's second largest exporter of oil) lead to a breakdown and depression severe enough to require a month of sick leave to recover. Being open about it to the Norwegian public earned him even greater respect. "I came through that bad time stronger and wiser about conserving my time and emotional energy" is how he summed it up.

The hour was up. His aide, never far from sight, moved closer to give him five minute, then three minute time signals with well practiced subtlety. I got the message, thanked him with a handshake, and he was off to his next appointment. It was an hour that I will not forget. For if it is rare for one person to be an ordained pastor and head of state, it is even more rare for that person to combine such a calling with theological depth and skill in statecraft. It is memorable that a gifted, forceful man with obvious charisma, can be humbled by a nervous breakdown and come through it stronger by going public with the lessons he learned from trying to do too much. It says something about the people of Norway, the church that formed Kjell Magne Bondevik and his spiritual pillars, and the power of family tradition, that this man can live out his calling in a manner that makes faith and politics not either/or but both/and. His continuing role as director of the Peace and Human Rights Center promises more to come in his role as a statesman in world affairs.

A weird moment occurred later in the evening, hours after meeting with Bondevik. I had stopped in a neighborhood convenience store for an item when an agitated man startled me by blurting out "What makes you so happy?" My awkward answer didn't deter him from walking to the ATM machine for cash to pay a drug dealer waiting outside. In the snippet of our time to talk he told me that his name was Einar, that he was once baptized and confirmed in a Lutheran church in Oslo, and that now he was free to sneer at my answer to his question about what brought me to Norway. Off he went into the night, a sobering reminder that in one of the world's pricier cities there are those who spend all they have on self-destruction as drug addicts. In a Norway where 88% of the 4.5 million population list themselves as Lutheran, there are the Einars—baptized pagans who have lost their way. Who searches them out? I wondered. Who, in this prosperous land with a pastor/prime minister, remembers Jesus' words about the other sheep, not yet of his fold, for whom he laid down his life and took it up again?

Sunniva Gilver has the inward drive and the outward appearance that suits her calling to reach people in Oslo not likely to be seen in church. She greeted us at the door of her second floor flat, bare footed, a diamond in her nose, her reddish hair loosely cut, wearing a black t-shirt imprinted "prest" (priest) front and back, and blue jeans. She was finishing off a call from London as she motioned us to follow her into her living room, her cell phone held to her ear by one hand as she herded her three young, curious children off to

Sunniva Gilver

their room with the other. Her phone call concluded, she noticed my attention to the crown molding and strikingly beautiful plaster work in the flat. That's her husband's handiwork, she explained, adding that though he is not yet a believer he is a good husband, father—and plasterer. In the first thirty seconds of being in her presence, I had collected enough first impressions to think I knew what I was in for theologically to match the appearance of the person hosting us.

I could not have been more wrong. Whatever her appearance, Sunniva Gilver, is thoroughly grounded in Biblical theology, and while creative in ways of reaching Norway's unreached, her creativity has a solid base. She grew up in the Church of Norway. Her faith matured in a steady process of growth throughout her teens, without sudden conversion experiences along the way. At sixteen she was an exchange student in Venezuela where she lived with a Roman Catholic family and saw close ties between their faith and lives. When returning she was hard pressed to interpret that to her Norwegian friends, and in so doing, followed the advice of pastors to study theology. In the course of her studies, what was normally a summer of practical internship in a congregation, became what she named as "a crazy and wonderful year of preparing sermons, visiting the sick, talking with street kids—really breathtaking in its intensity." Before completing her six year course of study toward ordination, she took a year out to study at Wartburg Seminary in the USA, and commented on the value of what she learned there about integrating academic, practical, and ecumenical theology.

Her pastoral vocation began in an affluent neighborhood of Oslo where her talent for innovative ways of introducing people to the faith took the form of creating forty eight programs that were used on national television in Norway. The first ten set the pace for the remaining series. They were filmed from the back seat of a taxi cab. She hailed people from the street to join her for conversations on sin, salvation, love, faith, life after death, etc. The agreement was that they could ride free if they agreed to get into the cab and talk frankly. Throughout the series she made it clear that she was a pastor and wore her clerical collar as a sign that it was not a stunt, but a serious effort to reach people in ways other than knocking at their door. The results surprised her. People recognized her on the street, spoke freely, with most of them reporting positively on the church as they experienced it. She credited the ecumenical team she assembled to write the programs for much of the success of the venture, though she had to draw the line occasionally with her Pentecostal collaborators. In general, however, the ecumenical make up was essential in bringing a variety of voices to tell God's good news to people surprised to hear it broadcast from the back seat of a taxi. Her recent years of ministry have been as a chaplain to university students, an assignment which has immersed her in Oslo's multi-cultural

Gronland neighborhood. She described it as the only real melting pot in Norway with its 8% emigrant population, including 70,000 Muslims who have moved in since Pakistanis started coming thirty years ago. She knew of at least twenty Muslim enclaves in the area and has participated in religious dialog, sometimes even being invited to preach in a mosque.

She had an interesting view of the problems of Lutheran passive dependency on outmoded forms of ministry in the State church in Norway. As one who knows the statistics of sparse church attendance, she's realistic about the huge challenges and fully invested in helping in her own way to overcome them. She also knows that there is much hidden belief and unspoken faith that surfaces when she engages people. Examples: the hours she spends with families before the baptism of children in which she asks such questions as Why baptize? What's ahead for the baptized child? What's expected of the family in helping form a genuinely Christian life in the secular city? How to avoid separating the baptized life from realities of daily living? These matters get a hearing as she goes to the homes of people, a work she loves because it gives her opportunities to connect all the goodness of God through this sacrament to children and families whom he loves. "Who am I to deny that love?" she asked me rhetorically, then went on to expand on her belief that God is not The Pal Upstairs but the One due our deepest reverence. She added that during her year in the USA she observed that Lutherans in Norway are not the only ones who get stuck in static ways that blunt creative outreach. In Wartburg, Iowa, she said with polite irony, it was not a state church that smothered needed innovation but "Mrs. Brown, frowning in the front row." Her closing comment expressed the joy she finds in singing with toddlers and mothers with whom she meets once a month, a welcome counterbalance in her ministry with students and emigrants and an upbeat commentary on her baptismal name, Sunniva, meaning "child of the sun."

Stavanger, on the southwest tip of Norway, is the port of departure from which hundreds of thousands of Norwegians set sail for a new life in the new world of America throughout the 19th and into the early 20th centuries. In the past twenty five years the city has doubled in population from 50,000 to over 110,000, due largely to the boom in offshore oil exportation evident in ships and tugboats churning up water in the busy harbor outside our hotel. My musings on what emotions those emigrants felt as they looked back for one last glimpse of their homeland were interrupted by the arrival of my guest, the vice-mayor of Stavanger. Bjord Tysdale Moe is a woman in her fifties, smartly dressed in a tailored green skirt and jacket; her smile, blond hair, fluent English combine to make her a charming person to meet. "We've fallen in love with Stavanger in just one day" I declared. "That's the way it's supposed to be" was her pleased response.

She described her growing up in one of the picture-book fjord towns with a white steeple church and prayer house, this one several hours north of Stavanger on the coastline of Norway. She spoke appreciatively of her solid spiritual background as the middle child in a devout family where hymns were sung, daily prayer offered, and where her carpenter father—a man of open minded piety—allowed her older brother to take tickets in the town cinema for pocket money. He also helped build the prayer house where those who gathered regularly at midweek were also members of the congregation which gathered in the white steeple church on Sundays. Both details about her father were commentaries on his open attitude in contrast to some Lutherans in this region sometimes called the Bible Belt of Norway. Attending movies, not to mention ticket-taking at the door, was not widely approved. Nor did those who went to prayer houses always get along well with those who prayed in white steepled churches on Sundays. Two months after her confirmation her mother died of cancer, a deeply felt loss that gave her an early awareness that life is short and is meant to count. Through her high school and college years she stayed active in church and community, discovering her organizational skills as a leader. She married a man of similar background and values, who was a graphic designer for publications of the International Fellowship of Evangelical Students in Oslo, where she had also worked in program administration. She took courses in theology and was into her second year toward a degree when, instead of taking her exams, she gave birth to the first of their two daughters, both of whom are currently studying art.

After four years the family returned to Stavanger where she worked in the same international student organization, this time as the youngest and only female on the staff. Among her colleagues were men active in the Christian Democratic Party. A national election was coming. They asked her to consider running as a delegate to the Party's caucus. Her husband encouraged her. She was elected. The experience galvanized her interest in public office; her next success was election to the city council of Stavanger where she relished her opportunities to improve services to elderly citizens. Following the arrival of her second child and succession to a second term on the city council, she advanced in leadership on health and social work challenges in a Stavanger rapidly increasing in size and complexity, including the inevitably of corruption with the growth of oil wealth. Six years ago she was elected as vice-mayor. Her satisfactions: being in a position to apply her holistic, egalitarian conviction that every person counts and has something to contribute. Her frustrations: balancing local government with national political priorities. Her motivation for service: the faith she learned as a child and saw demonstrated in her parents. Among her favorite Sunday activities: teaching Sunday school in the congregation where she and her husband participate. Our conversation took place on the same day I met with Sunniva Gilver, the pastor to students in Oslo. In outward appearance, Bjorg Tysdale Moe, the vice mayor of Stavanger, was a striking contrast. Her duties keep her busy not with university students' spiritual well being or with Muslim enclaves, but with city council members, oil and shipping magnates, health and welfare agencies, and much else that has to do with governance in a major seaport of Norway. Despite outward contrasts, both women draw from the same inner resource, Christ's lordship through his church at work in his world. Both do so impressively.

Still another facet of spiritual life in Norway was opened to us by Ivar Langen, the president of the University of Stavanger. Sitting with him as guests in his home, he explained that this fledgling university has had to battle for its recognition in 1960 as a recognized institution of higher learning in Norway's educational establishment. It surprised me to learn hear that it took the interplay of local groups to "build the university brick by brick" in Langen's phrase, by applying skills he characterized as typical of this region of Norway—community work, entrepreneurial skills, and an innovative approach—to become the first local institution to be awarded university status on the basis of academic merits. The present enrollment is 8,000. It is growing as it serves students through its Arts and Sciences, Social Sciences, and Science and Technology faculties. It was an enlightening moment in our conversation; I had never before thought of what it takes for a school begun locally to make it into the august ranks of a European university. Langen smiled at my observation, saying "every European city of any note should have a medieval cathedral, a university, and a championship football (soccer) team—we're two out of three and our Viking Football Club should soon make the grade." Stavanger's medieval cathedral more than qualifies; it was dedicated in 1125 and has not missed a Sunday service since.

Langen, a tall, middle aged man with an unassuming manner, served lefsa and coffee in the living room of his unpretentious home, tastefully decorated with works of art clustered around pictures of his four children and a bowl of fresh tulips on the coffee table. It was surprising to hear him describe himself as one who was raised in a devout Pentecostal family where he learned early on to affirm the feeling side of Christian faith and provide a basis to understand the place of the Free Church tradition in Norway's religious history. He was baptized at 17 and by age 27 had become "a Lutheran Pentecostal and Pentecostal Lutheran" which led to more comment on his belief in justification by grace through faith as a guard against overdependence on feelings. That central doctrine was why he joined the Lutheran Church as an adult. He spoke of the growing number of charismatic groups in Norway, and mentioned Oasis as an example of its positive impact among youth. His own children have taken part in the annual Oasis summer gathering which bring together four to five thousand young people for worship, Bible study, and fun. His son is an ordained pastor serving a congregation of the Free Church in Norway, separate from the State Lutheran church, but like all recognized free churches in the country, is supported by the government via the church tax levied on all citizens. The value of listening to this hospitable man was to see how easily he keeps his identity as one who chose to be a Lutheran as an adult without abandoning the best of the Pentecostal piety gained from his youth, who is glad for his children's' activity in Free Church congregations, and who integrates all of this into his calling as the president of the University of Stavanger. He embodies a well grounded spirituality that gives him freedom to honor the breadth of the Spirit's work without diluting the core of the Gospel or limiting its power to one ecclesiastical institution in Norway.

Kjetil Aano (pronounced Ohno) is the face of the missional vitality within the Church of Norway. He is the Secretary General of the Norway Mission Society, which was founded in 1842 as an independent society within the Church and now net-works to energize congregations for mission. The Society works on four continents where its 100 missionaries participate in three programs: evangelism where the gospel is unknown or marginally available, diaconal and development work in assisting national churches in administration and sustainability, and organizational management in building competencies for local efficiency in stewardship and social ministry. His family background has prepared him well for his present calling. He spent part of his boyhood in Tanzania where his father

Kjetil Aano

was a teacher and administrator in a school under the auspices of the Norwegian Lutheran Mission. This was in the early 1960's, an era of national liberation in Africa, and he recalled being old enough to understand the significance of his father's turning over his position as headmaster to the newly formed Lutheran Church of Tanzania to an African successor. Shortly after that he spent a year as a high school exchange student in California during the height of student activism against the Vietnam War. He returned to Norway to finish high school but was undecided between theology and medicine as his future. He could not envision himself as a pastor in a traditional congregation in Norway, and medicine, he decided, was too boring. A long talk with a respected pastor encouraged him to consider the NMS School of Mission and Theology in Stavanger and test his aspirations toward a missionary vocation abroad that he had held since his youth. He enrolled and stayed with the six year course of study to complete his degree, then marry Marianne Skjortnes, who was no stranger to the overseas mission, and accepted an appointment to Madagascar as an missionary evangelist.

The first year there, he said, was the toughest of his life as he struggled to learn the Malagasy language before he could be ready for work. He credited his wife who had learned the language as a child of missionary parents in Madagascar with helping him get through it.

After three years of his best efforts as an evangelist he recognized that he had neither the aptitude nor linguistic fluency to preach and teach. His gifts lay in organizing programs which trained local church workers to form new congregations, a work in which he flourished for three years before being called back to Norway to apply those same skills to energize Norwegian congregations in finding their role in the global mission beyond Norway. The transition was not easy, as he recalled, because of complications arising from regional differences in Norwegian Lutheranism. Congregations in western Norway were more open to the wider world of mission; the eastern churches, steeped in the narrowness of village church life, were less so; and the southwest Bible Belt corner of Norway tended to view its the Church of Norway itself as its mission. He was called back to Madagascar in the mid-1980's to teach in one of the Lutheran seminaries of a church that was rapidly growing. During that three year period he witnessed firsthand the unique spiritual gifts in the indigenous Lutheran Church of Madagascar, especially the Shepherd Movement of lay evangelists which grew from beginnings under a remarkable charismatic woman, Ninelevah, a story I had learned in full when in Madagascar a year later. Aano learned much about these from his students who experienced them first hand in their towns and villages. His years of teaching in Madagascar and his foresight in adapting Lutheran theology to new conditions there equipped him to return again to Oslo for NMS leadership in multi-cultural ministries to refugees streaming into Norway from Africa and the Middle East.

I asked him to assess the nature of the mission the church in Norway faces today. His answer began with this bottom line fact: all Norway is a mission field, as is all of Europe. People have difficulty people hearing the Gospel as good news for their bad situation. Norwegians are comfortable and affluent and are tone deaf to the message of sin and redemption. There are two factors at work culturally that the church must analyze: nominal affiliation in the Church of Norway without serious belief in its message and the new situation of religious pluralism in which Norwegians must discern what it means to live with a multitude of religions. For the 500 years since the Lutheran reformation reached Norway there has been one religious voice. That era is over.

I asked him for signs of hope. He answered by regarding the whole cultural situation of Norway as not only problematic but also filled with openings that the church must find and use. The example he cited was in accepting religious pluralism as a wake up call to Norwegians to see immigrants, especially Muslim men, going to their mosque on Friday nights and asking themselves why as Christians they have reason to go to church on Sunday mornings. Better stated: the church does not exist to produce Norwegianism but discipleship under Jesus Christ. Second, he sees signs within church leadership of a readiness to start over with a self understanding of itself as a community of transforming faith. Third, mission does not begin by crossing salt water but begins by crossing racial and cultural barriers in Norway. Without this, the church dies. Mission is at the heart of all the church does in all its varied ministries. Fourth: the church in Norway is being changed by positive influences from the USA (the Willow Creek program has been widely studied) and Britain, which stress understanding the times, evaluating church strategy critically, and risking fresh ways of expressing the faith. Fifth: take on controversial matters that have to do with real people in real life. The Church of Norway has completed a five year study on sexuality. To no one's surprise, including Aano's, the results have been divisive, with half the church convinced it cannot change its teaching on homosexuality and the other half convinced that in the liberating spirit of the Gospel the church must see that homosexuality can be a genuine expression of love and therefore open to gay persons. Till now, marriage of same sex persons is not sanctioned by the church. Will that day come? Aano did not speculate, but expressed the hope that the mission of the Gospel in the world will be the church's first priority and that all other matters be faced and resolved in the light of that priority. He is well placed as the leader of the Norway Mission Society to bring the full weight of his conviction and standing in the Church of Norway to see to it that mission comes first.

Something unexpected happened near the end of our days in Norway. Aano took us to the Stavanger airport for our flight to Oslo, thinking there was time to spare. But the airport was jammed, with long lines of frustrated people trying to get on airplanes. Aano sized up the chaotic situation and acted immediately. By sheer determination and rare Norwegian *hutzpah* he elbowed a path for us to the head of the line, with no time for parting formalities. As we were in the air for Oslo I realized that in the rush of things I was missing my camera with its year's worth of pictures. The next morning we arrived for appointments at the headquarters building of the Church of Norway, and as I stopped at the reception desk to telephone Aano to inquire about my loss I was startled. Through the entrance door walked Kjetil Aano, as if by magic. He put my camera in my hands (having found it in his car where I had left it, and tucked it into his brief case for his trip to Oslo earlier that morning), smiled, spoke a one sentence greeting, and was on his way upstairs for his engagements of the day. On the surface, a minor event, noticed only by me. Yet I saw in it a mini-parable on the efficiency, thoughtfulness, openness, surprise, modesty, hospitality, and practical help we had experienced from those who gave us their versions of the promise and the perils known by God's People in Norway.

The Church of Sweden traces its origins back to the beginnings of Christianity in Sweden with the baptism of King Olof in the 10th century. Five centuries later Luther's reforming movement arrived in the 1520's and the church took on its Lutheran confession of faith. In so doing, however, it retained the doctrine of the historic episcopate, i.e., the practice of ordaining its bishops in an assumed line of unbroken succession from the New Testament era. This compatibility with the ancient tradition of the church is also evident in its liturgy of the mass, vestments, miters, crosiers, music and art work in many of its church buildings. The Church of Sweden has contributed to world ecumenism and theology through notable leaders, Nathan Soederblom, Gustav Aulen and Anders Nygren among them. In 1958 it was among the first Lutheran churches to ordain women and in 2000 pioneered the separation of church and state in Sweden, initiating a change that has spread to other Scandinavian countries. Today there are approximately 5,000 clergy serving the 6.9 million Swedes registered in the Church of Sweden; they comprise 78% of the Swedish population of nine million. By the church's own estimate, approximately 2% attend worship services regularly.

Elna Sundqvist

SWEDEN

Elna Sundqvist, 48, married, and the mother of two teenagers, and an ordained priest (aka pastor) in the Church of Sweden puts a face on these statistics, a face we found smiling and hospitable as she welcomed us to her household and parish in Malmo, Sweden's southernmost city. We had met her a year before at an international conference in Bethlehem and now were the beneficiaries of her widespread contacts in the Church of Sweden in helping us arrange meetings with clergy and laity in Malmo, Lund, and Stockholm. Her own story of her path to pastoral ministry included one detail from her childhood that helped us understand the inclusive spirit that characterizes her ministry. She grew up in a household of spiritual disaffection due to an event her mother had experienced as a child. An overly strict Lutheran pastor publicly ordered her out of the church one Sunday for whispering during the sermon. She never returned. Elna's own spiritual upbringing was provided by her devout grandmother, a woman of prayer who took her to Sunday School and taught her to love Jesus and told her the stories of the Bible. When a new vicar replaced the inordinately strict pastor in her village near Malmo, he saw promising qualities in the teenage Elna and encouraged her to teach Sunday School, join in youth activities, and pursue her unusual aptitude for the church's outreach in social ministry. With his encouragement she began her preparation for ordination by enrolling in theological study at the University of Uppsala, one of Sweden's two paramount theological faculties (the University of Lund is the other, where she studied later). Her first year there in the late 1970's was a near disaster. At nineteen she was unprepared for the radical diversity of students and theological outlook at Uppsala and toward the end of her first year decided to drop out and think through whether she wanted a pastoral vocation or even leave the church altogether. What kept her from acting on that decision was the positive influence of a presiding bishop of the Church of Sweden at that time, as well as the impact of songs of courage and hope by South African Christians in their struggle against apartheid. She felt the wind of the Spirit afresh and completed her theological education after which she married, flourished in her first major pastoral assignment in a suburb of Malmo (and brought her two children into the world), plus taking further theological courses at the nearby University of Lund), then assumed the pastorate at St. Michels where she is now in her sixth year.

"About those statistics of 2% church attendance in Sweden—they are indeed troubling!" she acknowledged in a conversation in her home at the end of a full Sunday. She remarked that her best way of dealing with that national problem was to devote her best energies to the parish where she serves. In watching her engage people in her preaching, worship, and interacting with young and old that day, I gained glimpses of faith in action. A modest sign was the personal attention shown an elderly man helping his severely handicapped daughter find a place to sit in a well filled sanctuary before the service began. What caught my attention was her presence at the entrance door to welcome those who came, calling many by name. Although I could not understand the language of the liturgy and sermon, I could sense that in the unspoken body language of those present there were signs of healthy pastor-people rapport. While she was talking with young parents after the service (who were picking up their children from the immaculate and amply furnished nursery for infants and toddlers—another sign of outreach to young families in the neighborhood), I struck up a conversation with Arta Stepina, the organist and choir director, about her work at St. Michels and what Elna Lundqvist's ministry meant here. With surprising candor she spoke of the troubled family background in Latvia she left behind when coming to Malmo to study church music and the circuitous route of circumstances by which she had found a position at St. Michels. This providential turn of events meant support for bread and board as a budding church musician; even more important, she said, was the care and pastoral wisdom she was receiving from Pastor Lundqvist as she was finding her way through the uncertainties of romance and marriage. One Sunday of watching and listening in a congregation is brief, to be sure, and overly broad conclusions drawn from so narrow a base are risky. But it was enough to suggest that statistics that tell of 2% church attendance among Swedish Lutherans do not tell all. Pockets of spiritual vitality such as St. Michels hint that there is more behind the numbers than a one Sunday visitor could comprehend.

More insight into the life of St. Michels congregation came in conversation with Cenny Viktor Larsson, an overeducated young man (one degree in philosophy, another in theology at Lund, a year in a Catholic religious community in England, another year of research among Salvation Army, Pentecostal and Catholic communities in Canada) who is settling into a pastoral vocation under Lundqvist's mentoring as a vicar at St. Michels. He described his average work day which begins with leading prayer early each weekday morning with Taize songs, Scripture, and ample time for silent prayer in the strikingly beautiful sanctuary which is open to all. An average week often involved one or more funerals as well. He mentioned his practice of visiting the family of the bereaved in their home—for many it is their first visit by a pastor—and after praying with them inviting them to help select hymns and Scripture for the funeral Mass. This personal visitation has a two-fold purpose, to establish a pastoral connection that can continue beyond the funeral as well as to offset what he called "too much pushiness" by undertakers who don't realize that a funeral is a ministry more than a business. Regarding families who have long been absent from the congregation, he said he withholds judgment since he has little awareness of what their previous church experience may have been (he knew of Elna Lundqvist's story of her mother). He comes as one who brings Christ's Gospel and leaves the rest to the work of the Spirit. He said that families do not pay for the ministry of the pastors at funerals, baptisms or weddings. This prompted me ask him about clergy unions in the Church of Sweden and the information I had heard about fees for pastoral services in such circumstances, a surprise to my ears. He knows such arrangements exist, acknowledging that he pays his dues to the clergy union but has little to do with them otherwise. He described clergy unions as too much of a mirror of Swedish society in general and would not mind if they didn't exist. More urgent problems by far have to do with the pervasive individualism he sees everywhere. It takes this form in the church: "the homosexuals have their own Mass, the addicts have their own Mass, and the youth have their own Mass." All this is not bad in itself but it feeds the everybody-doing-their-own-thing malady, his phrase for what makes community impossible. His outlook on the next twenty five years surprised me. The Church of Sweden is cutting away from the World Council of Churches (which Nathan Soederblom helped found over a half century ago) and Lutheran World Federation because of controversies within both organizations. He didn't specify what they were nor did he define the nature of "cutting away." His desire is that the Church of Sweden recovers more of its theological soul and thereby do more than mimic what is current in public opinion. He spoke of the benefit he gains by airing such matters with Elna Lundqvist and does so regularly. He also noted how energized she was after returning from the Bethlehem conference with Palestinian Christians, the event which had begun our friendship with her. Over the year since she has sponsored programs at St. Michels with invitations for people throughout the area to become involved in the international network of information and exchange led by Christmas Lutheran Church in Bethlehem, and one more commentary on the evolving societal leaven of the faith that has characterized Elna Lundqvist's ministry from her earliest days.

A striking building that rises up forty-five stories to dominate Malmo's cityscape is aptly named the Twisting Torso, after the signature style of its celebrated Spanish architect, Santiago Calatrava. Not many blocks from it is a nondescript building which houses the Church of Sweden's mission to the homeless and addicts of the city. The director is Johannes Joergensen, a former Roman Catholic priest who found the loneliness of celibacy too much and married a Chilean woman he had known earlier in his ministry. Though no longer a priest, he is still Catholic but entirely happy to be continuing his ministry as a layman working under the auspices of the Church of Sweden. More important, he said, than his ex-priest status is his fluency in five languages he found useful during his earlier calling under the Missionary Oblates of Mary Magdalen in serving refugees coming into Sweden from all over. His ear for language continues to serve him well in his present work with the City Mission in Malmo, one of Sweden's most polyglot urban industrial centers. 27% of the city is non-Swedish, with up to 80% foreign-born, mostly Muslim refugees in some neighborhoods. He told us that the city is still noted for its anti-clergy spirit as a carry over from an influx of German socialists earlier in its history and now exacerbated by its present working class population of refugees from the Islamic Middle East.

Urban homelessness is a growing problem in Sweden as the gap between rich and poor widens. Increasing numbers of foreign workers, willing to work for less and often exploited as such, form part of the problem. Despite worker safeguards for Swedish citizens provided by the national socialist system, there are always some employers who prey upon immigrants as a source of cheap labor. Joergensen sees an increasing role for such ministries as Malmo's City Mission elsewhere in Sweden, especially in caring for the children of addicts and the working homeless. He regards the public sector as less well equipped to handle such matters, and cited as evidence the fact that street people seek out the City Mission because its reputation for caring, professional service to between four to five hundred people at any given time is well earned.

Since the elevator was out of order, he walked us up four floors to Café David, a large room with kitchen facilities for breakfast and lunch that is open for modestly priced meals served from eight till three on weekdays and for a Sunday morning breakfast service with liturgy tailored to reach a non-typical congregation. As he served us coffee he mentioned the fourteen guest rooms that are always occupied, as it is the only hostel in town where one can walk in off the street and get a place to shower and sleep. He works with addictive people from varied national backgrounds, forming them in groups according to common ethnicity, as well as the fact that belonging is essential to recovery and sobriety. Each group determines its schedule for coming together to hold each other accountable, select a work project (ranging from painting furniture to computer repair), participates in Bible study, and commits to ongoing contact after leaving the City Mission program. By such means each can build a new identity and help partners do the same, he said, and when conflicts inevitably arise, the group must find a solution to which all contribute. The City Mission ministry reaches within and beyond Malmo, as Joergensen maintains contact with deacons in surrounding parishes who send referrals and monetary support. On a rueful but not surprising note, he added that in the climate of middle class moralism common in the region, this reciprocal relationship of service and support does not come easily.

His emphasis was on the holistic ministry that the City Mission offers. This includes an inter-religious (Lutheran, Catholic, Muslim) team that works with youth in local schools with a focus on moral issues. Health care centers are also a part of each City Mission ministry, with one full time nurse on duty and doctors available twice a week for evening hours, a service of particular importance since most guests avoid hospitals. They choose City Mission medical services because the nurse or doctor knows them, listens to them, and treats them with a dignity not always found elsewhere. The team of religious, medical, and social workers combine to work toward healing that ruptured sense of being human, which is the ultimate price of addiction or homelessness. Joergensen told a parable on that concept of ministry quoted in a brochure explaining the history, methods, and goal of the City Mission. It is a story about a little animal that had two of everything— two pillows to sleep on, two bowls to eat from, two bones to chew on— but left his home searching for something more than double of what everything offers. It's the "more than everything" offered in affluent, comfortable Sweden that is the reason for the church and its City Mission expression, he explained. People, whether accomplished or homeless or addicted, are people with a dignity conferred by God in whose image all are made, and the calling of God's people is to serve this spiritual center of human identity in a way that includes the material and psychological, the individual and communal—whether those served believe in God or not.

Guests were coming in and walking out of Café David as we talked with the director, and despite our efforts to appear other than outsiders. But our dress and English language conversation gave us away. We walked back down to his first floor office for his concluding words which were all the more impressive for their brevity: "Our work here takes a long time to show results, some of which we'll never see, but we're here because we have a common mission to the poor whom God appoints to be the judge of what we do." With that simple yet profound statement to think about, we thanked Johannes Joergensen, and walked out of the Malmo City Mission with this to ponder: this former Catholic priest and those he serves may not be in the 2% of the Swedish population counted as church attenders, but they are the very ones Jesus shall call his own in the great surprises disclosed in his Parable of the Last Judgment (Matthew 25:3-46).

The short drive from Malmo to Lund takes only a half hour, but to enter the Romanesque, twin-towered Lutheran cathedral there is to step back a thousand years in time. In this sanctuary royalty were crowned in 1217, Franciscan monks were thrown out by rambunctious reformers in 1527, and in 1947 the Lutheran World Federation was formed within its hallowed, darkened walls. Through the centuries countless sermons have been preached, sacraments celebrated, weddings solemnized, funerals conducted, concerts performed, commencements held, and people from every part of Sweden and the world have entered to pray. On the day we stepped inside the massive brass doors depicting Biblical scenes, we noticed the 750 year old astronomical clock on our way to our seats with several hundred clergy of the Church of Sweden gathered for worship at the start of a daylong conference. Pastor Lundqvist gave us whispered summaries of the bishop's sermon on the priority of *Seelsorge*, the spiritual care of the soul, with emphasis on the soul care of the pastors themselves. It was a timely theme for a day of attention to the pastor's prophetic calling in a socialist paradise of satiety. Such a provocative subject made me regret all the more my inability to understand Swedish and follow the nuances of what was said. The day ended with our inclusion as guests at the Lundqvist family table where conversation in fluent English was shared by all, including a collegian daughter studying pre-med and a high school son with dreams of becoming a SAS airlines pilot. It was Swedish hospitality at its best and a sign of the Church of Sweden alive in those who embody the apostolic injunction to welcome each other as Christ has first welcomed us.

Our most critically penetrating look at the ups and downs of the contemporary Church of Sweden came in a lengthy conversation with David Olson, 68, an ordained clergyman, wearing blue jeans, cowboy boots, and a wool sweater suitable for the chilly second floor room of the Stockholm Cathedral where we sat for conversation. He is American born (in Phoenix, Arizona, where his mother's strong influence formed his spiritual foundations) and educated for the ministry at Augustana College, a Swedish Lutheran mecca on the Illinois side of the Mississippi River during its era of theological influence under the presidency of Conrad Bergendoff. He recalled Bergendoff's reaction of bowing his head in despair when learning that Olson had been posted to Stockholm for his first assignment out of the seminary. Bergendoff, the premier Swedish American Lutheran theologian educator, had never been allowed to function in the church of his ancestral homeland, Olson's voice rose as he explained further, "because he was not ordained in the apostolic order prized so highly here—part of the crap that keeps the Church of Sweden from the priorities that really count." Hearing that told me I was in for an assessment of the Swedish church that would be long on unvarnished candor and short on sugar coating. Before he got into that, however, he swung into a brief, biting critique of the American political right wing, a topic not on my agenda as I eased him into the subject of what it means to be a Lutheran Christian in Sweden today.

He is one with forty years of pastoral experience in the Church of Sweden, much of it the outgrowth of his first assignment as an assistant pastor in Stockholm. There he met and married his Swedish wife and centered his duties on preparing youth for confirmation. He could not have begun at a better place in understanding what he regards as the core problem of the church: unbelief. He saw its signs in his first two years of teaching Luther's Small Catechism to youth in their early teens. He recalled the day when a dutiful, well prepared confirmand interrupted his regular routine of catechizing students on their knowledge of Bible passages and Luther's catechism with this question out of the blue: "Pastor, do you believe

in God?" Olson was startled at first, then came to realize that the youngster was asking the only question that finally matters. The experience also
made him realize the extent to which a pastor is viewed as a professional
mouthpiece of the church, paid to answer questions nobody is asking. He
cited a parable by Soren Kirkegaard (1813-1855), the keen-eyed, caustic
Danish church watcher, who likened the church to a circus in which the
clowns enter from one side of the great tent to parade up and down to the
delight of all who clap their hands and laugh with approval as people being
royally entertained—but no one sees the fire starting from the other side
of the tent and no one has ears to hear "the tent is on fire!" That parable,
Olson said, fits as a judgment on a church that does its liturgical thing and
carries out its traditional functions as expected, but without hearing and
heeding that confirmand's urgent question of whether God is obeyed or even
exists. I asked him if his judgment was too sweeping. After a pause to take
the question seriously, his answer came in a reference to his seminary professor who would stand at the back of the classroom when students were
practice preaching and interrupt by shouting "So what?" His purpose was
to press vapid religious generalities back to the hard question of whether
God is or isn't in the truth being told. For Olson, whose passion is communication, the So What? question is really the at the core of the belief-
unbelief divide that runs through the heart of the Swedish population despite
its statistics of 78% membership in the Church of Sweden.

That discovery early in his ministry caused him to rethink everything
about how the coming generation can be reached. He wrote new confirmation materials that began not with putting a catechism or Bible in the
hands of youth but by seeking to understand more of their world as the
starting point. He took his concerns to the Central Committee of the Church
of Sweden and found a receptive response. Starting with where people are,
after all, was doing what Jesus himself did, especially in his teaching ministry of parables which begin with "The Kingdom of God is like…" and then
drew on images of a farmer planting seed or a housewife finding a lost coin.
As Olson began to publish such materials that were field tested in his own
congregation his work was more widely recognized; he was named to a
pan-Scandinavian Church Commission on confirmation. When surveys
revealed that 62% of the Swedish people consulted reported that the acts

of the church had nothing to do with faith in God, Olson saw his concerns validated. He wrote candidly that kids were baptized because Grandma made a new dress for the baby or a child was confirmed because Mom and Dad were confirmed. He did not withhold the judgment of the religious sociologist conducting the survey: "My only conclusion is that the Church of Sweden itself is the last protection *against* Christianity itself." His work became the standard for a whole new generation of publications used in congregations throughout Sweden, a development not without sharp criticism against Olson himself as an American-born interloper who could not appreciate tradition in the Church of Sweden. He has dealt with it by continuing to confirm youth in their early teens as has been the tradition for centuries, but to prepare them by creative methods that bring youth and parents together in intriguing ways. Example: using skits on the Parable of the Prodigal Son from Luke 15 in which the confirmands portray the wayward son (dark glasses, guiltless swagger, Dad-made-me-do-it outlook) or the unforgiving older brother (Get out, bum! No return till every dime repaid). Then, after the skit is fully acted out the youth form a half circle facing their parents, asking them what it means that the love of Christ binds them together in the church and what that love looks like in their homes. Twelve such skits were published and Olson spoke of powerful moments when parents and youth told him of breakthroughs to new levels of belonging in faith to Christ and to each other in love.

What's needed now, he said, is for the same kind of critique and renewal of presentation to occur with regard to the understanding of what the liturgical life of the church means for the lives believers live between Sundays. He cited two reasons why so few Swedes go to church today. One is that to do so is to be labeled "religious" and Swedish people do not like labels. Going to church regularly means making a statement, taking on a public identity that the vast majority turn away from because they perceive it as negative or phony, with no connection to their daily world. The second reason is that people have never been given a cogent reason for regularly assembling to worship God. Putting it another way (and in Olson vernacular), that people will go to church to see Charley confirmed, or a Boy Scout get a badge, or to hear the choir sing—then the church is packed out! But to *go back* to church and keep on in faithfulness—

that case has not been made. It must be made if people here are to know the fullness of meaning of the worship life that grows out of living the relationship with Christ in a way that is inseparable from belonging to others. To Olson, everything can become a means of reaching that "Aha" moment of realizing that not only does God exist, he exists for me, for us. He took an example from a Christmas Eve sermon preached in the Stockholm Cathedral in which we were sitting. Someone had spray painted "Into the shit with Christ" on the outside wall. The dean of the cathedral picked up on it in his sermon which began with the unedited graffiti and a tribute to the one who wrote it: "For once he got it right." That's what the Incarnation of the Son of God announces, and Olson added that no one dozed as the dean preached the Gospel with power. Again, Olson drew on a contemporary event outside the church walls. For nine straight years the movie One Flew Over the Cuckoo's Nest was the most watched film in Sweden; Olson sees such a response as an indicator of the spiritual longings that are latent among the two million Swedes who saw it and kept going back to see it again. He described his experience when seeing the film in a Stockholm theater and noted how silent people around him were after watching something so moving, as if waiting for someone to help them interpret their strong impressions. He risked breaking the silence around him in the theater that night by quietly suggesting that this film was about Jesus, a comment that did not bring offence or dismissal by those who heard it, but surprising responses by some who turned to him to say that they had never before thought of Jesus, love, and redemption in such terms before. He asked them "Why not follow up on what surprised you here tonight?"—a question the incurably pastoral teacher David Olson could not help asking.

In comments more broadly descriptive of the Church of Sweden he serves and loves, he spoke of the problem of wide swings of the theological pendulum. In pre-World War II days the church had veered to the political rightwing, siding with the establishment in turning its back on workers and those most in need of justice and care. That loss is still deep and damaging, left unresolved by the current swing to the political left and its issues of sexual identity, same sex marriage, and abortion. Though he is restless with church controversies that distort and distract from the Christ-given task of teaching and nurturing people in words and ways that connect to daily realities of life in Sweden, he is not without hope. "I'm too hopelessly Lutheran" he said, explaining that the primacy of Christ's grace in and over all things makes him so. He is grateful for generous collegiality among clergy and laity, and spoke admiringly of a woman, a lay person, who addresses business people regularly on ethics and the difference the practiced Christian faith makes in corporate life in Sweden today. He smiled when recalling this: "the room we were in was so jammed with business big wigs that she had to lecture while sitting on my knee." Olson himself has had ample opportunities with business people of all levels, as many as 500 at a time, who attend mid-day services at St. Jacob's Church where he serves. As we were leaving the *Storykon*, the Swedish name for the cathedral, he pointed out the magnificent wrought iron sphere suspended from the ceiling to within reach, with scores of small holders for individual candles to be lit and placed by those who come to offer intercessory prayer. "Last year alone 70,000 candles were lit here—that says more about religious faith alive in the urban wilderness of Stockholm than one imagines" was his closing word, followed by a warm handshake, and our gratitude for his time and straight talk.

Our last day of interviews in Sweden took us to the suburb of Solentuna and the parish church called Kummelbe. Awaiting us there was Gun Grundl, who laughed with us over my mistake of trying to find her phone number by looking under Solentuna in the directory. She is in her middle years of a lifetime with more than the average share of rough patches. I knew of her through our mutual connection with a friend in Chicago who suggested that she might have a significant life story about finding her way back to the church after years away. There was something about her appearance that suggested the rock-ribbed strength needed for raising her two children alone after her marriage failed. She said it was the mistake of her life to marry a man who mistreated her abominably, who would strike her and scream at her—after coming home from the Roman Catholic Church he attended. She got through it all by supporting herself as a teacher in an area high school and was rightfully proud of completing thirty years in her profession. Her married daughter was facing a divorce after being diagnosed—Gun Grundl learned this on her birthday—with a brain tumor that now required full time hospitalization plus arrangements for the care of her two young children. Her son is a civil engineer living abroad. She told me these things in the opening minutes of our conversation, her voice understandably wearied by recalling the events, her face marked with the lines that come from enduring hard years, yet her eyes still able to reveal a flash of humor despite all they have seen.

She smiled when recalling the circumstances several years earlier when she decided one Sunday that she would go to church "to sleep through the sermon so that I could be awake to enjoy the music"—as she put it. She likes music, she said, and if she ever went to Kummelbe Church at all it was not to worship, pray, or pay attention to the sermon but for the excellent music she heard there. On that Sunday on which she intended to keep her routine, and despite the fact that she was more tired than usual, she did not sleep through the sermon. The preacher was the co-pastor, Gita Andersson, whose sermon was nothing of what she expected, neither boring nor irrelevant, but a gripping testimony to Christ The Way from a text in John 14. She had a vivid memory of how startling it was for her to experience the wake up call the Word of God had for her that day. She went back, signed up for the Alpha Course (for which Kummelbe is a key congregation in Sweden), and for the first time in her life found a spiritual home through the Christ who had found her at a time and in a place she least expected. Looking back on the previous decade, she could now see signs of how she was being prepared for what happened that Sunday morning and the course of her life since. Music has been no small part of it, even in the persons of young musicians who have rented rooms in her home while studying in the Swedish Radio Music School nearby and whose talent she could enjoy as they practiced such songs as Nobody Knows The Trouble I've Seen. Without fully sensing it at the time, she can now see that God was speaking to her. She is now positively involved in the parish Alpha Course program, with its midweek suppers for those who now are where Gun once was. She can relate well to their quest, and in later conversation with Gita Andersson and her colleague, Pastor Staffan Stadell, I learned how much they value her renewed spiritual life and participation in the mission of the congregation through Alpha.

That phase of the congregation's mission was explained in detail by

Anders Litzell, 25, who is on the parish staff as a coordinator of the Alpha ministry at Kummelbe and in other parts of Sweden. He comes from a family of active Christians with Pentecostal church connections. Before graduating from the State University of Stockholm in computer technology he studied at Wheaton College in Illinois and through his dormitory room mate discovered in a nearby Episcopal Church the liturgical tradition he had missed in his homeland—"smells and bells, the whole nine yards, plus the fact that I didn't have to park my brain at the door" as he summarized it. He has visited London where the Alpha program began, as have Andersson and Stadell, and had seen its impact at Kummelbe and heard of its growing influence in the 153 countries of the world where it has been introduced. Its essentials are quite basic, he explained—taking Jesus' custom of table fellowship with all kinds of people and applying it to the mid-week meal at the church, with half of those around the supper table welcoming guests with informal conversation about changes in their lives, then a pastor speaking briefly about some specific theme of Christ's truth and what it means for life today. Gun amplified that explanation by Anders with her own experience, all of which have not been easy since her turning point Sunday. When I asked her what she would want for the Church of Sweden and all the people around her in Soluntuna, she simply looked around her at the Kummelbe Church surroundings and said: "I wish it could all be like this." A good answer, and one that offers hope as the parting word on what it means to live the faith in Sweden today.

In Finland, as some have said, the Chosen are largely frozen. Translated: in this nation of 5.2 million people, 94% of whom are baptized Lutherans, churches are sparsely attended on Sundays, especially during the short summer season when Finns head for the out of doors. While Sunday church attendance is not the only measure of a vital Christianity, some Finns see a problem when the privilege of hearing the word of God regularly and keeping it in the company of fellow believers is reduced to showing up at Christmas and Easter. Among them is Olli Valtonen, a pastor in Helsinki, who put the issue in a witticism worthy of Yogi Berra: "Everybody in Finland loves the church but nobody goes there." He has done something about it. Two decades ago he sized up the non-church attending person in today's Finland as a kind of latter day Thomas, the absentee disciples who doubted Jesus' resurrection. He was instrumental in a creative venture to reach secularized Finns by re-presenting the classic liturgy of the church that invited imaginative participation in its actions. The result was the Thomas Mass (Mass means the church service among Finnish Lutherans), a form of liturgical evangelism we experienced late one Sunday afternoon in a downtown Helsinki church.

Olli Valtonen

FINLAND

The first point Olli Valtonen stressed when speaking with us about the Thomas Mass was that he should not be called its founder. His involvement (a very significant one, I learned, as more of the story unfolded) was motivated, as he said, "by my own needs, but it didn't stop there." He meant that the push to do something about widespread dismissal of the church in Finland grew from his restlessness with too much static formalism in the church itself. That was at least part of the reason why there are so many baptized nomads—his term—in his homeland who have dismissed the church as a place where their hungry souls could be fed. He was also keenly aware of secularizing forces outside the church that contribute to the problem. He gained such insights as a journalist working for a major Helsinki newspaper before his call to the pastoral ministry of the Evangelical Lutheran

Church of Finland. As a pastor he initiated a process of outreach that combined openness to those with doubts and spiritual hang-ups of every kind with respect for the rich worship heritage of the church that has stood the test of time. He knew that such a quest needed firm theological grounding, and with that in mind invited, Miikka Ruokenen, a professor of dogmatic theology at the University of Helsinki, to be his theological mentor. He also knew that it had to be an ecumenical venture. To that end he called together a group of forty people representing the Orthodox, Pentecostal, and Free Church traditions in Finland to join him and other Lutherans in weekly meetings to search together for a way to engage Finns who are distant from the faith and the church and, not incidentally, to pray for the guidance of the Holy Spirit in this quest. What emerged from the "holy chaos" (Valtonen's standard term for the radical diversity of the planning group) was not a new church or a movement of liturgical elitism but—again quoting Valtonen— "a vital current flowing through the Evangelical Lutheran Church of Finland." To the surprise of the planners, 500 people came to the first Thomas Mass on April 10, 1988. Two decades later, more than 150 congregations in Finland have incorporated it into their worship practices. It has also been well received elsewhere in Europe, notably in Sweden and Germany. The genius of this rediscovery of the power latent in traditional liturgy is precisely that arises from the conviction that the Holy Spirit's power still comes through imaginative participation by the people in prayer, the Word, and the Eucharist— without dependence upon a sole charismatic leader.

Among the stories Olli Valtonen told us about the background of the Thomas Mass as he took us by car to a downtown Helsinki church was one unforgettably etched on his mind. It came from his days as a newsman-turned-pastor and illustrated, as he put it tartly, "the spiritual death by drowning in the church's rationalism that has left Finns fed up but not fed." It was customary for the Lutheran bishop of Helsinki to annually address journalists and media people on some topic of contemporary importance. On the occasion Valtonen remembered, the assigned subject was ethics in communication. The bishop went on for an hour in an abstruse treatise laced with theological jargon that sailed over the heads and wide of the interests of his audience. Then he left without taking questions. At that point, one senior newsman turned to Valtonen and with ill-concealed disgust muttered:

"At least he could have given us a blessing—goddammit!" Valtonen added that the next bishop of Helsinki often used the incident as a pointed lesson in the church's problem of non-communication. Even so, that moment had its riveting effect in driving Valtonen to do something more than lament the fiasco of what had happened.

When we entered the huge Mikael Agrikola Church (named after the first Lutheran bishop of Finland) shortly after four o'clock on a wintery Sunday afternoon, the vast sanctuary was empty except for a half dozen people gathered in a far corner of the nave—musicians warming up, we were told. We proceeded downstairs to join others for further Valtonen commentary, including the fact that between forty to seventy people participate in myriad helping functions in each service. He also prepared us for another moment of "holy chaos" coming, referring to that part of the liturgy when the prayers of the people are offered, not by the officiating pastor alone, but by everyone. At the invitation of the host of the Mass, all are invited to move from their pews to the side aisle nearest them. There, small prayer altars are available intervals up and down the aisle, each with a candle, a box with slips of paper, and a person standing by. Each worshiper then wrote a specific petition to God on a slip of paper and took a moment for quiet meditation before placing it in the box and returning to the pew. Valtonen said that this action will take at least a half hour, as a thousand people will be moving to and from a dozen or more appointed stations to write their prayers. During this time the musicians will lead singing drawn from sources ranging from Bach chorales to Taize chants to hymns set to jazz. "More holy chaos" he suggested, smiling. During this time, some may choose to go forward to the chancel rail and kneel so that a vested clergy or lay person could respond to whatever on their hearts needed offering up to God. When that time came in the Mass, I noticed many kneeling at the altar and counted sixteen men and women spread across the width of the chancel to listen and console.

At five o'clock we went upstairs to the nave. I was astonished to see the church already filled, with latecomers hurrying in from the extra tram cars to accommodate the Thomas Mass crowd—courtesy of the Helsinki Public Transport Service. It struck me as a Helsinki counterpart to American mega-church parking lots. The service began with a procession of several dozen lay and clergy participants, led by the crucifer carrying a large processional cross given by the Taize Community in France. The liturgy followed as Valtonen had described it. I did not find holy chaos in the movement of hundreds to and from the prayer altars in the aisles. It was an unhurried, deliberate action by people, showing courteous consideration to each other in waiting their turn. Another impressive moment came when the persons assigned to attend each prayer station came forward to pray aloud one selected petition, chosen from the many placed into the box for its poignant expressiveness of what people beg God to heed and answer. We were told that another volunteer group comes each mid-week day to offer to God the hundreds of petitions left unspoken at the Sunday Thomas Mass. The sermon, which was by a guest preacher from the United States, was an embarrassing disaster—a textless, overlong meandering from the obvious to the irrelevant. Noting my discomfort, Valtonen whispered "We can handle this; the people come for the Eucharist rather than the sermons." Holy Communion was celebrated and distributed at a dozen stations with dignity and dispatch. Following the benediction, the majority stayed on for coffee and conversation in a large downstairs assembly room distinguished by the Finnish genius for turning the wood of the walls and ceiling into a work of art. Over two hours had passed since the Thomas Mass had begun. I saw no one clock watching, nor did I.

The next day, after a visit to the widely known Rock Church with its unique underground sanctuary carved entirely from granite, and a stop at the Lutheran Cathedral with its rounded green dome dominant on the Helsinki skyline, Valtonen was generous in meeting with us again for more insight into faith and culture in Finland today. He spoke of those who have left the church because they found it boring or irrelevant only to find how empty life is when all they have is a thoroughly secularized culture. He has seen signs of spiritual hunger among Finns through those who have found that their doubts about God do not bar them from the welcome they experience when attending the Thomas Mass. Not infrequently he has seen stoic absentees long alienated from the church come to tears by the profoundly moving experience of being accepted, as they are, by others who understand their dilemma. Because he knows the depth of that longing for reunion with God, he has found that it cannot be met with abstract doctrine. "The

Good News of Jesus Christ must move from the head to the belly" he asserted. It happens when the Gospel gains ground through ritual, experience, symbols, signs, and stories that communicate Christ's grace. He knows that Finns who are church dropouts sometimes drop in to an empty church on weekdays "just to breathe."

Valtonen used the phrase with care for the Biblical meaning of breath—*ruach* in Hebrew means breath, or spirit. It refers to the Holy Spirit whom Christ sent to give birth to the church at Pentecost with vivid signs, and still comes with power. As a Lutheran, Valtonen said that he has learned much from the Eastern Church which has always had an important presence in Finland. In the 1980's when he was just underway in what developed into the Thomas Mass he spent hours with Orthodox priests and learned to appreciate their seriousness when praying "Come Holy Spirit" in the Eucharistic liturgy, then believing that the Holy Spirit comes. Those preparatory years also included ecumenical sessions with Pentecostal and charismatic clergy along with the Orthodox. "I would ask them to write their ideas for input on a piece of paper, and then collect them in a bag—time and again this was done. It was more "holy chaos!" he said, returning to his favorite phrase in describing how the Spirit works. "We Finns need to loosen up our traits of unemotional austerity with the leavening of the Spirit" he said. As an example he recalled his first time he preached to a congregation as a newly ordained pastor and risked including a slight note of humor in his sermon, hoping that it might be well received. But when an older woman came to the sacristy afterward to reprimand him with the warning that "The one who smiles in life will cry eternally!" he realized that this dour view of Christian piety can be a thick shell for the Spirit to penetrate.

I asked him what the church would look like if Christ had his way. "A far more welcoming community where his grace holds sway" was his answer. Lutherans in Finland are not welcoming communities, he lamented, and wondered if that stems from a view of God that sees him as only and always angry with sinners. He said that a recent trip to St. Petersburg gave him an experience he wished for everyone. He had two hours to spare before returning to Helsinki, and took a cab to the Hermitage Museum. There he spent the time he had sitting in silence before Rembrandt's masterpiece, The Prodigal Son, based on Jesus' parable of the welcoming father who opened his arms to his wayward, tattered, undeserving son. There the whole story of God's love for his children is depicted in the gesture of welcome—those open arms and the depth of self-giving love that Christ himself embodies and offers. This is the love that the Thomas Mass seeks to offer. Valtonen sees that power at work in his current ministry as director of the Helsinki City Mission where people who need healing of every sort are received in the spirit of Christ. He finds ways to express that transforming love in the columns he writes as a regular contributor to Finland's premier magazine. His persistent restlessness in exploring new venues of the Spirit took him and his wife to London to study the diaconal work at the famed congregation of St. Martin's in the Field. "Handel and Mozart once performed there. Think of it, there's still a concert there every day! On Sundays there are six services offered, two of them in Chinese. The International Amnesty program started there. The idea of public libraries as well. We've got a lot to learn." We left him feeling that if there are obituary notices posted anywhere about the church in Finland, Olli Valtonen is too busy with "holy chaos" to heed them. Are his efforts and those of like-minded Finnish Lutherans making a difference in the wider circles of leadership in the church? A positive clue comes from the response of the Lutheran bishop of Helsinki when Valtonen came seeking his blessing on the Thomas Mass: "I cannot stop you—thank God."

Seppo Rissanen and Risto Ahonen carry a potent leaven for good to the church through their respective roles in the Finnish Evangelical Lutheran Mission, which, since its founding in 1859 has maintained a direct link with every congregation of the Evangelical Lutheran Church of Finland. Rissanen, is the executive director of FELM and brings a broad background of vocational experience (parish pastor, missionary in Egypt, writer and scholar of Muslim-Christian relations) to

Seppo Rissanen and Risto Ahonen

his work of overseeing a staff of 475 persons, 240 of whom are missionaries serving in over twenty countries around the world. When he gave me that statistic, I had to stop him and ask if I had heard him correctly. It struck me as extraordinary that a Lutheran Church of a nation of just over five million members, most of them nominal rather than active, would have a mission arm that connected every congregation to the 240 missionary partners overseas, with a support staff of that same number working in Finland. Also, it is notable that the FELM goes about its task with theological seriousness. Risto Ahonen serves as the theological consultant of the FELM. He has done so since 1996 and before that was a professor of missiology at the University of Helsinki for ten years. His most recent book, *Mission in the New Millennium*, reflects the significance the FELM places on solid theological grounding for the rapidly changing global context in which the church proclaims and lives the Gospel. Both men were generous in hosting us for conversation on trends in the Finnish church which inquirers like us need to understand. Primary among these, they said, is the gap that widens between church and people, especially in Helsinki where one fifth of the Finnish population lives. Too many in the ranks of clergy and laity are still in denial of this reality, though the Thomas Mass is a welcome sign of fresh beginnings. While Finnish Lutherans may be the least church-attending believers anywhere, the signs of faith still appear as Rissanen spoke of people who do go about their daily lives with an awareness that they are baptized Christians. Much of this stems from renewal movements in the past, the latest of which was in the 1980's. Summer festivals for spiritual renewal are well attended. Hospital and prison chaplaincies are active. Some 64,000 children are in Sunday Schools of the 580 parishes of the church. Women have been ordained since 1988; now over half the clergy of the Evangelical Lutheran Church of Finland are women, active in preaching, counseling, and diaconal services. The church in Finland is one of the richest in the world, but the problem remains that the church tax system replaces personal stewardship as an integral act of worship. Both Seppanen and Ahonen stressed the importance of bringing the immense vitality of African and Asian Christian churches back to Finland where it is needed. The FELM, with its connection to Finnish congregations is the key channel for this to occur. Also, it is a unifying leaven between pietist and high church elements of the church as it keeps mission, both local and global, as the purpose for which the church exists.

Meeting and listening to Seppo Risstanen and Risto Ahonen, both in Helsinki and in our home in suburban Chicago during their USA church trip visit, left me with this impression. These men do things well, with a thoroughness and modesty that is, like their language and culture, uniquely Finnish. Their calling keeps them focused on the larger scope of the global mission and the theological soundness which empowers it in Africa, South America, Europe, and Asia. Who are their missionary colleagues in distant corners of the earth? Quite by chance we met such a person in an unexpected place, the FELM mission house in Helsinki, a missionary home on furlough some ten thousand miles from her assigned missionary post in Papua New Guinea where she has served for over thirty years. She was busy with an activity that would be an unlikely item on her reports to FELM leaders—knitting. Her story puts into personal perspective what the FELM does and why it is important.

Pirkko Luoma, was sitting with her needle work in the day room of the FELM mission headquarters building, a multi-story building that houses the administrative offices, meeting rooms, a well maintained museum of its mission history, a refectory, and guest rooms for returned missionaries and other visitors. Beverly and I were enjoying a break in our schedule as guests there and were relaxing in the day room when Beverly and Pirkko noticed each other, each busy with a knitting project. It was a natural opening to conversation which turned from knitting to her years in Papua New Guinea under the auspices of the Finnish Evangelical Lutheran Mission. Pirkko (she insisted on our using her first name) is 57, highly committed to her specialized calling abroad, and blessed with a wiry durability in persisting in her work despite recurring health problems that have plagued her along the way. It was clear that she wanted to talk not about knitting or back ailments but about rendering heretofore unwritten PNG dialects into written form and then translating selected portions of the Bible.

She was born in a small town in the northeastern corner of Finland and grew up in a family where evening prayers were the rule, although church attendance was mostly a Christmas and Easter event. However, the Bible stories she learned as a child were well taught by teachers in her school and by the pastor who prepared her for confirmation as a 14 year old. Such details were not insignificant as I thought of Pirkko and her family as church attendees only at major Christian holidays, yet as people who prayed together as a family, shared the Scriptures in their home, renewed their baptismal faith at the time of confirmation—experiences which were not uncommon in the small towns and rural areas of Finland. Her best friend was a girl affiliated with a Jehovah's Witness congregation in the community, with whom Pirkko would often spend summer days discussing but not arguing religion. Such conversations stirred her to greater attention to explore her faith. Three years later, at a Christian skiing camp (sponsored by the revivalist wing of the Lutheran church which made good use of the Finnish mania for skiing) she became more deeply aware of belonging to Jesus as her living Savior. When returning home to her Lutheran congregation, she was disappointed to find it more of a social club than a place of spiritual power—another note for my understanding of what weakens the church in Finland. Undeterred, she and four other girls met regularly for Scripture study and prayer, an activity which carried over into her decision as a university student to concentrate her studies in linguistics as a preparation for her calling as a Bible translator. She studied in Germany and England, and then entered the Wycliff Bible Translator program in Finland and followed its rigorous discipline of rendering unwritten languages into written form so that the message of the Bible can come to people who have never heard it before.

As a missionary of the FELM, her first assignment was in 1978 when she was sent to East Sepik, a region of Papua New Guinea, with a fellow missionary for further language work. She and the other linguist (FELM sends missionaries out in pairs) for a first year devoted to learning Urim, one of the 800 unwritten languages of the wider region. The Wycliff program requires extensive study of the culture as well as the oral language of tribal groups, followed by four years of rendering Urim into written form in a vocabulary that is culture-specific. Then came a furlough year in Finland to attend to scoliosis and foot paralysis problems before returning to PNG for her second four year term of translating portions of the New Testament as well as Old Testament stories into Urim. Now, she said, she looks with satisfaction on her years of service among people she has learned to love and respect. Her greatest joys, she said, were when her Bible translating became the channel of converting people to Jesus Christ as Savior and Lord and her biggest problems were with people who confused their conversion with the expectation of automatic material prosperity. "There's lots of asking for things—so much so that some missionaries can't handle it" she said with the authority of one who has learned to handle it.

I asked her to help us imagine a day in her life as a Bible translator in northwest PNG. "Well, the first thing is just getting there, it's a two hour plane ride in a single engine Cessna from the nearest airport." She went on to say that three villages are part of her town area, separated from each other by an hour's walk. Her house is mounted on stilts, with a wooden floor and walls, and palm fronds tightly woven to form the roof. Food is brought to her door daily by those who make their living by marketing the products of their gardens. Greens and vegetables are staples, sometimes pork as well. Drinking water is safe as it is rain water saved in the roof tank. She cooks on a combination propane and wood burning stove. Loneliness is not a major problem. Her days are well filled with her translating work. Currently she is working on II Cornthians and Hebrews; she was pleased that her translation of the Book of Acts has been successfully completed. Three nationals work with her on the translating. Faithew, one of the translator workers, took a second wife and therefore had to leave his work in the church as a youth leader and fellow translator. But Sam, another worker, and his wife, have completed their four year studies at the Christian Leaders'Training College recently. She spoke of the great joy she found in hearing him preach the Word to his own people when he was doing his practical term in the village where Pirkko lives. Another notable event was the appearance of people who walked (for three days, one way) to her area for help with their Bible translation work. They reported building seven schools with bush materials plus a translation office. They have placed thirteen teachers in the newly built school rooms, and even completed an air strip in the hopes of establishing outside connections. Now their hope is for translators who can produce parts of the Bible in their Pahi language. Such things, she said, come as reminders of the hunger for God's word in their own language and the promise of the Holy Spirit who is at work through such people. She turned the conversation back to her own gratitude to be living and working where she has been assigned on this latest (her sixth) missionary term. How closely she and villagers can bond was evident in her story of a visit by one of the women of the village. Pirkko had received news of her mother's health problems back home in Finland. The visitor 's own mother had recently fallen ill and died—Pirkko knew the deceased mother well. As they spoke together, tears welled up in her visitor's eyes. Then she began to weep copiously and wail as a lament of sorrow for her own mother and empathy for Pirkko's. "Such are the moments of deep connection" Pirkko said, and then added another story about the enjoyment she and her co-worker find in taking children to a nearby river for lunch and playtime—and a little help in bringing back firewood to her house.

Meeting Pirkko Luoma by chance in the day room as she and Beverly began a conversation around knitting, was one more unplanned encounter among many we have experienced. Pirkko is only one of 240 FELM missionaries, all with experiences that can be multiplied that many times over as one thinks of the remarkable breadth and depth of this single missionary agency based in Finland where the light of the faith is said to be waning. Witnesses like this diminutive woman with her knitting, her back problems, and her three decades of commitment as a linguistic scientist and missionary translator suggest no waning of the Gospel. Nor is that apparent in the administrative calling of Seppo Rissanen and the theological contribution of his colleague, Aho Ristanen. Olli Valtonen and the Thomas Mass show how creative faithfulness can help doubting Thomas's discover what they are missing. These Finns know the problems of the church well enough. But their faith at work in the face of such obstacles has a parallel in something distinctively Finnish. Maramekko artistry in cloth is admired worldwide for its clean lines and graceful blend of colors which are stunning in their understated beauty. Those who received us with hospitality and taught us much in a short time suggest such a tapestry of more lasting beauty.

PART 5

INTRODUCING
CENTRAL AMERICA

Lutherans in Central America, perhaps more than any other among the millions of Lutherans throughout the world, "bear in their bodies the marks of the Lord Jesus." That is New Testament talk (Galatians 6:17) meaning torture and martyrdom for the sake of the Gospel. This is one of the themes that stand out in the testimonies of what men, women, and youth in El Salvador, Nicaragua, and Costa Rica, have experienced personally under brutal regimes that sought their destruction. Such stories could be multiplied from witnesses elsewhere in the Caribbean region, particularly from those in Guatemala and Honduras, whose stories are yet to be told. Another theme is the distinctive meaning of mission as *accompaniment* with the poor and marginalized of society, an intentional theological direction that makes the quest for social justice inseparable from proclaiming Jesus, whose saving work at the cross brings good news to the poor, release to the captives, sight for the blind, and freedom for the oppressed (Luke 4:18). Two more characteristics of the churches here are worth noting: the predominance in the congregations of the generation under 35, and the leadership roles assumed by women at all levels of the church. American missionaries who began Lutheran work there in the post World War II years built strong foundations of sound theology and healthy ecumenical relations—often the fruits of suffering together for the sake of the Gospel. Now, the accent of the church there is thoroughly Spanish, as their Latino witness enters increasingly into the wider circles of global Lutheranism.

A unique cross adorns the wall in Resurrection Lutheran Church, located in a blighted neighborhood of San Salvador, the capitol city of El Salvador. During the civil war of the late 1980's, parishioners victimized by fighting made a large wooden cross, wrote upon its white painted surface a list of the atrocities they had endured, and then mounted it on the wall for all to see. Later that year, on November 16, 1979, the Somoza regime's death squads came to the church for Medardo Gomez, the pastor of the congregation. His outspoken preaching against the government regime and his care for its victims had made him a marked man. When the troops stormed the church, only to learn that Gomez had taken sanctuary in the German Embassy, they removed the cross from the wall as proof of "subversive material." In that act they gave the cross its name, the Subversive Cross, and started it on a mission they did not intend. In the government building where it was kept, people grew curious about the atrocities it named and took note of its message holding the perpetrators accountable before God. In 1992, after the Peace Accords were signed, Bishop Gomez asked the American ambassador and other international leaders to join him in appealing to the then President Cristini for the return of the Subversive Cross to its rightful place. It was returned to the wall of Resurrection Church where its message still resonates today.

Medardo Gomez

EL SALVADOR

On a Sunday morning, the day following our arrival in El Salvador, Medardo Gomez interrupted his preparations for worship to give Beverly and me a warm hug of welcome, Latino style. Before he began explaining my part in the liturgy, he pointed out a large wooden cross mounted on the wall off to one side of the sanctuary, and assigned his young American intern, Dan Beirne, to tell us its story. We listened with interest, but since time was short, asked to hear more later. I had come to El Salvador to learn more about Medardo Gomez and his prophetic leadership as a churchman whose ministry directly confronted "the rulers, the authorities, the cosmic powers of this present darkness" (Ephesians 6:10-17). That Sunday morning was my first opportunity to meet him. He is a short, stockily built man, with a frame proven sturdy through the years of bloodshed and tears he has weathered. He smiles easily. His broad face, wide set eyes, and jet black hair reflect his *mestizo* roots in an Amerindian and Hispanic ancestry. He is outgoing, without airs, and yet imparts an authority earned through years of serving fellow Salvadorans who have been brutalized, killed, maimed, and driven into homeless exile as wartime refugees. He has had his own share of attacks on his own life. One in particular stands out.

On a fateful day in 1983 the un-surprising upshot of his subversive cross ministry came in one terrifying moment, just as he was exiting the San Salvador airport after seeing off a church delegation returning to Norway. He was seized by a death squad dispatched by the Salvadoran government, thrown into the backseat of an unmarked car, blindfolded, and driven to a secret holding place. There Gomez was tortured for four days and nights with electric prods, beaten at intervals, given neither food nor water, and questioned incessantly about his alleged ties to the "contras"—the Salvadoran guerilla army fighting for the overthrow of the Somoza dictatorship in El Salvador. Medardo Gomez was indeed a contra, but in the specific sense of obedience to the God of the Biblical prophets whose crucified Son had called him to speak truth to power whatever the cost. Why was Medardo Gomez spared the fate of countless others who were summarily shot to death after torture did not break them down?

He reflected on that question and other turning points in his life during a Sunday afternoon conversation following the morning Service (led by women and honoring women whose lives were examples of mission and service). We sat together on a spacious porch overlooking San Salvador while several dozen young adults finished off their picnic lunch with songs, laughter, and friendly chatter. The cheerful ambience of the setting was in contrast to the somber subjects Gomez opened up in a conversation that began at mid-afternoon and continued till sunset. He started with the question of why he was not murdered after the airport abduction. Mennonite missionaries in San Salvador, he learned later, became aware of his abduction within hours of its occurrence. They sent word immediately to church leaders in Europe and America who protested the Gomez kidnapping to the Salvadoran government. But more effective, he surmised, was the apparent intervention by Edward Meese, the attorney general of the United States (a Lutheran Church–Missouri Synod member), who had heard what had happened and somehow sent word to the Salvadoran government to back off. They did, and thus Medardo Gomez was spared the fate that befell so many of the *desparacidos* who were never seen or heard from again. Gomez was sure that these quirky, spontaneous interventions were by God's doing, though he did not expect to ever learn the specific details behind them.

He went on to recall his birth and upbringing in a Roman Catholic family in the town of San Miguel, where he was confirmed by Oscar Romero, the senior priest of the congregation. Romero was the priest who moved from the comfortable security of a traditional hand-in-glove relation of the Catholic Church hierarchy to the Salvadoran state to become the courageous archbishop, whose denunciation of government corruption led to his assassination as he celebrated mass at a hospital chapel altar. Romero made a lasting impression on young Medardo and was the source of his early aspirations to become a Catholic priest. He had advanced to the point of applying for admission to a Catholic seminary when he learned that his application could not be considered until his parents, who had been married in a civil ceremony, would be married by a priest in a Catholic Church. When Gomez asked his father (a mechanic) and mother (a teacher) if they would comply, the father's heated "No!" followed by "You're crazy to want to be a priest!" ended his thought of following Romero's advice. He described his entry into the Lutheran Church in San Miguel not as a conversion but as a continuation of his baptismal covenant with Christ. That move was influenced by his closest childhood friend, David Fernandez, a Lutheran pastor's son, who had helped him explore Lutheran teaching and practice. David Fernandez' later martyrdom by a death squad was a grievous loss to Gomez and became a catalyst for his deepened commitment to carry on in his friend's stead as a Lutheran pastor. It was also important to him that his parents supported his decision. He could still quote their words which proved prophetic: "whatever you decide, do it with sincerity and strength, confidence and surety, so that you don't turn back."

He studied theology in the Lutheran seminary in Mexico City for five years. There he learned Lutheran teaching under a faculty that served an ecumenical student body of 200 (thirty of whom were Lutheran) and where he learned to think openly about such subjects as liberation theology, an emerging Roman Catholic theological trend which combined prophetic Biblical theology with elements of Marxian social analysis. It is best known for its watchword "God's preferential option for the poor." He said that while Lutheran theology connects in many ways with that phrase, it is too limiting because of an implied discrimination against those who are better off. God discriminates against no one but loves all, whoever they are, and whether they are poor or prosperous. He preferred his reformulation as "God's preferential option for the needy" and explained it with an example from his own family. He and his wife have six children and eight grandchildren. They love them all equally. But special attention goes to the smallest, sickest and most vulnerable—and then he paused to ask me if it isn't that true of good families everywhere. Gomez thought it obvious that in the context of Salvadoran life, past and present, the most needy were impoverished women. The preferential option for the needy took practical form in the Salvadoran Lutheran focus on ministry to and with marginalized women. It was exemplified in the Resurrection congregation worship that morning, and its results were apparent in the growth of the church through its care for women and others who have nowhere else to turn.

Gomez said that his cross-centered theology has been forged through constant engagement with those who seek justice and God-given renewal for life in El Salvador. He identified it with neither the political right or the left, but said that it shows in such examples as medical aid and humanitarian work among fallen guerillas and beleaguered anti-regime demonstrators who have none to care for them. Such a mission of accompanying those most in need exacts a price, he noted. The death threats that he, his family, and the people of Resurrection Lutheran Church received were frequent, but Gomez turned them into stark reminders of what it means to experience "conversion to the poor," a phrase he picked up from Archbishop Romero. These constant pressures caused him to reach out with increasing frequency to world Lutheranism and ecumenical contacts to help him stay alive. When in 1983 he preached an impassioned sermon before tens of thousands gathered in the city center (at the national funeral for six martyred Catholic priests and two women housekeepers), he could no longer be safe in his homeland. Through United Nations channels he found sanctuary in Mexico. Once again his life was saved but this time it troubled his conscience since he had to break the vow he had made never to leave El Salvador after his providential deliverance from assassination following his airport abduction.

How is it now for him in El Salvador? I asked. He said he was relieved that he no longer had to live in daily fear of assassination. He was grateful to be immersed in his ministry to and with the poor, and for new challenges in this new time. Among them is accompanying those who serve people with AIDS and others who help immigrants get their bearings in El Salvador. He spoke of his concern that one third of the nine million Salvadorans live outside the country because they cannot find jobs in their homeland. He thought it scandalous that an estimated 500 Salvadorans leave the country *every day* to seek work elsewhere. It's no surprise, he added, that the many unemployed youth become fair game for gangs. On the brighter side he is heartened by growth among the sixty-two churches, or communities, as they are called in the Salvadoran Lutheran Synod. Among the 50,000 baptized, some 11,000 are confirmed. Youth ministry is strong in El Salvador as well as throughout Central America. There are sixty-five pastors, eight of whom are ordained women. Pastors have primary responsibility for preaching and teaching. Next is the office of presbyter (academic studies completed but not yet ordained). Then come deacons, evangelists, and catechists. The Salvadoran Lutheran University is the primary educational institution of the church with a curriculum that includes continuing pastoral education for clergy. Fiscal sustainability is a primary challenge. Organizational improvement is needed. Loyalties are not as strong now as during the war a quarter century ago when sheer survival held people together closely. His summary of statistics and trends was brief. It was the end of a long day. He was tired and so was I.

The sun had now set. It was time for Salvadoran food. The Gomez's and Luekings, joined by interpreter Dan Beirne (a Valparaiso University graduate, essential to the purpose of our visit) were ready to push back, enjoy supper and swap family stories. Dessert was good, but Gomez' offer to meet with another person the next day was even better. Gomez gave me a hint as to the person we would meet—a onetime boy guerrilla who led the music of the liturgy earlier on the Sunday we were just concluding.

Christian Chavarria, the person Gomez mentioned the night before, welcomed us for a visit and began with a sentence that was striking in its seriousness and brevity: "My life has been a painful life, yet one that has been blessed by God who has been ever near." He then launched directly into his experience of the violence that descended upon Chalatenango, his hometown north of San Salvador, nearly thirty years before. Families, knowing that the death squads were coming, gathered their elderly and children into their homes, thinking that they would surely be safe. Christian was four years old at the time. His parents were away. An aunt and uncle were looking after him in the house when the troops came. They dragged his aunt and uncle out into the yard and shot them. Then they re-entered the house to find Christian cowering in fear. They grabbed him and threw him down with such force that his head was split open. They left him for dead, then went back outside to paint a white hand on a tree, a sign that they would later return to kill his parents. When Christian revived. he was alone in the house for two days, too young and dazed to understand what had happened. He remembered throwing stones to ward off the dogs that had begun to eat the flesh of his dead relatives. His parents returned to the carnage, barely evading the returning troops who were delayed because they were burning down houses along the way. His father and mother gathered up their traumatized child and fled to the forests beyond the town for temporary refuge from the militia. They continued on, walking by night northward to the Honduras border, joining other refugees as they went. Chavarria could not tell his story to this point without stopping to cry at intervals. When he pulled himself together he explained that his parents later pieced together the parts of the story he was too young to remember. As validation of the truth of his story he showed us the scar on his head from that day of horror. It was proof we hardly needed as we listened in respectful silence.

For the next six years he and his family made the best of refugee life in a huge encampment under United Nations sponsorship. The schooling he received came at hands of his parents. The Honduran government, aligned with the Salvadoran regime, was grudgingly tolerant of the refugees in order to avoid censure by the international community. At first the Chevarrias lived in a tent, then in a tiny house surrounded by barbed wire in an encampment where escapees were shot and survival depended on international aid. In 1989 he and his parents made their way back to El Salvador where all three trained for guerrilla warfare. "It was all we knew how to do—learn to shoot and kill those who tried to kill us" he said in reference to what drew them to the guerilla cause. At age 11 he was given a Russian rifle, longer than we was tall, and when firing it for the first time the recoil knocked him to the ground. All of his friends signed on for training. Of the fourteen who started, all but two were killed in their first months of fighting. One of the two survivors lost both legs, an arm, both eyes, and his faith in God—all this before he was 16. For Christian it was different. He did not lose his faith in God. His mother's words kept coming back to him when he saw the dead and dismembered bodies, the destroyed houses, and devastated land. "Don't blame God for all this evil which humans bring on each other." While in the refugee camp in Honduras a Catholic priest would occasionally come. But it was Medardo Gomez and other Lutheran pastors who came who proved to be the mainstays in helping him sustain his faith. From them he learned to associate the word Lutheran with protection. He was ready to leave the fighting, glad that "though I shot at everything and everybody in sight, I never hit anyone." Battle lines were never clear, he said, soldier sometimes shot at each other, so chaotic was the confusion.

Thus did a traumatized young child become a boy soldier, motivated by terror turned into vengeance, a story repeated countless times in Central America. Beverly asked him how he got through it. He paused again to repeat his opening sentence on God's faithfulness despite monstrous evil. He added that he would like to think that there are lessons that can be learned to break the cycle. But they are not cheap lessons. Justice, shared power, compassion, integrity, and a will to reconcile differences are costly qualities, he said. Yet these are the things that make for peace and that is why peace must finally be the work of God through the hands of those who serve him.

He resumed his story. When returning to San Salvador, he wanted to become a lawyer. His father agreed to this but told him he had no chance for such a profession. Undaunted, he worked as a bag boy in a supermarket daily, from seven in the morning till six in the evening, trying to manage night school as well. It wore him down. At 15 he was at the point of exhaustion, when, as he put it, "God went to work in my life." A turning point came about through a Lutheran pastor doing his grocery shopping, whom Chavarria recognized as one who had accompanied Gomez on visits to the refugee camp. Subsequent conversation prompted the pastor to ask him what he wanted to do with his life. "Make crosses" was the surprising answer. Impressed, the pastor helped him find a course in art and crafts, where he discovered the talent he did not know he had. He began to produce and sell crosses and wooden plaques painted in brilliant yellow, red, orange, and blue—symbolic of his growing sense of what he and many in the Salvadoran Lutheran Synod speak of as a theology of life. Christ's cross is the base for a theology of life, he said, smiling, and the vivid colors he used represented joy and hope in the renewed life that he found.

His promising new direction was suddenly interrupted in 1993 when a classmate, with whom he had been photographed as a fellow guerilla, was "disappeared." The killing was a reminder of how fragile the peace accords of 1992 were, and when he received a death letter signed in blood eight days later, he knew he had escape. Then, when his picture appeared on the front page of a prominent newspaper as an accomplice, his plight was desperate. Bishop Medardo Gomez helped him gain status with the United Nations High Commission On Refugees. At 16, alone, and not knowing his destination, he was taken secretly to the airport and put on a plane bound for Sweden. He remembered crying from fright and loneliness all the way. However, after a few days of misery in northern Sweden, he told himself to stop crying, accept his situation as a gift of God, learn Swedish, make friends, get into school (where he had to deal with his first experience of racism), and prepare himself for his future. Three years later he was no longer eligible for sanctuary in Sweden. Putting fears aside and with no money in his pocket, he returned to San Salvador and devoted himself to an intensive study of English. He flourished under the mentoring of Bishop Gomez and, as a volunteer, he helped provide emergency aid when earthquakes and hurricanes struck. He was determined to complete the cycle from child survivor to boy soldier to artist in the service of the church. When I saw him several days later at the Lutheran University of San Salvador he came out of a class in session for and conversation on how he can market his crosses abroad He continues as a leader in Resurrection

Lutheran Church in San Salvador where his musical gifts are well used and where he leads a group of twelve people in Wednesday night prayers and planning for outreach into the neighborhood.

When I asked him what message he would like to send to us in the global North, he hesitated before answering. With my urging to hold nothing back he said: "When we had nothing to eat in the refugee camp in Honduras, we saw a program with Ronald Reagan interviewed in a beautiful house, with barns and horses, and lots of land. But he led a policy of your country's sending arms to those who tried to kill us, and they did kill my older brother, uncle, aunt, cousins, and closest friend. I am really afraid when leaders like that stay in power." He said he did not mean to indict all Americans by his words and that he is grateful to those who support his artistic calling in the church. Despite his disclaimer, his message holds and must be heard. The scars on his body show what happens when it is not.

The most recently formed Lutheran church in the world is in Nicaragua. It began in 1990 with a remnant from among the 25,000 Salvadoran refugees who fled the civil war in El Salvador in the 1980's for sanctuary in Nicaragua. Among the handful of Salvadorans who chose to remain in Nicaragua was Victoria Cortez, whose preparation for her eventual calling in the church was formed through the hardships of seven years of refugee camp existence. Harsh though those years were, they proved essential to her spiritual formation as a pastor and now bishop of the Lutheran Church of Faith and Hope, as Lutherans are known in Nicaragua. On a sweltering day in Managua, she received us in her office on the first floor of the church's Central Community building, just off a main street in Nicaragua's capitol city.

NICARAGUA

To reach Bishop Cortez's office required walking through the chapel of the church's headquarters building where several dozen sizeable bags of grain seed were stacked up in the rear of the room. Our guide, Annie Bjerke (a young American assisting as translator and coordinator for church programs) explained that they were stored in the chapel not only for the convenience of farmers who would pick them up, but also as a sign of the church's mission as a companion with the poor. As we walked on she diverted us to a side aisle, pointing out that the center aisle was reserved for use during worship services as communicants approached the altar. The seed bags and side aisle path through the chapel were subtle signs of how the church here sees its holistic ministry of connecting seed for the soil with the seed of the Word. We would have missed the insight were it not for Bjerke's thoughtful commentary as we made our way to the bishop's office.

Victoria Cortez received us cordially. She is a striking woman in her mid-fifties, dressed in slacks and wearing a spring green blouse. She showed us the courtesy of greeting us in English before continuing on in her native Spanish as she turned to subjects connected with our visit. I had written to her earlier to ask her permission to interview a cross section of laity and clergy in various parts of Nicaragua for their experiences and insights. Through Annie Bjerke, on loan from the Global Mission of the Evangelical Lutheran Church in America, she had responded graciously and already arranged a full itinerary for our daily contacts. Before turning us loose among her people, however, she made sure that we had at least a modicum of background for what lay ahead. She showed us a well produced film with scenes documenting the formative events of the newly formed church. It included scenes of the raw violence of the 1980's civil war between the leftist Sandinista government forces and the right wing remnant of the previous regime, the plight of refugees, and footage from the historic founding of The Lutheran Church of Faith and Hope. Near the end of the film I pointed to the screen and called out the name of my seminary classmate and long-time friend, Kenneth Mahler. I recognized his face among those shown in this historically important service. Together with Cortez and her husband, Ilo Utech, he was the third in the trio of witnesses present at the birth of this newest member in the body of world Lutheranism. My good luck in spotting him was well received. The fact that I had known Mahler well and expressed admiration for his lifetime work as a seasoned churchman in Central America made it easier for Cortez to give her blessing on our roaming about among the flock she carefully tends.

After commenting on the orientation film, I asked her for an overview of major turning points in her life. She answered with a rapid fire string of autobiographical events that kept translator Annie Bjerke hard put to keep up. She was born in San Salvador, El Salvador, into a family of nominal Roman Catholic parents. By age ten she had found her own way into youth participation in a nearby church, even dreaming of one day becoming a nun. Her father disapproved. Her early aspirations were further blocked by a lazy priest who was less serious about confession and communion than she was serious about these sacred acts. Her teen years were times of spiritual drift. At the National University in San Salvador she majored in economics, excelled academically, and after graduating won a scholarship to the Patrice Lumumba University in Moscow where promising Third World students were trained for a future as revolutionaries. She learned Russian, flourished in her studies, and three years later returned to El Salvador, thoroughly immersed in Marxist political ideology. As she put it, she *plunged* into rural reform projects, working under an organization formed to bring down the repressive regime of Anastazio Somoza in favor of a socialist paradise. She worked clandestinely under life-threatening conditions. But with the passage of time, she said, she began to have second thoughts about violent revolution as the answer to violent repression. As much as she hated the death squads of the Somoza regime, she began to be equally appalled by the heartless tactics of opposing rebels under Augusto Cesar Sandino (called Sandinistas) and their organizational fractiousness. As her quandary deepened, she heard of a Lutheran bishop with a passion for justice among the poor with whom she was working (while living with a farm family and writing poetry idealizing her wretched circumstances) and sought him out as one who might help her resolve her inner conflicts. Meeting Medardo Gomez was a turning point in her life. She immediately found common ground with him in his commitment to the poor. But the deeper gift he gave her was witness to God's grace as the power stirring beneath her yearnings for an alternative to what she had learned in Moscow. He taught her a Biblical framework for liberation through God's truth which could sustain her in the hard work of turning nonviolent change into a political reality in Nicaragua.

With Gomez as her mentor she became a Lutheran. She promptly put her considerable organization skills to work by forming a Salvadoran Lutheran Relief program for the poor, using funds from the Norwegian Evangelical Lutheran Mission. This also gave her a valuable introduction to working with the international Lutheran community. By 1983, however, El Salvador was fast becoming too dangerous a country in which she could remain and work. With thousands of other Salvadoran refugees she fled to Nicaragua for seven years of organizational and relief work among fellow refugees crowded into huge camps in several locations. During that time she met another Lutheran who would play a key role in her future, Kenneth

Mahler, the missionary theologian from the United States whom I had recognized in the orientation film. With Medardo Gomez and others, he helped her build a sound theological base for her eventual calling in the church.

Beverly asked her about life during her early years as a Salvadoran refugee working in Nicaragua. It was hard and dangerous. As she explained why Nicaraguans resented Salvadoran refugees flooding into their country. Their country had once been the second richest in Central America after Costa Rica. Then came three decades of war, political corruption, and natural disasters of hurricanes and earthquakes. The influx of Salvadorans from the north imposed an added burden that contributed to Nicaragua's descent to the poorest nation in the region next to Haiti. Little wonder, then, that she and the Salvadorans like her lived as resented refugees from 1983 till 1990. On one occasion, she recalled, a mob of a hundred angry Nicaraguans from the neighborhood in Managua where she had started a congregation came to destroy the temporary space they had rented, as well as to attack anyone inside. After reaching Bishop Gomez by phone to ask for his prayers, she sent her terrified members out a back exit and stood alone in the doorway. As the mob closed in with knives and clubs in hand "they kept yelling terrible things at me" she said, "so all I could do was stay silent and put myself in God's hands—thinking they would surely kill me." For reasons she could only attribute to God's intervention, the mob did not kill her but after mutterings and more threats, drifted away. That harrowing experience prompted her to contact the German Embassy in Managua for help in gaining access to the president of Nicaragua in the hope of gaining government protection against further outbreaks. The Nicaraguan presidential staff replied that there was no Lutheran church in the country. This was true in the sense that an official registration of the Lutheran Church of Faith and Hope had not yet occurred. The German Embassy staff took Cortez's plight to heart, however, and pledged sanctuary in the event of a similar recurrence. The whole experience taught her that some Nicaraguans who were opposed to reforms initiated by the leftist Sandinista government thought that Lutherans who worked among the poor were stooges of that government. The mob at the church was made up of "contras"—those opposing the Sandinista regime whom the USA equipped with arms via the Iran—Contra scandal in Washington. She said no more about the impact of that scandal on Nicaraguans, perhaps in deference to us as Americans. She chose instead to speak of what those turbulent events had taught her about seeking justice for the poor. "It is dangerous to live the truth of our God who takes the side of the oppressed against oppressors" she said in a tone almost matter of fact, then added after a pause, "it has cost many among us their lives."

Her account left me wanting to hear more. But she had finished that subject and turned instead to facts she wanted us to know about the Lutheran Church of Faith and Hope. It had grown to 8,000 baptized members in its first two decades. Three quarters of the fifty pastors serving in the sixty "communities" (community means congregation in Nicaragua) are women. The predominance of women pastors gave her a sense of pride in their effectiveness as examples for women to follow in a culture of male dominance long conditioned by the Roman Catholic Church. She said that although Lutherans were small in number in her nation of five million population, we would see their potent influence among the people she had arranged for us to visit. Another important statistic was that the majority of baptized Lutherans are between 12 and 30 in age. Then, shifting abruptly from abstract statistics to real people, she suggested that we go upstairs to meet a young person waiting for us in a library room. The conversation with Bishop Cortez gave us a glimpse of her manner of leadership. She came across as practical, pastoral, unapologetically focused on the poor, realistic about problems, yet filled with hope in the power of faith to sustain a youthful church, now and in the future. We walked upstairs, with Annie Bjerke leading the way.

Hellen Rios, 21, was reading a book when we entered. She rose to greet us in English, understandably a bit nervous about conversing with foreign visitors she had not met before. Recognizing that, Beverly then did something that has proved valuable everywhere we've traveled. She opened a small album of family pictures to put Hellen at ease, and for good measure, complimented Hellen on her artfully decorated T-shirt with "Sublime Senorita" stenciled on. In minutes Hellen was comfortably started in telling of her birth and upbringing in Managua, in a family which was nominally Roman Catholic (she was not baptized until she was 11). Nothing of note followed her baptism, she said, until she saw her friends' activities in a nearby Catholic community. It was her first awareness that baptism had consequences.

After her second year as a psychology major in the university her spiritual life took a new turn. She met fellow students who were active in a cooperative ecumenical ministry known as Action by Churches Together and was impressed by their work of organizing street fairs to disseminate AIDS prevention information to street kids. This was all new to her. She admired their effective means of reaching youth through live bands set up to play music on street corners where youth gathered. Hearing music they liked, kids were drawn in close enough to notice tables displaying clearly illustrated pamphlets on a disease they vaguely associated with sex. The irony, she explained, was that in Nicaraguan homes and schools any open talk about sex was taboo—while in the nation at large AIDS was already an epidemic. Another attractive feature of the ACT ministry was their use of youth camps. She had recently finished her fifth session in a camp near Managua with a hundred youth, ranging from 14 to 25, gathered for a week of games, Bible study, talent shows, and talk about things on their minds. These were her pathways into the Lutheran community, where she also was given the opportunity to travel to Honduras to visit AIDS patients. She spoke of how deeply it affected her to converse with people facing death, as well as the satisfaction she found in returning to tell her experiences in youth gatherings in Managua.

How did she envision her future? we asked. She expressed the hope that after finishing her university degree in psychology she would find a way to work in the church—including the possibility of becoming a pastor. Like students everywhere she worried about finding any kind of job in the meanwhile. She said it was common for Nicaraguan students to dream of working in Costa Rica or the United States but many would settle for places less attractive to them, like Honduras or El Salvador. It was a revealing comment on biases evident among Central Americans. She told of brief contacts with Pentecostal and evangelical groups and attributed their growing popularity to "being much more animated than we are, with lots of excitement such as speaking in tongues and trances." What did she see as the place for Lutherans in Nicaragua? "We try to do things that please God by helping others worse off than we are" was her summary of the mission of the Lutheran Church of Faith and Hope. She spoke also of how much the close fellowship in the community meant to her, and when listening to her stories we had the sense that she spoke for many. As we walked downstairs, we stopped momentarily at Bishop Cortez's open door to say we were well started in our week of visiting. She responded with a thumbs up and broad smile.

Later that day, conversation with 21 year old Mario Cesar Leiva opened up insights into how fast some teenagers must grow up under harsh circumstances in today's Nicaragua. He never knew his father. He was raised by his mother who had to make the hard decision to leave her children and travel to neighboring Costa Rica when Mario turned 16. That was the only place she could find employment as a teacher. Shortly thereafter, his older brother left to look for work in Mexico after a fruitless search throughout Managua and its environs. This meant that at age 16 Mario had to assume the responsibilities of the care of his younger sister as well as an aged grandfather who could no longer look after himself. We asked how he did it.

He began by commenting that his circumstances were not unusual in Nicaragua where many families are split apart because employment is so hard to find. Then he pointed out that it was the Lutheran community that saved him. Before becoming bishop, Victoria Cortez was the pastor of a community in which his mother had found her spiritual home and opportunities to use her teaching skills in a night school for poor children. As a 13 year old, Mario had joined his mother in the same community through the rite of confirmation. When she and his older brother had to leave Nicaragua for work elsewhere, Mario was supported by the community which made sure he had enough to eat. They also kept him motivated to finish high school and enter Martin Luther King University in Managua, a school founded a decade earlier by a group of churches which included The Lutheran Church of Faith and Hope.

Early in his university study as an engineering student who kept up his active participation in his Lutheran community, two unexpected events had a lasting effect on is future. The first nearly cost him his life. Once when he was on his way to night classes a gang of roughnecks beat him up badly, took his watch and cash, and could have killed him with the knife one of them wielded. One of the assailants knew Mario through his effort in his community to organize a youth program as an alternative to drugs and alcohol for kids on the street. "Sometimes the guy you think has learned to respect you has other ideas in mind" he said with rueful wisdom. Then came his more telling reflection on the experience: "I really think that God was with me and spared my life that night." He expanded on his conviction with a moving witness to his deepening faith in "a God of love who loves people who don't care about him, who sent his Son to die for everybody, who is here with us and bigger than our all our troubles." It was important for me to record his words exactly as he spoke them with measured conviction and an open amazement over the providence of God in his young life. He could thank God that his mother left him in the hands of the church and not elsewhere or nowhere. He did not judge his mother's decision to leave for Costa Rica, saying that God alone can know why things go as they do. He said his duty now was to pray for her daily, thank her for the money she sends him, and wait for her return.

He had to learn the hard way what can happen when Nicaraguans try to visit family members working in Costa Rica. He had saved enough money for the airline ticket and proper visa and boarded the plane for the Costa Rican capitol. But when his flight arrived at the airport in San Jose he was treated badly. After waiting in long lines for clearance to enter, even paying bribes to insure entry, he was rejected. For no other reason than that he was judged as being of the wrong nationality, he had to return home without seeing his mother. That could have left him bitter, but a second providential turn came shortly after he was back in Managua.

It was an invitation to join a student delegation traveling to Germany for three weeks of home stays with Lutheran families in various cities. His observations of that experience were both appreciative and candid. Germans were punctual, good at analytic discussion, and keenly observant. Also, their churches were nearly empty, the youth were missing, and support from the church tax seemed to be on the way out. He cited the main outcome of the trip as a push in the direction of becoming a pastor in the future. He hoped to complete his remaining two years of study at Martin Luther King University through a scholarship he had earned. He saw that as another sign of God's hand guiding him. Meanwhile, he said, his priority was to give his younger sister the best family life possible. Now that she was 16, and with no mother or father at her side, it would fall to him to talk with her about values and warn her about the *machismo* in boys she would have to deal with. He needed all the help he could find to keep the home base strong for her and for his grandfather. His summing up came in these words: "I've received so much help from Pastora Cortez and others that I think it's my turn to be a guide for my sister and others like her." It was remarkable to hear a 21 year old big brother, deprived of so much family in his own growing up, speak with a tenderness and maturity that parents twice his age might envy. We were getting clearer about the Lutheran Church of Faith and Hope not as a church with a youth program but one in which youth are the church.

It required six hours of hard driving in a jeep that had seen better days for us to reach the farm home of Gerzan Álvarez and his wife, Emperatriz Valasquez, situated among low hills and scrubby farm land not more than eighty miles northwest of Managua. Even for our driver, the trusty Beto, this remote location tested his knowledge of the region plus his driving skills over unpaved roads with potholes that made it as rough as any we've seen anywhere. Some delays along the way were a charming diversion, however. We urbanites from *El Norte* do not often

Gerzan Alvarez and Emperatriz Valasquez

get to see columns of Brahmin cattle ambling along at their own pace, impervious to the prodding of cowboys on horseback (some wearing ball caps with various USA team logos) who paid little attention to the honking jeep. Nor could we imagine how oxcarts *that* loaded with watermelons could ever make it to market for the small profit their patient drivers could make. Finally, we did reach the Alvarez farm house where a hospitality awaited us that was worthy of every minute of every mile to get there.

This Lutheran pastoral couple live in surroundings worth noting in detail as a commentary on their commitment to ministry. Gerzan built his house of sturdy brick walls and clay tile roof himself. Emperatriz swept the earthen floor, which she kept immaculate. Window openings at both ends of the room let in natural light, as there was no electricity. A mirror, a calendar, family pictures (including one of Gerzan in his graduation cap and gown) were mounted on the interior walls of hardened clay. A bike leaned against a side wall. One cross was placed on the wall above it. Another cross stood on the floor in the corner, placed there for reasons we would soon learn. A bag of sand hung on a rope from a rafter, "for working out," as Gerzan explained. Opposite the blue plastic chairs on which we sat was a table with a simple green cloth covering. The darling Miurel, age 9, was pleased to tap out her name on my laptop so that I could spell it correctly. Another older daughter, bothered by a toothache, lay in her hammock on one side of the room. Gerzan was dressed in blue jeans with a blue checked sport shirt, and looked trim and fit for his 51 years. His well tanned face was leathery from his combined vocation as pastor and subsistence farmer. Emperatriz, 44, is also a pastor. Her round face was topped by jet black hair drawn up in a bun. Our guess was that her red sleeveless blouse and black skirt were her Sunday apparel, chosen for this weekday visit from American guests.

Gerzan was animated in describing his pastoral work. "God provides for our needs. Look at our house. It has a tile roof over our two rooms. See all the things God gives us. He makes the beans and other crops grow—people don't make it grow. Look out the door at the well at the bottom of the hill—we can draw clean water anytime!" He then went on to describe how thankful he was for those who come to the two services he conducts on Sundays. They walk to worship in all kinds of weather, he said, and the same was true for those who come for prayers and Scripture on Friday evenings. The average attendance is fifteen. Holy Week was coming, which meant foot washing on Thursday, a Good Friday liturgy based on Jesus' Seven Words from the Cross, and special Easter worship of the combined house churches on Sunday. He wanted to do more with youth, but getting around on his bicycle made it hard, especially when rains turn the roads to mud.

He told us that his own education for ordination was mainly at the Central Community in Managua where he learned the books of the Bible, especially the Gospels and how the good news of Jesus' death and resurrection was the center of preaching. Then he turned in his chair to point to the wooden cross standing against the wall in the corner of the room. There was a reason, he said, why he did not put its base into the earth but stood it up on the surface. "Jesus is not in the ground. He's risen! He puts his power in the words we say about him" he said, pointing to the cross and then to his own lips to make the point even clearer. He went on in explanation of how trips to the Central Community in Managua several times a year enable him to keep learning more about preaching and liturgy. As he spoke my mind stayed fixed on the utter simplicity of his manner of speaking the faith. Where else in the world, I wondered, do pastors discourse on the doctrine of creation by pointing to a tile roof overhead or to the bean crops growing outside? And where else is the central truth of the faith explained by a cross whose base was standing on, not under, an earthen floor to proclaim the resurrected Jesus who puts his power into the preacher's words?

Emperatriz joined in as the conversation turned to more about training, saying that the professors in Managua emphasize the theology of the cross. That was new to her. In her experience growing up as a Roman Catholic, the cross of Jesus was about the suffering his people must bear with him. But now, she said with a lift in her voice, they were learning how Jesus' cross is about his death which brings life and love. He is not in the ground anymore, she repeated after her husband, but risen to put joy in her heart and hope as one called to be a pastor. "Now we carry the cross not as our suffering but to join us with Jesus as he makes people free." My question about what that meant in her ministry led Emperatriz to talk about her work with women and children, few of whom have had the opportunity learn to read or write. The practical ministry they both provide is what first attracted them to the Lutheran community. When the devastation of Hurricane Mitch in 1998 destroyed what they had, Gerzan met Lutherans who came to help storm victims rebuild. Among them was a pastor who conducted a service that so impressed Gerzan that he became interested in knowing more about what he had heard. After further contact him and those helping hurricane victims, the pastor surprised him by asking if he would start a new community among his neighbors with similar needs. Gerzan agreed. Twenty families came to the first worship service—Gerzan pointed out the door to the tree under which the people gathered.

Then Emperatriz summed up the events that drew her to wanting to be a pastor. She put it in her own words which caught the heart of the Gospel: "We always thought that it was our works that made God look our way with favor in his eyes, but then learned that it was God's work that gave us what we're now doing." She and her husband serve without a regular salary. The people in their communities are too poor to support them. Like their neighbors, the Alavarez couple live on what they earn as farmers, with the minimal offerings of the community used for trips to Managua for their continuing education.

Gerzan talked of his war memories from the late 1980's. Everyone had to serve in the military under the Sandinista government. He was among those who had to learn to use rifles and grenades to fight against the "contras" who were better equipped with weapons supplied through the USA. It was a hard time. Many had to leave their families for half a year or more to fight in battles he always dreaded. He was glad to come home alive so that he could marry Emperatriz whom he had known since both were young-sters. They were together for three years, then went to the Catholic Church for the wedding. When the events of Hurricane Mitch led to his calling, Bishop Victoria Cortez encouraged her to join him in the training classes as well. Emperatriz now serves two communities on Sundays, both within walking distance. Together they serve four communities, all meeting in houses. When asked about joys she found in the work, she answered that it comes when people listen to the Word of God and live what they hear. Gerzan said that his satisfactions come when he can bring back more learn-ing from his classes in Managua and apply them to the communities here. He never liked to study when young, he said, and remained illiterate until his life was turned around by Bishop Cortez. As he recalled that chaotic time of his youth, he said that he had always tried to "be somebody" by wild living (which included going to Mass when he was drunk). That's why his main joy now, he said with feeling, is that Jesus has forgiven his sins and given him a future beyond anything he could have imagined.

What were problems in their work? Beverly asked. Emperatriz' answer was not what we expected. "We have no mail service here nor a phone line either" she said, and added that she knew of no plan to bring electricity to her house. The idea of a cell phone to reach Managua when necessary was a good one, but batteries are necessary. The absence of electricity to keep them charged ruled that out. She hoped that solar power units she had heard about in the region might be introduced closer by. But nothing like that was in sight, and while they appreciated our offer to help, there was no reason for them to accept a gift for cell phones. This turn in the conversation prompted a question I had not thought proper to ask: "Do we seem like rich people to you?" Their answer was that because we had come to them to share our mutual faith we were all rich in the same way. A visit like this was a something new, they added, and even though they knew nothing of the way we lived, it was good to come together as people who love the same Lord.

Before we left we experienced one more surprise, thanks to Alvarez hospitality. How they procured two bottles of Coca Cola they set out on the table for us, cooled by water drawn from the well, we had no idea. But the refreshing drinks were a kind of secular sacrament, conveying a sign of friendship established in a few hours of listening and learning about what we have in common despite the obvious differences. Before they walked us down the hill, past the well, to the waiting jeep, Miurel typed her name one more time on the laptop. Her two older sisters emerged from wherever shyness had kept them during our visit to greet us and told us their names. And the oldest sister declared that listening to the conversation from her hammock made her toothache better. She insisted on getting up and walking down to the jeep with her parents to see us off.

We arrived in the town of Somotillo as night was coming on and the absence of street lights made it hard to find Immanuel Community of the Lutheran Church of Faith and Hope. When we did arrive, the church was semi-darkened. Pastora Anielka Carmen Martinez had started the mid-week Lenten service. The building was of simple, concrete construction, with windows and doors open to let in the cooler evening air. A group of about fifty were seated in white plastic armchairs in a semi-circle in the middle of the room. All appeared to be youth in their teens and early twenties. Two mothers with their small children were present. Pastora Anielka sat cross legged on the floor at the head of the semi-circle of worshipers, a lighted candle burning before her. Her voice was so soft it was hard for me to hear, not to mention understand her words in Spanish. Annie Bjerke's whispered translations of the homily told us that the message centered on the mystery of Christ's presence. The main wonder, she was saying, was not in the darkened, mystical atmosphere around those gathered in the room but in the redemption Jesus has lavished (Ephesians 1:7) upon us in the forgiveness of sins through his blood. It is Jesus' voluntary self-giving, she pressed upon her youthful listeners, that liberates us from sin. (We heard the word liberation often from her and from all Nicaraguans to whom we listened). She used it as the key to putting away the weakness of sin and finding in Christ's victory what it takes to live freely despite poverty. Her application of the text was clear and uncomplicated. We honor Christ in Lent not by making our lives harder than they already are but by turning ourselves over to him in the freedom to love him as he has first loved us. After speaking she called for a time of silence, then asked for spoken prayer if any wished to pray aloud. Several did, in barely audible words. The music of the service was Latino in style, with texts celebrating liberation through Christ the hope of the oppressed. After the benediction was spoken the youthful worshipers walked from the dimly lit sanctuary into the pitch black night, many holding hands as they found their way. When Beto flashed on the jeep lights to help them see, some turned around to smile and wave their thanks.

The next morning at 8:30 Pastora Anielka met us for coffee on the porch of a motel in Somotillo. She is 27, the single mother of her young daughter, and smartly dressed in bright red slacks and white sleeveless blouse. She did not smile easily; there was the hint of sadness in her eyes, perhaps the sign of some earlier heartache that lingered. When she did smile, however, her face was brightened by dimples that brought out her natural attractiveness. She came from a family of devout Lutherans, she said, and her parents and grandparents wanted her to know the goodness of what they had found in the Lutheran community in Somotillo. But when she became a single mother she was afraid, thinking she would be rejected. However, the persistence of the pastor, Ramon Rodriquez, in seeking her out and inviting her finally won her over. She did find acceptance in the community under Rodriquez's pastoral care. Tears filled her eyes when she said, directing her remarks to Beverly whose presence encouraged her: "It's hard to be a single mother in Nicaragua, like having a hole in your heart.

But when people accepted me that hole began to heal. I found a place where I could be close to God." Rodriquez recognized her gifts and arranged for her to go to the Central Community in Managua for formation classes in theology. She did well and began working with adults and youth in Somotillo. Then came these animated sentences: "It was marvelous! Nobody looked at me as a single mother. I was a sister and friend. I felt God calling me. It was during a week with youth in a camp near Somotillo. It was so wonderful I never wanted to go home—but I did. And here I am." This was her third year as pastor of Immanuel Community where we worshiped the previous evening.

At this point she introduced her church member Yaritza Rodriquez, who looked younger than her 18 years. I asked Yaritza what it meant for her to be a part of the community under Pastora Anielka's care. She answered readily, saying that she had wanted to meet us after the Lenten service the night before but was too shy. Now, reticence set aside, she wanted to show, as well as tell us what the church meant to her by taking us to another part of the town. With that our morning conversation on the motel verandah ended (happily, since noisy eighteen-wheeler transports, smaller trucks, motorcycles, cars, oxcarts and mounted cowboys herding cattle were already churning up clouds of dust from the unpaved road a few yards from us). We stuffed ourselves into the jeep for a short ride to a location where ten new houses were going up. This was the work of the Lutheran Church of Faith and Hope that Yaritza was eager to show us. Her own family had been among the thousands of Nicaraguans who had lost their houses in the calamitous Hurricane Mitch nearly ten years earlier. Now the church had led the way in finally securing funds for ten new dwellings going up, one for Yaritza and her family. They were helping mix cement for the foundation footings when we met them. Her three younger siblings in the family were standing by, too young for work assignments. As we all shook hands and took pictures, I wondered about schooling for the youngsters since it was midmorning on a weekday.

Yaritza chose that time and place in front of the construction site to speak of the profound changes in her life that had come through Scripture classes, youth camps, the three year confirmation instruction under Pastora Anielka, and God's closeness in worship such as the Lenten service the previous evening. She was proud to add that her Lutheran Church of Faith and Hope was living up to its name also by making it possible to people to help in constructing the houses going up before our eyes. Although the leadership of the Central Church in Managua was necessary for a project of this size, the youth of the Immanuel Community in Somotillo initiate smaller projects on their own and use the money to help others. She explained that they sell soft drinks at the soccer stadium, use their bikes to taxi people here and there, and make tortillas to sell on street corners. "This makes us forget our own problems and work for something bigger," she said with pride in her voice. She explained that the money is used for various purposes, including bus fare to visit youth in other communities. The point she was emphasizing was that most of the Immanuel Community members are alone in their families when it comes to being active in faith. They need each other.

Before leaving Somotillo I asked Yaritza what message she wanted to send to the USA. She deferred to Pastora Anielka, smiling as she added "because she's been there and knows what to say." Her reference was to her pastor's earlier trip to South Dakota and home stays with parishioners there. Anielka Carmen Martinez did have a message to offer. It was centered in the sufficiency of Christ's liberating grace to unite us, different though we are, in one faith and life of service wherever we are. Here in Nicaragua, she said, a welcome awaits everybody who comes. Amidst poverty there are believers here who are rich in faith and hope and are happy to share that wealth.

Her words stayed with me on our return trip to Managua for a concluding visit with Bishop Cortez. During our summary conversation she mentioned a coming event that might interest us. The Lutheran School of Theology in Chicago would, in two months hence, confer on her an honorary Doctor of Divinity degree. She was excited about it as an occasion to lift up the work of the Lutheran Church of Faith and Hope as well as receive an honor as its bishop. Later, in Chicago, when I did attend the commencement she had mentioned, I had no trouble finding her shortly before the ceremonies began. She was among the graduates taking last minute pictures, donning their mortarboards, and preparing to join the academic processional. But before stepping forward to greet her I waited a few paces back. I wanted to fix this scene in my mind and try to imagine the extraordinary span of events in her life since that other commencement, years before at the Patrice Lumumba University in Moscow. That commencement and this one were distinctly related to revolutionary causes. One sought a new political order through violent means. The other announces the dawning of another kingdom through the cross of Christ's suffering love. Victoria Cortez and many in the church she serves know first hand how *revolutionary* Christ's suffering love is, how directly it confronts the sinful powers of darkness, and how opposed it is to domesticated religion. Nicaraguan Lutherans know the weight and glory of such costly discipleship. Their witness, which we heard and saw again and again in our days with them, makes us hopeful that their rare gift will be recognized and cherished throughout the global church. More than many of us realize, we need it.

Costa Rica's reputation as a place of natural beauty and abundance dates back at least to 1502 when Christopher Columbus reached its Caribbean coast and called it "costa rica"—rich coast. Our early impressions upon arrival at San Jose confirmed his description. The first two hours' drive north from the capitol city brought gorgeous sights at each turn. The lush landscape was alive with flowers, hills blanketed with greenery of every kind, waterfalls, elegant resorts, and excellent roads for the flourishing tourism industry. The last hour of our journey showed us a different Costa Rica. The roads were wretched. The flat landscape was dominated by banana plantations, their fruit clusters wrapped in blue plastic bags for protection against a freeze. There were no resorts. Towns were few and scattered with no direction signs to help us reach our destination. It was a small chapel, freshly painted in two shades of green, situated at the far edge of Jardin, a village too small to appear on a map. Over the doorway a sign (with the Martin Luther logo prominently displayed—a blue cross at the center of a red heart against a white and blue field) read Iglesia Luterana Costarricense identifying it as a chapel of the Lutheran Church of Costa Rica.

COSTA RICA

Pastor Stephanie Quick was too busy to greet us when we pulled up at mid-afternoon on a Sunday. She was concluding Bible story time with a group of children gathered in the yard outside, and was about to move them inside the chapel for worship where she would lead worship shortly. It would be her second service of the day after serving a community (community means congregation) in the larger town of Guapiles where she lives. She is in Costa Rica at the request of the ILCR, the acronym for the Lutheran Church of Costa Rica, as a mission developer from the Evangelical Lutheran Church in America. In current church parlance, her pastoral work in Costa Rica is accompaniment, a key word in the new vocabulary forming around today's global mission of the Gospel. The term implies a difference in the relationship between those once sent as foreign missionaries by a home church to evangelize and those whom they evangelized who were kept subordinate. Thus, a half century ago, Lutheran missionaries from the United States, Finland, and other countries came as servant leaders to Costa Rica to proclaim Christ and form Lutheran churches. Now Costa Rican pastors and laity lead the Lutheran Church of Costa Rica.

Stephanie Quick accompanies them and serves at their request and under their direction. It is important to add that international exchange is a two way street in this new era in which the mission of the Gospel is everywhere. Christian missionaries from what were once termed "heathen lands" in Asia, Africa, and Latin America are now in Europe and the United States as partners in building the faith and handing it on to others.

Estebana Orozco was among the adults arriving early for the 3 p.m. service. She is 41, the mother of three children who were among those outside in Pastor Quick's Sunday School circle. Through our interpreter (Krystal Obermeyer, recent college graduate, fluent in Spanish, on loan from the USA) we made good use of the time before the service by introducing ourselves and inviting her to sit down with us. She was glad to oblige and told us that she is president of the community and lives close enough to help look after the building during the week. In addition to worship each Sunday afternoon, with an average of twenty children and eight adults attending, she described weekday classes for adults on subjects ranging from studies in the Bible to catching snakes and extracting their venom for medicinal powder. "The medicine is good for combating cancer and neurological problems" she added with a tone of authority that made us wonder how she learned the process in this area where she grew up. Her contact with the Lutheran community came about through a women's meeting in a house close by. She was a lapsed Catholic at the time, but the group's openness and practical work of taking on useful projects impressed her. When the call went out for helpers to paint the chapel she was glad to accept, and added how pleased she was to decide on the two shades of green. With her prior experience in making purses she was ready to start teaching that craft as an addition to the weekday class schedule. Plans for a class in computers had stirred interest, but were deferred due to the theft of the recently donated computer. She spoke freely of her love for God and her confidence that he led her to this community where she and her family have found a spiritual home. "One way I show my gratitude is baking bread for communion" she said. She went on to express her hope that her bread-making talent might lead to starting her own bakery and a business, a matter that depended on getting a bank loan. Her more immediate concern, however, was to save up for a two dollar bus ticket to travel to her sister who was ill. With that comment it was time to rearrange our chairs for the liturgy about to begin, and try to digest a well filled half hour of conversation with the first person we met in Costa Rica.

The next day's return to San Jose brought meetings with two people, each with different experiences and insights into life in their respective communities. The first was with Brenda Rivera, 20, a striking young woman with eyes that made us think of Jesus' word of the eye as the light of the body. She had a quiet presence, a dignity combined with reserve, and though she did not speak English she was forthright in Spanish as she told her story. She was born in Nicaragua and remained there until she was twelve. At age 8 her mother had to leave the family for work in Costa Rica. Her father cared for her and her two older siblings until she was 12, when both parents decided that Brenda needed to be with her mother in Costa Rica. All this was difficult and confusing for a girl entering her teens. Brenda saw it as one more version of problems faced by so many Central American families split up by necessities of finding work wherever possible. She had been baptized a Catholic but it meant little. What had begun to give her an inkling of what the baptized life might mean came through an invitation from a friend who belonged to the community where we were conversing. Through her friend she met an older couple who led youth activities and taught catechism class, the Umberto's, whose kindness and commitment were a major influence for good at a crucial time in her life.

She was impressed by the way in which the Scriptures were taught by the Umberto's. "Everyone really tried to get something from the Scripture readings by drawing pictures of Jesus' parables and then talking together," she recalled. This early enthusiasm did not last. She was not sure why she drifted away but thought it might have been caused by the fallout from her early years of family disruption and the discomfort of being a Nicaraguan youth in Costa Rica. She went to an evangelical church because she liked the music and had heard that they were growing fast in Costa Rica (they now represent 14% of the population in which 76% are Roman Catholic). But the people were critical of her, so that did not last. Finally she returned to the community, as she put it, like a black sheep looking for a place back in the fold. Her pastor, a Brazilian, received her warmly. She appreciated his intelligence as well as his pastoral care. Markus Rodriquez helped her regain her self-confidence lost along the way. This happened through her training as a youth leader, a good experience for her that she was glad to see repeated in other communities. Young people get the chance to lead other young people. She said that an average of twenty five youth meet weekly for Scripture study, crafts, traditional Nicaraguan dance, mime, drama, and teaching Bible stories to the smaller children. On the last Saturday of each month the youth prepare and present a worship service conducted entirely by youth. Her voice rose as she spoke with excitement about a major event that had occurred the previous year. She went with several other youth of the community to Sigtuna, Sweden, for a three month exchange experience. She was grateful for the chance to live in the homes of several host families, and gained new ideas when visiting youth ministries of the Swedish church in various congregations. It also meant opportunities for her to tell Swedes about the many good found things occurring in her community as well as in others she knew in San Jose. What surprised her about her experience in Sweden was the fact that many Swedes do not believe in God. Nor do Swedish young people talk much about God when they are together. As puzzling as this was, she was careful not to make sweeping judgments after less than a month in another country (where she was excited to see snow for the first time). Her visit to Sweden, she said, did make her glad to return home "wiser for going, grateful to the Lutheran Church in Sweden that made it possible, and all the more determined to make my future count in Costa Rica."

The second person we met was Ledia Teresa Guadamuz, a peppy, red haired woman wearing a bright yellow dress, who was volunteering in the day nursery of the LaCarpio Community of the Lutheran Church of Costa Rica. She is 51, married, the mother of two sons, and the grandmother of three. Though raised in a Roman Catholic family where the faith was lightly practiced, she told us how she came to her strong conviction that God has a definite plan for each person. Fifteen years earlier she was living in a neighborhood with poor housing and her place was, as she put it, a dump. She heard of a political campaign to enable her and people like her to move to better quarters, even to someday own a home. She and her husband took the risk of preparing to leave their shabby location in anticipation of a new start in better surroundings. Then the campaign sponsors pulled out with the cash they had pocketed and the whole plan proved to be a scam. By God's grace, she said, she learned to trust his promises as never before "and when I prayed my knuckles turned white" she said. They were able to get temporary housing in the meanwhile, but a decisive turn came when the Lutheran Church of Costa Rica intervened. She noted that she kept hearing the word *accompaniment* as the Lutheran leaders helped them get an attorney who took their cause to the city government and also explained how they could inform the news media of their bad experience of being swindled out of decent housing. They were thrilled with the outcome of having a better place in which to live and seeing the church intervene for justice. This drew her to join the ILCO community and volunteer in what she was doing.

Ledia Guadamuz paused in her narrative in order to show us around the well equipped, brightly painted nursery, and then said she wanted to return to her story to emphasize the main thing about the church's accompaniment. It was what she felt in her soul as, for the first time in her life, she found a connection between what she was doing during the week with her worship on Sunday when God "spoke to her in plain Spanish." She had heard the Bible before when attending Mass. Her husband even had a Bible and tried to teach her its meaning. That didn't work. Things changed when leaders from ILCO came to her neighborhood with help that rescued her family from homelessness. When she saw that, the words of the Bible came alive when she went to meetings for study and discussion in small groups led by the pastor. There she could ask questions and get answers, all of which was new to her. She said she had a great deal more to learn about the Bible and what it meant for people in her neighborhood. In order to do that, she was proud to say that she was completing high school after years as a dropout. In that connection, she said she was preparing for a coming test in a difficult subject and asked me if I would pray for her. Then and there we concluded our conversation as I offered prayer for a 51 year old candidate for a high school diploma, unabashed about her jitters in passing an exam, and equally unhesitant to ask for the Lord's help in getting to her goal.

On our way to meeting Melvin Jimenez, the president of the Lutheran Church in Nicaragua, Beverly reminded me of something I had not noticed.

Every person we had interviewed in El Salvador, Nicaragua and Costa Rica had been baptized in the Roman Catholic Church but had lapsed into inactivity. None had reported being proselytized. Each had been drawn from spiritual drift by the example of people they found appealing because their actions spoke so directly to life problems. None had been rebaptized, nor had any been required to renounce their former affiliation. Most were young, alone in renewed spiritual life in their families. All were from the economic underclass. With these observations in mind, formed from conversations limited to the comparatively few with whom we spoke, we were interested in sharing them with President Jimenez for his broader, deeper perspective.

Melvin Jimenez

He met us in his office in the modest two story headquarters building of ILCO in San Jose, easy to recognize with a large, multi-color banner posted above the entrance that announced the coming twentieth anniversary celebration of the founding of the church body. I had not met him before, but found his manner friendly as he rose from his desk to welcome us. He is a man nearing sixty, if not already there, with his gray open-collared clergy shirt a good match for his thick gray hair and a carefully trimmed mustache. He knows English, but as one more at ease in expressing himself in his native Spanish, chose that medium for the entirety of our time with him—and thus interpreter Krystal Obermeyer was fully engaged throughout the hour. Behind him on the wall were crosses which caught my eye, and as we sat down with him I commented on the strikingly colorful Latino style of each. The remark gave him a point of departure that proved useful in his response to inquiry about the Lutheran presence in the predominantly Catholic Costa Rica. He said that the crosses were gifts from Roman Catholic that symbolized trust and mutual respect in his ecumenical relationships with them that have grown from working together among the poor. I asked whether Ledia Guadamuz's story we had heard the previous was one that exemplified ecumenical accompaniment. He knew it well since he had participated in the cause and was glad for cooperation with Catholic priests and others. He went on to make the larger point that the Lutheran missionaries who came from the United States in the early 1960's, Robert Gussick and Kenneth Mahler were named among others, brought good theology and sound churchmanship to their founding work. They were Missouri Synod Lutherans whose Gospel-centered belief and practice presented Lutherans as a leaven in the church catholic that is confessed in the Apostles Creed. Not all Catholics received them well, to be sure, but the field of workers among the poor was never overcrowded. There was always more work to do than Lutherans and Catholics combined could accomplish. Another positive factor he mentioned was the radio ministry of the Lutheran Hour, begun by the Lutheran Church–Missouri Synod in 1960. Costa Ricans of all religions and no religion responded in sizeable numbers, and the materials sent them put Christ first and urged affiliation with local congregations wherever possible. After two decades of sound ecumenical doctrine and unified practice by Lutherans from the States, however, the last two decades have been a regrettable departure from promising beginnings. Missouri Synod controversies in the United States in the 1970's were reflected in a narrowing of their work in Central America, Costa Rica included. Fledgling congregations were left leaderless, he said, with a noticeable tone of sadness in his voice.

Melvin Jimenez himself was adversely affected by the withdrawal of the Missouri Lutherans from cooperative efforts. It was difficult for him as a young man in the 1970's, just entering training with the Lutherans for a future of visionary pastoral leadership. His earlier experience as a lapsed Catholic had left him in a spiritual vacuum. He tried going to a youth group of an evangelical denomination but found it too narrow in legalistic rules and without attention to the needs of the poor. Without going into details that would have interested me, he said that he found his way into the Lutheran community, studied theology, was ordained, and served as a pastor in the young church that was formally constituted in 1988 as the *Iglesias Lutheran Costarricense,* ILCO by its acronym. By its twentieth year the church's outreach ranged from urban San Jose with its million and quarter population to Jardin, a village of less than a hundred. The number of those listed on the church roster as baptized and confirmed members is 1,200. He gave a brief explanation of the three levels of church organization. The first is the community, formally organized and under authorized leadership of a pastor or catechist. Next is a community under development—the one we visited in Jardin was an example. Third were points of service, i.e. places with promise for future mission.

Jimenez was elected president in 2000. He named these as his goals for ILCO: a Gospel-centered focus in interpreting the Holy Scriptures with direct relation to the life situations of believers, the unity of the spiritual with the physical needs of people, and the front line of mission as the laity rather than the pastors of communities. To reach these goals he mentioned four emphases: striving to make the church a family knit together by practical means of holistic mutual care, showing openness to the many Costa Ricans who are lapsed Roman Catholicism looking for Christ-centered discipleship, maintaining unity in ILCO as one Lutheran church in Costa Rica rather than splitting into contentious divisions, and keeping worship vital in enabling believers to "enter to pray and exit to serve."

I asked him for his view of current problems ILCO faces. He mentioned the high percentage of youth in the communities of the church body who need more training for the leadership they are assuming. Brenda Rivera was an example. While her personal commitment is indeed promising, she needs deepening in an educational institution of the church for her future service. ILCO cannot accomplish that on its own; it is an ecumenical challenge that must be carried out in cooperation with other churches with similar needs. Finanical sustainability is another key problem. The Lutheran Church in Costa Rica has chosen to work among the poor. Its own modest headquarters and community buildings are part of its credentials. But money is still needed for the church's ministry and there is a lack of it. Third on his list was the inadequate use of the media to promote the church's mission, especially in finding its voice for justice in public affairs both local and national.

Did he find joy in the work? I asked. He does find his calling blessed with joy as a major gift of the Spirit. He spoke of how moved he is when he sees people on the margins of life, with no standing among others, come into their own as confident believers who have found themselves—"because they have been found by Christ" was his phrase with a theological nuance. This is particularly important because there are many Nicaraguans in Costa Rica who are scorned as outsiders. Another occasion of joy in his calling is when he sees women finding a new dignity and strength from their community. He mentioned Dietrich Bonhoeffer's Life Together as book used here as a model for how people of faith belong to each other. I asked him what message he wished to send to the church beyond Costa Rica. After pausing and suggesting that he would need more time for a more considered response, he responded in two short, thoughtful sentences: "The love God gives us is not ours alone but always to share" and 'Let's help each other recognize Jesus in the faces of the poor he calls us to serve'. Our time was up. We thanked him and walked from his office across the hall for our concluding interview with Costa Ricans.

Roger Forbes is 35, courteous, fluent in English, and well prepared to move with ease into the substance of a subject that came up as a surprise. In my limited correspondence with President Jimenez explaining what I hoped to accomplish, I had sought his permission to meet with people whose practice of the faith might illumine the wider context of the church and society in Costa Rica. Roger Forbes was an unusually good choice. After the pleasantries of mutual introductions, he said: "For me, the word journey is the right one to describe my story." It was hardly a cliché.

He began with the familiar litany of baptism and growing up under parents whose Roman Catholicism was lightly practiced. Despite that, he had felt a desire to know God more personally in order to get at something deeper in him that confused and troubled him. For that reason, he said, he began attending Mass regularly in his early teens and

Roger Forbes

responded well when a priest put him in touch with a church youth group that met weekly for catechism instruction and attention to questions about life. At one of the meetings a friend wanted to open the subject of sex. The leader refused. This was particularly disappointing because Roger had just turned 16 and it was beginning to dawn him that he was different. He felt an erotic attraction to other boys which filled him with guilt, so much so that on one occasion—after struggling a full day and a sleepless night—he found the courage to go to a priest for confession. He remembered an over-whelming dread that swept over him as he entered the confessional booth and continued throughout an agonizing half hour as he stammered out his confession. During the entire time, the priest kept looking at his watch and said nothing. He was so distraught after emptying his soul that he could not hear the priest's words of a mechanical response, but had to guess if he was right that his penance was to say three Hail Mary's and two Our Father's.

That moment left him with a feeling of rejection deep enough to set him adrift from the Roman Catholic Church. Though he expected pun-ishment, he was surprised by the sense of relief that came instead, even a certain exhilaration at the prospect of finding his way forward on his own. "God is everywhere" he recalled from his catechism instruction, "so even if I pray alone he will hear me" he concluded. He continued in this way for several years through times that were hard for him and his family. They lost their house. His mother had fallen seriously ill. By age 20 he had survived other problems and entered the university in San Jose. His secret problem of confused sexual identity remained unresolved, but he kept hoping for some way to overcome the dilemma within. It did not help, he said, that his father was a *mestizo*, a Jamaican of mixed blood from a culture that was violently homophobic. He had separated from Roger's mother, and he could recall hearing his father sing Jamaican songs that told of killing gay people because they were less than worthless. Added to the fear he felt from his father's bias against homosexuals was something his mother had once told him, not in suspicion of his orientation, but as one more notion from her hodgepodge mixture of magic and Catholicism. "There is good luck and bad luck," she said, "but the worst luck of all is when a mother has a son who is a homosexual." Despite his fears of being discovered, plus the hardships of living in a hovel with of his family, he completed his degree in industrial engineering and learned things in the process that he could not have learned any other way. I asked him what he meant. He answered by remembering how his mind could conjure up fantasies of going to Disneyland but realism would jerk him back to the fact that he hadn't eaten all day.

Then the predictable happened. He fell in love with another man, a Jamaican, who had fled from Jamaica to Costa Rica after losing an eye in a vicious attack by a bigot who beat him up because he was gay. Roger had befriended him, first out of compassion, but then more complicated emotions set in. Though Roger was still living at home, trying to save enough to live on his own through a promising job he had recently landed, he had still not told his secret to his mother or sister (who needed his financial help for travel to Spain to become a nun). His secret trysts with the Jamaican lover continued, as did the pressures he knew would one day explode from living a lie. The triggering event was a phone call one day from a caller with a Jamaican accent asking if this was an apartment for gays. After taking the call his mother began putting things together and confronted her son with a barrage of cursing such as he had not heard before. Roger responded with anger, telling her "if you're against him you're against me." She told him he was a sinner who could not behave and dress like a woman and live at home any longer. It was not her angry order to get out that surprised him. It was her cursing him as a son rejected by God that gave him the deepest grief. He gathered his things and ran away to another part of San Jose where he found a room. He told me that he got over his anger with his mother whom he still loved, but what cut him to the quick was that she put her ersatz religion over any love she had for him as her son.

The desolation of the break with his family stretched out into a first year with no contact with them whatsoever, followed by seven years of irregular communicating by phone. He recounted the sordid details of his resumed relationship with the Jamaican, which had to end finally because of the psychosomatic outbursts from his lover who was still traumatized by beatings he had suffered earlier. Roger's mother had finally taken him back in after one attack so severe that his head wounds required surgery, yet she would tolerate no word about his deeper, unresolved suffering. He had reached a point, he said, where he knew he could not live on without finding help. He sought it first at a Methodist Church which proved fruitless after a month. His second effort at a Pentecostal congregation was even shorter lived. After that he gave up on churches. His concern about testing positive for HIV prompted him to go for a clinical test which meant a month of waiting for the result—which was positive. "Why are you crying—it's your fault" was the doctor's reaction to his tears when learning what he faced, followed by more lecturing from the doctor about infecting others. He told her he was not promiscuous, fell into a depression, and made plans for his funeral.

Then, for reasons unknown, he began to fight for his life. He kept his job and started a daily discipline of running. He joined a gym program for regular workouts, and as an act of faith, signed on for an experimental three year program offered by a medical drug company, not knowing whether he would live to see the outcome. He read books on AIDS and joined a group of gay rights activists which ended his secrecy about his sexual orientation with his family. He was telling me all these things, he said with apologies for its lengthy detail, as prelude to the event in his life that came as a turning point when least expected.

The gay activist group with whom he was associated had planned an art show. Because he was a skilled portrait artist himself, he was put in charge of one of the exhibits. Among the visitors attending the show was a Swedish missionary who had come to Costa Rica to serve San Sebastian Lutheran community. She wore her clergy collar for the event, and as Roger put it, "looked like a church person ready to take it out against gays." He could not resist approaching her for conversation in which he had his argument lined up, point by point. He remembered the shock he felt when hearing her first words: "I want to ask you to forgive all of us in the church. We have made you invisible. We have hurt you." In that vein she continued, without condemnation, but asking forgiveness. "Wow! What a surprise" was his response, quoted in much the same wonderment with which the Swedish pastor heard it first from him. She received him into his new spiritual home at San Sebastian community not long thereafter. It is open to all, gays, lesbians, people with HIV, as well as those who are none of the above. Forbes travels much in his engineering work (including to a conference in India two years ago), but said that he rarely misses the Thursday evening and Sunday services. He is grateful for opportunities to share what Pastor Katarina labeled his "resurrection experience" wherever he can, especially among students at his alma mater. Before finishing the interview he showed us the six types of pills he takes daily to maintain him in a productive life.

His closing word to us were deceptively simple : "Though people may abandon us, God does not." The quiet authority with which he spoke them came from a faith tested but proven sufficient for the worst he had endured. We thanked him for opening himself to us in a way that gave us insights into life in Costa Rica that could not be found in tourist brochures. He and others to whom we listened were witnesses to a beauty that struck us as more rich and durable than the vaunted natural lushness of Costa Rica, the land of the rich coast. We caught glimpses of it in their stories of justice sought and found for the homeless poor, of spiritual sanctuary for Nicaraguan immigrants stung by prejudice, of a church leader's joy in those who enter church to sing and exit to serve, of a gay man's odyssey from darkness to light, and—not the least—in the stories of those who learn the Scriptures as they share ways of turning snake venom into life-saving vaccine.

PART 6

INTRODUCING
SOUTH AMERICA

North Americans, as one Chilean Lutheran put it in a mildly acerbic comment, need to remember that America is a term that includes an entire continent lying to the south. She might have added that South America is not only larger and more populous than its neighbor to the north, but is where Christians are growing (due to Pentecostal influence) and in transition (loosening ties between Catholicism and national regimes) as never before since the first missionary priests arrived with Columbus in the late 1490's. Lutherans are part of this larger story, in ways unique to their history in the five South American countries described here. The prevailing pattern of Lutheran churches as islands of immigrants separated from their Hispanic and Portuguese surroundings since their mid-19th century arrival—most often from Germany—has gradually changed to a decidedly more indigenous South American identity in recent decades. Brazil is an example. In Bolivia, Lutherans have an altogether unique story to tell, with implications for the global church. Chilean Lutherans have found their prophetic voice through leadership tested under totalitarianism. The role of women is notable in the young church in Peru. Argentine Lutherans have pioneered theological education through ecumenical cooperation. The witnesses to these things, heard in the stories they tell, make the labors of the church in South America well worth appreciating rather than neglecting them as an afterthought.

The Good Friday procession re-enacting Jesus' trial and crucifixion began under a hot noonday sun in Lurin, a village perched
on a steep hillside rising up from the Pacific Ocean coastline, an
hour's drive south of Lima, Peru. Young people of the local Roman
Catholic congregation were properly costumed for their parts in
the passion story and a crowd gathered as they began the solemn
procession around the town square, interrupting a soccer game by
sweaty youngsters who took a time out to watch the simulated
scourging of Jesus with strips of cloth substituted for whips—red
dye poured on to add realism. The wailing of those portraying Mary
and the women was the only sound that broke the silence as the
pageant moved slowly around the square. When the procession
reached its ending point the young man taking the part of Jesus
was stretched out upon the cross which lay flat upon the pave-
ment, his hands were tied to the crossbeam and his legs were likewise fastened near the base of the cross. A footstool was placed under
his feet to support his body as the cross was raised upright. Then
with much feeling for the meaning of each of the sentences, he
uttered the last seven last words of Jesus from the cross. All looking
on were silent throughout, whether from pondering the vast mystery
of Christ's atoning sacrifice or from wondering how long the young
man could bear the strained posture of a simulated crucifixion.
And then it ended. The actors dispersed. The hum of normalcy
resumed in the cafes and shops around the town square. All of us
were left to make out for ourselves what meaning Good Friday has
for our lives and our world as it was played out in Lurin as well
as in other places in and beyond Peru.

PERU

Such a tradition of re-enacting Christ's passion in the town streets has deep historical roots in Latin America. Undoubtedly, it makes a salutary impact on countless lives in ways impossible to measure, especially among people who may have had little opportunity to read its message from the New Testament but who can see and hear it acted out in public. Good Friday's meaning, however, cannot be left to watching a mock crucifixion. It calls for belief and application to the ups and downs of life amidst the daily rounds. That was what a group of Peruvian parishioners did later that afternoon as they welcomed us into their circle of conversation intended to connect Christ's redeeming work with their lives now. We found a shady place alongside Filadelfia Church, as Lutherans have named their place of worship, a one room building which one older man present could remember helping build decades earlier. After introducing themselves (through an interpreter), Ana Morales, a bouncy 64 year old woman without a gray hair in her head began the conversation by getting straight to the point: "The Lord gave himself for us; with him we lack nothing." She went on to fill out that terse declaration with specifics. She spoke of bringing fifteen children into the world, then being abandoned by her husband, then holding on in faith to the Lord's promise who has kept her in body and soul through the support of her children. Kelly Lescano, 15, the youngest in the circle, followed by saying how much she liked coming together on this holy day to talk about God's word, something she's done at other times with other kids who would first gather for games and then get around to their questions about the Bible when their pastor joined them. Honorato, 69, the man who helped build the church with his own hands, volunteered his help as a way to thank God for bringing him through an illness he was told he would not survive. Gary Lescano, 20, began by speaking in Spanish but then found courage to switch to English, pausing only for occasional help from the translator to say that while he admired his Catholic buddies for participating in the Good Friday pageant, the better thing was to help each other live the good news of the cross in Lurin where the bad news of poverty, joblessness, and crime is all too evident. One man whose name I missed said that what he appreciates about the Filadelphia congregation and the pastor is that nothing is forced but people want to come here for worship. Amelia Flores, 50, summed things up as the time approached for a 4 p.m. service in the church: "he died for us, we live for him." This hour of conversation with a half dozen people of varied ages was memorable for its openhearted simplicity. I could not recall one quite like it among all my Good Friday experiences through the years.

It was through an invitation from their pastor, Adita Torres, that they knew of my desire to meet with them. She is 48, born in Lurin, single, and remembered the beginning of the congregation founded years before by an American missionary, Frederick Wolf. She met him through an invitation from a friend to see how Lutherans might rekindle her faith that had lagged since her baptism as a Roman Catholic in her childhood. Especially appealing to her was working with children in the Sunday School, something new to her that became her entrance into wider participation in the fledgling congregation. From those beginnings she went on to Bible School and seminary in Chile, then spent four years of ministry with a Methodist congregation in Lima. From there she returned to Lurin to serve with a Peruvian Lutheran pastoral couple who specialized in medical aid to those who had none in the area. Adita had contracted tuberculosis when she was younger and through that trial had learned the importance of God's healing grace through medicine coupled with prayer. She came to Lurin in 1999 as one of the first women pastors of the Evangelical Lutheran Church of Peru. Now there are ten pastors in the church body, five women and five men. She serves without salary, dividing her time between preaching, leading worship, and training lay leaders with her position paid as director of an ecumenical church organization in Lima where she travels by bus three days a week. She told me of the problems of her people—domestic violence, joblessness—especially among youth, and the ever grinding pressures of living on several dollars a day. She loves her work nonetheless and was proud to describe the Lutheran church initiative in bringing to the people of Lurin the first system of safe drinking water in its history. This conversation took place as we sat together in her second floor flat with the windows open to a magnificent view of the Pacific Ocean. Between the noon hour procession of the cross and the later conversation with church members she treated us and other guests to a sumptuous meal with specialties for Good Friday. Her meal was not in denial of the Lord's sacrifice but served, as she explained, as a sign of the abundant life he wants for all. Some choose to fast on Good Friday, she said without criticism, but for her the day is best kept by sharing generously with others the meat, vegetables, and Peruvian baked bread that convey the generosity of the risen Lord.

Irene Ponce and Alicia Cuyotti were also among the first women ordained as Lutheran pastors in Peru. Both received seminary training in Brazil. Both are experienced in serving congregations in poor neighborhoods of Lima where the priority is on outreach to youth. Ponce, who is pastor of Belen congregation described meeting with parents who force their children to sell drugs. Shortly after moving to the neighborhood she saw a boy lying in a drugged daze on a street corner who called out to her. She did not recognize him in his advanced stage of addiction but did what she could in helping him to his feet and taking him to the church for food. Some months later she was called to help with a funeral and when she went to pray with the family she learned that the deceased youth was the one she had found on the street. Police had shot him to death on his 18th birthday when he was caught stealing. He had once been a child in the breakfast meal ministry served at Belen congregation. His fate was a tragic example of the way life is for youth and families in the slums of Lima. Irene, who walks with a slight limp due to the after affects of polio as a child, said that the worst family problems she encounters in her ministry make her all the more determined to reach youth before they are lost to drugs and an untimely death. She has established a partnership with *Nuyos del Futuro,* "Children Of The Future," a foundation that provides nutritious meals for specific age groups of children. Around fifty come each morning for breakfast and early afternoon for lunch on their way home. Through this agency Pastor Ponce seeks men who become a spiritual father to children who have none. On Sundays there is worship and Sunday School for these children and the few parents who come. There is no other weekday ministry in the neighborhood like that at Belen, nor any spiritual nurture for youth and families so battered by poverty and the constant lure of turning to crime. That is why Lutherans are here, she said, when people wonder what non-Roman Catholic Christians are doing in an overwhelmingly Catholic country. The need to reach people struggling just to survive is immense. Those caught up in that struggle do not ask about denominational differences.

Easter Sunday worship in Cusco, a city of 300,00 in the high Andes of Peru, an hour's flight southeast of Lima, was another experience of the Lutheran Church of Peru's dedication to serving those no one else serves. Pastor Ofelia Davila took us with her to Talitha Kum Lutheran Church located in a slum area of Cusco at the end of a bumpy dirt road. It is a nondescript building of modest size, with galvanized metal roof, mud brick walls, and earthen floor. We were welcomed by a half dozen women and a group of children from 6 to 16. Pastora Davila donned her white alb and stole to lead the service according to the Lutheran liturgy. The hymns were sung without musical accompaniment. Scripture, sermon, and prayers all in Spanish, of course. Christ was praised as the risen Lord and although we could not understand the words we could sense the spirit in which those present offered worship to God. At the end of the service most stayed for answers to my questions about what it means to be a Lutheran Christian in Cusco. As in Lima, women of this congregation take turns in serving a breakfast each weekday morning to children on their way to school. Ofelia Davila has found the resources to make that possible. She is 46, slender, wiry, and blessed with a combination of high commitment and wisdom that has grown since she was drawn to Lutheran theology by reading the life of Martin Luther. That experience, nourished by youth ministry contacts along the way, led to her confirmation in a Lutheran congregation and theological study—interestingly enough, in a Catholic seminary in Lima in 1982. When that faculty was overtaken by the Opus Dei ultra-

Ofelia Davila and church members

right wing movement she lost interest. She had gained enough of a taste of liberation theology under the prior faculty, however, to sustain her determination to find a place of serving in the church among refugees in Nicaragua. Civil War erupted there, forcing her to return to Peru where a friend informed her of the Lutheran seminary in Sao Leopoldo, Brazil. It is a commentary on her granite-like dedication that she scraped together enough money for a bus ticket to Brazil, a trip that required eleven days and nights of non-stop travel. Her companion was Irene Ponce. The two studied and worked part time, finishing their seminary work after five years of demanding effort to qualify for ordination. How she went about founding a congregation in Cusco reveals what it takes for ministry among the poor to become reality. She told me these highlights following her leadership of Easter worship.

She welcomed her assignment by the Evangelical Lutheran Church of Peru to Cusco because no other Lutheran work was underway in the poorest section of the city. At the end of her first year of frustrating work, the single family that showed promise of becoming a nucleus for a congregation stopped coming. At that point she remembered a Peruvian saying that "God squeezes but does not strangle" and kept meeting people wherever she could find them in homes and coffee shops. From those associations she formed a group of women who came together regularly to speak about their lives and problems and seek help for changing their lot. A new pathway of promise opened when she met leaders of an organization formed to bringing basic services such as water and electricity to neighborhoods without them. Davila brought news of this group to women of the area, now grown to nineteen in number, with whom she had begun Bible study. This led to worship in her home and questions about the Lutheran church and its beginnings in the 16th century Reformation. As a testament to her teaching skills, she explained the reforming purpose of the Lutheran church by comparing it to what these women did each August when repairing the walls of their homes and re-thatching their roofs to prepare for the coming rainy season. Lutherans did not come to build a new house but to make the old one livable again. That was clear enough, and led to further questions whether Lutherans gave away Bibles and food to those who attended Bible class and worship, as was customary among evangelical and Pentecostal congregations. She took care to explain that while Lutherans welcome everyone, gifts are not used to attract people. The better motive is to come seeking the loving kindness of God and thus to find the dignity and self-respect that lasts. She taught that God is present in the histories of all who go under the banner of the cross his Son carried, and Ofelia Davila would continue to be a friend and sister in Christ to each person, whether they joined the congregation or not. As Bible study and home worship continued, the women attending began to speak more of what they faced at home, especially domestic violence. As those stories became more frequent, the group resolved to do something that took courage. They went as a group to the house of an abused woman and helped her file a complaint with the police. Pastora Davila often went back personally to such families to counsel both the abused and the abuser. Meeting people at such points of their acute need brought depth to her ministry as well as an increase in numbers. Her confirmation class for youth and adults included a sewing workshop to help women learn skills that could help the family survive. When the numbers grew too many for her to accommodate in her house, a room was rented for this burgeoning work of the congregation. The time came to find a name for this new congregation. The New Testament story telling of Jesus' raising the daughter of Jairus found in Mark 5:41 where his sovereignty over death is expressed in his words, "Daughter, arise!" became the text of choice. The name of the congregation was taken from the Aramaic in which Jesus spoke the command—"Talitha kum." Our Easter morning worship with the people of Talitha Kum congregation was an experience of the risen Lord at work in this tiny, faithful community of faith. In the midst of the harsh realities of life surrounding them and their pastor, we could gain a memorable glimpse of how well rooted they are in the Gospel and how skillfully they receive and practice it in ways that make sense in a vibrant Andean culture.

Cusco is the starting point for the two hour train ride to Machu Picchu, the fabled lost city of the Incas and one of the grand tourist sights known throughout the world. The day trip was worth the huffing and puffing up the last leg of the zigzag footpath to the vista where the stunning sight unfolds below. The Incas built their city on a tiny patch of ground surrounded by dramatically steep mountains and cliffs, kept green by the mists and rains that alternate with moments of bright sun breaking through. In the latter half of the 15th century the Incas made this remote location their refuge from the Spanish conquistadors who sought to vanquish them and their remarkably sophisticated feats of engineering, architecture, astronomy, and agriculture. Why they abandoned it for what they thought would be some safer location deeper into the eastern Andean highlands remains a mystery. The sad irony was that the Spanish finally found and destroyed them anyway. The site was discovered in 1911 by an American geologist, Hiram Bingham, and is now a Peruvian national park. After several hours of strenuous tramping through the well-kept ruins of Machu Picchu, stopping often to catch our breath at such a high altitude, we were ready to nap during the train ride back to Cusco. But the steady appearance of skilled entertainers parading up and down the aisle kept us attentive and smiling with their songs, skits, and finally a fashion show of fine woolens. Machu Picchu was well worth the extra time it took on our schedule and we were grateful to visit this celebrated site. But it was the faithful Peruvians of Lima, Lurin, and Cusco, whose ministries are inspiring in their dedication to the poor, who are never seen in tourist brochures, who made the most lasting impressions.

Two things make Bolivian Lutherans unique in the global Lutheran family. First, 98% of the pastors of the Evangelical Lutheran Church of Bolivia are self-supporting. They draw no salary from the congregations they serve or from the church body, but, like Saint Paul who earned his keep by tent making, so these pastors work at secular jobs to support themselves. Nearly all of the 100 plus pastors are farmers; the remaining 2% are city dwellers who work in commercial or professional occupations. The president and the mission director alone are salaried by the IELB, as the church body is known through its Spanish acronym. Secondly, this Lutheran church (the largest of four Lutheran bodies in Bolivia) has from its beginnings in 1938 concentrated its mission not to ethnic Germans but to the Aymara Indian population in the Bolivian highlands and La Paz. Now, 70 years later, the 22,000 baptized gather in 135 congregations, which makes it the largest Amerindian church in the western hemisphere. Despite impoverished conditions which limit the annual income of its members to around $1000, this church has learned to do much with little. During its first thirty years it established an orphanage and a Bible Institute which has sent thirty Amerindian pastors to preach the Gospel to their own people in their own language. In 1972 the IELB was officially organized and three years later became a member of the Lutheran World Federation. Despite its modest size and specialized constituency the Evangelical Lutheran Church of Bolivia offers a compelling model of sustainability to Christian churches throughout the developing world, indeed throughout global Christianity, where the challenges of supporting the ministry of the Gospel are everywhere and urgent.

NB

BOLIVIA

These generalizations about the IELB came to life during a Sunday visit to a congregation in Calasaya, a village situated on a flat plain at 13,000 feet elevation, about an hour and a half drive from the Bolivian capitol of La Paz. The drab, mud-walled houses, each surrounded by a garden and farmyard for animals, have as a commanding backdrop the magnificence of the snow-capped Andean peaks, some reaching an elevation of 20,000 feet. The first thing that caught our eye as we approached the village was the Lutheran church with its bright turquoise front wall and red brick sides as a sign of the Bolivian love of color. The half dozen bicycles leaned against the church wall indicated how some get around. The majority walk to church or take a bus from longer distances.

Two lay pastors greeted us with smiles as we climbed the steps—slowly and with shortness of breath due to the thin air—to the second floor entrance. David Wunsch, the invaluable American ELCA regional representative and our guide in Bolivia, is fluent in Spanish and Aymaran and thus communicated easily with those who welcomed us. Inside the sanctuary, furnished with a rows of plain wooden benches, three young men in their late teens were warming up on musical instruments (two wooden flutes and an electronic keyboard), preparing to accompany congregational singing. On the opposite side of the room, one of the two welcoming pastors was in charge of a large, white bass drum used to beat out the rhythm for the hymns. As people were arriving, a woman began leading hymn singing, some sung in Spanish and others in Aymaran, which continued through the first half hour of the service. Wunsch explained that such extended hymn singing was common in congregations and served as a substitute for the more traditional Lutheran liturgy. The Scriptures were then read, the sermon preached, and before Holy Communion was celebrated the officiating pastor introduced me for my words of greeting.

Following the Eucharist, the pastor announced a special ceremony marking the one year anniversary of the death of the former pastor. The family of the late pastor came forward to stand with heads bowed and hands folded to hear a memorial tribute read. Then the entire congregation came forward to surround the bereaved family, crowding in close behind them, some close enough to place a hand in blessing upon the late pastor's family. After prayers were spoken, the pastor took a vase from the altar, removed the handful of white flowers it held, and lightly sprinkled the remaining water over the family. Later, I asked if this was as a baptismal remembrance. It was not, I learned, but was requested by the family as a custom from Aymaran native religion, perhaps adapted for Christian usage but more likely received as a connection with something deep in Aymaran lore. The ceremony of remembrance, with the whole faith community gathered close in around the family, provided a powerful moment. It did what liturgy, "the work of the people," is intended to do as the word implies. On that Sunday in Calasaya the action of the entire congregation brought comfort to a family in need of the tangible bonds of Christ's love present conveyed to them through touch and consoling word.

Wunsch told me that there are reasons behind the indigenous form of worship we witnessed. It has come down from the Lutheran missionaries of the World Mission Prayer League who arrived from the United States in the 1930's. They brought zeal to proclaim the Gospel among the unreached Aymara Indians of the Andean highlands without imported forms of liturgical worship from North America which they themselves had already laid aside as too Catholic. Moreover, they did not come assuming that impoverished Aymaran Indians could support their own pastors. From the outset they envisioned and carried out a unique policy of training pastors who supported themselves as subsistence farmers. The practice of these two key principles, a self supporting clergy and an indigenous way of worship, put the World Mission Prayer League stamp upon the mission which flourished in the Andean highlands and La Paz during the four decades following its beginning in 1935. Then, in the late 1970's the American missionaries of the Prayer League did one more thing essential for indigenous church growth; they put the leadership of the church in the hands of Aymaran Lutherans and left the country. Before and after leaving, their unique work was not without inner stresses, conflicts, and inevitable problems. Yet, this young church body was blessed by pioneering missionaries with rare vision and the creative will to carry it out. They laid the foundations of an indigenous church that was not top heavy with a missionary-dominated organization impossible to sustain by its Asmara constituency. The Bolivian Lutherans are to this day a unique expression of sustainable church life in an area of the world where the faithful do not have cash resources to support those who serve them in the Word. Why should that be so unique in the 21st century church? The Christians of the first three centuries of church history would have had thought it normal.

I learned of these and other historical developments while listening to Christobal Alejo, 41, the recently elected president of the IELB during a bumpy, six hour northward from La Paz in a pickup truck. Our conversation was interrupted frequently by the eruption of thick clouds of dust kicked up by an eighteen-wheel trucks laboring up the steep, unpaved road ahead of us. Or it was silenced (at least on my part) when our vehicle was squeezed to within a yard of a thousand foot precipice on the outside rim of the road when another eighteen-wheeler coming down the mountain claimed its right to the inside lane. I did not need Alejo to remind me that some regard this road into the high Andes as the most perilous in the world.

Our destination was Teoponte, a town of 1,700 where the church had joined with local authorities in a project to bring safe drinking water to the people in this remote community. Alejo told us that this area had received a memorable visitor in its more recent past. In 1967, Che Guevara had come to Teoponte intent on making it an outpost for his cause of justice for the poor. He was by that time well on his way to becoming a global symbol of radical reform through his struggle to replace capitalist monopolies and neocolonial imperialism with Castro-inspired Marxism he had learned in Cuba. His venture was short lived. On October 9, 1967, he was cornered by Bolivian police and assassinated not far from Teoponte. As Alejo told me of that unexpected visitor in the recent past of the region, the thought came to me

Christobal Alejo

that he also came to bring change but through a different means. I wondered whether the townspeople were expecting the president of a church body to arrive in blue jeans, plaid jacket, and a New York Yankees ball cap on his head. It was a useless question. They were perfectly at home with Alejo as he moved with ease among them, chatting and sipping coffee while preparing details for the water project dedication. When all was ready, he led the procession up the mountainside to a site above Teoponte where a system had been constructed to pump up clean well water and deliver it down long bamboo pipes to the townspeople below. Alejo read a passage from John 4 on Jesus as the living water and applied it to the occasion. This was followed by prayer, lengthy speeches of appreciation by various town officials, and concluded with firecrackers popping loudly as a bottle of champagne was ceremonially smashed in celebration. During the long pickup truck ride back to La Paz, (down the same nerve-wracking road, this time in the dark, with Wunsch, Beverly, and myself in the jump seat, knees to our chins) Alejo began to tell the story of his origins in an Asmara Indian household. Before he got very far he announced that he was too tired to say more. It was unnecessary for us to say we were too tired to listen.

We met with him the next day in his office where he picked up the thread of a narrative that told us much about himself, the church, and growing up as an Asmara Indian outsider in a Bolivia with its biases and class distinctions. His first contact with Christianity came when he was a boy of 8. He was on his way to play a game of soccer with other kids he when he heard singing from inside a church as he passed by. He stopped to listen, was invited in, and, as he put it, "for the first time in my life was made to feel like a real person." by the WMPL pastor and congregation. He described himself as a teenager with a wild streak that sometimes turned up in outbursts of singing, dancing, "and all kinds of charismatic carrying on—so much so that the pastor got fed up and kicked me out!" He tried a Pentecostal congregation but found its legalism too much for him. Chastened in mood, he returned to the Lutheran congregation, grateful that he was received back for another chance to belong and grow in faith. He studied sociology after high school, intending it as a broadening background for his real interest which was theology. After high school he studied at the Institute of Evangelical Andean Theology, an ecumenical seminary in La Paz, and following that he continued his education at the Latin American Biblical Institute in San Jose, Costa Rica. He returned to Bolivia for service as a lay pastor and just two years previous to our pick-up truck interview was elected president of the IELB. It was a commentary on the significance of lay pastors in the church, he said, that he was elected to the presidency. He expressed the hope to be ordained in time for the seventieth anniversary of the founding of the church body coming a half year after our conversation.

Alejo characterized the present time in the church as a test period of transition, by which he meant the challenge of retaining the solid grounding in the Biblical faith taught by the early missionaries while opening the church's overall ministry to a deeper integration into Aymaran life and culture which the American missionaries had largely rejected. In connection with this necessary and hopeful transition, he spoke of his admiration for Umberto Ramos, a Bolivian Lutheran with unusual theological gifts and charisma for leadership that sometimes put him too far ahead of those he served as president of the church body. Ramos was killed in a car accident in 2004. In the years since the IELB has struggled to implement his vision of a Bolivian church growing into a more holistic mission and better related to the international church through its membership in the

Lutheran World Federation. Alejo also referred to theological training and leadership development as key to the strategic planning for the long term future of the church. Previously, the lay pastors received their education at the Lutheran Educational Center in Sucre, in a school associated with the Andean Lutheran Theological Seminary which is administered by the Norwegian Mission, with ties to the Missouri Synod in North America. Its courses centered in a basic understanding of the Bible, Lutheran doctrine, with a conservative bent that strictly rejected any appearance of syncretism. This strand of theological education continues to influence the practice and outlook of many of the pastors now in their middle and later years. Another strand of theological education that has entered into the IELB is the one offered by the Ecumenical Andean Theological Institute. It has a contrasting theological curriculum which Alejo summarized as one which presented universal Christian teaching through the lens of Latin American, specifically, Bolivian culture. Ramos, prior to his death, had striven to strengthen the ties of the IELB with this theological school, and the current leadership is following the same track. Alejo emphasized that the future Lutheran identity of the church body he serves depends on how the IELB deals with these two contrasting programs of theological education.

I asked him about the unique IELB tradition of self-supporting pastors as a model for adaptation elsewhere in Latin America. He has not been consulted on that policy, he said, and added that he has little time to promote the Bolivian experience since this practice is not self-perpetuating and needs constant attention to maintain its viability amidst new circumstances. At present he and other church leaders are working on more careful attention to bi-vocational training for prospective pastors, by which he meant giving students a wider range of new vocational skills which they can use to support themselves as they carry out their ministry. He noted that in Bolivia, as elsewhere in the world, people are leaving farms to seek work in towns and cities, a trend the church must heed. The present and future picture of the IELB also calls for a larger measure of funding provided by the Lutheran World Federation for projects such as potable water in Teoponte, solar greenhouses for increased crop yield, and the expansion of such innovative ventures as an IELB-sponsored ranch which owns one hundred head of cattle for church income purposes. Christobal Alejo saw himself as but one example in this transition era and urged me to talk with others about the church in Bolivia as they experience it. It was not difficult to find others who were generous with their time and had important stories to tell.

Abdon Condori, 52, has served the Apostle Paul congregation on the outskirts of La Paz long enough to cite examples of the ups and downs of his calling. Several years ago some of his members, reflecting the widespread influence of Pentecostal evangelists on radio and television, began calling for baptism by the Holy Spirit as necessary for full standing as a bona fide believer in Jesus Christ. Condori saw a congregational split brewing and warned those given to charismatic exuberance against the temptation to make their experience the measure for everyone in the congregation. Besides having no depth, the real problem with these measures is that they do not call believers to persist in trusting Christ's grace and love under his Word as the assurance for their acceptance by God. This doctrinal conflict led to another issue, this one concerning the ownership of a plot of land given to the congregation. How did he and the fifty or so members get through it? He answered that here is where the three staples of the Lutheran reformation tradition were basic—grace alone, faith alone, Scripture alone. Not only did these provide sufficient guidance for solving the immediate issue (the disputed land was across the wall from where we were sitting); it laid the groundwork for facing other problems. Condori told me that by dealing squarely with doctrinal and property issues he was gaining confidence to meet new problems the congregation was facing in its mission to an increasingly urbanized Boliva. It concerned him that people coming in from the countryside are ill prepared to avoid crime, gangs, and drugs in cities like La Paz, where "people can kill for a cell phone." Finding a spiritual home, he said, can sometimes make the difference between life and death amidst new and intimidating problems. He is firm in his belief that God works for good in all things, including Aymara cultural traditions that help sustain a sufficiently strong sense of identity among those he serves. He cited as an example the meaning of "ayri," an Aymaran word meaning to help each other. He illustrated it by describing such events as weddings in which the entire congregation is invited to share in the food and dancing that are part of the celebration. This would not have been the case a half century or more ago when, under the WMPL rejection of all things Aymaran, "ayri" would never have been recognized, let alone honored.

Nelida Kapquique

Nelida Kapquique, 45, is the mother of five children, and an example of the growing role of women in the IELB. We met in the church headquarters building in La Paz. My first impression of her was that she was a traditional Bolivian woman, her strong face framed by jet black hair combed back tightly and her colorful, full length skirt, warm sweater and shawl gave her the look of representing the past rather than the future in the place of women in the church. As I soon learned when listening to her story, my impressions were far off the mark. She is an elected member of the six person governing council of the Lutheran Church in Bolivia. She spoke of her passion to help the church welcome and deploy the abundant gifts of the Holy Spirit to women of faith. She has credibility for her cause as one raised in a flagship congregation, the first one formed by Lutherans in Bolivia in which she and generations of her family have been active for seventy years. Her parents were illiterate until WMPL missionaries taught them to read and write. Her husband has been the president of a church district. Until now, women have not been ordained in the IELB, but she said that it an unavoidable issue before the church now. She hopes that current discussions will lead to accepting women for the ordained ministry soon after the church marks its coming 70th anniversary. Ten years ago there were no women were in any positions of leadership. Nelida Kapquique is one of a growing number of women who are now in elected positions of church leadership and are contributing their gifts to the widening of the scope of the IELB mission in Bolivia. She told me not to generalize too freely from her experience, however, but to get a broader view of how other women see their role in the church at this time. It was good advice that brought my mind back to an event follow-ing the Sunday service we had attended earlier.

The event was a congregation meal, picnic style, outside the brightly painted church building in Calasaya. Coming down the outside steps from the second floor sanctuary to the church yard, the people sat down on the grass in two long rows facing each other, men on one side and women and children on the other. Between them a long strip of blue plastic was rolled out, flat on the ground. wide enough for two men carrying bags of pota-toes to empty them onto the plastic as they walked up and down on either side. That was the meal—potatoes. They were home grown, washed, and boiled by the women of the congregation before being bagged and brought to the church dinner. Somewhat to our discomfort as the only ones served a special treat, we nonetheless enjoyed the helping of delicious goat cheese added to our supply of potatoes—as all looked our way to see how the del-icacy was received. Furthermore, chairs were brought for us and for David Wunsch, a courtesy that we appreciated as people unpracticed in sitting cross-legged on the ground for any length of time. After all finished the potato meal, the two men serving the first course of potatoes returned with two more sacks, this time filled with a Bolivian version of popcorn. Again, they poured out the dessert of pink popcorn on the plastic covering so that all could reach for handfuls, while paper cups went around for the orange drink offered. Modest and different though the menu was to us, it was still a festive event that the adults and children thoroughly enjoyed, while at the same time keeping an eye occasionally turned our way to see how we were faring We fared well. Hospitality is hospitality no matter the food or the setting. The bright noonday sun helped warm the chilly high mountain air but I noticed that most of the colorful ruanas worn by the women stayed around their shoulders. When one of the older women was bold enough to offer her derby hat and multi-colored shawl for Beverly to try on, the smiles and giggles of encouragement from up and down the row of onlookers were incentive enough for her to give it a try. Despite her best efforts, however, Beverly could not make the hat stay on at the half-jaunty angle at which Bolivian women somehow manage to keep them firmly fixed.

In such moments something memorable happens. Vast cultural dif-ferences seem less vast. People separated by thousands of miles and lifetimes in different cultures experience ever so briefly a taste of what it is to be children of God who are redeemed by his Son and united in his Spirit. We become a spiritual family in which acceptance, love, and good humor happen on the spot.

Chile is a land of contrasts. Its string bean shape hugs the Pacific shoreline for 2,650 miles from north to south; from east to west its widest point is just 267 miles across. The snowcapped Andean peaks at its northern end stand in silent grandeur; howling winds and wildly churning seas are the trademark of Tierra del Fugo at its southern end. Its barren deserts of volcanic rock and sand are a moonscape of forbidding wilderness where nothing grows; its lush vineyards produce world class wines that are the envy of vintners everywhere. As it is with contrasting topography, so it is with the Lutheran story in Chile. German Lutherans kept themselves culturally separate from the their Hispanic Chilean surroundings for a century after their arrival in the 1860's, importing their pastors from Germany to insure their ethnic insularity. As they prospered as hard working farmers and business entrepreneurs they became increasingly remote from the Chilean underclass that was chafing under centuries of injustice. By the 1960's reform was in the air, especially land reform, which threatened all well-established Chileans, Lutherans included, and set the stage for the Pinochet reaction to reform with its military takeover of the reformist government on September 11, 1973. That crisis split Lutherans into two groups. On the one hand was The Lutheran Church of Chile (ILCH by its Spanish acronym), the bearer of the bourgeois tradition, which welcomed Pinochet as the savior of Chilean order from alleged communist disorder. On the other hand was The Evangelical Lutheran Church of Chile (IELCH), which resisted the military dictatorship and by standing with the victims of the military coup began new directions of Lutheran ministry among Chileans of non-German origins. The story of what happened in both churches during the trauma of the coup and its aftermath is traced here through key figures whose lives mirror how the church is changing from isolation toward integration into Chilean life.

CHILE

Helmut Frenz, who at different times was leader of both churches named above, is an obedient rebel. He was obedient to the Biblical Word that propelled him to controversial leadership in the tumultuous weeks of late 1973. He was in the eyes of not a few Lutherans and establishment Chileans a rebel who should be tightly reigned in, if not removed by means fair or foul. His name was revered in and beyond Chile by those who admired his courage as a Lutheran bishop who confronted the ruthlessness of the dictatorship of Augusto Pinochet. He was loathed by those who saw him as an ecclesiastical meddler who should have stayed in the pulpit and off the streets. Now in his late seventies, his weathered face reveals the tell-tale lines of what discipleship costs and is still recognized by those who remember him from the front page accounts of his prophetic ministry throughout the seventeen years of the Pinochet dictatorship. I met him in Santiago, Chile, for a lengthy conversation covering his version of pivotal events from the tumultuous 1970's and following. It was a period in which he grew into his calling to strip the church of its trappings as an enclosed religious/cultural enclave which tyrants love to domesticate to their own evil purposes. His leadership, together with others who shared his vision, has helped Lutherans in Chile to deepen as a member of Christ's body in the world by caring for all regardless of ethnic boundaries. He made it clear to me in our conversation how perilous it is to expose the evils which underlie oppression and how utterly dependent upon God one must be in overcoming demonic powers with good.

Frenz was born and theologically trained in Germany. In 1965 he was sent by the German Lutheran Church to be a pastor to a congregation in Concepcion whose duties were to keep his flock soundly Lutheran and thoroughly German. He was told early on that it was not necessary to learn Spanish, which was true as far as his pastoral work among middle aged and older parishioners was concerned. But it was not true for his work with children and young adults who had trouble understanding his confirmation classes, preaching, and general conversation which was in German. After a year of becoming increasingly aware of this dilemma, he spent three months in Buenos Aires to learn Spanish. He came back to Concepcion with enough facility in the langue not only to reach young people but also to begin outreach to Chileans in poorer neighborhoods and refugees who were flooding into Chile from neighboring countries. Thus began his awakening to realities of what Chileans of non-German heritage faced as an underclass locked into a social/political system that offered no way out. Frenz was quick to perceive the implications of another sign of change when Salvador Allende, after three unsuccessful runs, was elected president of Chile in 1970. He was unsettled by it, for in one sense it gave oppressed Chileans a sign of hope but in another it was the introduction of the "Chilean Experiment" as it was called—socialism with a Marxist affinity yet based in a democratic system.

In early 1970 Chile was an island of liberal socialism for political refugees fleeing autocratic regimes in neighboring Argentina, Brazil, Paraguay, and Bolivia, a fact which made Allende even more popular with his constituency at home and more stoutly opposed by Chileans with no taste for reform. While Allende was not a professing Christian, he respected the Biblical ethic of those who welcomed the foreigner in the land and approached Frenz and other clergy with the request that they lead in caring for incoming refugees, many of whom arrived with ongoing regional political reform still in mind. When Frenz accepted the request he was dubbed The Red Pastor by those who saw him as a departure from the traditional Lutheran pastor. They resented him as an activist collaborator with a new government bent on threatening reform—all this in addition to his pastoral ministry in Concepcion. He brushed off the label, immersing himself ever deeper in caring for his congregation while steadily expanding his ministry to include refugees, as well as honing his skills in raising support from the prosperous Lutheran Church in Germany and generous Lutherans in the United States.

Despite determined opposition to his new directions of ministry for Lutherans in Chile, he was elected bishop in 1972, a surprise action that, in his words, "I can only explain as the work of the Holy Spirit." This meant a move from Concepcion to Santiago, the capitol city, and drew him closer into the impending crisis between haves and have-nots in the nation at large, as well as exposing his activism more directly to the Pinochet regime. Yet he never carried out his ministry under any political banner. He never joined the Communist Party. "I was on the side of the victims" was his summary of motive for his controversial work. As a bishop with a pastoral heart for differing groups within the church, he recognized the plight of prosperous Lutherans and other capitalists whose large copper and other mining corporations were nationalized under Allende's reform legislation. He listened to pastors and laity caught up in the crunch of sudden social change and spoke out publicly against extremists on the far left who exploited Allende's reforms as an excuse for violent takeover of property. The Chile of 1972 was a nation slipping out of control for reasons he could not yet know. He told me that he later recognized it as part of a calculated covert destabilization under the CIA of the Nixon administration in the USA. It was all part of a cynical strategy by those opposing Allenda to spread enough economic chaos and social anxiety to enable the military takeover to be welcomed as the restorer of law and order.

On the night of September 11, 1973, the military coup led by General Augustin Pinochet took over. Allende died of gunshot wounds the next day—self inflicted according to the official report, by assassination according to others. In any case, Chile awakened to life under a de facto dictator. Frenz said that many welcomed the coup, not only right wing ideologs, but masses of people who feared the rising chaos as uncontrollable anarchy. Frenz paused in his narrative, and leaned forward to underscore these words: "And among those who welcomed General Pinochet was Bishop Helmut Frenz." He thought the coup was a temporary but necessary measure for the elections that would surely follow, and his approval was widely published in the national and international media. He mentioned two experiences that changed his initial acceptance of Pinochet as a temporary necessity. He had been asked by Allende to join Roman Catholic bishops in preparing a Te Deum, a specifically Christian liturgy of celebration for the upcoming September 18 National Day observance in Santiago. The coup and Allende's assassination was timed to occur just short of September 18, aimed to blunt the violent events by a May 18th day of celebration of national sovereignty and patriotism. He learned from the Catholic bishops what was going on even as they were meeting, how—on orders from Pinochet—political refugees were being rounded up, tortured, shot, or "disappeared" (i.e., drugged, tortured, loaded onto cargo planes and pushed out to disappear without a trace). Frenz was shaken by what he heard and all the more conflicted by his initial response which he interpreted approvingly for the press at home and in Germany. What should he do now as a bishop responsible for leadership in his church and concern for his own life as a father with a family of seven children. "My soul was split" he said.

Then came the second and decisive event. Just days after the coup, while walking on a bridge across the Mapocho River running through Santiago, he looked over the railing to see bodies floating down the river. He stopped, aghast at the site, and counted seventy corpses before he could take no more of it. It changed him, as he said, "from the inside out." From that moment on his initial view of the necessity of the coup was radically reversed and his direction of prophetic leadership determined. He threw himself into new projects aiding refugees and accepted the request by the UN High Commission to preside over UN work in Chile. Within two weeks after the coup he joined with Roman Catholic bishops in forming an ecumenical Committee To Cooperate for Peace in Chile to contend for human rights. This association led to his subsequent collaboration with the Argentinian Nobel Peace laureate, Adolfo Perez Esquivel, in opposing the years of military oppression under Pinochet.

As expected, this sudden leap into prophetic leadership on a national scale enraged right wing Lutherans who not only clamored for his ouster but plotted to bring it about. The new rules under Pinochet were established to take care of all opposition activity. Labor unions were dissolved and banned outright. Elections in all other organizations were forbidden, the church included. Pinochet himself appointed replacements. Knowing that, those bent on deposing Frenz called an extraordinary synod in March, 1974—a deliberative meeting of pastors and lay delegates from every congregation—with the single aim of dismissing Frenz and keeping Lutherans passively compliant under Pinochet's dictatorship. The effort failed for two reasons. In defiance of the scandalous measure whereby Pinochet would appoint a new Lutheran bishop, Frenz preached a powerful sermon on a text from Isaiah 43 with its image of the suffering servant on which he based his call to the church to follow the Christ of the cross. It reached the hearts of a sufficient number of delegates to gain courage in opposing outright capitulation to dictatorial tyranny. Frenz named that as the first miracle. The second occurred when, amidst venomous accusations against Frenz as a Lutheran bishop misleading the church by siding with "Communist guerillas sent to kill us," a delegate arose to ask for the floor. Prompted by no one, he read aloud a letter from the Chilean Minister of the Interior thanking Bishop Frenz for his refugee work. The letter was actually a political ploy by the government to showcase Frenz and his refugee work favorably in order to blunt international criticism of Chile under Pinochet. The result was a vote to sustain Frenz as bishop by a decisive margin. The victory was temporary, however. Eight months later the power bloc bent on ousting Frenz took a new line, more sophisticated this time. They had politicized the delegate list, working carefully to insure a majority vote to dispatch their arch-enemy. Again a synod was called in order to "deal with the bishop who is still in place, supporting communists." Again Frenz preached, convinced that God had a word for his church. No sooner had he said Amen then a move was made to replace the stated agenda with a new motion calling for the bishop to resign. Debate followed, centering on the opposition's claim that Frenz's support base of *those Spanish-speaking people* did not represent the majority, i.e., the German speakers, who were touted as the bearers of bourgeois cultural tradition. These were the ethnic Germans, largely from the south of Chile, who were comfortable with the status quo and uncomfortable with disturbing it for a larger justice. The vote was taken. Frenz was supported by a two to one margin. He counted it as another miracle. The hard liners walked out, taking eight congregations with them to form a new Lutheran church. The eventual organizational division of Lutherans into two church bodies had its beginning in these events. The IELCH was formed around Frenz and continued his spirit of holistic ministry to all Chileans, especially to those still caught up in poverty and injustice. Frenz can be candid in his criticism of this Lutheran body in which he is still a member, however. He was blunt in his disapproval of current trends in his church body of leaning too heavily on financial support from Lutherans in the USA and Germany, calling it "the elephant in the room" and asking rhetorically why a tiny church body of less than 3,000 baptized should have a full salaried president, secretary, treasurer and office functionary, all accommodated in a suite of five rooms in a public office building. He has lost none of his quality as an obedient rebel who can still afflict the comfortable as well as comfort the afflicted.

Rolando Holtz is the president of the Lutheran Church of Chile, the successor body to the church founded by immigrants from Germany in the 1860's which has kept its German identity through the century and a half since its founding and has largely been resistant to change. But the ILCH (its Spanish acronym) has shown a capacity to change by its 2005 election of Holtz as president. We talked together in a sitting room of the parsonage of Redeemer Lutheran Church in Santiago, where he is also the pastor of the congregation that has played a large, if ambiguous, role in its 120 year history within the church body. Frenz had told me that Redeemer was a flagship of support for Pinochet during the 1973 crisis. Some 95% of its members welcomed the takeover, four of its parishioners were members of the military junta itself, as was the chief of secret police and the head of the Santiago airport security force. Some members were expelled from the congregation for being alleged Communists. That was all true, Holtz affirmed, but his point was to indicate that the congregation today is not a carbon copy of what it was four decades ago. His quiet manner in telling his story conveyed a depth of thought together with candor in expressing what he thinks. He was at ease with foreign guests like us who came to learn and ask questions. These qualities now serve him well as leader in a church body in transition from its Germanic past toward becoming, in his words, "a church that enters more fully into the culture of Chile, something we're not yet doing."

Rolando Holtz is 60 but looks younger. His life story reflects a trajectory of slowly emerging change in the church he leads. He was born in the coastal city of Valparaiso, an hour west of the Chilean capitol of Santiago, the son of a Lutheran father and a mother who was earnest in practicing her Catholic faith. He was baptized a Roman Catholic and went to Catholic schools throughout his teen years, including three years of pre-seminary training for the priesthood. Three obstacles kept him from going on to ordination, the vows of celibacy, the rule of obedience, and the doctrine of transubstantiation. He recalled the wisdom of a priest mentor who told him when he was an uncertain 19 year old that he should take time away from the seminary to think things through more carefully, and assured young Holtz that the door was still open if he decided to return to the seminary. He switched to the university in Valparaiso, finished his degree in education and became a teacher. Heart problems required him to interrupt his work for rest and recovery. He had continued study of theology in a Catholic university along the way, and came into his first real contact with Lutherans when his son was to be baptized. He had come to know the pastor of a nearby Lutheran congregation who impressed him favorably. That congregation was small and needed help. He volunteered to assist in ways that stirred an interest toward a pastoral future in the Lutheran church. To that end he enrolled in seminary courses in Buenos Aires, Argentina, and over a five year period of distance learning completed requirements for graduation from the Lutheran seminary and was ordained in 1983. He served for 21 years as the pastor of Santa Cruz congregation in Valparaiso and then came the surprise election which moved him to Redeemer congregation in Santiago and the presidency of the ILCH. While he knew and admired Helmut Frenz for his work among the poor, he said he has chosen to stay out of political entanglements with the Pinochet government. Frenz had told me of his high regard for Holtz as a pastoral theologian, a good sign of improving relationships between the two Lutheran church bodies. In further comment on that subject, Holtz stated his puzzlement over why the Evangelical Lutheran Church in America does not maintain contact with The Evangelical Church of Chile. His church is interested in people who are poor and marginal and wants to establish church relations with the ELCA in areas that have nothing to do with money but have everything to do with the mutual gain from such ties. I left the conversation with the feeling that the kinship between Holtz and Frenz bodes well for a future in which Lutherans in Chile will be more closely aligned in matters of faith and practice.

The two hour trip west from Santiago, the capitol of Chile, to the coastal seaport of Valparaiso is a beautiful drive through a fertile valley, notable for its vineyards and elaborate vintner plantations that appear, one after the other, along the express highway that links Chile's two major cities. Our destination was Santa Cruz Lutheran Church, a historic congregation located atop a steep cliff overlooking the Valparaiso harbor. When we arrived on a weekday afternoon, Pastor Rodolfo Olivera Obermoeller was occupied in conversation with a group of visitors. I noticed the time he took to welcome them with a cup of green tree that is hallmark of Chilean hospitality, as we sat down in a back pew to rest and savor the atmosphere. The magnificent Sanctus from Bach's B-Minor

Rodolfo Olivera Obermoeller

Mass, heard over a speaker system, filled the sanctuary with glorious sound. Above us were thick wooden arches which were distinct against the white plaster ceiling. To one side was a balcony with a Psalm verse inscribed in German, a reminder of the German emigrant origins of Santa Cruz over a century and a half ago. Behind and above us was an impressive pipe organ which, we learned later, came as a gift from Queen Elizabeth II of England after she had made an identical gift to the nearby Anglican congregation.

Speculating on why her generosity reached across the street to include the Lutherans was our light entertainment as Pastor Obermoeller was readying to welcome us.

"Call me Rudy" were his opening words, delivered in fluent English that went well with his spontaneous and warmly outgoing manner. He knew beforehand of the purpose of our visit and for that reason, perhaps, launched immediately into a much-detailed history of the Santa Cruz sanctuary, bell tower, and other matters that were well beyond what we needed to know. When I suggested as much, he was unperturbed, and in good humor switched to another set of facts about Lutherans in Chile. They number 15,000 altogether, among whom his branch, the ILCH led by Rodolfo Holtz, count approximately 6,000 members, and yet more details about organizational matters than I could handle. Once more I interrupted as a pastor twice his age and more, this time to steer him to his own story. And once more he took my urging in stride, and, without missing a beat, kept up his galloping pace—this time focused on his life story to date.

Rodolfo Obermoeller is 30, his wife is named Sylvia, they are parents of a three year old daughter and infant son. He described himself as a headstrong, feisty son in a nominally Lutheran family where he was confirmed only because his mother "held a pistol to my head." He detested the church for its stuffy formalism, its terminally boring sermons, lack of hospitality toward non-Germans and studied neglect of youth. In a church camp (where his mother sent him as a punishment) he experienced his first flicker of life in his soul. A counselor took him aside for a daylong listening and talk session, drawing out of him the buildup of anger in him against all things authoritative. Afterward, he walked alone for hours on a moonlit night and saw in the beauty of nature a hint of God's grandeur which he had been too bottled up inside to notice. He told his family none of this. But while studying electronics at the university in his native Valparaiso, he followed up on his camp experience and volunteered for youth leadership in the congregation he had largely neglected before. To his surprise he discovered how satisfying it was to find 80 kids attracted to the creative Bible studies and service activities he initiated. He also argued with other leaders, fought with the pastor, quit, came back, went off to a camp in Argentina for leadership training, which led to six years of theological study in Buenos Aires. During those half dozen years of supporting himself as a student at the Ecumenical Institute of Theological Study (ISEDET in Spanish acronym) he learned to apply his classroom learning to what he saw in the streets of Buenos Aires, with its harsh realities of poverty, hunger, homelessness, urban crime, diverse sexual orientation, alcoholism. He supported himself through temporary jobs and said that his constant struggle with authority did not let up. He received his theological diploma in 2002 and returned to Chile to marry his sweetheart, Sylvia, who was his spiritual and emotional anchor throughout his bumpy ride to maturity. After several short term assignments in various congregations in Chile and Argentina, he was called to be pastor at Santa Cruz.

Could he sketch for me an average week of his pastoral work? I asked. He answered with words of gratitude for the generosity of the members who provide his salary plus parsonage and car. Mondays he arrives early to open the doors of historic Santa Cruz congregation and keeps the sanctuary open for visitors whom he greets—not a common practice for pastors on Monday, I thought, nor was the open church in a large city something to be taken for granted. Monday afternoons are for visitation and leading worship—in German—in a nearby retirement home. Tuesday he teaches German and religion in a public school from 8 a.m. till 4 p.m. He follows with a Bible study for a women's group, and often concludes the day conferring with his Catholic and Orthodox clergy friends on projects for the poor. Wednesdays are open for visiting members at their homes, which sometimes includes preparing couples for marriage over a series of five to eight meetings. He has thirty weddings a year, a third of which are among those with no church connection, thus becoming a major mission outreach opportunity that Obermoeller welcomes as well worth his time and effort. He knew of no other parallels among pastors of his acquaintance. Thursdays, after taking the older of their two children to kindergarten, is his day off that he and his wife enjoy together. But not an evening off; he meets another study group after supper with the family. Fridays he meets with the church secretary who prepares materials for the coming Sunday, helps him with his correspondence, and sends out his pastoral letter at three month intervals. He also writes regularly for

Valparaiso newspapers on matters of public interest, and is written up from time to time for controversial stands he has taken. I noticed an article posted on his office wall that named him as the Person Of The Year in Valparaiso, a commentary on his civic engagement. Youth meet in the church on Friday afternoons at four, something he particularly enjoys. Saturdays are busy with teaching a confirmation class for 13 to 15 year olds and another for young adults from 17 to 23 years. He bases much of the faith formation curriculum on the Sunday service liturgy, amplified with Scripture, Luther's Small Catechism, and the Augsburg Confession. Weddings are on Saturday afternoons. He always goes to the reception parties following for at least a brief time with bride and groom and their families. On Sundays he is up early to open the doors at 8 o'clock, put on music in the sanctuary to help prepare himself for worship, as well as to catch the attention of passers by as an invitation to come in. Before leading worship at 10:30 he takes a walk around the block to clear his mind and focus his prayers. When preaching he follows an appointed text from an outline, and in his words "flies into the sermon" with a fifteen minute limit so that he can't waste words. The Eucharist is celebrated every Sunday and the Lord's Table is open to all the baptized. He likes to balance singing and silence during the service. A new hymnal is coming. Hymns that have stood the test of time are favored, though new ones welcomed. The organist has high standards for good music and makes good use of the pipe organ of royal origin. Dues as assigned to all members. A door offering as people leave is directed to special causes and averages $60 per week. Educating people to think of the church when developing their bequests is slow going. It is customary that after the service around 80 remain for coffee and conversation, an important opportunity for increased fellowship that Obermoeller is happy to see on the rise. Easter attendance averages 180. On Christmas Eve and Day 600 attend.

I asked him how the current members of Santa Cruz congregation regard the Pinochet era. He began by saying that the older members who were present at the time of the coup in 1973 told him that the congregation was split down the middle when it happened and the wounds are still unhealed. This made him properly cautious about reopening a subject so volatile. Yet he knew it had to be faced and the only way to do it was to place the Pinochet era within a soundly Biblical framework. His method was to invite the congregation to join him in a Scriptural study centered on how the Jews have suffered as the people of the Covenant as a template for the Chilean experience in the 1970's. That approach nearly exploded in his face, however, when those participating—most of them from German heritage—complained that it was "too much about the Jews." But Obermoeller answered that he has the same background and kept insisting that in any case the church cannot have Jesus without the Jews. It took sheer persistence on his part, he said with feeling, to hold the group together as it moved from the saga of the Jews to a history of Chile and how the country reached the crisis that Pinochet sought to solve with his "either me or chaos" oversimplification. He paid thorough attention to the idolatry of depending on the *caudillo,* the autocratic strong man, to put down anarchy instead of turning to God who judges impartially and offers grace and truth for real solutions—in this case to the alleged failure of the "Chile Experiment" of a socialist approach to a democracy. Obermoeller's experience with his own father (who took strong offense to the simple statement that the Pinochet government was a military dictatorship) was an example of the struggle at the congregation level, which included, of course, those equally passionate in their denunciation of Pinochet and the tyranny of his ways. What has happened since? Beverly asked. He said that the effort to lay a Biblical foundation in which to think the problem through has stood on its own merits. Though far from resolved, there is hope for progress because people once unable to even mention the subject can now listen and speak with more awareness of what the Scriptures mean as a word of the living God to the present time. Pastor Rudy—he repeated his invitation to address him by his nickname—is well practiced in taking heat for his leadership. He remembered that when he was a student in Argentina he was threatened with death on occasion because he was objective about Augusto Pinochet and his deeply mixed legacy—revered by those who held onto their economic and social privilege because of Pinochet and those who suffered more loss, further injustice, torture, and death at his hand. As Obermoeller described the congregational process, its pain together with its purpose, he could not do so dispassionately. In his own person he embodies the tensions that will take years to resolve. His courage as a young pastor, fearless in diving in where most prefer the safety of benign neglect, make him a symbol of hope for how Chile can be cleansed of the blight of this darkest hour in its history.

We could hardly expect that the wealth of insight gained from the three clergy, Frenz, Holtz, and Obermoeller, would be matched by our limited conversations with lay persons. Renata Obermoeller, an aunt of Pastor Rudy's, and Vilma Zimmerling, gave us several hours of their time for conversation on their experiences. Vilma is a retired teacher, a life-long Lutheran who studied at the Roman Catholic College of St. Thomas where she was well served by capable priest-professors. She continued a degree program under this faculty until she chose to interrupt her education for marriage and motherhood of her three daughters. Ten years later she decided to finish her studies in philosophy and did so with the encouragement of a faculty who did not regard her Lutheranism as an obstacle. When she graduated with her family at her side, her advisor for her dissertation told her something she remembered with a smile: "You have two titles, mother and teacher—in that order of importance!" Renata, a Chilean by birth, went to Germany for five years in the 1980's during an unhappy time in her life for reasons she did not disclose. But when she returned to Chile she found her spiritual home again. She told us of her gratitude to God for recovery from serious illness, and spoke with pride about her sons—one working as an electrical engineer in Germany and another son as a mining engineer in Mexico. I asked both women to comment on two questions. The first: what was your experience of the Pinochet time? Both affirmed the strong feelings on either side of the subject and acknowledged that opinions continue into the present younger generation, though to a lesser degree. Both denounced Allende as a communist leader whose policies brought Chile to the brink of ruin. They remembered being hungry, helpless, and anxious; then Pinochet came and order was restored. They portrayed Pinochet as a military general who was not a dictator nor did he try to be, but was the man for the hour who made a difference for good in their lives. When inquiring about persecution or torture of Chileans under his rule, their answer was "We saw no evil." Our feeling was that they spoke for many more.

My second question was about their hopes for the future. Vilma began on a personal note, that her three children, nineteen, seventeen, and thirteen, would be baptized by Pastor Rodolfo Obermoeller. Renata's hope was for a greater unity among separated Lutherans. Then she added this afterthought: "I also hope that your fellow countrymen in the United States, when speaking of Americans, will remember that the word applies not only to you who live north of the equator but to the millions of us in South America as well!" I shook her hand as a sign that she had won her first convert.

The Lutheran University of Brazil (ULBRA by its Portugese acronym) is a phenomenon in world Lutheranism. It began in 1966 when a young pastor and his congregation in Porto Alegre faced a painful decision. Should they terminate the congregation's dying elementary school or find a viable future for it? Under the prodding of their visionary pastor, Ruben Becker, the choice was not only to retain the school but to give it a future beyond anything remotely imagined at the time. St. Paul Lutheran School became the seed (and eventually the legal owner) of what is now a first class Brazilian university, indeed the largest Lutheran university in the world. The statistics behind its forty year growth are astonishing: 156,000 students are enrolled on thirteen campuses scattered around the nation, 24,000 of whom study at the main campus in Canoas, a suburb of Porto Alegre. Behind the statistics, however are some sobering lessons which are part of the larger story. But first, how did ULBRA happen?

BRAZIL

That was the question on my mind as I entered the office of ULBRA'S president, Ruben Becker for a tightly packed hour of conversation late one morning. He was informally dressed in an open collar shirt and sleeveless sweater, and for a man in his 70's, he is unusually fit. We began our conversation in English but after a few introductory sentences he asked that we switch to German, his second language after Portuguese. Becker is a man of no-nonsense formality, impatient with small talk, and perhaps for that reason hoped that the language switch might shorten the visit of this stranger from Chicago. Our conversation continued quite smoothly in German, however, and he grew increasingly forthcoming when learning of my interest in global Lutherans and a book on the subject. On the wall opposite his ample, slightly elevated desk which dominates his regally furnished office are two oil paintings. One is of the original St. Paul School, a simple one room wooden building as it was a century or more ago, with several pupils in 1890's dress standing outside the door. The other is of his four children in their earlier days, two daughters and two sons. These side by side portraits symbolize the twin passions of his life, his family and the university. The growth of ULBRA, with its seed-to-giant-oak saga, could be seen outside the window where twenty eight building were visible across the spacious university grounds. The paintings suggest a counterbalance to one commonly held view that Rector Ruben Eugen Becker is entirely about authoritarian leadership with no capacity for emotional empathy. In my brief time with him, however, I found him gracious in receiving me for a visit on short notice and affirming of my intention to attempt to broaden our North American awareness of the global church. Not surprisingly, his authoritarian ways have made him a controversial figure in Brazil, both loathed and admired. But on this point all agree: Ruben Becker could not have accomplished what he has done in the past four decades without an obsessively strong commitment to founding a university with a clearly Lutheran identity. He has personally raised enormous amounts of money for his cause, a skill that reflects both to his genius and his undoing. He has moved adroitly, if at times ruthlessly, among financial circles where Lutheran clergy are rarely found. He has learned what it takes to assemble a quality faculty in order to maintain the high academic standards by which the university is known. These were my early impressions as he went on to tell more of how the university grew from the improbable beginnings of a nearly defunct Lutheran elementary school to the prestigious institution that it now is.

He spoke of the first financial breakthrough in starting the university. He persuaded a Swedish Foundation dedicated to funding Christian higher education institutions to provide a sizeable initial grant which covered 75% of the cost of the land chosen for the Canoas (a suburb of Porto Alegre) campus. Becker's skill as a negotiator with the Brazilian government showed in his convincing the national Ministry of Education to fund the balance. From that point on, he said, the 1970's became a decade of one fiscal success after another, as Becker stoked the meteoric growth of ULBRA by seeing to it that the fledgling university boasted a championship soccer team— the best way to promote its reputation in a nation that idolizes the sport. When I asked him about tuition, he said that it ranks at the top among Brazilian universities, which means that its students are drawn from the economically elite families of the country. Recently, he added, that circumstance has been altered through the introduction of weekend courses, e-learning curricula, and financial aid programs have enabled students from lower economic circumstances to enroll. Less then 1% of the heavily Roman Catholic Brazilian student body are Lutheran. He cited this as a prime opportunity for the school to serve a wider spiritual mission to students with only a nominal Christian faith or none at all. At Becker's insistence, every entering student must take a course entitled "Religious Culture" for an overview of the world's major religions with a strong emphasis on Christianity and Lutheran teaching. Moreover, each entering student receives a Bible, a copy of Luther's Catechism, and a book highlighting Lutheran faith and practice. Every plenary faculty meeting as well as departmental committee meeting begins with Scripture and prayer. From his office window he pointed out the central location of the chapel on the campus as a symbol of his emphasis on the primary importance of the Word of God in shaping the minds of students as they prepare for their role in Brazil's future. The building is of striking circular design with floor to ceiling glass exterior within which are handsome oak pews row upon row around the altar. It has one of the finest pipe organs in the country which is used for worship as well as for concerts by musicians from throughout Brazil and beyond. Three full time student chaplains carry on a vigorous ministry on the main campus and were helpful in giving me their overview of the university and arranging for an interview with the rector.

It was a privilege to meet the rector, tour the campus, and speak with the chaplains during two separate visits to ULBRA and experience something of the amazement of its story. Yet there were lingering questions in my mind about the overreaching dominance of one man's vision, the temptation to mingle personal gain with his funding efforts, and the key issue of who would follow Ruben Becker as rector (rumors were that a son was next in line). With sadness, but not with surprise, a year after my visit I learned that Becker had abruptly submitted his resignation. In answer to my inquiry as to what happened, the president of the Evangelical Lutheran Church of Brazil, Paulo Nerbas, stated that under Becker's direction ULBRA had assumed too many businesses besides its main business of educating students (a professional soccer team, a large health plan, the purchase of five hospitals, and other real estate enterprises). When some of these failed, the resulting debt threatened the existence of the university. Becker was questioned by the board of directors but could not provide satisfactory answers and resigned. A new rector was elected. The relation to the hospitals and other businesses was terminated and, as Nerbas said in a concluding understatement, "the educational work of the university is going on after much hard work and prayer." The sobering lesson learned through the experience of a gifted, driven pastor-become-founder of a university is not hard to see in retrospect. Power became addictive. When used without rational controls and accountability, it turned a visionary founder into an autocrat who could not share power wisely and remain accountable. In Lutheran theology there is a built-in warning about human nature as *simul justus et peccator*—both saved and yet still sinful. Rather than blame Ruben Becker for refusing to recognize the excesses of his personal power, it is better to apply the saved-and-yet-still-sinner truth to oneself and, having done so, find the courage to warn another who is teetering on the brink of disaster.

Martha Heine is another unique Lutheran in Brazil with the zeal of a founder. But in her case she had the grace to initiate and sustain a ministry among children of the slums of Porto Alegre in which many collaborate as leaders and workers. She does not look her 80 years nor does her pace show signs of easing up as an octogenarian. She was born in Brazil, the daughter of a Lutheran pastor, who discovered her aptitude for teaching when she was in her early teens. Her father sent her to a Lutheran high school and college in Porto Alegre where she completed her studies, a rare accomplishment at the time. On one occasion, when visiting a destitute family of nine children who were without a mother and whose father could not support them, Martha heard the cry of an infant from a crib somewhere underneath the foundation of the house—the coolest place available for the infant beset with multiple problems. She adopted the child on the spot, and brought the newborn home to announce to her husband (a pastor's son whom she had married several years earlier) that since they could not have children of their own, this would be the way they would

Martha Heine and children

become parents. Four years later she received another needy child and raised him as her adopted son. With her husband and two children the family migrated to the USA after World War II, settling finally in Chicago among relatives who helped them build a new life. At age 66, after the death of her husband, she was searching for a new calling in her life and found a hint of it through an offhand question from her 9 year old granddaughter whom she took with her on a trip back to Porto Alegre. The child asked why the children she saw on the streets were so poorly dressed and held out their hands for food or a coin to buy something to eat. That question set in motion an idea that, seed-like for two years, finally sprouted in the form of ministry to street children through cooperative efforts with a pastor and some teachers who were serving street children.

What was unique about her burgeoning ministry was her method of support, which by her choice was independent of any funding from Lutheran churches already hard pressed to meet their budgets. Since she had regularly divided her time between Brazil and Chicago, she started gathering donations of used clothing for children and mothers during her Chicago stay and shipping them off to Brazil where she sold them at affordable prices to low income families. Her house in Porto Alegre soon became well known as a resale shop for good clothes at prices within reach. For the past seventeen years she has grown her calling as a late-blooming Lydia to the point where she now contributes $35,000 annually to fund ministries among children in nine slum schools. This means connecting with some 5,000 children and teens year by year. A portion of her earnings is also used for needed projects at a Lutheran home for the aged on the outskirts of Porto Alegre. When once visiting there she found conditions so intolerable that she pushed for new leadership (which happened) and new standards of care for older men and women who have nowhere else to go. The signature event of her ministries among children, now organized as *Amigas,* with oversight boards in the USA and Brazil, is the annual Christmas party for children and parents. It centers around the story of Jesus' birth enacted in full costume with songs, stories, games, and food in an abundance that underfed children remember.

When moving fast to keep up with Martha Heine while following her during several days of visits to slum schools, a pattern emerged as she went from school to school. Upon seeing her arrival on the school grounds, timed when the children were outside their classrooms, they flocked to her side with smiles, excited shouts for her attention to their latest doings, and curious side-glances at the two strangers she brought along. She knew most of the children by name and would tell us in English about individual youngsters with special needs through such asides as: "Here is Rodolfo—he's 11 but much too small and malnourished" or "This child's mother must protect her from her father who comes home drunk." It was a sign that her compassionate heart combined with can-do practicality has multiplied the benefits of her outreach to over nine schools serving Brazilian street kids plus the residential care center for seniors with no home. Such programs of care, I learned when talking with teachers in the schools involved, range from all-school hot dog lunches to school supplies to repainted classrooms to new additions to school buildings.

There are slightly more than a million Lutherans in Brazil. They make up the membership of two main Lutheran church bodies, the Evangelical Church of the Lutheran Confession in Brazil (c. 716,000 baptized, the largest Lutheran church in South America with 1,810 congregations and 1,162 preaching points, 719 pastors, and a seminary of 250 students in Sao Leopoldo, and the Evangelical Lutheran Church of Brazil (c. 300,000 baptized, in 1,500 congregations, 500 mission stations, served by 603 pastors, seventeen social service institutions, also with a seminary in Sao Leopoldo). The relationship between the two is cordial, I learned, though not formally established by organizational unity due to the latter's more conservative Lutheran doctrine and its disapproval of women's ordination. Diaconal ministries have a significant role in both Lutheran churches. Each has drawn from the resources of the Wheat Ridge Ministries, an inter-Lutheran agency based in the USA with a long history in a broadly defined mission of seeding ministries of health and hope worldwide. An example is the Wheat Ridge sponsored Eliezer Project which is based in the large, public Conceicao Hospital in Porto Alegre, offering spiritual support to terminally ill patients and their families who have no health insurance. This palliative care program is something new in Brazil and well suited to the longstanding Wheat Ridge practice of providing start-up grants for medical and wholeness of life ministries that continue on their own. Another Wheat Ridge initiated ministry is Vila Petreira (Portuguese for "the other side of the tracks") in the town of Esteio. Earlier it was a notorious slum, lacking sewage facilities and electrical power and so ridden with crime that police would not enter. Among the Brazilian pastoral leaders in transforming this *favela* from a dangerous slum to a livable neighborhood is Bruno Rite. His commitment to social ministry in Brazil is reflected in his role as a regional representative of the Wheat Ridge connection to various social ministries through the years. In the northern Brazilian city of Rio de Janeiro, with its contradictory symbols of the luxurious Copacabana beach hotels back to back with the worst slums in this city of fourteen million, is the Good Samaritan Service Center for children whose average life span is twenty years. Pastor Mozart Noronha and a deaconess worker are based at Good Shepherd Lutheran Church, a congregation with a 180 year history in Brazil and one of the largest with a membership of 1,200 baptized. The two have led this congregation-based ministry of the Center for 28 years, opening its doors to children and their families as a haven of safety and hope.

It is not often that one finds a 22 year old university graduate who already has four years of experience behind him as an elected official of a city council. Marcel Van Hattem is such a young adult whose reputation as the youngest political figure in Brazil is known in the capitol city of Brasilia, as well as in his home town of Dois Irmois—"two mountains" in Portuguese—just over an hour west of Porto Alegre. We met him after a Sunday morning service in the congregation in which he and his family participate actively. His Lutheran church is 200 meters down the street from the other Lutheran congregation in the town of 8,000. The two buildings are almost identical and have stood within sight of each other since 1903 when a doctrinal dispute (which no one remembers anymore) brought about a separation. A bar now separates the two places of worship.

Marcel's mother is an architect, the daughter of a retired Lutheran seminary professor. His father is a mechanical engineer who was born in Holland and came as a child of seven with his family to Brazil. The Van Hattems have five sons, all handsome enough to qualify with the middle son as a model for young men's clothing. Each is fluent in English with an interesting story to tell. Marcel was the focus of my attention because of his unique participation in public affairs that began when he ran for office as an 18 year old. His motivation, he said, was his impatience with the people of his town who did nothing about corruption in their government. He was university freshman enrolled in a course in public affairs when he decided to convert a term paper assignment into a campaign for office. He searched out details of mismanagement, published them in a newspaper he began on his own, won the election and took a seat on the city council. Since then he has been fully occupied with his civic duties in addition to finishing his university degree. When I asked him what he brings to his experience as a rising star in Brazilian political life he responded from his Lutheran roots in a manner that impressed me. Lutherans, he said, have a foundation in God's work for the wider good of civic order through his law. Distinct from God's law is the Gospel of his saving work through Jesus Christ. The Gospel motivates him for serving others, he said, and he needs its liberating power to keep him going. Liberation, he went on, is an important word in Brazil. He mentioned familiarity with remnants of the Roman Catholic liberation theology of the 1970's and following, but was disappointed that it had lost its spiritual heart and become too identified with political strategy. Lutherans, who in his view are generally far too indifferent toward active participation in government, owe it to apply their faith in working to liberate places like Dois Irmaos from entrenched malpractice in public affairs. Although some pastors have looked down on his activism, others have encouraged him. Even the president of his church body, the more conservative Evangelical Lutheran Church of Brazil, gave him a personal endorsement but stopped short of making it public. The satisfactions he spoke of from his experiences so far centered around the friendships he has made in the city council of his town and in the capitol at Brasilia. As an example, he mentioned his effort to gain support for a trip to Holland to learn of a project in city management there. It fell short initially and he was disappointed. But when he used his newspaper to issue a call for help, the needed funds came through. He made the trip and returned better equipped to advocate constructive change on the basis of what he had seen in Holland. As to the things that irk him, he mentioned news media owned by wealthy Brazilians who equate their money with wisdom for statecraft and are shameless in exploiting through disinformation. It is a lesson he has had to learn as a novice in office but he expressed the hope that he would never settle for indifference to such disservice to the electorate.

He surprised me by saying that he has not ruled out the pastoral ministry as his future calling. Both his grandfathers are ordained clergy. He asked me what my years of experience have taught me about the public role of the ordained minister. I answered that my guiding motif for my calling is based in St. Paul's words in Ephesians 4 to the effect that God calls pastors to equip his baptized people for their daily ministry in the world, serving the wider good as parents, teachers, workers, leaders, etc. It was a new insight and led to further conversation with him about his future.

A day with Mario Lehenbauer, veteran pastor and church leader in Brazil, provided varied glimpses of church life in Brazil through the eyes of one who has spent decades in varied aspects of service. He listed several matters of key importance in understanding Lutheranism at present. Urbanization is changing the face of Brazil and all its societal institutions, including the church. This is more apparent in northern Brazil, he explained, where there is a more adaptive culture in play. In the church that means a growing influence of Pentecostalism that affects things as varied as theology to hand-clapping in worship to the kinds of hymns sung during the service. The south of Brazil is more traditional, and Lutherans are found mostly in that region where the implications of new cultural forces are slower to be recognized and met. Regarding Lutheran unity, the general picture is one of polite recognition but not yet dealing with more basic theological matters of difference. The more conservative IELB does not ordain women, based on a different way of interpreting Scripture from that of the IELCB which does ordain women and holds membership in the broader ecumenical Lutheran World Federation and World Council of Churches. In speaking of women in the church in general, however, Lehenbauer spoke appreciatively of congregations of his church in more remote mission locations where women do preach because there are no men who can or will. Such default practice, he acknowledged, is only a substitute for the real work which is yet to be addressed.

Lehenbauer treated us to something no visitor to Brazil should miss. It was a noon hour spent with a *churasco* meal of choice cuts of meat served on skewers by waiters who seemed radar equipped to return to the table for yet one more slice of sirloin or tenderloin or other temptation to delicious gluttony. Brazilians know how to live well and eat heartily. Our only problem with the *churasco* extravaganza at noon was a supper hour repeat of the same. We took the Vitor Mahler family to dinner, whose hospitality in their home made our Porto Alegre stay an experience of the apostolic invitation in Romans 15 to "welcome each other as Christ has first welcomed you, to the glory of God."

An intended morning tour of Buenos Aires, the Argentine capitol celebrated for its grand boulevards and historic palaces, had to be scratched for two days of hectic taxiing back and forth between the United States and Brazilian embassies. The purpose was to obtain a visa for Brazil that circumstances prevented us from acquiring one a month earlier in the USA. The process took twenty-five separate steps through the thicket of bureaucratic red tape. Our frustrations, however, were minor when compared to what happens when citizens of politically conflicted countries apply, particularly when their place of residence is distant from an embassy. Copious attention is given to filling out application forms, followed by travel to an embassy, which can mean a wait for hours or days, only to be turned down without explanation. When that happens deserving people with much to give are deprived of participating in international gatherings, teaching exchanges, family visits—all of which are mutually enriching for the global community. Hearing such stories from clergy and laity of all denominations put our mini-saga in perspective. In this era of international travel afflicted by terrorism, the fact to remember is that 99.9% of the visa applicants are well intentioned people who pose no threat to anyone but must bear with extensive security measures imposed to detect the handful who are a threat and must be denied.

Alan Eldrid

ARGENTINA

Our introduction to church life in Argentina began with a visit in the office of Alan Eldrid, the president of the United Evangelical Lutheran Church (IELU), a man in his middle years, hospitable, informal in manner (he greeted us in shirtsleeves and open clergy collar) and generous in giving us time on his well-filled schedule. He is also a man of interesting surprises, the first of which was his fluent, British-accented English which came easily to our ears as non-Spanish speakers needing interpreters more often than not throughout our South American journey. He explained his bilingual gift as the boon of growing up in a bilingual household where his parents spoke English as readily as Spanish. Another surprise was his name, which seemed non-Spanish enough to make me wonder if he might be a transplanted churchman from England or North America. No such thing, he commented with a smile, noting that in the melting pot that Argentine society is, his name is no oddity requiring a more Spanish makeover. As our conversation moved to my inquiry about his pastoral experiences and how he came to be president of his church body, he provided the third and most novel surprise: "Perhaps by mistake" he said with a half-serious, half-humorous roll of his eyes.

He was referring to the moment in a church conference several years earlier when the sitting president of the IELU took him aside to say that it was time for a leadership change and that Eldridge would be a good successor. Flabbergasted by such a prospect out of the blue—he was happy in his pastoral ministry in a congregation with no desire to change—he asked if there might not be some mix up. But the president was serious and persisted. His name went forward. After being elected he had ten minutes to accept or decline. Still in a daze, he accepted and was installed on the spot. His purpose in telling this story was to make the larger point, that in this church body, the smallest of three Lutheran groups in Argentina, choosing new leaders is not heavily politicized nor is it a much contested process. The ad hoc process says more about the ministry that is done by the people rather than the person serving as president. What followed his election provided another point for us to understand about Lutherans in Argentina. They take more seriously who their local pastor is than who the church president is. To illustrate he cited his experience in arranging for an interim pastoral worker to fill in for him temporarily. She was a young woman intern from the USA. When arriving at the church for her first Sunday morning on duty she was confronted at the entrance door by five irate women of the congregation who demanded: "We want to know where our pastor is!" When things settled down enough for him to confer with his former parishioners on what they were seeking in a new pastor, their tart reply was "one just like you—except for the things we don't like about you." In recalling these events, Eldridge's sense of humor showed as a useful quality among his range of gifts in handling the unexpected. His self-effacing manner of not taking himself too seriously helped explain why he is well received among the twenty eight pastors of the IELU who serve the 10,000 baptized listed on the church roster, a list which Eldrid said needed pruning for a more realistic account of those who are active and those who need to become active.

Church leaders don't always speak with such candor about statistics, nor have I ever met one with a story quite like his on how he came into leadership. What made his comments more than anecdotal was the contrast Lutheran style and structure present to the vertical, top down authority in the Roman Catholic Church which has dominated religious life in Argentina for five centuries. He wanted us to understand this contrast in the light of the long tradition of strong-man rule from the time of colonialism begun by the Spanish conquistadors in the early 16th century and continued to the present after Argentina gained its national independence in the 1820's.

Lutherans came into this heavily Roman Catholic milieu from Germany, Denmark and Sweden in the 19th century to form close knit communities which, until recent decades, remained largely separated by language and culture from their Hispanic and Indian surroundings. Eldrid's own IELU church origins were from North American Lutheran missionaries, sponsored by women's missionary societies in congregations in Pennsylvania. They came shortly after World War I with a plan of forming congregations around Lutheran elementary schools. They settled along railroad lines being built in the 1920's. They formed neighborhoods of closely connected enclaves in which babies were baptized, children were schooled, youth were confirmed and thus well-grounded adults forged the backbone of congregations with a strong Lutheran identity, often with a son in the family set apart for pastoral or teaching ministry.

The IELU was formally constituted in 1948, in time to expand its mission to the new wave of eastern European immigrants from Hungary, Latvia, Estonia and Lithuania who fled Soviet-style Communism that had taken over eastern Europe following World War II. The refugees who found their spiritual home in Lutheran congregations were soon challenged to cooperate in opening the door to more newcomers who spoke strange languages and brought new customs. Eldrid saw an irony at work in the effect refugees from Communist lands had on Lutheran congregations in Argentina. Their understandably vehement anti-Communism set them up for exploitation by right wing Argentine government regimes who mouthed anti-Communist slogans while suppressing legitimate movements for justice and reform in Argentina and in the surrounding region during the 1970's. A growing approval for lockstep military regimes made Lutherans passively obedient to ideological systems in their new homeland that repeated the oppression they suffered in Eastern Europe. They continued the tradition of isolation from the mainstream of Argentine life that had been the Lutheran pattern for a century and a half. Pastors had their hands full in maintaining the status quo and were overtaxed in serving the flood of incoming refugees. Thus Eldrid characterized the situation affecting what it meant to be Lutheran in Argentine on the eve of a new era that brought change.

Juan Cobrda, a name I heard repeatedly when listening to Lutherans in Argentina, embodied that change and was a major figure in enhancing it in the decades following 1960. He was born in a village in the north central region of what is now Slovakia, and as a boy of 17 was a son in a family fleeing Communist oppression in Slovakia. The family was first slated to settle on a farm in France and would have done so if the parents would have agreed to leave their younger son behind because he tested positive for tuberculosis. They refused, keeping their son, Jan (later changed to Juan in Argentina) with them as the close-knit family waited for their placement after spending time in an Austrian refugee camp. During that period an event of consequence occurred when a Jewish carpenter (an escapee from a World War II Nazi concentration camp) befriended the family by providing food and a job for the father in the household. That experience of practical compassion made a lasting impression on the 17 year old Juan. It enabled him in later decades to understand what it means to be a stranger in a new land and it motivated him to shape his own ministry and that of his church toward compassion and justice for immigrants in Argentina and beyond.

Soon after the family's arrival in Buenos Aires in 1948 he joined the Argentine navy and in the short span of five years rose to the rank of captain, gaining an international perspective through naval voyages to Asia, Africa, and the Middle East. A Lutheran captain on an Argentine ship of near total Catholic crew of sailors was uncommon enough, but even more uncommon was his practice as the captain of reading of Scripture and leading prayers on a regular basis—with attendance required by all hands aboard. When in a foreign port, he found not only a bar with good beer but on Sundays a congregation at worship. On one occasion of attending worship, an offhand comment by the pastor that he might consider a vocation to the pastoral ministry set him on the path of pursuing the idea when he returned to Buenos Aires. In 1954 he enrolled in seminary for a new start in surroundings markedly different from those he enjoyed as a Navy captain; he was one in an incoming class of six students in a Lutheran seminary in Buenos Aires. Four years later he completed his studies with distinction and received a scholarship from the Lutheran World Federation for two years of graduate theological study at the Hamma Divinity School in Ohio.

His studies there ended after his first year as the IELU summoned him back to Argentina to take over pastoral duties in a congregation in Rosario, 300 kilometers north of Buenos Aires. There he met a striking young teacher who became his wife. After less than a year he was sent to Grand Bourg, a new experiment in community in Argentina, comprised of 4,000 houses built to accommodate the tide of incoming refugees. Remembering his early years as a refugee and the impact of the Jewish carpenter, he realized that before he could concentrate on forming a congregation he had to address the problems of a new community without water, power, or any plan for establishing schools. He appealed personally to the Argentine Ministry of the Interior and showed determined leadership in seeing to it that the government took action in meeting the basic survival needs for 10,000 new settlers, an initiative not commonly associated with Lutheran pastors traditionally oriented to looking after the spiritual needs of those already settled in congregations. His advocacy of a larger vision of ministry was tested for seven years before he was satisfied that living conditions were adequate for Lutherans and non-Lutherans alike. This included planting a system of schools, the first of which began with six students and grew to 1,500 seven years later in 1967, the year in which he was elected president of the IELU.

Cobrda's vision of the church as servant of holistic ministry to immigrants inevitably began to put him in conflict with those who saw him as a threat to their comfort with the status quo, much as Helmut Frenz had experienced in Chile (both men knew and respected each other). This surfaced when he was elected to chair an ecumenical committee for refugees and led in settling 200 Chilean newcomers, some of them of Indian ethnicity, to settle in largely Lutheran communities. Remembering what it meant to be an outsider with tuberculosis, facing separation from his own family, he met the agitation of threatened residents with tact and forthrightness, first by housing them in a nearby vacation spa after dividing them into groups of twenty to avoid public confrontation when going en masse to and from meals. When that proved unsatisfactory he managed the purchase of a plot of land ten kilometers away and engaged other Lutheran clergy to help him in the pastoral care of those who found themselves everywhere unwanted.

This took place at a time and in a region wide area of political unrest. The once popular president Juan Peron had been exiled to Spain after the death of his wife, Evita, considered by many as the real power behind his showmanship exterior. The military takeover regime did not favor taking in refugees from Chile, where Pinochet had assumed power in 1973. The kidnapping of those challenging the status quo made life increasingly hazardous for those like Juan Cobrda, who was accused of being a Communist and threatened with the same fate as some 20,000 Argentines who had been "disappeared" by 1974. His own brother had been arrested as complicit in Cobrda's ministry and armed police had come to his parents' residence at midnight demanding information about the work and whereabouts of their sons. Cobrda's ties with the chaplain of the Buenos Aires police force, who had warned him about his own impending arrest and the prison location in Patagonia where his brother was confined, may well have saved the lives of both men.

As these crises deepened, Cobrda realized that his presence was too great a threat to his family and his pastoral work in behalf of refugees. For that reason he did not contest his deportation from Argentina, the first of two that followed later. With his wife, who had given birth to their son one day before, the family left for Trenton, New Jersey, for three years of pastoral ministry among Slovak Lutherans there. In 1978, when Argentina won the World Cup soccer championship, the military junta, desiring to present a positive face to the world, allowed Corbrda and family to return to Buenos Aires where he served as pastor of El Redentor Lutheran congregation. His installation was sobered by his knowledge that on the same day the Argentine president received the World Cup trophy, fifteen dissidents were assassinated in another part of the city and the fate of some 20,000 more disappeared remained unknown to their grieving families. Cobrda's returned to a mixed reception in his own church body. Those who favored his ministry of welcoming care for refugees and prophetic defiance of dictatorial violence against refugees sought to restore him to leadership in the IELU. Those of the opposite view declared that they would leave the church and incite opposition against him from the outside. Faced with those choices when asked to stand as a candidate for the office of church president, he decided against it and continued as pastor of El Redentor congregation, broadening its outreach to new arrivals in Argentina as well as to those on the margins of urban society. He left Argentina a second time in 1983 for years of pastoral ministry in Akron, Ohio, and Chicago, where he recognized the gifts and potential of a Argentinian graduate student with Danish roots, Willi Hansen, and encouraged him toward a future as an influential theological professor in Buenos Aires, a development touched upon later in this chapter.

In the course of his years of churchmanship in Argentina, Juan Cobrda extended the witness of South American Lutherans to international circles where it was lesser known before. He represented his church at World Council of Churches and Lutheran World Federation assemblies in Europe and South America, and participated in negotiations for the care of refugees in Asia, the Middle East, and Africa. In 1970 he was elected vice-president of the Lutheran World Federation which meant regular visits to Geneva, Switzerland, with international colleagues, a position held for seven years. From 1973-1975 he was Chair of the Argentine Committee for Refugees from Chile, an agency working under the sponsorship of the United Nations and World Council of Churches as well as the Lutheran World Federation. In 1980 he chaired the planning committee that formed the Ecumenical United Seminary in Buenos Aires, an amalgamation of faculties from Presbyterian, Methodist, and Lutheran seminaries and now known as the University Institute-ISEDET. Even in this academic endeavor Cobrda was called upon to deal with crises that nearly aborted the seminary before it could begin. One was financial. An amount of $800,000 from USA and European church sources had been gathered to launch the new seminary, but due to the spike in inflation in 1969, the investment committee had placed the money apart from banks at the time—and lost it all. His first task as chair of the founding committee was to fly to Geneva, meet the representatives of the sponsoring churches, explain the dilemma, and return with another check for $800,000. The second crisis was of a different order. The 300 students who moved into the new seminary quarters had to evacuate hurriedly before classes were underway. A fire bomb had been planted in the building, and Cobrda was of the strong opinion that it had been placed there by government forces hostile to a new Protestant seminary strengthened by the union of several theological institutions. He went to the Minister of the Interior personally to protest the action and was not surprised to meet a wall of denial. Cobrda, well seasoned in such matters, made his point, however, by leaving an empty suitcase in the office. He returned later to claim it and told the official to his face: "If I had left a bomb for you in that suitcase, you surely would have come after me!" It was partly tongue-in-cheek combined with his sense of realism about what happens when an Argentine regime flexes its muscle through intimidating actions. But there was nothing tongue-in-cheek about the fate of a promising young theologian, Mauricio Lopez, called to teach at Ia Buenos Aires seminary in 1980. He never made it to the campus. Somewhere en route he was disappeared for his active protests for human rights in Argentina. His body was never found. The military report on his murder took the cynical format used to describe him and others who suffered a similar fate: "Lopez is among those who went to Europe and now he has a good life there."

After a decade of service as bishop of the Slovak Zion Synod in America from 1993 on, he now lives in retirement in the Chicago area. Juan Cobrda's half century of ministry as a Lutheran leader in Argentina offers more than anecdotal interest; he mirrors the wider course of an entire body of Lutherans in Argentina seeking throughout the latter half of the 20th century to grow toward greater maturity in the height an depth and breadth of Christ's love, finding that his lordship is not only personal but communal, enduring the inevitable hostility of afflicting the comfortable while comforting the afflicted, and finally winning through to small and large victories of reconciliation and fruitfulness in discipleship.

The first thing to catch our eye when arriving on a Sunday morning at Holy Communion Lutheran Church in a lower Middle Class neighborhood of Buenos Aires was a trio of buildings that represent the course of ministry there since German immigrants founded the congregation in 1948.

The parsonage, a sturdy two story structure that housed pastors and families who conducted worship in the adjoining chapel with a capacity of up to 100 worshipers. Nearby on the same property is a larger dormitory style building for the purpose of housing homeless women and their children. Our hosts for the day were the American couple, Kate Lawler, the regional representative of the ELCA in Argentina and Chile, and her husband, David Wunsch, her counterpart in Bolivia and Peru. He translated my homily preached as the guest preacher from Chicago, during which the pastor of the congregation, Angel Furlan, arrived for a front row seat in the congregation he has served for twenty three years. He had come directly from the airport after attending a conference of Lutherans from Central and South America in Honduras and after delivering a brief report to the congregation led us to a meeting room nearby which is rented out during the week as part of a primary school. There we sat down with a circle of several dozen women who are residents of the community house and a few men of the congregation who were interested in our purpose in coming. One by one, they told their stories. Christina began by telling how she came fifteen years ago, homeless and jobless as a single mother with her ten month old child and through the supportive encouragement of the community has found a home and family for the first time. She has moved from housework to sales to her present job in business management in a not-for profit agency. Her chief satisfaction, as she said, has been to pay back what she has received here as she helps welcome and encourage new arrivals who come with problems she knows from experience, summing things up with this sentence: "We're a big family here, and being together makes the problems we face not so big." A woman in her late forties, slender and pert, she spoke as one who has leadership qualities for getting things done, and set the tone for the others as they readily spoke up. Ceferina, named after her grandmother, saw the sign of welcome to the Community House of Holy Communion congregation when passing by one day, looking for a haven after her young daughter had died and her husband left her. Emelia, a dark haired single woman who smiled easily, was employed in making leather purses when the economy collapsed in he early 1990's. A friend told her of a house next door where she tried without success to find work; just as she was leaving she heard the person who gave her the bad news call out: "There might be something for you next door"—and that put her on a road back to self-support through the $50 a month she earns by housework as a member of the community. As the stories continued, the sadness of women hurt by domestic violence was a consistent thread, along with witness to the healing atmosphere that each woman had found. Sarah and her husband, Jacob, also spoke as a married couple in residence; she was nursing her infant who had recently been baptized by Pastor Furlan. Sofia, seated next to us, looked too young to have been the mother of the thirteen children she has borne, the oldest now 31, and the youngest, six. She had been abandoned by her mother and the father she never knew. At Holy Communion Community House she has begun a new life beyond her dreams and her striking brown eyes sparkled as she spoke of her hopes for her children with whom she keeps in contact.

The community is self-supporting, helped by a one time gift by the Lutheran Church of Sweden to build the dormitory. Holy Communion congregation is an average size parish of 100 families, sixty of whom are active. The residents of the dormitory are the backbone of the congregation. Pastor Angel Furlan is a distinguished looking man with a pensive face, set off by graying hair and dark eyebrows that give him an almost plaintive look. His quiet aura of knowing what this unique ministry requires came through in his description of his pastoral calling as *accompaniment*, the term often heard among Lutherans in Central and South America for those seeking bread for soul and body. His is not a pastor-centered ministry, he said, since "the women are the most effective ministers to each other." When asked what issues are presently before the Holy Communion community, he named the challenge of what membership here really means. Is it putting a name on a membership list or participating in worship wholeheartedly, caring support of each other, and seeking mission and ecumenical partnership with surrounding churches. As he spoke, one woman added in a firm voice: "God should please not send us a legalistic shepherd, but one who will help us grow and will feed us as our shepherd so that we can do our part for others when they come!" Furlan went on to speak of the huge burden that HIV AIDS lays on top of those caught in poverty. Those with AIDS cannot get work. Hospitals cannot serve the growing numbers. The government provides free medication, but lack of housing and food, plus drug addiction, add up to problems that are crushing. He lamented that too many people die, not from AIDS but from the lack of food or job or family to care for them, and sometimes even the lack money for bus fare to a hospital to die in some kind of dignity. He concluded the Sunday afternoon gathering on a note of gratitude, however, affirming that after 23 years of serving the Holy Communion congregation and Community House, he is eager for whatever each new day brings. He is continually uplifted by the powerful demonstration of the priesthood of all believers through the actions of women who come in despair but find hope for a new start through the Gospel alive in their midst.

Willi Hansen, a tall, sandy-haired, 46 year old is a Lutheran theologian who teaches at The University Institute-ISEDET in Buenos Aires. Hansen's ethnic Danish roots, name, and looks give him the appearance of a character straight off the page of a Hans Christian Andersen novel. Spanish is his first language as one born in Argentina, and as one thoroughly immersed in the culture of his native country he has given scholarly attention to the need for a more culturally contextual ministry of the Lutheran church here. His broad theological education in Argentina, Brazil, and the United States, coupled with his international experience as a consulting theologian with Lutheran World Federation projects in Asia and Africa, made me an eager listener as he spoke. In short order he listed these themes as essential in understanding Lutherans in South America:

- Lutherans in the Latino context have a lively connection with Martin Luther's theology since the conservative Roman Catholicism predominant in South America is not far removed from the 16th century Catholicism that Luther confronted.
- The mission of the Gospel is seed on rocky soil in urbanized South America where cities are highly secularized and Freud dominates in middle class minds.
- After Vatican II in 1963 many Roman Catholics did what Lutherans and other Protestants have sought to do, conduct worship in the vernacular and seek a new role for the laity—thus reducing the appeal of the heirs of Martin Luther here.
- The tumultuous social and political upheavals in Argentina and beyond during the 1960's and '70's created a split among Lutherans and other

Christians who were ill-prepared to move beyond their own liberal/conservative divisions which still inhibit their ministries.

- Lutheranism in its Latino dress cannot be packaged re-do of its European and American forms. How to work theologically as Lutherans in a South American context is a work in progress, needing powerful connection with symbols and life situations here.

It was this last insight that was particularly provocative and Hansen provided two examples to expand his point. Devotion to Mary, the mother of our Lord, permeates Latin Catholicism, and if Lutherans are going to touch the soul of the South American, then Luther's own deep reverence for Jesus' mother must be recovered in preaching, teaching, hymnody, and art that can reach the person on the street. Secondly, now that Pentecostalism has arrived with whirlwind force throughout Central and South America, appealing to millions who have found Catholic formalism arid and Lutheran head-theology bewildering, Lutherans have much to learn from them. This includes, in his way of speaking, "discovering what makes people tick." He explained that this involved understanding and integrating human emotions in worship, and presenting the public face of the Lutheran tradition with integrity and flexibility in forms of worship and community. Hansen sees hopeful signs of such things at work among younger pastors, with much still needed for the future.

Another interesting response came when I asked Hansen about financial sustainability in the churches in and beyond Argentina. He has regularly conducted workshops on the subject in which he calls for a decision for the people of the church in a given place to carry out their mission under the Gospel within their economic means to support it. Another issue is where the church's mission should be centered. Should it be in the cities where middle class Lutherans live who are not accustomed to moving among the poor and where property and living costs are prohibitive? Or should it be on the outskirts of cities and towns where the poor who come from the countryside can afford to locate and who need a way of being the church that Lutherans have not yet found. Without my asking he went on to a related topic of how the several Lutheran church bodies in Argentina can work together more effectively. In his view, the three separated Lutheran churches (four, if one Union church is included) are a waste of resources as each tries to do too much on its own. A unified Lutheranism is needed. A new confessional basis is not necessary; Luther's Small Catechism, the Augsburg Confession and Leuenberg Agreement are all available. The Reformed have lost much of their theological identity and look to Lutherans for theological leadership, a fact that he has seen at work within the ISEDET faculty and student body where he teaches.

His comments on the appeal of Lutheran theology among ISEDET students from a variety of backgrounds prompted me to seek out a group of them for conversation in an empty classroom. Raquel, 36, the daughter of a Pentecostal pastor, is comfortable with her theological study at ISEDET. She enrolled through a recommendation from an Assembly of God pastor and spoke appreciatively of the freedom of the Gospel found in Lutheran theology. Luis is from Colombia, of Catholic parents, who survived the dangers of gang warfare as a youth. Now an ordained Baptist minister, he was drawn to ISEDET by the quality of its graduate education program. Veronica, 46, came from an unusual background. She has dual Ecuadorian and French citizenship, worked as a journalist in Europe and South America, was at one time employed by World Vision, aspired to be a nun when she was 15, and has been at ISEDET for a year. Juan is 23, from a Waldensian Protestant mother and Catholic father in Montevideo, Uruguay, just across the broad estuary of the Rio de la Plata River, spoke of a tragic suicide of a family member had moved him to search for God as a teenager. His Waldensian/Lutheran co-pastors in his home congregation gave him comfort and inspiration for a pastoral future and have supported his coming to ISEDET to prepare for his future. Ivan, also 23 and from Uruguay, came from a Catholic family who were put off by having to pay the priest when he was confirmed as a boy. A Lutheran pastor visited his school and invited him and his friends to youth activities. There he learned more of the Lutheran church and came to ISEDET to prepare for pastoral ministry. Marcia is from a village several hours from Santiago, Chile, where she did well in school, decided to study chemistry, worked for five years, when the death of her brother set her on a path of seeking God. She had been confirmed as a child in the Lutheran congregation, drifted off, returned to her Lutheran heritage, and earned a scholarship for theological study in Leipzig, Germany. She is looking forward to the new experience of a two year vicarage before completing her studies at ISEDET, a five year program altogether.

This potpourri of students with their widely varying backgrounds covered several evenings of conversation and reflected the draw of the Lutheran tradition in the theology taught at ISEDET. I asked them whether there is such a thing as a Latin American theology. They answered along these lines: the South American situation is markedly different from the USA and calls for different questions with answers that fit the Latin context. Theology must be practical for parish ministry and home grown, something each one who had studied abroad was quick to emphasize. Theology in South America must be seen through the eyes of the poor in the developing countries of the continent, as well as in the Roman Catholic context that has prevailed for centuries. Some spoke of cooperative work for human rights in various countries and the need to help people confront the power structures that oppress rather than serve. Each evening's conversation closed with prayers by each student around the circle, and with words of appreciation from Beverly and myself for their gift of time and interest in letting us in on their thoughts, experiences, and hopes as part of the coming generation of pastors in Argentina and beyond.

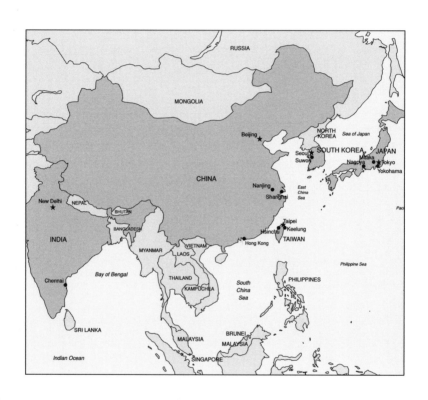

PART 7

INTRODUCING
NORTHERN ASIA & INDIA

The five countries included in this geographic grouping include China and India, which together comprise over one third of the world's population, and present examples of unexpected, exponential Christian growth (China) and perseverance among Christians who follow Jesus' command to serve the outcast (India). Two more countries are included in which striking contrasts are apparent, the dramatic increase of Christian numbers and influence in South Korea and the opposite circumstance of minimal statistical growth in Japan where Christians are known by their well educated laity and the establishment of quality schools ranging from kindergarten through university graduate school. Taiwan is part of this northern Asia cluster as an example of the Christian calling to be peacemakers amidst the sharp nationalist tensions dividing Chinese on both sides of the South China Sea. The Lutheran presence in these five Asian nations is as old as three centuries in India to the late 1950's in South Korea, and the form of Lutheran ministries is shaped by differing conditions in each place. Notable examples are the response to the crisis of refugees (South Korea and Taiwan) and the story of how one Lutheran pioneer's vision of reaching Buddhists in China led to a theological research center that continues its unique witness from a beautiful hilltop location overlooking Hong Kong.

Lutherans in Japan number about 26,000, not quite 2% of the 4.7 million Japanese Christians of all denominations in a land of 127 million population. Missionary work by Lutherans began in 1892. A temporary surge in Lutheran and other outreach work by all Christian denominations occurred in the post World War II period. But the emergence of a plethora of new religions in this era has returned Christians, including Lutherans, to the pattern of slow growth that has characterized the course of Christianity in Japan since Francis Xavier's arrival as the first messenger of the Gospel in 1549.

JAPAN

I wondered if other visitors experience what I felt when entering the campus of the Japan Lutheran Theological College and Seminary in the Tokyo suburb of Mitaka. What came over me was a wave of relief to see green grass, trees, and flower beds after the rapid transit ride out from central Tokyo through some of the world's highest urban density in the world's largest city. Skyscrapers, high rises, commercial buildings, houses, noodle shops, neon signboards, cars, trucks, and streets crowded with people all passed by in a blur as a numbing reminder that this metropolis is home to 35.3 million people, a fifth of the total Japanese population of 127 million squeezed into an area the size of California.

We were luncheon guests in the faculty residence of seminary director Naozumi Eto whose hospitality was well remembered from previous visits. Also present were retired professor of systematic theology, Chizuo Shibata, a friend throughout the fifty-five years since our student days serving a Lutheran congregation in Yokohama. A senior faculty member, Hiroshi Suzuki, was present who in modesty would not have told me that he recently completed translating Jaroslav Pelikan's five volume history of the development of Christian doctrine. With justifiable pride in his colleague's work, Dr. Eto informed me of the accomplishment which symbolized the high standard of what the seminary provides its students.

Toshifumi Uemura

The special guest was Toshifumi Uemura. I had heard beforehand about this newest faculty member who has a spiritual DNA unlike any other Japanese I've met. He devoted several years of his life toward becoming a Shinto priest but after completing all requirements chose not to be ordained. Instead he responded to a long germinating and deeply held belief in Jesus Christ and, while retaining the wealth of his accumulated Shinto learning, turned in a new direction which led to his baptism and ultimate vocation as a Lutheran theologian and educator. Eto introduced him briefly and he proceeded to tell his story in fluent English and with a tactful ease that enabled him say enough without talking too much among his seniors.

Uemura began by briefly sketching his upbringing as the second son in an affluent family which had prospered in the business of producing and marketing salt. He grew up in a household well furnished with the accoutrements of traditional Japanese religion, both Shinto and Buddhist, but these figures merely gathered dust as cultural relics due to his atheist mother's exclusion of any religious practice in any form in the household. He recalled that his mother had agreed to marry his father only on the condition that there would be no prayers to the gods or to the ancestors in the Shinto wedding ceremony. Against such a background of aggressive hostility to all things religious it was not surprising that Toshifumi Uemura, as a boy of 10, would explore on his own a world forbidden to him by sneaking out of the house to attend a Christian Sunday School in a church nearby. Two things stuck in his memory. The first was what he termed the sweetness of the church atmosphere and the kindness of the pastor who taught him a song about Jesus. The other was his one word summary of the Bible stories he heard about Jesus and his miracles—"nonsensical." He did well in school through his teen years. As the second son in the family he was excused from taking over the family business which was the duty of his older brother. This left him free to enter a prestigious Tokyo university to pursue a major in international studies.

He jumped ahead in his narrative to recapture the moment of meeting a person named Mita in a house in Tokyo. Before entering the door he chanted a *norito*, the Shinto blessing at the beginning of a ritual. She received him and before he could explain who he was and his purpose in coming, she declared in an authoritative voice: "whether you believe or not, God exists." Then came even more startling words. She declared that Jesus Christ is the only Son of God. The impact was stunning enough to bring Uemura to realize that she left him no room to doubt. He dates his belief in Jesus as the Christ of God from that opening moment of meeting Sueko Mita. He hardly knew what it meant to believe in God as revealed in Jesus his Son nor did he know how this unlettered Shinto woman could be such an authoritative witness to Christ. It was all a mystery, but magnetic enough to draw him to continue commuting to her house for ten years as her disciple. While deepening in his knowledge of Shinto, he recalled that as he kept his grounding as a believer in Jesus he could ask Mita why Christians are so eager to do mission work. He heard her declarative answer— "Christians *must* proclaim the gospel if they believe and do not doubt who Jesus is." He remembered another time when he asked her about faith. She answered with similar directness that faith "is the assurance of things hoped for, the conviction of things not seen"—a quote straight from Hebrews 11:1 in the New Testament Scriptures.

As transformed as Uemura was by his confession of Jesus as the Christ of God he was also drawn to a deeper immersion into the distinctive teaching of Mita as a Shinto master. Over a ten year period following his university study, he commuted to her house to absorb all he could under her spiritual tutelage. Her method was like nothing he had experienced before. She forbade religious texts of any sort, nor would she allow disciplines of fasting or meditation. Her method was dialog, only questions and answers after her formal lesson was completed. After his university study, and in contradiction to Mita's declaration that Christianity was the only proper path for him to pursue, he entered Kokagukuin College for aspiring Shinto priests in order to deepen his grasp of Shintoism. But the more he probed the greater disparity he found between Mita's teaching and the Shinto precepts taught at the university. He finished his studies which qualified him for ordination into the Shinto priesthood but he realized he could never become a priest in a religion he found so complex and at odds with all he had received from Sueko Mita.

This left him in a dilemma. He was nearing 30, with two university degrees and no sense of direction as to his future. He was a believer in Jesus Christ. He had gained considerable knowledge of the complexity of the Shinto religion. He rejected the prospect of becoming a priest. He had devoted ten years to the teaching of a reclusive woman whose doctrine was at odds with the Shinto establishment. In a state of thorough confusion, he took a month to seek direction. Answers came, soon and in abundance. He gathered with Christians, first in an Assembly of God congregation where the preacher who impressed him administered baptism. He then met a woman who later became his wife. She was an organist with a love for Bach, a love which he shared and found in Bach a connection to the Lutheran tradition. Through the Lutheran pastor in the congregation where his wife served as organist he received catechetical instruction, and later was powerfully influenced by the legendary Japanese Lutheran exegete and seminary professor, Sennen Kishii. He convinced him to enter the Lutheran seminary in Mitaka where he did field work near a Shinto shrine known to him during his previous university studies. It was there that he forged his vocational focus as one uniquely equipped to prepare Lutherans and other seminarians to build bridges to Shinto adherents by emphasizing the preeminence of the love of Jesus Christ. Later he continued his theological education at Luther Seminary in St. Paul, Minnesota. He Joined the Tokyo Lutheran Seminary faculty in 1995.

His closing words were in praise of the mystery of the Holy Spirit's freedom to choose a Shinto Master, Sueko Mita, as a vessel of service, an uncredentialed recluse whom he nearly passed by, yet a person through whose witness his life in Christ began and who set him on a path of deep study of the Shinto religion that so dominates Japanese life and culture. He asked rhetorically whether the Holy Spirit works only through Christians and answered his question with his own affirming testimony. Uemura believes with St. Paul that no one can say that Jesus is Lord except by the Holy Spirit (I Cor 12:3). He also knows that the Holy Spirit chooses his own witnesses in surprising ways and unexpected places. His unique odyssey makes him invaluable within and beyond the Lutheran church in Japan. As if to accentuate the cloak of mystery that hovers over so much of his story, he answered my question about what has happened to Sueko Mita with her own cryptic message to Uemura: "I will suddenly disappear from the community." And she has.

It was but a few minutes' walk from our hotel in downtown Tokyo to the Tokyo Lutheran Center, the headquarters building of the Japan Lutheran Church, the other main branch of Japanese Lutherans. It was surprisingly unchanged from the building I remember from a two year internship in Japan in the early 1950's as a seminarian from the USA. Those were boom years of hope for an openness to accept Christianity as part of the new reality in Japan immediately after World War II. General Douglas MacArthur had urged American churches to send missionaries, and many came from China after the Communist government expelled them in 1947. Many Japanese themselves assumed the conquering Americans would bring Christianity with them. It had been the practice of Japanese conquerors to impose their beliefs on peoples they conquered all along the Pacific Rim. That hope proved ephemeral with the emergence of homemade Japanese religions in the 1960's which fit hand in glove with the truly conquering religion of the era—material affluence produced by an exploding Japanese economy.

A polite, hospitable young woman stepped out of her office at the Center to greet us. I asked for Rev. Masahiro Ando, the director, who was off to Hokkaido together with other key staff people of the Center. I introduced myself to Emi Okada and explained our purpose, making an on-the-spot decision to ask her if I might interview her for her story. She kindly obliged after apologizing for her English—apologies which turned out to be unnecessary as she spoke with poise and insight. Like so many Japanese in their late 20s, she grew up in a family with Buddhist/Shinto grandparents, but her parents espoused no religion at all. Her first connection with Christianity came as a student at a Lutheran high school near Tokyo. Among her teachers there was Rev. Osamu Nomura who was also pastor of the Hanno Lutheran Church. From Nomura she learned Christian basics and responded to the positive examples of faith in action she saw in her mentors during her six years of schooling. She was baptized as a young woman of 20. No one in her family attended her baptismal service, but neither did her parents oppose her becoming a Christian. She mentioned the positive impression Pastor Nomura made by visiting her home and personally explaining what baptism into the Christian life meant. This was timely since many Japanese throughout the 1990's readily lumped Christianity with the violent actions of fringe sects like the Aum people who were terrorizing the nation with bombing threats. When naming her chief blessings she began with friends who shared faith in Christ with her, not surprising as one who was the sole Christian in her family. Next was the blessing of receiving the Eucharist in fellowship with others in her congregation—not a large number but significant as a closely knit community of believers. Third on her list of blessings was attending an Asian conference of the Lutheran World Federation which was her first contact with Lutheran Christians from throughout the Pacific Rim. When asked about problems she named the minority status of Christians in Japan (2%) and the Lutheran minority within that minority. When I asked about her hopes for her future, she surprised me with her thought that she probably will not marry, but then added with a shy grin that what she meant was that she had no such plans presently. She spoke of her appreciation for her undergraduate education at the International Christian University near the Lutheran seminary in Mitaka, the school well respected by Japanese academia since its beginnings initiated by Douglas MacArthur after World War II. Almost casually she added that she especially enjoyed her major in classical literature and had mastered Greek and Latin to read the classics in their original languages.

Listening to Emi Okada taught me things held in common by Japanese Christians. She was born into a non-Christian family. Her first contact with the Gospel came through a Christian school. She was baptized without immediate family present to share its meaning. She has strong congregation loyalties and is particularly grateful for employment among fellow believers. She is keenly aware of the minority status of Christians in Japan. She is actively engaged in continuous learning both within and beyond the congregation.

Marutei Tsurunen is one of a kind in Japanese history. He is the only non-Japanese ever to become an elected member of the Japanese Diet, the Japanese counterpart to the United States House of Representatives. His blue eyes and light hair tell of his birth in Finland where he grew up and completed his degree with a social welfare major. He came to Japan in 1967 as a Lutheran missionary specializing in child welfare ministry. After mastering Japanese he became a translator of classical literature while shifting his vocational focus to educational administration. In 1979 he became a naturalized Japanese citizen and married a Japanese woman. As his interest in public office grew he combined it with agricultural and forestry concerns about which he wrote widely and spoke often. He was first elected to public office in 1992 in local government and in 2002 became a member of the upper house of the Diet.

He was easy to meet and readily hospitable as he welcomed us to his office overlooking the spacious parliament building grounds in downtown Tokyo. My first question was about his motive for moving from his Lutheran missionary beginnings to his present calling in politics. He answered that his Lutheran belief about vocation was the reason. He felt God's calling to a position of wider influence in addressing major problems of environmental conservation in one of the world's leading industrial nations. He recalled Martin Luther's teaching on the Christian calling to serve in government which is a holy work to be taken up with due reverence for God's will that all should care for the neighbor and the earth upon which all depend. Was his non-Japanese birth a political liability? He smiled when answering that losing four election campaigns before reaching the Diet taught him that he had to overcome prejudices against him by means of extraordinary persistence in demonstrating to skeptical farmers that his expertise in organic agriculture served their long range good. It was because he was smart and honest that he won office, finally, not because of his race and nationality. He told me of his book written to relate the ups and downs of his years of struggle to reach a position where he can make a difference for the good of Japan, aptly titled *Here Comes A Blue-Eyed Assemblyman*. In his ten other published books he described the varied facets of what an adopted son, an outsider-insider, experiences when traveling the unusual pathway to public service.

When it was time for our late morning visit to conclude, he excused himself after instructing a staff member to give us a packet of materials which highlight his environmental interests. We thanked him for his time and insights. He in turn thanked us for coming to his office with interests and questions he had not heard from American visitors before. I wondered when the next time would be that I would spend a morning with a Finnish born, blue eyed, naturalized Japanese citizen, environmentally concerned legislator who brings his Lutheran theological convictions to bear upon his calling.

Yoshiro Ishida, well known as a Lutheran theologian and pastor in and beyond Japan, was a torpedo factory worker in his teens when the tide was turning against Japan in the mid 1940's. His religious life centered on living for the emperor and such practices as banging a Shinto temple gong 108 times on New Year's Eve to drive off evil spirits in the coming year. At age 17 he was drafted to teach fourth grade until 1945 when World War II ended. Then an uncle helped him enter Doshisha University in Kyoto by inventing fictitious academic credentials needed for his acceptance. As a university student he began to read more in the Bible he had received from a Buddhist priest several years before. In that unlikely gift from an improbable giver he was particularly struck by Jesus' parable of the prodigal son in Luke 15, with its promise of God as a father who not only welcomed his renegade son but embraced him joyfully with an unconditional love. That Gospel seed deep within him prompted him to search out and find a Methodist missionary who baptized him and later introduced him to Sennen Kishii, an influential pastor and professor among post WW II Lutherans. He had developed a theology of the crucified and risen Jesus that grew out of the severe persecution he endured at the hands of the fanatical Japanese nationalists during the war. Through Kishii he was instructed in Martin Luther's Small Catechism as a dependable primer of the Christian faith. Kishii's influence was not only strong as a teacher. As a preacher his sermons could move young Ishida to tears on occasions. In the late 1940's, when Kishii was named to the presidency of the Lutheran seminary in Nakano, he followed his mentor to the first post-war classes in a building that, ironically, had only been spared destruction by American bombers because the Japanese secret police had arranged a cross in prominent display on its roof. When he finished the seminary, which was devoid of sufficient books, living quarters, adequate food and heat during winter, he had a serious case of tuberculosis which made him too weak for pastoral ministry. An American nurse, Annie Powers, had learned of his plight and took over his care. Two years later he was ordained, served a pastorate in northern Kyushu for five years, then came for a year of challenging graduate study in a Lutheran Seminary in the Chicago suburb of Maywood. That gave him a grounding for wider theological study and a rich career of service in teaching, pastoral ministry, as Secretary for Asia in the Lutheran World Federation, and finally as president of a Lutheran college in Kumamoto, Japan.

I met Ishida at the door of the parsonage near Nagoya, Japan, where he and his American born wife, Gloria, received us cordially. No sooner had we finished a cup of tea when he suggested that I join him for a pastoral call on an older woman in the congregation he still serves in his active retirement. We took a taxi for the fifteen minute ride, a reminder of something common in Japanese congregations—parishioners do not commonly live close to the church.

Takako Ohashi, now in her mid-70's, nearly blind and unable to walk, insisted on serving us tea as she greeted us hospitably in the tiny, single room where she lives alone. Though surrounded by spare furnishings, Miss Ohashi was uninhibited by such externals when speaking with animation about how she came to faith and service as an evangelist and Bible teacher in earlier years of her life. She was one of five children, growing up in a Buddhist family where she lost both parents by age 7. She was raised by older siblings who saw her though high school. Her first contact with Christianity was through an office worker where she was employed who was a good example of lived Christianity. She responded to a radio broadcast of the Lutheran Hour offering a correspondence course. In the early 1950's she became acquainted with a Lutheran mission congregation, housed only in a tent at first, but later housed in a small church building in which she was baptized. Her family disapproved, telling her not to attend any family gatherings now that she was a Christian. She attended a Bible School in Shizuoka, passed an exam to become a Lutheran evangelist in the Nagoya area, where she worked in handling Lutheran Hour correspondence. In the absence of a resident pastor in her congregation, the pastoral care of the congregation fell largely to her. When health problems curtailed her activity, she continued attending Sunday worship without missing for over two decades despite her ailments. Rather than complain about her personal problems she emphasized instead the happiest ten years of her life during which she presented programs of Bible stories to children in the public schools of Kariya, the Nagoya subub where both principals and parents knew and respected her. When I asked her about current matters among Lutherans in Japan, she was candid in recounting some of the terrible times she had encountered with Lutheran clergy who did not accept her as a valid co-worker in evangelism. She was glad that there are now seven ordained women serving Lutheran congregations in Japan, but added that she still worries that too much professionalism and too little evangelism work is done by Japanese Lutheran clergy, male and female. She worried that she is the last of those trained to be evangelists as she was, but then added with a sigh that her worries serve no good end. It is better to pray and entrust the church to God, grateful that she has in Yoshiro Ishida a pastor after the Lord's own heart.

Hiroko Kato lives with her family in the Yokohama suburb of Ofuna, and represents the place of women in positions of lay leadership in the church I met her in the early 1950's when she was a youngster in a family which opened its home to me for weekly Scripture study and prayer with a dozen neighbors. She was among those who were baptized and formed the nucleus of what is now a flourishing Ofuna Lutheran Church. She showed an early aptitude for music and took her university degree in organ study in Japan, followed by graduate work in choral music at Concordia University in the Chicago suburb of River Forest, where she was also part of our home and family for two years. She now serves on the Executive Council of the Lutheran Church of Japan.

How does it happen that a congregation of seventy baptized members can develop, sponsor, and administer a pre-school program of over 600 children, served by 120 teachers in three spectacular school facilities in the environs of Yokohama, Japan? The answer is the grace of God at work through a pastoral leader with a keen understanding of how much Japanese parents value early childhood education as key to their children's life trajectory. Kazuteru Matsukawa, now in his seventies, is as tireless today as he was in 1964 when, as pastor of a fledgling mission congregation, he combined pastoral leadership with a nursery school ministry. After careful study of national trends showing

Kazuteru Matsukawa

more mothers working outside the home during Japans' exploding economy in the 1960's, he made promotional visits to families and schools in his neighborhood and in 1964 opened the first congregation sponsored nursery school in his town of Ofuna with sixty children taught by six teachers. Matsukawa also saw the importance of including one English speaking foreign teacher on the staff, knowing how strongly Japanese parents want their children to learn to speak English under a teacher whose first language is English.

Matsukawa grew up in Hokkaido, Japan's northern island, as the oldest son in a Buddhist family where he was expected to carry on his father's business in the repair of watches. His life took an unexpected turn, much to the dismay of his family, just as he was completing his university degree in business management. For the first time in his life he heard a proclamation of the good news of Jesus Christ via a radio broadcast of the Lutheran Hour. He was determined to learn more about such a compelling truth and sought out a missionary sent to Sapporo by Missouri Synod Lutherans in America. Rev. Hugh Auw instructed him and later baptized him in secret rather than force him to face at that time the ire of Matsukawa's family. He worked for two years in the Lutheran Hour office in Hokkaido in the early 1960's, a period when this radio ministry of Gospel proclamation and teaching was rapidly reaching tens of thousands of Japanese listeners.

During his years in Tokyo he learned about a fledgling mission congregation in Ofuna, an hour by train south of Tokyo which he served while studying for the ministry. By 1964 he was the twelfth part time pastoral worker to come along in the dozen years since the congregation began with a Bible class in the home of the Ohta family. Yoshie Ohta, the mother in the household, was also a teacher who actively advocated a strong outreach to young children. Matsukawa stayed and now, four decades later the congregation is the administrative center of Japan's largest pre-school under Christian auspices. A tenth of the present adult membership of Ofuna Lutheran Church are alumni of the pre-school program, while many others have carried the good news of Jesus with them into their lives of worship and service elsewhere in Japan.

I asked Pastor Matsukawa how non-Christian parents regard the curriculum that integrates Bible stories, prayers, and daily worship into what their children experience daily. He answered by inviting me to attend a school sports day in which he and the teachers were personally engaged in leading the children in games, singing, and thoroughly enjoying the day as much as the children themselves. When it was snack time I noticed how naturally the children joined in the prayer of thanks for food and fun. The sports day was a sample of the basic premise underlying the four pre-schools administered by Ofuna Lutheran Church. The Gospel is not an optional add-on but integral to the whole learning experience given the children through teachers who show in their relationship to the children the love of God which they believe. Parents do not object, Matsukawa said, and added that they pay well to enroll their children. Each school has a waiting list. Those school fees form the financial support of Ofuna Lutheran Church.

An additional point of importance, Matsukawa observed, is the fact that church membership in Japan is aging. More younger believers and younger families of the faith are needed. In the Ofuna congregation over one half of the baptized are under forty, a statistic that makes it an exception in Japan. Another factor of Japanese society that Matsukawa watches is the declining birth rate and its implications for the future of pre-school outreach programs such as his. As he keeps a full schedule as pastor, school administrator, and participant in wider Lutheran church life in Japan, he has hopes for continuity in his wide-ranging ministry through his son,

Kajiyoshi Matsukawa, now the pastor of the Ofuna congregation. The Matsukawas are the only father-son pastoral team in Japan, but if these two are a symbol of the commitment and creativity of pastoral leadership to come, the future is bright.

Hirotaka Tokuhiro knows from experience how vulnerable Japanese youth are to ersatz religion as an answer to an inner longing to believe and belong. He is in his thirties, neatly dressed in shirt and tie that matched his suit (dressing down has does not play well in Japan) and hospitable in making us feel at home in a comfortable meeting room adjoining his desk as communications and mission director of the Japan Evangelical Lutheran Church. He quickly sketched his background: born in Kyushu, Japan's southern island, in a family in which his mother was active in a Pentecostal church, his father an atheist. He grew up restless with the extremes his parents symbolized, seeking but not finding, ever in search of some kind of certainty and identity for his young life. While out walking one day, not long after he had finished his high school in Osaka, he met a young person who appeared to be a Christian with her timely, tactful invitation for him to join her and others in conversation about God and belonging. It began a web of increasing involvement in what he sensed was the Reconstruction Church, better known as Moonies, which indeed it was. He had nothing by which to measure or withstand the gradual process of turning over to those who sought to own him body and soul. He was hooked after six months. He dropped any further plans for schooling and even became a group leader for a time.

Throughout this time, he said, he held onto a corner of himself that reasoned thus: God is using this weird experience to prepare him for something better ahead. His parents were, like all parents of Moonies, desperately trying to pry him loose from the cult life, and arranged a three day return home to Kyushu as a rescue operation. He slipped out of his house at midnight and returned to Osaka. But his career as a Moonie ended, finally, when he tired of his superiors constantly dunning him to collect money as the measure of Moonie truth (for which he received nothing). His breakaway point came by his own decision. He simply did not show up one evening at an event he was to lead. An eight year nightmare had ended. His greatly relieved parents accepted him as their son again.

Through his mother he heard of the theological program at the Lutheran seminary in Tokyo, and because he had gained some interest in Martin Luther prior to his Moonie years he found a Lutheran congregation and was later baptized. The one positive side of his cult experience was meeting his wife, also a devotee of Sun Myung Moon who left disillusioned but chastened by the experience. During his second year of theological study he experienced a breakthrough to inner peace and resolution. It revolved around the paradox he learned from St. Paul in Romans 7, that the believer is at one and the same time justified by Christ yet a sinner nonetheless. Then, as he put it to me, he stopped being an observer of theology and become as one immersed in the Biblical truth. He was ordained and called to serve a Kyoto Lutheran congregation, ironically enough, in the very area where he had spent earlier years as a Moonie. Later he accepted a call to a Tokyo congregation and in 2003 took on his new work as mission director.

As his chief joys he cited his service as organizer of youth camp and work camp activities. He has been to India several times with groups of Japanese youth serving the poorest of India's poor, the dalits. In this aspect of his work he is assisted by his colleague who joined us for the conversation, Noizumi Otomori, whose nickname Cindy identified her as one who spent four years in Los Angeles, becoming fluent in English. She has been to India four times leading groups of Japanese youth She spoke of these trips not only as service but as seed-planting of the Gospel in young hearts of youth who saw life differently after witnessing living conditions far different from their affluent Japanese surroundings. Both Otomori and Hirotaka were eager to lead a crew of Japanese Lutheran youth to Palestine for service projects side by side with Palestinians. With a touch of humor he commented that since Japanese travel everywhere, why not turn travel toward a deeper purpose by linking young Japanese with people and places which show God at work in his world.

An unplanned event on our last day in Japan was an experience that both touched me and tied me back to my first time in Japan as a seminary intern in Ofuna from 1951-1953. I had finished my morning coffee in a hotel dining room which was empty except for one other person and myself. He greeted me in English and I surprised him by responding in Japanese.

We struck up a conversation. One thing led to another as we conversed, but he brightened up when I mentioned the writings of Uchimura Kanzo, founder of the No-Church Movement among Japanese Christians in the 1930's and onward. Our conversation took a deeper turn as he spoke of the influence of Uchimura on him, something that he prized especially at this time when he was facing a serious illness and a hard path of treatment ahead. Before we parted with mutual good wishes he surprised me by doing something rare. He gave me a hug, then declared that our chance visit was not by chance. "Rather, we can thank our God" was his parting comment. Both the hug and his "our God" choice of words made the parting memorable.

Lutheran missionaries the United States arrived in South Korea in 1958, when the chaos and trauma of the Korean War and its aftermath were everywhere evident. A nation had been sundered at the 38th parallel, the Communist North completely sealing itself off from the South and the rest of the world. Into that dire need for healing and unity, Lutherans entered with distinctive theological and material contributions that have leavened the larger society and ecumenical Christian scene. After nearly a half century, Lutherans presently number about 5,000 baptized, served by 52 pastors in 39 congregations.

Won Yong Ji

SOUTH KOREA

Won Yong Ji is one of a kind in American Lutheran mission history. He is the first to have a leading position in planting and guiding the Lutheran mission from its beginning in the nation in which he was born. Not only was Ji a Korean by birth, with all that implies in matters of language, cultural affinity and racial identity with those served. More significantly, he lived through what millions of his fellow Koreans suffered in the first half of the 20th century—families split apart by the greatest catastrophe to befall Koreans in their long history. The nation itself was split in half, each fearful of the other, and suspended in virtually intractable mutual isolation. These profound dislocations of war and refugee survival became the anvil on which his spiritual capacities and leadership qualities were forged. His span of life, now reaching into his 80's is a roadmap for understanding how Lutherans have found a unique place in the larger picture of Christianity in Korea, the land of the Morning Calm.

He was born in 1923 in a village in northern Korea, where, early in life, he experienced the love of family from a father who taught him discipline and a mother who gave him affection. From his parents he and his siblings gained the character traits of responsibility, determination and the dream of an education and the passion to acquire it despite daunting odds. A Presbyterian missionary introduced the family to the Christian faith. Won Yong was baptized at age 17, just at the time when his dream of further schooling faded as the Japanese military occupiers shipped him off to Japan in the early 1940's as a conscript in the dangerous work of spotting American aircraft on their bombing runs over Tokyo. He was among the Koreans who survived and returned after World War II to his ancestral village in Korea, only to face the new threat of Russian troops invading from the north, bringing an ironclad Communist rule with them. Thinking that an escape to South Korea for an education would mean only temporary separation from home and family, he slipped out of his house in the dead of night in December, 1945. His younger sister's appeal for him to bring her back a pair of red shoes was the parting memory he has of the family he would not see again. Then came a harrowing escape from Russian soldiers at the 38th parallel, who caught him with a dozen others, robbed him and the others of all they had, and would have shot them on the spot but for the flashing headlights of American army jeeps close by. That was enough to distract the Russians sufficiently for Ji and his fellow escapees to scatter and run for their lives toward the Americans who received them, interrogated them, and allowed them to proceed south to Seoul and safety in South Korea.

Seoul and all South Korea offered but minimal safe haven in the winter of 1945. The 22 year old refugee became one of thousands, later to swell to millions, of those who escaped to South Korea not only from the North but from China, Japan, Manchuria, and other places as well. Penniless and with no family, he put into practice the hard-earned lessons of discipline and resourcefulness he learned in his boyhood, and managed to survive by picking up any odd jobs he could find, including tutoring high school students and helping in the Sunday School of a local church. One day while walking through the crowded streets of Seoul, he glanced upward to see clouds in the sky, which he took as a metaphor for his life, adrift without a destination. That experience moved him to a new determination to make something of his life, perhaps as a teacher or, as it turned out, as a pastor.

Through the encouragement of friends he began theological study for ministry in the Presbyterian Church at Chosun Theological College and Seminary. He graduated with honors and had his first taste of a pastoral calling by starting a mission congregation. He continued his education through further study of English in a Korean government school staffed by Americans, passed the exams for study abroad, and via the diplomatic and financial support of American military and chaplain personnel, sailed for America in March, 1948. Divine providence continued to guide his years in America through friends who helped him gain entrance to colleges in California. He read Luther and Lutheran theological works which were powerful in shaping his spiritual formation. Through the support of Lutheran laity and clergy who recognized his gifts he entered Concordia Seminary in St. Louis in the fall of 1950, just three months after the outbreak of the Korean War. Though deeply torn by the desire to return immediately to South Korea, he postponed it until he had further prepared himself by completing his studies at Concordia Seminary, plus a year under the theological faculty of the University of Heidelberg, Germany. He was ordained into the Lutheran ministry and commissioned by the Lutheran Church–Missouri Synod to return to Korea in September, 1958, to join three fledgling Missouri Synod missionaries with whom he was to work in missionary partnership, Paul Bartling, Maynard Dorow, and Kurt Voss.

Now, nearly fifty years later, it was a boon for me to meet and talk with him in the living room of his faculty apartment overlooking the campus of the Luther University in Suwon, forty five minutes south of Seoul. He has taught in the theological faculty of this school of the Korean Lutheran Church for the past twenty years, combining it with regular commutes from St. Louis where he also teaches at Concordia Seminary. I found him as warmhearted and intellectually lively as the young Korean arrival in America that I remembered from our seminary days together in St. Louis in 1951. When I asked him how Lutherans in Korea have kept faith with their founding vision of complementing rather than competing denominationally he answered in an orderly sequence: 1) production of Biblical studies that reflected a solid Law/Gospel method of interpreting Scripture, 2) emphasis upon the sacraments of Holy Baptism and Holy Communion as means of Divine grace, 3) prayer and forms of worship that reflect the centuries of Christian tradition, 4) the relevance of the Epistle of James—somewhat surprising for a Lutheran, since Luther himself labeled it an epistle of straw—as vital for maturity in faith for Korean Christianity which has expanded outward rapidly but needs more inward depth, 5) social ministry of the Gospel related to the increasing secularism in South Korea today, 6) the centrality of the Gospel in relating to new and non-Christian religions in Korea.

He also spoke warmly of the close and fruitful partnership with the American missionaries who were fellow leaders from the early years of Lutheran work onward. Paul Bartling was instrumental in establishing the Lutheran Hour and Bethel Bible series as tools of evangelism useable by all churches in the land. Maynard Dorow and Hilbert Riemer were veterans of over forty years of missionary leadership, especially in theological education. Both have served with distinction as president of the seminary and the theological college. He wondered aloud where the counterparts of these long term missionaries are today, those who come not for one or several years but devote their lives to loving the Korean people while serving them, who master the language and learn the culture so vital for effective ministry, who by their foreign citizenship witness to the global people of God among whom there is no east nor west. Where, indeed, are they? Now that Korean Christian missionaries are serving throughout the world, there is still need for long term missionaries from overseas to leaven the churches of Korea, and Lutherans need to be among them. Ji reflected on his years of service with the Lutheran World Federation as secretary for Asian Lutherans, living with his wife in Geneva and working among burgeoning Lutheran churches throughout the Pacific rim. This broadened his ecclesial horizons and deepened his sense of Lutherans as a leaven in the one, holy, catholic, and apostolic church confessed in the ecumenical creeds that began in the western church but have been adopted by the faithful throughout the world.

What problems in the Korean Lutheran Church concern him? He spoke candidly of things which disturb the whole Lutheran community and upset the faith of the common people. He named power struggles and scandals of financial mismanagement as a blight upon the church. He noted that Lutherans are a minority but should not try to be mega-churches of tens of thousands of members such as are found among the well publicized Pentecostal and Presbyterian churches of Korea. Lutherans must work on quality not quantity by concentrating on depth in maturity of faith well anchored in the Biblical Gospel rather than emotional excesses. What Lutherans have to contribute is the theology of the cross, based on God's revealing himself in his crucified Son rather than a theology of glory that obscures the cross. Here is solid ground on which the faithful can stand in contrast to the traditional Korean concept of the opposing play of *ying and yang* life forces which offer no solid ground. Critical days of challenge lie ahead, Ji stressed, formed not only by nuclear threat from the North, but enclosed in the more subtle forms of western materialism rampant in the land. The average Korean annual income is between ten and fifteen thousand US dollars, but, are people happier? He learned otherwise, he commented, adding reminiscences from his own childhood. The rapid growth in Christian numbers during and after the Korean War has slowed. Much of it was fueled by the influx of refugees from North Korea. That generation has passed. New competition has emerged from an older religion like Buddhism, which now imitates Christian methods with hymns, choirs, and television outreach.

We walked from his flat on faculty row to one of the campus dormitory meeting rooms where one of Dr. Ji's former students, now a Korean pastor, introduced himself to me as my Korean host for my visit. Jun-Hyun Kim is in his late 30's, dressed immaculately, warm in manner, fluent in English, and generous in giving his time and hospitality in organizing conversations with Koreans I should not miss. His own faith story had some unique turns that helped me understand more of what students experience in Korea. Entrance exams for university admission are notoriously stressful. Kim attended a church-sponsored retreat designed to help students settle their nerves and be at their academic best for the ordeal of qualifying. It was in that setting that he gained far more than settled nerves to write exams; he gained a new life, begun in Christ's acceptance as one fully known, fully forgiven. His conversion was not well received by his parents, who wanted him to study law. He had failed his entrance exam. Kim later saw that setback as providential, showing him his lack of maturity for university level study. He went to the army for his two years of required service, and upon completion took the advice of his pastor to apply for theological study at Luther College, an institution that his Presbyterian pastor had heard about through the Bethel Bible series which the Korean Lutheran Church had shared with thousands of Protestant clergy in South Korea. His parents were dubious about a pastoral future for their son, but the pastor's act of personally visiting them to explain the excellent reputation of Luther College and Seminary put them at ease. He completed four years of theological study in 1995, then traveled to America for another four year period of study in St. Louis, then finally a year of English language concentration at St. Louis University and a graduate degree in Old Testament studies at Concordia Seminary. His wife was with him throughout this time, with their young son and another son born in St. Louis. His father helped with support for his overseas study, an important mark of parental progress in accepting Kim's conversion and vocational training. While in St. Louis he began work among Koreans living across the Mississippi River in Belleville, Illinois. He had recently returned to Korea and was ordained only a few weeks before I met him. His assignment was as an assistant pastor in a congregation near Seoul. With his graduate work in Biblical studies completed he is open to combining seminary teaching with pastoral ministry. A few days with him gave me the feeling that he will be an asset in either role, or both.

The Lutheran Church Korea (LCK hereafter) was established as a national church in 1971, just fourteen years after its missionary beginnings as a partner church with the Lutheran Church–Missouri Synod. During the next three decades it had established the Lutheran Hour as a major radio evangelism outreach throughout the country, and enrolled some 700,000 lay and clergy participants in the Bethel Series program of Scriptural study, founded its own government-accredited theological college and seminary for the training of workers in the LCK, and moved from American missionary church leadership to Korean leadership.

Hyun-Sub Um, the 60 year old president of the LCK, has a life profile similar to many Lutherans who have helped grow the LCK from its missionary beginnings. He was born into a non-Christian family, felt the tragedy of the Korean War early in his childhood through the loss of his father, first heard the Gospel as a Presbyterian Sunday School lad, made his initial contact with Lutheranism through enrollment in a night school theological study program combined with his daytime university classes, then shifted to full time seminary study and ordination into the pastoral ministry of the LCK. After years of pastoral service at Trinity, the mother congregation of the LCK and the location of the administrative offices of the LCK in downtown Seoul, he was elected president. His cordial welcome in the reception area outside of his office included a brief overview of his life story which, he noted, overlapped with the past half century of unprecedented growth of Christianity in South Korea. In 1905 Christians numbered .05% of the Korean population. Now, a century later, 42% of the 48.3 million South Koreans identify themselves as Christians. The showcase congregation, often cited as the largest in the world, is the Full Gospel Church in Seoul with its membership of one half million (some claim it is closer to a million). Um, while respectful of the passionate evangelistic leadership of its charismatic pastor, Paul Cho, said that Lutherans serve best by contributing quality theological influence rather than compete in quantitative numbers. His own life story was an example. It was sound Biblical doctrine centered in Christ's justifying grace that drew him to his calling and still constitutes what Lutherans have to offer to Christ's people in Korea.

His concerns were pointed, however, about present challenges facing the LCK, which is stuck in no-growth doldrums and needs to discern new forms of evangelism for new times as well as mature in stewardship toward greater self-support among the two thirds of its congregations not yet at that level. Um named three historical factors in understanding the exponential growth of Christianity after 1945: the identity of the Korean churches with the nationalist struggle for liberation from the oppressive Japanese military occupation from 1905 on, the servant role of churches in meeting massive survival needs of the millions of fellow Korean refugees fleeing the Communist invasion of the northern half of Korea in the early 1950's, and the relevance of 120 years of strong Protestant schools and universities whose graduates have leavened Korean society at all levels.

That explosive church growth has now tapered off, he explained. Um documented the comment by citing the two million member decline in

Protestant church membership recently, something he attributed to an overly subjective theology centered on personal experience that lacks strength in sustaining faith and discipleship from generation to generation. Another factor is the pressures of living under the constant threat of attack and destruction from the North. Lutherans faithful to the Gospel centered in Christ's justifying grace have a treasure to share, Um said, and he spoke of ways the LCK needs to step up its efforts to do it: more vigorous production and dissemination of sound theological materials and Bible studies aimed at the new generation of secularized young Koreans, plus greater congregational outreach to youth in the middle and high school level. The stewardship challenge was made visual as he showed me the model of a proposed multipurpose high rise building complex on land owned by the LCK for years, now greatly multiplied in value in the booming real estate market of downtown Seoul. It was within sight of his desk, a daily reminder of the wide range of the daunting tasks and promising new ventures that are before him and the entire LCK in these times.

"Sometimes I hate this job" was the candid observation, offered partly in humor and partly with an honest sigh by Il Young Park, the president of Luther College in Suwon, a forty five minute drive south of Seoul. Now in his third year as president he expressed the loneliness at the top known by all leaders; in his case it is heightened by responsibilities in a forthcoming major expansion of LCK theological education. The project has a typically Korean-size scope, to increase the student body by five-fold, from 150 to 750), the faculty accordingly, and the Luther College academic buildings and dormitories on the prime twenty-five acre campus which is now only one third filled. The 50 million dollar plan, he explained, is subject to rigorous government regulations for academic accreditation and the educational facilities that go with it. The size of the task helped me appreciate his stated longing for a return to earlier, easier days when his primary vocation was teaching systematic theology in the classroom, while others lay awake nights with expansion worries. This conversation took place in a restaurant where he hosted us in a small room off the main western style dining area, featuring fine Korean food and tasteful ambience—all thoroughly enjoyable except for sitting cross-legged on an immaculately polished floor with my knees hard to fit under the short legged table.

Kim's mother was an ardent Methodist Christian who shaped his early life with pre-dawn prayers and regular Scriptural devotions, the spiritual matriarch in a household where his father neither affirmed nor opposed the Christian faith. Both his parents had left everything behind when fleeing North Korea as refugees who had to struggle to make ends meet in Seoul where they settled. He grew up in poverty, with meager resources for a university education toward the pastoral ministry to which he felt called as a high school student. Just at that time, in 1966, the newly formed Lutheran Theological Academy began night courses in theology and Biblical studies. His Methodist pastor heard of it and urged Park to enroll. He was the first student to complete the course. From there he excelled at Hanshin University. With support from a Lutheran scholarship program, did further graduate work in systematic theology, completed his mandatory two years of military service, and after ordination in the LCK served a congregation for five years, after which he went to Concordia Seminary in St. Louis for two years and a Masters Degree. In 1991 he returned to teach at the Lutheran seminary. Luther University is the result of combining theological education with courses of study in the humanities, counseling, social work, the performing arts, and other areas in which it qualifies as a university. Dr. Il Young Park looks younger than his mid-fiftiess. His gifts are needed for his challenging position at the vortex of Lutheran higher education in South Korea. He has a personal manner that combines modesty with warmth, plus a memory for things like my previous visit to the campus soon after its dedication in 1982. The salt and pepper thatch of hair on his head belies the demands of his daily calling. When asked how he is handling them, his answer began with "I pray for God to be our strength and sufficiency" and said it with a note of trust in his voice that is a fitting commentary on the half century of Lutheran life and witness in a Korea that will not be defeated.

Spending a Sunday at Dobong Lutheran Church in the greater Seoul area was an experience of an LCK congregation in full stride from early morning till late afternoon. At 5 a.m. the pastor of the congregation and a handful of very early risers were in the sanctuary for a pre-dawn liturgy of Scripture, song, and intercessory prayer. This is customary for virtually all congregations in South Korea, not only on Sunday but on each day of the week. Korean Christians, at least those we met, are among the most disciplined and impassioned in prayer to be found anywhere, and Korean Lutherans were quick to adopt the pre-dawn custom of prayer from the beginning. All night prayer marathons are known throughout Korean Christian churches but not among Lutherans in my brief stay.

Reaching BoDong Lutheran Church took nearly an hour by car from the seminary campus, along an express highway running through cluster after cluster of high rise apartment and condo buildings that had once been low income housing. Now they are expensive places to live as the metropolitan area of greater Seoul expands outward, increasing the gap between the haves and have-nots in the process. Dotting the landscape everywhere were steeples capped by crosses, some put up temporarily on rooftops of commercial buildings in which smaller congregations have rented rooms for worship until they can afford to build. Other crosses adorned huge church buildings, mega-church complexes purchased and put up before land prices skyrocketed. Immense, bright red, neon-lit crosses are prominent on the walls and rooftops of these churches; seeing them when they light up the night sky is a visual reminder of the growth of the Christian population in the land.

The BoDong church has neither a temporary steeple nor a mega-size neon cross over it; its appeal as a building symbolizes the place Lutherans occupy in the larger picture of Korean Christianity—stable rather than temporary, modest rather than ostentatious. Just off the entrance-way and up one story is the flat where the pastor and family live. Pastor Eun-seob Kim and his wife came down to meet us just as our van eased into one of the three parking places (parking is now holy ground for urban churches worldwide) that substitute for a mini-lawn. His hospitality made us feel welcome immediately as he showed around the sanctuary and introduced us to several parishioners who were there early, but none as early as Pastor Kim himself. He had been up since 5 a.m. for a pre-dawn service with a handful of those who come to pray, sing, and hear Scripture.

Kim is a former business man (a banker for eight years), whose conversion to Christianity and vocation as a Lutheran pastor had unusual origins. His wife, whom he met during their university years, came from a strong

Christian family. Her father saw in his son-in-law qualities for the pastoral calling and encouraged him to move from his well paying bank position to study theology at the Lutheran Theological Academy. He took the risk of faith, not to the pleasure of his own parents who as non-Christians were not so much bothered by their son's conversion as the prospect of the loss of his banker affluence to help support them later in life. He told me of these things in brief snatches of Sunday morning time, including tea served by Mrs. Kim in their living room, while preparing for the main morning Service.

As the 11 o'clock hour approached, Pastor Kim donned his white alb with green stole and stationed me, the preacher of the day, beside him as we stood together at the back of the nave. Lined up before us was the choir of eighteen singers, ten men, eight women, robed in white gowns. Ahead of them, with the processional cross in hand, was a tall lad of high school age prepared to lead the processional down the aisle to begin the service. For a half hour previous the sanctuary was gradually filling up as those arriving took their places and joined in singing with full voice and mostly from memory the many gospel songs known and dear to them, without need of the Protestant hymnal in the pew racks (which was sparse in hymns from the Lutheran tradition). The liturgy was traditionally Lutheran in form but Korean Lutheran at several points. Two women—elders, I was told—were robed in special vestments and supervised the receiving of the offerings. I noticed that most present had their envelopes prepared and ready for the purple velvet receptacles as they were passed from row to row. The offerings were received by the deacon at the altar, who prayed a lengthy prayer after receiving them. Likewise the pastor prayed an *ex corde* prayer, which I was told included special petitions for special needs, in preparation for Holy Communion. Music, both by the choir and congregation, was abundant and spirited. My homily was translated paragraph by paragraph by Pastor Kim who had asked for a copy of it several days before. From time to time the parishioners responded with a softly murmured Amen or an affirming nod to themes which resonated. Following the benediction Pastor Kim introduced both Luekings and presented us with a thoughtful gift. When asked to respond I spoke my one word Korean vocabulary, *komapsumnida*, or thank you. That brought smiles and applause for its brevity on a Sunday when all were ready for lunch and four more hours of activity ahead.

The lunch that followed featured *kimchi*, cooked cabbage with spices that is the staple of Korean cuisine, both delicious and healthy, and made all the more enjoyable by the friendly talk and laughter around the room. We were seated alongside a lay member with a doctorate in agriculture, a mother and daughter eager to talk about America where the daughter would soon be studying, and the daughter's boyfriend who had to work at being enthused over the distance that would separate them for several years. The afternoon Celebration Of Praise was a special event occurring often throughout the year. Various groups of various ages took part, one after the other, singing to keyboard and guitar accompaniment, some of the music richly melodic in the Korean style, some sacred, some happy-clappy and all of it offered to the delight of those filling the pews. At the end of nearly two hours, a good natured rating followed. The prize went to the men's chorus whose gig started out with a somber Hallelujah, then broke into fast-paced jazz, complete with text and lively gestures, a hands-down winner.

The fabled Korean capacity for persistence in doing things they value came home to me at the 4 o'clock hour. Instead of concluding the day that had begun at nine that morning, several dozen stayed on for a question/answer session with me on my global journey to date. Their questions and comments were thoughtful, especially as older Koreans present related my impressions of the church in Japan from which I had just come to their own memories of harsh experiences they or their parents had endured during the Japanese occupation prior to 1945. The freedom from revenge that is the fruit of Christian forgiveness was prominent in their observations and all agreed to the importance of further personal contacts with Japanese Christians, Lutheran and otherwise.

By six in the evening it was time to conclude the day with prayer led by one of the elders. I was struck by the fullness of that Sunday at BoDong Lutheran Church and wish that it could be a pattern for similar congregational fellowship among people of faith everywhere. As I thanked Pastor Kim for his hospitality from morning till evening I asked him if he was tired by the non-stop nature of his pastoral activities since before dawn that morning and ready for a quiet remainder of the Sabbath. He smiled as he took my arm and explained that there was one thing more to enjoy before we parted, supper at a Pizza Hut nearby. With that we were off with his family, amazed at their unflagging cheerfulness at the end of a memorable day.

Interviews with seminarians provided a cross-section of the varied backgrounds of candidates and the diverse experiences that shape the context for their current theological study toward a pastoral future in the Korean Lutheran Church.

Jung-Ho Choi is 40, unlike the average seminarian in age but much more unlike his fellow students in his weird odyssey to conversion and vocation. In his early teens he first heard the Gospel from his young friends. But inner demons kept troubling him with a persistent question "Who are you?" for which he could find no answer. His quest took him to Christians and Buddhists, to political activism and finally to years of working on a tuna fishing boat that took him everywhere but to an answer to his inner anguish. On his third try at suicide he waited till midnight to jump from his fishing boat into the sea off Guam. To this day he cannot account for his survival as anything but the grace of God at work through crew members of a passing boat who plucked him from the waters at dawn the next morning. Renewed contact with siblings helped him rediscover his selfhood, but the primary power that helped him gain his new self was Christ whose answer to his long bedeviling question was: "You a forgiven man." After a brief foray of several months on a Christian mission in the Philippines he returned to Korea, and found Luther University on the internet. He gained entrance at Luther College and Seminary based on a transcript that was minimal academically but maximal in experience. He is married, the father of two children, is in his sixth year of theological study, and expressed a desire to establish a specialized ministry of healing of the whole person, built around a pastoral counseling center. He brings rare credentials toward fulfilling that vision.

Byung-Hue Ko, 34, was converted through the witness of Campus Crusade workers. He majored in surveying and was on his way in a career when a huge iron crane fell on him and severely injured his leg. He spent months in the hospital recovering; when released he saw a sign board announcing theological studies at Luther Colllege where he applied and was accepted in 2002. His parents, while unhappy about his decision as non-Christians, nevertheless did not block his intentions. He was particularly drawn to Luther for its emphasis on the theological foundations of Law and Gospel, justification by grace through faith, and the theology of the cross. He had Full Gospel Church years of membership in his late teens and twenties, but found its subjectivism lacking. He has completed his third year of study at Luther and spoke with eagerness about his coming year of internship. The LCK will assign him a church where he anticipates duties in teaching Sunday school, youth work, worship leadership, home Bible studies, dawn prayer meetings, and occasional preaching under a supervisory pastor.

Sung Yuan Rohm is 28, single, brought up as a Christian family in Seoul, who was deeply influenced by a pastor in charge of his college age student group who was skilled as a teacher of Scripture. In his last year of college his pastor took him to a clergy conference where the sincerity of faith among the participants helped prepare him to grasp the heart of the Gospel in Paul's Ephesians 2:8 witness to salvation as God's undeserved gift. Riveted by that key passage, he followed the encouragement of his Presbyterian pastor to transfer his university credits and enter Luther as a junior. He has now finished his undergraduate studies and is into the second of his four year course toward a Master of Divinity degree and readiness for ordination. When asked about challenges facing the church in today's Korea he noted that the rapid growth of earlier years is tapering off. As South Koreans grow more affluent, the temptation to idolize material abundance grows. His sense was that too many Koreans seek an overly subjective religious experience. The "I" becomes central. Luther's emphasis upon the objective basis of Christ—for –us is needed as the LCK contribution to the wider health of churches in his homeland. His comments were thoughtful as we spoke and it was clear that he takes his faith and calling seriously. What may be ahead for him in ten years? I asked. After pausing to think, he spoke of an anticipated shrinkage in conversions as the mission of the Gospel faces harder times ahead. But he cited Ephesians 2:8 once again as the motive for hope as he looked forward to serving God and people in the future.

Hilbert Riemer has devoted his adult years in mission service in Korea, both as a full time Lutheran missionary as well as partial service as a United States military chaplain to American forces stationed on the Korean peninsula. He is one of a diminishing number of today's missionaries who, with their spouses leave their homeland, go abroad, learn the language, absorb the culture, proclaim the Gospel, teach the Biblical faith, help establish an indigenous church, train gifted nationals for leadership, and all this to "work themselves out of a job"—as the slogan of the missionary's vocation puts it. Why are there fewer such missionaries than fifty or more years ago? The rise of nationalism in countries formerly colonized by westerners has closed the door to lifetime missionaries. The emergence of indigenous leadership, the very goal of the mission, accounts for the sea-change in relationships between first and third world Christians in the global church. The current pattern of sending short term missionaries to assist in specialized tasks means fewer stay long enough to learn the language and identify deeply with the culture and church in that place. Furthermore, the more recent and increasing numbers of Asian and African churches sending missionaries to the secularized continents of Europe and North America illustrate the two-way traffic of exchange that replaces the one-way mission assumptions of a century ago.

These factors were not abstract but lived realities in the person of the man who welcomed me for conversation in his Luther University office. As I listened to Riemer, I thought of his American missionary colleagues who had preceded his Korean arrival by several years in the late 1950's, Paul Bartling and Maynard Dorow. The global church is poorer for the retirement of these long term missionaries whose faithfulness bears witness to the global character of Christ's family of believers across the face of the earth. They defy the caricature of the missionary as the vanguard of a western imperialism that still burdens Third World peoples. Their counterparts are harder and harder to find today and that made me all the more desirous of making the most of the conversation with Riemer while I had the opportunity.

I asked if the initial vision of Lutherans as a uniting movement within the body of Christ in Korea has held true as the LCK nears its fiftieth year. He answered Yes—though imperfectly. His documentation of how Lutherans moved from a "clean" beginning (not competitive with but contributing to the larger Christian good in Korea) included these factors. Lutherans demonstrated by fraternal outreach that they were not suspect as crypto-Roman Catholics. With strong emphasis on Christ's justifying grace,

Lutherans became a leaven amidst Reformed legalism and Pentecostal excesses. Early on, the Lutheran Hour effectiveness through radio evangelism brought a boon to all Christian churches; listeners were regularly encouraged to seek a local congregation for a spiritual home. The Bethel Series, through the late LCK president, Won Song Ji, was trusted and widely used because the Lutherans who offered it were a statistical minority of a few thousand baptized and no threat to the older, established churches. LCK theological education was ecumenical from the outset, receiving students from other denominations and enriching them through its graduates. The criteria for admission all along has been the certification of baptism and a letter of recommendation from a local pastor. The LCK has fostered ecumenical participation and began a new umbrella organization for greater cooperation among church leaders. At present the LCK does not ordain women to the pastoral ministry, and Riemer added—at least not yet. The church body has said neither Yes nor No to the matter. In its comparatively young life, Riemer surmised, the LCK has been wise not to take on more than it can handle. Lutherans are continuing to deepen in maturity in order to continue to be a leavening and unifying presence in an increasingly secularized society.

Qi Gui Shi is a man in his late seventies, the semi-retired pastor of Mu En (Flowing Grace) Church, a historic, multi-story brick building prominently located on priceless real estate opposite People's Square in downtown Shanghai. We were easy for him to spot as the only non-Chinese among those arriving for what we learned was "Honor Those Over Eighty Sunday." He summoned his granddaughter to guide us to the last seats available in the sanctuary that accommodates 1,600. She found a bilingual hymnal from which we sang along in English during the ninety minute service that included Scripture readings, prayers, a sermon by Pastor Shi on honoring the elderly, and anthems sung by the twenty-four voice women's choir. The theme of the day was highlighted when teen age youth escorted a half dozen octogenarians to the altar platform where each spoke briefly, followed by another from their number who sang "Nearer My God To Thee" in memory of the millions of Chinese lost during the catastrophic Cultural Revolution from 1966-1977. What that era meant for Pastor Shi and his wife was among the topics I asked about as we and our wives sat together for tea and conversation in a church reception room after the service.

Gui Shi and church members

CHINA

Knowing that our time to talk was brief—there are four Sunday services in this congregation of 8,000 members—I got right to the point by asking Gui Shi what an average day is like in his ministry. He launched into it but was soon off on a tangential observation that "the younger pastors don't work as hard as we did, now that prosperity has come to Shanghai." From there he diverted into more of his own story of his birth in 1929 (the year the church in which we sat was built), his graduation from the seminary in the late 1950's, and his coming to the pastoral staff of Mu En Methodist Church in 1966 when the chaotic decade of Mao Zedong's Cultural Revolution began. He recalled the day when a gang of young toughs burst into the church, announced themselves as the Red Brigade vanguard of the new China, and smashed the piano and organ before stealing whatever they could carry out the door. During the thirteen years that followed, the church remained locked and empty. Shi was deprived of his pastorate and forced to work making furniture in a plant in Shanghai. His wife fled the city to her parents' home in a rural area.

He could have gone on at length about those years but chose instead to describe the Sunday in September, 1979, when the church was re-opened. People began gathering outside the doors well before dawn for the re-opening service. He wondered how they knew of the re-opening since the membership records had long since been destroyed, but guessed that the few he could reach passed the news on to others. Six hundred people came on that memorable Sunday. Shi recast the scene as though it were yesterday: scores of people embracing each other with tears of joy, looking at each other incredulously, many asking in astonishment, "Are you still alive?" The opening hymn, "Joyful, Joyful We Adore Thee" needed no accompaniment, nor was any available, as people sang from memory without the hymnals that were no more. His recall of that day was more than anecdotal. It was his version of what happened throughout China as the late 1970's as Xiao Peng's reforms enabled beleaguered Christians to assemble in re-opened churches to hear Good News after the dark years of denunciation from 1966–1976, the decade of the so-called Cultural Revolution.

With an eye on my watch, I switched to other questions which he answered in tantalizingly truncated phrases. I asked what freedom means for Christian in China today. He answered that the main problem now isn't Communist oppression but the runaway consumerism that is sweeping the land. I asked him the clarify the present church situation in the People's Republic of China. He answered that Roman Catholics are divided between those loyal to Rome and those who cooperate with the state. Protestants, too, are divided by registered and non-registered churches. The registered churches, also known as the Three Self Patriotic Movement (TSPM), are self-governing, self-supporting, and self-propagating, have a measure of freedom under the government that varies according to geography. The non-registered churches (which emerged in the late 1940's in opposition to the TSPM policy of cooperation with the government) meet in the homes of believers and are generally more conservative theologically. Shi explained that the two groups are not as divided as before. The real split is between prospering city congregations and rural churches mired in poverty. I asked about his hopes for Christians in China's future. He answered that they are high, noting that the estimated seventy million (some put the number well over one hundred million) Chinese Christians already equal the number of Communist Party members and will surpass it in a decade. We were out of time. He had to meet a couple preparing for marriage. I thanked him for a memorable Sunday morning in one of the flagship congregations in the People's Republic of China.

We took a cab through Shanghai's afternoon traffic to the impressive campus of the Concordia International School Shanghai (CISS), where Tang Xiao Hong is the school nurse. We had met her several days earlier during a conference of Asian Lutheran educators and were intrigued by her nickname "Starry." She loves the art of Vincent van Gogh whose famous painting of a starry night so caught her fancy that she made it part of her name. Her story is representative of many younger Chinese Christians to whom we listened. She had no religion during her upbringing in Shanghai, but how she came to sense what she was missing occurred in an unusual way. As a nurse working on the obstetrics ward of a large Shanghai hospital she had come into contact with a new mother. The American woman's husband surprised her when saying how much his newborn son meant as a gift—and here she quoted his words that struck a responsive chord—"from the loving Father of us all." As she learned to know the couple better, they asked her if she would receive a gift Bible from them. She agreed, and heard another phrase from them that caught her attention. It was to read the Bible "as a love letter from the Father whose heart is open to all." Their further advice was two-fold. The first was not to get stuck in parts that baffled her but concentrate on the Bible's main message of God's saving love. The second was to read the Bible in the company of those who put its truth into practice. A Chinese Christian friend invited her to a Bible study where she not only heard words but began to see changed lives among those around her. When she read the Gospel story of why Jesus freely accepted death on the cross, she wept at the thought that he was 'God's love letter with her own name on it." She said all this without embarrassment. Since that time she has grown in awareness of new signs of faith at work in her life following her baptism.

She now continues to worship on Sundays when she is not on duty and mentioned her enjoyment of ongoing fellowship in her Bible study group.

At this point she asked if we might like to meet a doctor in her fellowship circle who had a unique story to tell. Twenty minutes after her cell phone call to assure the doctor of our interest in meeting him, pediatric oncologist Stephen Liang arrived. He was still in his hospital scrubs (green cotton slacks and coat), and after brief introductions, he highlighted his rural upbringing as the youngest child in a family with his four sisters, smiling as he told us that he was "pretty much spoiled as you might guess." He excelled in elementary and high school, went on to medical school, and after a three year residency in pediatric oncology was licensed for practice. It was during a later term of special studies at the Duke University Medical School in the USA that he had his first contact with Christians whose approach to medicine as a calling under God showed Liang something essential that he had missed. "It was loving my patients—something that simple— but it was never mentioned in medical school" he said. The impact of his medical colleagues' faith revealed to him what he knew he needed, especially in his specialty of working with children terminally ill with leukemia and with their families. He returned to China to move beyond, as he put it, "a resentment of sick children because I could not heal them to loving them with Father's love that healed in ways deeper than a medical cure." His way of speaking of God as Father, anarthrously, as in "Father called me to Jesus through those Duke doctors" or "Isn't Father amazing in his love for sick kids!" was new to me and it struck me with its emphasis on the intimacy of his trust in God. He then opened the laptop he brought and show an eight minute DVD he had made himself. Entitled "A Window To Heaven" it showed the faces of children he served (and one of whom he adopted) as his voice was heard in comment on each child. At my request Liang transferred the disc to my laptop I have shown it often to audiences elsewhere.

We came to Shanghai to meet attendees at a conference of the Asian Lutheran Education Association hosted by Concordia International School Shanghai. The school itself has an intriguing story. It was begun with major cooperation from Lutheran educators in Hong Kong who brought an expertise gained from their years at the Hong Kong International Lutheran High

School. The government of the Peoples Republic of China welcomed the venture because it wanted a model of western educational excellence available to the children of international corporation executives (including General Motors Asia, Dow Chemical, Texas Instruments, Kodak, and others). In ten years the school has grown from twenty two students to eleven hundred, with a waiting list of applicant families ready and able to pay the annual tuition of $20,000. During a break in the conference program, I found the man I most wanted to see as a key person in founding Concordia International School Shanghai.

Fred Voigtman sat down with me during a lunch break in the conference to tell me the story of how it happened that a group of Lutherans, with no official standing in the Peoples Republic of China, were able to buy property and build the school into its present form. He told it in an understated manner, with little reference to himself as the essential liaison to the Chinese government. He is a modest man, shorter than average height, and his only exterior distinguishing mark is his thatch of jet black hair and matching mustache. That

Fred Voigtman

surface impression changed, however, once he started revealing the passion, intelligence, and rare skills he has developed in his fifty years of life to date. He is American-born, the son of a Lutheran pastor and grandson of a Lutheran school teacher. His immersion in Lutheran education began in kindergarten and extended through his graduation from the Valparaiso University law school. He was an Air Force officer assigned to intelligence during the Vietnam War and told me how much he hated the year of intensive Chinese language study he had signed up for. That year of language study proved purposeful beyond the discomfort it caused, however, beginning with his military intelligence assignment in Taiwan. That, in turn, led to frequent trips between Taipei and Washington to learn the intricacies of diplomatic relationship with the People's Republic of China. His wife, Paula, turned their Taiwanese posting into an opportunity to found an adoption agency for orphans, a work which eventually led to an early retirement from the Air Force and new purposes for his fluency in Mandarin Chinese and his diplomatic/legal experience with the PRC government. As a born and bred Missouri Synod Lutheran he was well known to those who had made the Lutheran high school in Hong Kong a pre-eminent school; he joined them as they collaborated on the new school in Shanghai. He was among the few persons equipped linguistically and tactically to thread his way through the bureaucratic maze of the Chinese Ministry of Education –an eight year marathon—to finally convince the Chinese authorities that it was in their best interest to permit Lutherans to do what they do well— build a quality school for the families of international businesses arriving in increasing numbers after 1996. Voigtman told how me how he overcame the government's resistance. He showed them the names of the those willing to serve on the school's board of directors when permission would be granted. It was a list representing a cross-section of blue chip corporations from America. The PRC government wanted the economic boost such companies would bring. Capitalist profits prevailed over Communist political ideology and the governmental permission was granted. When the USA Missouri Synod Lutheran headquarters could not muster the funds needed for the purchase of land and building construction, Voigtman, and his fellow Lutherans from Hong Kong, found the needed money and Concordia International School Shanghai was born. In its first decade, Voigtman stressed, the school's commanding reputation was established by its educational philosophy of high academic standards joined with a strong community spirit between teachers and students. These values were carried out by a carefully chosen educational staff that understood the necessity to avoid proselytism in a student body of diverse religious backgrounds. Voigtman's dream is that the Shanghai Concordia can become a model for similar schools located within the three hundred mile radius around Shanghai where three hundred million Chinese live (more than the total population of the United States). In his view, Christian schools are a potent leaven for widespread good amidst the problems of rapidly surging urbanization in eastern China. More than that, such schools demonstrate the Good News of Jesus Christ by their quality of education, motivation of teachers, and commitment to students. He summed up his vision by quoting the six words he overheard as a fourteen year old student was showing his parents the CISS campus: "This school has changed my life." Persons of Fred Voigtman's depth and capacities are rare, I thought after listening to him, but such surprises are among the hallmarks of Divine grace all through the centuries since 635 A.D. when the first Christian missionaries reached China.

Ruth Zhang Yu, 35, is a seminarian nearing the completion of her five year course at Union Protestant Seminary in Nanjing, the premier theological school of the TSPM. Her specialty is rural ministry, in her case among Chinese who must survive on $15 a month or less. Most will never travel more than a few miles from their farm or village. In such regions, money for school fees for children depend

Dean Lueking, Ruth Zhang Yu, and Zhang Jing

on whether a rice crop fails or flourishes. She explained that her people represent that half of the Chinese population left out of the booming urban prosperity widely touted by the government. Through an interpreter she told me of ambitious arrangement to train laity to lead her village congregation (which now numbers 4,000) in southwest China while she finishes her seminary training. Her husband remains back home where he is in the army. She explained that he, like many Chinese Christians who are soldiers, keeps a low profile in order to avoid expulsion both from the army and from the Communist Party in which he must keep a token membership. When ordained, she will be among the four hundred women pastors in the church, who, with their 32,000 male pastoral counterparts serve the twenty million Christians of the TSPM, the statistic quoted by the government. Unofficial estimates put the number at between fifty and sixty million believers.

Ruth was one among a dozen seminarians we interviewed in the student body of 250 men and women at the Nanjing seminary. She came from a Christian family and could remember when her parents would open their home as a house church during the tense times of the Cultural Revolution. She did not consider herself a believer until a turning point changed her life. She had suffered a painful ankle injury and sought out the local Buddhist priest for healing. The priest treated her according to Buddhist tradition, which was to set out a bowl of water and after stirring it, sprinkle it on her ankle. But the pain only grew worse. She told her mother of her plight and was instructed to kneel in prayer, repent of her sins, and trust Jesus Christ to help her. In that moment, she said, she experienced what she described as an all-embracing, holy presence as the pain left her. She was baptized and began attending a local Bible school. Even before finishing her course, she was teaching up to four hundred people each week from among the local migrant workers whose hunger for acceptance and belonging drew them to the Word. Her TSPM congregation anticipates her return after her graduation, she said, and added that many rural congregations without a pastor share that hope. Meanwhile, she sends them Bible correspondence course materials plus directions on how to carry out pastoral functions at weddings and funerals, which are major events in which the believers participate in practical ways. She cited the example of how her members follow up after a funeral. Once a week a delegation from the congregation visits the family to comfort and encourage the bereaved, until the family releases the visitors from further visits. Many of the believers she serves are farmers who can manage their time for such lay ministries better than urban people she knows in Nanjing. Among the dozen seminarians with whom I spoke, Ruth's sketch of her life and work as a village evangelist-becoming-pastor was the most informative as an example of one among the varied settings in which Chinese Christians are at work among China's 1.28 billion population.

The Nanjing seminary visit included a renewed acquaintance with Chen Ze Min, the former vice-president of the seminary, who at age 90 still comes to his office regularly. Beverly and I had met him on a previous visit to China and Nanjing in 1983. He insisted that we see the new seminary campus and arranged for a car to take us to a new area of Nanjing. It is almost a new city in itself as the site for various schools of Nanjing University, including a half dozen buildings under construction for the new seminary that will accommodate double the present number of seminarians. It had been twenty-four years since we had talked and, as he put it, "the wind changed." What he inferred was that Christianity is generally more favorably viewed today than four decades ago and that the seminary is more open to western Christian authors and their theological contributions. With regard to the registered and non-registered churches, he said that both need each other, not as hostile competitors but as partners and learning from each other in carrying out Christ's mission. As an example he said the state-approved TSPM churches can learn more about evangelizing from the non-registered churches, and the house churches need to learn better from the registered churches how to combine knowledge with zeal in their public witness in China. Communism, in his view, is increasingly discredited, though any public denunciation of its authoritative rule brings punishment. The church must see its mission now not as an alternative to Mao's Little Red Book of Sayings which was discredited decades ago. Now it is the lure of Wal-Mart, strip malls, and the mania to own a new car that is the new challenge. How to meet it? The ways are many, he said, but living the ethical life that reflects the power of the Gospel in its Chinese dress is essential to all the varied ways Chinese Christians bear their witness. Echoing what I heard from the pastor of Mu En Church in Shanghai, he expressed a hope for a promising future for Christianity here if the church will live up to its calling. He was encouraged to see more and more intellectuals interested in Christianity and ready to hear what Christians bring to the staggering challenge of being God's people in this largest nation on earth.

I was able to meet Professor Chen, the seminarians, and faculty through the assistance of Zhang Jing, or Cathy, as she introduced herself. She is the director of international relations at Union Protestant Seminary and arranged every step of our campus visit with flawless efficiency. She went beyond the call of duty in her willingness to share her personal story, which began with her parents who took their Buddhism seriously as well as their dedication to the ideals of Communism as an alternative to the endemic corruption and class divisions that have plagued China for centuries. Her father knew the poverty side of those conditions as one in a family of thirteen children. Despite the hardships which both her father and mother knew from youth on, both were highly disciplined people with demands on themselves and Cathy in order to help their impoverished relatives however they could. She initially resented her parents' dedication but outgrew her adolescent selfishness and developed an admiration for what she termed as her parents' nobility, an esteem she still holds highly. Regarding her father's principled agnosticism she quoted his comment when first seeing a Biblical placard with the Ten Commandments: "I agree with all but the First." In her teens she read everything she could get her hands on, in quest of an inner peace that eluded her in Buddhism. Her problem was that Buddhism called for an inner purity she felt impossible to reach. Her early experiences of reading the Bible were disillusioning; Jesus was simply one more "energy magician" of which there are many in Chinese religion. She majored in American literature in her university studies and was drawn to Emily Dickinson and the author's freedom to get angry with God because of her physical ailments—and still survive.

She began talking to Christians she knew who aided her deepening search for the elusive inner peace she had always sought, and, through closer contact with practicing Christians, took her first real leap of faith. She left a better paying job as an interpreter for similar work at a lower salary with the China Christian Council office in Nanjing. It impressed her that she was hired on the basis of her merits for the job, though she was not yet a confessing Christian. It was in the writings of Bishop Ting, widely regarded as the voice of more recent Chinese Christianity, that she found needed guidance in weaving together the many strands of Chinese tradition and religious thought into a form which connected her to the grace of God revealed in Jesus Christ. Bishop Ting's intellectual gifts were important, she said, but more important in her breakthrough to faith were the hymns sung in the services she attended. They became the primary channel of the Holy Spirit's gift of a peace that was deeper than intellectual understanding. She remembered being moved to tears when first hearing hymns—especially those written by composers who themselves expressed what she had sought and found—and added without hesitation that she can still weep openly when singing hymns that speak to her heart. She was baptized when she was 31 and thereafter determined, in her words, to "look to God and not to man." Her long journey to faith was marked by stations along the way. She studied theology at Eden Seminary in St. Louis for a year and found the connection between theology and society challenging. The Eden experience taught her to think critically and not be hesitant in finding her way when living the tension between what God's law demands and what Christ's saving love provides (a comment that came easily to my Lutheran ears). When returning to China she married and now has a 12 year old son. The combination of her professional efficiency with her personal sincerity in disclosing the deep things of her heart gave us a memorable glimpse through her eyes of the mysterious ways in which the Spirit of God works in China. When we parted at the seminary gate, after she made sure the cab she ordered had arrived, she was off into the night on her motorbike, weaving her way through Nanjing traffic after a twelve hour day, one hand on the bike handlebar, the other pressing her cell phone to her ear.

Hong Kong, while politically included as a Special Administrative Region within the Peoples Republic of China since 1997, still carries the aura of its one hundred sixty years as a colony of the British Crown. It remains an economic juggernaut as one of the financial and trading centers of the world. It is said that its 6.8 million populations has more Rolls Royce owners per capita than anywhere else in the world. Lutherans are among the Christian churches with long Hong Kong histories; the two Lutheran bodies total 22,600 baptized, and have weathered decades of war, Japanese occupation, and the influx of thousands of Chinese refugees from the mainland from 1948–1951. The Hong Kong International School, with its enrollment of twenty eight hundred students and forty five million dollar annual budget, is the flagship Lutheran high school in the world and its leaders had a key role in establishing its Shanghai counterpart in the late 1990's. The seminary of the Evangelical Lutheran Church of Hong Kong and Tao Fong Shan, a research center for inter-faith dialog, are but a few hundred yards apart atop a steep hill with a magnificent view of the surrounding area. The distinctive Chinese style of architecture of both institutions creates a strong impression as one enters either campus. Here Lutheranism lives and works in its Chinese dress.

Tao Fong Shan, "holy wind" in Cantonese, is a one-of-a-kind Lutheran ministry evolving from the vision of a German missionary, Charles Reicheldt. He came to China in the late 1920's, and was soon restless with superficial mission work carried out with little knowledge or interest in a predominantly Buddhist context. He learned classic Chinese and walked to Buddhist monasteries in native dress to learn their religion and form friend-ships with monks—all this to raise the level of the Christian mission to Buddhists to a level unknown before. The wars in China during the 1930's caused him to relocate his mission base in mainland China (he barely escaped with his life on several occasions) from Nanjing to Shanghai and finally to Hong Kong. There he chose the quiet beauty of the hilltop loca-tion as a suitable place for a new start. His theology of mission took as its theme the opening words of the Gospel of John which speaks of the eternal Christ, the *Logos*, as the true light that enlightens everyone. Building upon that theological foundation, Reicheldt began a mission that worked along-side but distinct from traditional church channels. His legacy accounted for the various stages through which Tao Fong Shan has emerged to its present form, now owned and supported by the Areopogus Foundation based in Oslo, Norway.

John LeMond is an American theologian and scholar who has been a leader on the Tao Fong Shan ministry staff since 1991. We met him at an early Morning Prayer service he conducted for a dozen or more students in a small room hewn from rock at one corner of the grounds. Afterward, he sat down with us in his office to tell of the way stations of his journey, from his Southern Baptist beginnings in Florida to his becoming a Lutheran at 26 after finishing university studies in journalism. As a part of his train-ing at Luther Seminary in Minnesota he interned in Taiwan, after which he completed doctoral studies in mission, ecumenicism, and the history of religion at Princeton—and learned Chinese in preparation for his work at Tao Fong Shan. I asked him what he took from Martin Luther that spoke to his present vocation in inter-faith dialog. He answered readily—"Luther's theology of the cross." He elaborated on his response by saying that since God has come to us once and for all the crucified rabbi from Galilee, he can and does come to us under the forms of other religions as well. This was his point of departure that gave him freedom to truly engage people of other religions without eroding his own foundation of faith—and leaving the outcome to God. Too many non-Christians, he remarked, approach dialog with Christians suspecting that it will be a one-way exchange with their conversion as the goal. That deprives Christians of discerning how God, the living God whose Son is the Light that enlightens everyone, works in and through the dialog partner. LeMond is open to the other precisely because the Christ whom he serves is the *Logos*, the Tao, incarnate and crucified Lord for the redemption of the world. This is the basis for the witness Tao Fong Shan seeks to bring as a center where trust has been established between dialog partners over a long period of time. That task has been complicated, he said, by four centuries of domestic conflict and western imperialism since the Jesuit missionary, Matteo Ricci, arrived in 1600. All too often the church has been part of western imperialism that has poisoned its mission. He named three elements needed for bridge-building: love, humility, and patience as the truth works its way through long standing barriers.

There are hopeful signs. LeMond mentioned regular contacts with such agencies as the China Academy of Social Sciences, a group that exchanges consultations with Tao Fong Shan scholars in order to keep well informed on the status of religious polity of the Chinese government as it is applied throughout China. The continuing consultations themselves receive no official opposition, but LeMond showed me a specific example from a current news item describing police harassment of a Christian community for alleged subversive activity. The overall attitude of Communist Party leaders is negative toward Christianity, yet Tao Fong Shan maintains regular contact with faculty members of the departments of ethics in twenty leading Chinese universities who share concerns over the increasing ethical vacuum in contemporary China. Such contacts are significant. These are faculties in premier universities which do impact students and influence their future through continuing contributions from people like LeMond and his colleagues. Another purpose Tao Fong Shan serves is that of helping Christians, especially of the non-registered house churches, to be better equipped to get assistance they need in broadening their witness beyond homes (once secretive but more open in recent times) to the public sphere of life in China. The younger generation of believers does not carry the baggage of earlier betrayals and hurtful conflict that burdened relationships between registered and non-registered churches in previous decades. This has improved ties between both in present times. In fact, LeMond observed, there is a third church emerging, especially in the cities—he cited an example in Beijing from a recent visit—in which house church and registered church Christians freely mix together for pragmatic reasons. Registered churches must shift all their financial accounts to the government while the house churches do not. It does happen that people attend a registered church on Sunday morning and a house church in the evening.

His point was that the church situation in China is fluid and not fixed. Government pressure is less in the cities. The greater problems there are finding well trained pastors and a building in which to worship. Many pastors hold two jobs in order to support themselves while serving. At the same time there is a large TSPM congregation in Beijing with a gifted pastor who preaches the Word freely, has started a charitable foundation, organizes cultural events, and sends Chinese missionaries to outlying areas in China. Roman Catholic Christianity in China is moving toward a more unified body after decades of disconnection from the Vatican. When the papal nuncio moves from Taipei to Beijing, the effect can be that an increasingly solidified Chinese Catholicism. That trend can also stir Protestants toward greater organizational efficiency. The China Christian Council is one agency that works toward that goal, though its function is limited to registered churches. He documented the remarkable growth of TSPM churches since 1979. There are an estimated 20 million believers currently, served by 3,700 pastors, 27,000 evangelists, and 150,000 lay volunteers. There are 18 seminaries and Bible schools in China, with 1,800 students enrolled. In the two decades since 1988, 50 million Bibles have been published in China.

LeMond insisted that I meet his Chinese colleagues for a deeper, broader view of the work of Tao Fong Shan. He introduced me to Him Tung Chan, 40, married, a convert to Christianity when in his teens, and well educated in China, Taiwan, the USA, and Hong Kong. He had recently come to TFS to develop educational programs and materials intended to further integration of Christian witness with Chinese culture and tradition. He also introduced me to Daniel Yung who works with pastors and laity taking short term residencies in leadership development. He expanded LeMond's comments on contact with universities in the People's Republic of China by describing his collaboration with ethics faculties of 30 educational institutions in China to address the vacuum in ethics created by Marxism on the wane and consumerism on the rise. He made it clear that

PRC ethicists are not interested in a re-introduction of the western Christian evangelistic methods of the previous century. Nor is that the purpose of Tao Fang Shan. Instead, both groups realize the importance of mutual consultation on how best to teach ethical values to a new generation of Chinese. He edits the presentations made in consultations held at Tao Fang Shan and makes them available for wider publication. He said that the Lutheran theological emphasis on the freedom of Divine grace as the power for ethical living is well received in the interchange with ethicists who recognize its promise within the deep Confucian tradition of living by rules. The Lutheran contribution can, however, meet real needs only if it sheds its western trappings and relates more effectively to the Chinese mind and soul. That comment by Young made me think that he and his colleagues are unusually well positioned as Chinese Lutherans to serve that purpose in providing values that can influence the world's largest population into the future.

China is so vast and complex that any effort to summarize it all in a single statement is futile, unless it is the paradoxical maxim I heard at TFS that "everything said about China is both true and false." The glimpses of faith and life given us by unfailingly hospitable Chinese Christians made me confident of this overall conviction that God's promise never to leave himself without witness holds true here. Those who told us their stories and showed us their work believe that promise. In the hidden workings of the Holy Spirit they are part of the future of the church in China that holds astonishing prospects. By 2050, experts say, China will be home to more Christians than anywhere else on earth.

The new and impressive library building is the latest addition to the campus of the Lutheran Theological Seminary, located in the city of Hsinchu, a forty minute ride by high speed express train from Taipei. The welcome given us by the seminary president, Dr. Thomas Yu, included an informative slide presentation on the seminary (forty full time students, fifty more part time, plus 200 "Grass Roots" students —the title of an innovative three year study program for men and women without previous formal education but zealous for non-ordained ministry), a faculty of eight professors plus guest lecturers from overseas and the support staff. We were grateful to meet with pastors and lay leaders of the Taiwan Lutheran Church, both at the seminary and at the church headquarters buildings in downtown Taipei. Chinese names can be a problem for westerners to pronounce, let alone remember. Something distinctive about each one is noted in this chapter as a way to recognize their distinctive part in the life of the church.

TAIWAN

Chien-Min Yao, a retired captain with thirty-two years of service in the Taiwan Navy, wore his gold braided captain's cap as he sat down with us for an interview. He is a fourth generation Christian, who, after finishing high school went on to the Taiwan Naval Academy, was commissioned as an officer and went to sea. During his career he commanded a fleet of twelve destroyers with 260 sailors under him but his modesty made him reluctant to talk at length about his years of patrolling up and down the coastal waters off mainland China. His sense of humor came through in a comment that he often enjoyed a glass of beer when on shore leave in ports around the world—without getting drunk. He also mentioned his custom of visiting local congregations when he was in port on Sundays—and remembered once in the Solomon Islands when a pastor there put him to work helping paint the interior of a church before sending him off with a blessing. His response to our question about what it meant for him as a Christian to be in command of a crew with many non-Christian sailors was forthright. "I ordered the removal of all pictures of an idol famous in Taiwanese native religion that nervous young sailors brought on board for protection against the many dangers of patrol duty." At times, he remembered, crewmen would come to him for advice about their worries and he welcomed those openings to share his Christian faith.

But the subject that brought him here was not his past but his present as a deacon and chairman of the Church Administration Committee of the Taiwan Lutheran Church. His responsibilities cover the usual range of practical matters pertaining to insurance for church workers, health care, pension, retirement, and other needs. Housing is part of the usual package for pastors, he said, and sometimes a car as well. Mandatory retirement is age 65, and he spoke of his concern about whether the $1,000 per month pension coverage is sufficient. When asked about present challenges, he mentioned the need for more younger clergy, and added that as a grandfather he hopes his grandchildren will outgrow their impatience with the more traditional Lutheran liturgy he prefers. His hopes for the future? A coming generation with soundness in faith to meet all the quirky challenges of life in Taiwan. Listening to the retired navy captain, we recognized that the TLC is well served by this layman who brings unusual and sophisticated gifts to his calling in the church.

It was helpful that Lee Hung-Jen, 58, introduced himself as the Double Bliss man in identifying his ministry in the TLC centered on marriage and family life. He was neatly dressed in a black turtle neck sweater that set off his silvery gray hair—fashionably long—and prompted me to tease him about his movie star good looks. He responded with a grin and thumbs up gesture but moved directly to the serious challenges of his pastoral calling. He explained that the Double Bliss name for his work (established and supported by a TLC foundation) implies that happiness as we humans generally think of it is not sufficient to withstand all that life brings. The Gospel—the lasting bliss—is needed as the heart of all of God's gifts and is the center that holds everything together. His ministry is devoted to the many Taiwanese couples in which the bride is from Myanmar, Thailand, Malaysia and other Asian countries. These immigrants need programs of cultural adaptation and language training, he said, but words are not enough. He emphasized that the heart must be opened by Christ's love and thus evangelization is integral to the Double Bliss man's calling. He explained that because of class differences,

Taiwanese women do not readily marry a man beneath their economic and social level. That means that some 300,000 Taiwanese men must seek their brides from other Asian countries, with the result that one out of every six babies born in Taiwan is of mixed parentage. Over the past five years he has traveled the length and breadth of Taiwan to carry out the work of establishing counseling centers and training others to help mixed couples integrate into Taiwanese life. The government has been interested enough in the problems he recognizes to provide its own program of matchmaking and charges a hefty fee which must be paid by the bride's family, thus limiting the numbers who apply.

At this point I asked him how such marriages generally work out. His answer: poorly, as a rule. That's where the Double Bliss ministry fits in, for most of the foreign brides have no assurance of a good life; they feel inferior in Taiwanese society, and take it out on their Taiwanese husbands who are, in any case, not well regarded for seeking a foreign bride. How does Double Bliss address such huge numbers? Through the Foundation, he answered, adding that he oversees fellow workers in seven geographic zones of the country and trains workers who are gaining trust and meeting needs through classes offered in towns and villages. Congregations fit well into this picture, although the government is more at ease working through the Foundation. Lee himself knows something about life without bliss of any kind. Though born of Christian (Presbyterian) parents, educated, and married in his late thirties, he lacked commitment and was caught up in too much bribery in his work as manager for a sizeable industrial factory. At one point he wanted to take his own life, but while walking along a street in his town he heard a word from God: "Child, you can come back to me and I will give you peace." That was a turning point that led him to enroll in the seminary in Taipei and start life anew with his spouse and family. In 1997 he was ordained a pastor of the TLC and served a congregation for a decade. Now he is several years along in Double Bliss ministry. Problems? As director of a Foundation he has more paper work than he wishes and financing responsibilities are wearing. Joys? The feedback from foreign brides who have not only found a good husband, but have been found by Christ, the Bridegroom to whom the whole church belongs.

It helped that Tzeng, Li-Chu Chou suggested that we call her Judy as our conversation began. Her bright red jacket and matching plaid skirt went well with her pleasant manner and, with her jet black hair swept back to reveal a few streaks of gray, she made an impressive appearance. She explained that she was an evangelist/preacher (but not ordained pastor, another level in the TLC order of ministerial offices). After apologizing for her less-than-perfect English she then launched into a perfectly fluent account of her place on the staff of Truth Lutheran Church, Taipei's leading Lutheran congregation. Beverly asked her if her work was primarily as a counselor. She answered by implying that in the TLC the term carries a deeper meaning. She is in ministry to over one hundred "sisters," i.e. women whom she counsels and seeks to lead to the lordship of Jesus.

When asked to describe an average day, she began by saying how important an early, quiet time to talk with God is before talking to people. Judy, 54, married with children, lives only a ten minute commute from Truth Lutheran Church, an imposing multi-story building located on prime real estate in downtown Taipei. She is the first in her family line to become a Christian and remembered that when she told her mother she was considering baptism, the tart reply she received was "over my dead body." When her father learned, however, that her inclination toward embracing Jesus as Lord came from the positive example of Judy's husband, a devout Christian, he reflected the deep rooted Chinese tradition that made the wife subordinate to her husband. She spoke at some length about her arduous and lengthy journey to the faith during which her primary obstacle was her own stubborn pride and rebelliousness. Her husband's family kept providing a witness that was the primary channel of the Holy Spirit, especially her mother-in-law, who raised her husband and other siblings without her husband who abandoned her for another woman. She did heavy labor in a factory, asking to double the loads she hoisted on her shoulders so that she might add to the pittance salary she took home to support her children—deforming her shoulders in the process. Judy's mother-in-law mentored her in Christ-like attitudes and ways of living and taught her to pray before she could truly believe that her words were heard by God. Her husband's love and faithfulness to her were fruits of his faith which caused her to recognize the source of his devotion. Thus she was led to wholeheartedly embrace the Gospel and was baptized together with her first child. From then on she has sought to deepen her spiritual gifts, including completing her theological education at the seminary and accepting a call to the staff of Truth Lutheran Church in 1996.

She told a story of an experience not often heard anywhere, anytime. A woman came to her who was a flight attendant for a Taiwanese airline and thus was frequently away from her home and marriage due to overseas flights. One day she came back to find the apartment empty. Not only had her husband left her; he took everything with him. When Judy heard her story and reached out toward her for an empathic hug "it was like embracing someone stiff and cold as a stone"—and unable to say anything, as Judy recalled. As the weekly counseling sessions followed, Judy's counseling skills and wisdom in handling the turbulence of human emotions were well grounded in the transforming power of Jesus' love. The flight attendant was led to profess Jesus Christ as Lord and was baptized, and thereafter stayed in contact with Judy while working through the challenge of forgiving her husband. She reached the point after a year where she could make contact with him and, in fact, invited him to Truth Church. He accepted—and brought his new wife with him. This created an unexpected turn of events whereby the second wife of the man became more aware of unresolved issues in the present marriage that were left over from his problematic past. When those two divorced, Judy told of the truly rare circumstance in which the first wife led the second wife to become a baptized Christian and now both are participating members of the same congregation in Taipei. Rare as such stories are, Judy said, the need for marriage counseling among Taiwanese couples grows as the corrosive effects of materialist prosperity take their toll on marriage and family life. Before concluding our time together, I asked her again about the number of women she reaches in her ministry— and she reminded me that it was over one hundred. My parting words of thanks included the suggestion that she might find ways to spread the stories of her calling, and that with her permission I would take the flight attendant's witness home with me and share it wherever I could. She nodded Yes and sent us off with her blessing.

Fang Chung-Yi is an 82 year old man who, half a century ago, was a soldier in China under Chiang Kai Shek. This once and former soldier was on the losing side of the 1940's civil war in China that deposed the corruption-ridden Kuo Ming Tang government and replaced it with the revolutionary Communist rule of Mao Tse Tung, who presided over the death and disruption of the lives of countless mainland Chinese. We were immediately drawn to him as a spry and articulate octogenarian who kept our interpreter working hard to keep up with his narrative. He fled his homeland as a young soldier in his early twenties, leaving behind his parents, many siblings, and a grandfather (the sole Christian) in a large, rural family in which no one could read or write. He came to Taiwan, seriously ill with heart problems and depressed over the thought that he would be dead within a month. Just at that time, however, he came into contact with Christians who visited him and persisted in their invitation for him to see what their fellowship of faith could mean to him as one more homeless refugee—without the family ties that are essential to being a person in the long reach of Confucian teaching in Chinese history. That connection proved life-giving during his two years of recovery. He said he could never have survived without the prayers of his visitors and their love was a primary means of his healing. He made contact with a Presbyterian congregation and gained the reputation as a "Jesus freak"—it took our interpreter some time to finally hit upon this term we could understand. What happened was that in his zeal as a new convert he brought forty-five people within a two week period to overflow the house church space for Bible study. The group had to be divided into two sessions.

His experience in a two year period of leading one hundred people to know and follow Jesus as Lord prompted a Presbyterian missionary to encourage him to enroll in a Bible college in Hsinchu and following that, to accept a Taiwanese Lutheran pastor's invitation to hire him, as his reputation as an evangelist was rapidly spreading throughout northern Taiwan. During the next twenty-nine years he continued his vocation as an evangelist in various places, but what interested us most was his continuing activity in an unusual retirement ministry. He returns to his native China for several weeks every year, preaching primarily in the "non-registered" house churches that have grown exponentially in China, He also has maintained personal contact with the registered, or Three Self (self governing, supporting, propagating) Church movement in the mainland that is officially recognized by the Communist government. He spoke of meeting Bishop Ting, the redoubtable leader of the Three Self Church with a strong message for western Christians to leave Chinese Christians to their own ways of relating to the realities of life in the Peoples Republic of China. Our octogenarian dialogue partner had muted enthusiasm for Ting and the Three Self Church movement as he has experienced it. His voice rose and his gestures grew more animated as he described preaching and church planting among simple peasants in the countryside he knew as a youth, people whose roots resembled his own and are more concerned with making a living than arguing the fine points between registered and non-registered churches.

I asked him for an example that stood out in his mind and without missing a beat he told of one of his evangelism forays into the PRC. He gathered a group of twenty-four believers, ranging in age from 18 to 25, two thirds of whom were women, and sent them to another province where they stayed in the homes of people prepared to take them in. Over a period of six months these two dozen people visited homes during the daytime and led evening gatherings to preach the Gospel to those who had never heard it before. He beamed when saying that the half year evangelism campaign resulted in a new network of house churches now numbering 170 new believers. Experiences like this make him firm in his conviction that the TLC in which he still serves as an actively retired evangelist should devote its mission resources primarily to fellow Chinese in the mainland. Despite whatever political differences pertain, he has never allowed such things to distract him from his conviction that the Gospel carries the power of Christ that transcends human barriers of every kind. He is an indisputable witness to that truth with his personal life story that began in China, and now, over eighty years later, continues with regular returns to the people and places of his birth.

His smartly tailored black sport jacket was the thing that set apart Chen Chi-Neng in our mind, a pastor with fourteen years behind him at his congregation in Keelung, about a forty minute drive by car from Taipei. His care about his appearance became a commentary on his care in the choice of theological literature he brought with him in a book bag slung over his shoulder as we sat down to talk together. He explained that in case of a delay in our appointment, he could fill in the time by further reading in the copy of Augustine's *Confessions* which he drew out of the bag to show me as an example of theological classics he's promoting among his pastoral colleagues in Taiwan. He also had books by Henri Nouwen and Thomas Merton with him; I meant to ask him about his readings in Asian theology but he was too intent on turning the subject to his pastoral work. His congregation is average size in the TLC, around 100 baptized people. When I asked him how he connects his theological interests to his pastoral work his answer was forthright: "what we're here to proclaim is salvation by grace—the truth that's much needed among Christians in Taiwan." He went on to explain that the problem of blunting the good news of Christ's grace by legalistic practices is especially a temptation in a culture so steeped in the Confucian tradition that stresses proper behavior but not the mercy of God that produces it. When churches cater to this tradition, he said, it might be easy to grow fast but it comes at the cost of the truth. He cited the primacy of God's grace in an unusual pastoral experience with a man who was deep into idol worship coupled with a psychological disorder so severe that he could not work. He was taken into a cell group in the congregation where he was surrounded not by accusation and bias but by love and acceptance as he was. He continued associating with people in this circle and as he did so, the Holy Spirit worked powerfully against the demonic spirits tormenting him. Pastor Chen saw the gradual movement toward healing and change taking place as the troubled man took on voluntary work initially and then became a salaried worker for the Garden of Eden organization, a Christian group focused on ministry to the handicapped. He still has trouble handling money, which he has turned over to the pastor for his oversight. But this gradual return to being a whole and functioning person was the sign of grace that Chen used to continue to encourage the man who had been at the point of despair. The pastor in the black jacket, well stocked in theological reading, expressed concern about the growing inroads of Pentecostalism with its lure of spontaneous emotional exuberance and claims of instant healing. That is why he favors a deepening appreciation of the sacraments as basic to the life and mission of those who are in Christ. Baptism, which includes infant baptism, answers the question of how one becomes a child of God by receiving the grace that God reveals through his crucified and risen Son. And the Eucharist is bread for the journey of life with the congregation of believers. Through his presence in bread and wine, Jesus feeds his people and calls his church to be an accompanying community to others who are learning The Way. His use of the term accompaniment for mission made me think of what how Lutherans in Central America often describe their experience in outreach to the marginal in society. Chen came to these convictions the long way around. He was brought up in charismatic church connections, then was a Mennonite for a time. After that he came under the influence of the Korean evangelist Watchman Nee, but found it too legalistic in prescribing exactly what Christians should do in striving for perfection. He found his spiritual home in the Lutheran seminary after a long spiritual search and is well settled in pastoral ministry where Divine grace keeps him at peace with God, with others, and—not the least—with his restless self.

Thomas Yu is the president of the Taiwan Lutheran Seminary. He had led the institution for fifteen years and is particularly well suited to relating this school to its surroundings in the city of Hsinchu, the Silicon Valley of Taiwan where 300 major national and international technology companies are headquartered and where the University of Taiwan—famed for its science department—is located. Yu was himself an electrical engineering major at the university but intentionally broadened his educational path by including psychology and philosophy as majors before he finished his degree over an eight year span. He is a born leader with a keen intellect and a gift for relating to people of varied interests and backgrounds, a capacity which serves him well as a churchman and educator who has been at the forefront in the planning and development of the new seminary campus. He is in his late fifties, married, with a son who is in computer technology in Houston and another son who is a musician

Thomas Yu

in Taipei. He is a first generation Christian, who came to the faith when living as a university student in a Lutheran student hostel. It was the witness of Christian students that caused him to inquire further into this faith based in "such a strange God who was willing to take on flesh and even enter suffering through his Son"—as he spoke of his conversion. He quoted from a Confucius saying in the Analects: "If I know God in the morning, I am ready to die for him in the evening," a typically Chinese way of saying that to discover a God of love was to be totally engaged in him for life.

After his conversion he studied theology and in 1969 received a Lutheran World Federation scholarship to attend Hamma Divinity School near Kent State in Ohio, just at the height of the late 1960's campus unrest which Yu described as "weird and totally puzzling." He left Hamma after a month and found his way to Luther Seminary in St. Paul where he finished a master's in theology. His church called him back to serve in Taipei as student pastor for six years, after which he taught briefly in Hong Kong, then earned his doctorate at Boston University after five years of study there. He wrote his dissertation on filial piety in the Chinese tradition in relation to pastoral care and counseling in Taiwan. After another teaching stint in Hong Kong he came home to Taipei and joined the seminary faculty in 1989. It was, as he said, the answer to his prayer that he could have a vocation in which he could, as he quoted the late Scottish theologian, John Baillie, "know and serve God from the top of his head to the bottom of his heart." He expanded on the quote by affirming the heart relationship to God as primary, but not at the expense of the loving of God with the mind. Though we cannot grasp the hiddenness of God we do have responsibilities to use the gift of intellect and develop ways of thinking that reflect the distinctive Christian life. Reflecting on discipleship as a Taiwanese, he said he did not want to be a western Christian alienated from his Asian heritage, but rather a Chinese Christian and a Christian Chinese. What that meant, he went on to emphasize, is avoiding the individualism that characterizes western thought and culture. He commented on the Asian concept of family which stresses that to be a person one must belong within a family, a community. And as a Chinese Christian, he thinks of being a person through belonging as a reflection of the Trinity, the Holy Family of Father, Son and Holy Spirit united in an ultimate filial love. Through the Gospel, that Divine community is imparted in all its transforming fullness to our relationship to our heavenly Father ("How precious that is!" he exclaimed as we talked) and share it with each other. Because the family system is eroding in Taiwan under the pressures of modernity, the church is given this treasure that is urgently needed. In carrying out its mission, the church needs no shaming performances or demands of piety in order to win the favor of God. All rests on what Christ has first done for us. Then the church is the welcoming, beloved community in which the individual does not stand alone but is fulfilled by serving with other believers so that the world may know the truth that sets it free. Thomas Yu has the gift of expressing himself without theological jargon, but with that quality of practical earnestness that makes him the leader that he is. Since our time with him was short, there was much more to the man than we could absorb in a brief visit. But whatever more there is, it only confirms and deepens the impression that here is a churchman educator whose broad international training gives him a global perspective for his immediate calling of leading a seminary in which men and women learn to know and love God 'from the top of their head to the bottom of their heart.'"

The bishop of the Taiwan Lutheran Church, Juan Kuan Chen, a congenial man with an outgoing manner, came well prepared for our conversation with four pages of information on the TLC, past and present. He commutes to his Taipei office early each Monday morning from Chayi, a city several hours south where his wife (born in Kuala Lumpur) and two daughters live. After his earlier years of ministry as a hospital chaplain and seminary professor, he was surprised to be elected bishop of the TLC three years ago and regards himself in his present position as an interim leader who will be replaced in a year. He explained that his heart is in hospital chaplaincy to which he hopes to return in Chayi, and thus ease the strain of the weekly commute as well as extensive travel throughout Taiwan for pastoral visits and congregation contacts. He was born of non-Christian parents but lived with his maternal grandmother who was a fourth generation Christian whose early life influence on him has been lasting. He was baptized at 17 in a Methodist congregation, studied law as a university student, and became a Lutheran through a campus student group that welcomed him for Bible study. After completing the mandatory two year military service requirement, he entered the Lutheran seminary where a course in clinical pastoral education turned him in the direction of hospital chaplaincy. When he took up this calling at the thousand bed Chayi hospital with its staff of 2,400 he knew he had found the specialized ministry for which he was gifted and to which he is eager to return. His chaplaincy training and experience have served him well during his term as bishop. He illustrated it by referring its usefulness in working through the inevitable problems and conflicts in which his help was sought. He noted that relations with the other Lutheran Church in Taiwan, the Evangelical Lutheran Church of Taiwan, are cordial as the two churches work together in common endeavors of social mission and theological education.

It was noticeable that the subject of the relationship of Taiwan to the People's Republic of China came up rarely in our week of conversations and contacts. Many of the Taiwanese Lutherans we met have personal family ties on the mainland and the fact that they are free to travel back and forth to China for church purposes is in contrast to the sharp political tensions that divide the two populations and keep the subject of their political relationship perennially sensitive and potentially explosive. The free exchange between Taiwanese and mainland Chinese families, though less publicized, is nevertheless an important and hopeful sign of connection between the 1.3 billion mainland Chinese and the 22.5 million Taiwanese. Every connecting link that is not barbed with hostility and suspicion is needed and welcome. Once more, this Biblical truth comes to the light amidst the darkness of strained international relationship: God does great things for the many through the remnant, the few, who are called to be a light, a salt, and a leaven in the world that he loves. Seven of them gave us their witness to that larger truth: a naval captain-become-church administrator, the Double Bliss man reaching those of mixed marriages, the evangelist/counselor in her smart red jacket with more than a hundred women in her remarkable ministry, the spry 82 year old whose annual, self-supported evangelism trips to the mainland builds bridges of faith and the peace that lasts, the pastor with the book bag of theological classics who reaches those too often neglected, the seminary president exceptionally gifted for his calling as an educator, and the interim bishop returning to his first love of hospital chaplaincy. These are a composite of the much larger community of the faithful, keeping their grounding in the Gospel while serving a nation whose relationship with the mainland to their immediate west is uncertain. Whatever form the political future of that relationship takes, God means well for those on both sides of the narrow strait that separates them. Those with whom we spoke live in that hope and work in the trust that as they entrust their labors to the promises of God, they are not in vain.

Chennai, formerly Madras, is India's fourth largest city with a population of nearly seven million. It lies on the southeast coast of India, not far from where the first Lutheran missionaries arrived in 1706. It is a densely populated place with streets jammed with bikes, busses, trucks and cars, all careening in and out and around each other, honking incessantly and largely to no avail. An occasional sign on the back of a truck or cab that reads "Please honk horn" seems hilariously irrelevant. Along one of those busy thoroughfares is an imposing gate that opens onto the campus of Gurukul College, a major Lutheran theological center in India. One of the buildings houses the office of the Chennai Slum Women's Advancement Program, a ministry under the auspices of the United Evangelical Lutheran Church in India, one of the eleven Lutheran church bodies serving the 1,741,000 Lutheran Christians who are part of the twenty-six million Christians in India, a nation of 1.3 billion people.

INDIA

Vydha Rani is 44, diminutive in appearance, her dark eyes and intelligent face set off against the white sari she was wearing as she welcomed us into her pleasantly cool office—a welcome relief from the scorching heat outside. Though slight of stature the demands of her calling require physical and especially emotional stamina to persevere in working with some of India's most vulnerable people, slum dwellers who are women struggling to eke out an existence against towering odds. After I described my purpose in coming to visit her and mentioned the brevity of our time in India, she asked me how I proposed to gain reliably sound insights into the scope of Christian work in India in little more than a week's time. Her question was not off-putting. I welcomed it as a sign that she was serious about allowing me entrance into the scope of her work, but first wanted to make sure I would not distort it by superficial treatment. She seemed relieved when I answered that my wife and I came without illusions of instant expertise, but sought, rather, to listen more than speak and try our best to see through her eyes the things that can be conveyed through stories that transmit meaning. With that, she indicated approval by an affirmative nod of her head and was off with introductory comments on how she came to her calling. She was born in a devoted Christian family, blessed with a good education all the way through university, began her career with a YWCA position in youth service, followed it with similar work under Lutheran auspices, and then made a surprising switch to slum ministry as the result of attending a World Council of Churches Assembly in Canberra, Australia. She was well into an overview of what her work was like when she paused, as if deciding in mid-sentence that any lasting impact of what slum women go through could not be delivered through talking more about herself or reciting statistics on urban slum realities in India, but rather by setting before me a real person, with a name, a history, and a story that exemplified her plight and that of the many more like her.

A young woman, whom I will call "Remi" was her person of choice. She was born in a village several hours south of Chennai. Her mother died when she was 10. Being the youngest daughter in a large, poor family, she had to stop attending school because if the sudden welter of new duties that fell upon her. Then, at age 13 the second catastrophe struck her young life. She was raped by men in her village. When found pregnant, her father demanded that she have an abortion and took her forcibly to have the procedure performed. After that he gave her some coins, put her on a bus for Chennai, and told her that because of her shame she could never return.

Wrapped only in her skirt and a shawl, she arrived in the vast, noisy bus terminal in Chennai, too traumatized to move from her seat to go out alone into a huge city where she knew no one. The driver found a woman passenger who helped her off the bus and found a shelter, the first of many. How she made it from day to day and from shelter to shelter—often sleeping in the streets and always begging for the next day's food—is a saga blurred of clear details by the daily misery that became her routine—like that of the

"Remi"

many Remi's trying to survive in the slums of Chennai. Providentially, Vydha Rani came across her about a year later and after hearing her story, decided to do something she had not done before. She made arrangements for Remi to move from the slums to the care of the matron in the dormitory of the Women's Centre at Gurukul, only a few minutes from Rani's office. There, for the first time in her life the teenager could go to sleep in safety and awaken the next day with assurance that there would be food for her and something useful to do in helping clean the Women's Centre premises. Rani's office was close by, enabling her to see her often, and monitor her adjustment to the first semblance of stability she had known in her life. She was not taken by surprise, the told me, by the rage that finally began to emerge in Remi as she slowly emerged from the numbing events that had enveloped her life as a motherless teenager who had been raped and sent abandoned by her father and family to the slums of a city she never knew existed before. On one of Rani's visits she told her mentor of her determination to return to her native village and kill those who had abused her with unspeakably evil acts. Rani was ready when this smoldering fury finally surfaced. After listening repeatedly and at length to Remi's full venting of a resentment, now turned into a roiling torrent of hate, she began a process of slow, carefully calibrated steps of presenting to Remi why violent revenge was no solution. Rani explained to me her concern that too precipitous advice could backfire and cause Remi to slip away on her own and commit murder back home. Moreover, Christian professionals serving through church programs based on campuses such as Gurukul must take care in bearing witness to the transforming power of Jesus Christ to persons like this young woman, lest the best of Christian intentions be taken as manipulation by those in the government suspicious of Christian motives. Step by step she laid the groundwork for Remi herself to come to the point where she could ask for an alternative to trying to kill her abusers. When that point was reached, Rani began setting out the markers of the more excellent way of walking in Christ's love, now disclosed in words that explained the deeds of those who surrounded her daily since her arrival more than a year earlier in the Women's Centre.

After hearing that long story, rich in implications for the wider picture of the ups and downs of Vydha Rani's calling, I asked if we might meet this person since she was living so close by. Rani agreed, but only if Remi would be willing and if we would keep our words brief. Beverly's presence was surely a clincher in making it happen that two strangers from half the globe away could meet a young girl who was not an oddity to be stared at but a person still in the tender stages of healing from all she had endured. Down to the ground level apartment of the matron we went, and after Rani prepared the way with an explanation of our request, the matron disappeared into her tiny quarters to ask Remi if she would allow an American couple to greet her, emphasizing that the wife would take the lead in the conversation. Remi came out to meet us, shyly at first, but with polite words in English that made it possible to converse. After a few minutes of awkward attempts at conversation, Beverly's voice and manner won her trust. She told us that she was attending night school nearby and was grateful for all that she was receiving under the care of the matron—who was hovering within earshot to make sure this unexpected intrusion was going well for her charge. We took her picture, wished her well, and were on our way. Later that evening, as we were in our room in another part of the dormitory, there was a soft knock on our door and to our full surprise there stood Remi. We invited her in for further visiting and counted on a sure bet to make things easy in such a moment—family pictures. The visit was relaxed, informative, and memorable. As our taxi arrived to take us to an evening appointment she walked us to the gate and before parting gave us the gift that she came to our room to deliver. It was a pocket New Testament in English—where she got it I have no idea—but what is certain is that it will be a permanent reminder of my gratitude that Vidya Rani did not smother us with statistical abstractions about the Chennai Slum Women's Advancement Program. Instead she introduced us to Remi who gave us a glimpse of a larger realm of ministry through meeting one person we will not forget. Looking back through the rear window of the taxi I saw the face of our new found friend as we pulled away. She made the shy wave of her hand a gesture of pleasure at being able to give something to us, people from another land and another life with whom a bond was established in a few short hours. She was smiling.

Moments like these, anecdotal and fragmentary though they are, nevertheless symbolize the power and promise of the ministry of one woman,

Vidha Rani, at work in one service arm of one church, the United Evangelical Lutheran Church, among the tens of thousands of Christian ministries of the twenty-six million Christians who comprise 6% of the population in India with its 1.3 billion people. Such moments count anywhere and everywhere in the world, but especially in India where the sheer massiveness and intractable complexity of problems could easily keep Remi invisible instead of becoming a living sign of God's power to do infinitely more than all that we ask or think.

A short walk from the Women's Centre dormitory where we were visiting is the administration building where Dr. Samuel Meshach, the principal of Gurukul College, has his third floor office. In the course of our mutual introductions, I was happily surprised to learn that just over a century earlier his great grandfather, a convert to the faith, had heard of Lutherans in the United States eager to begin mission work in India and sent off a telegram of invitation for them to start in his area at the southern tip of the sub-continent. I had known of that eventful beginning from my doctoral research many years earlier. And here we were in the presence of his great grandson who had recently become principal (president, we would say) of one of India's premier Lutheran institutions of theological education! After mutually enjoying our serendipitous common interest, he described Gurukul according to the meaning of its name from the Tamil language as "an extended family of teachers living with students in community" and the place it has in the broader picture of Lutheran church life in India today. He cited two facts of importance in the school's vision of its mission: 80% of the members of the Lutherans in India are women and 80% of the Lutherans in India are *Dalits*, the name designating the caste at the lowest rung of the social ladder. That set the tone for much of the remainder of the time as we listened to him spell out the significance of both facts in reshaping the curriculum of the college toward more contextual education. He was candid about the problems the school had encountered since its founding in 1927 when it began as a seminary for Lutheran students preparing for ministry in Lutheran churches. However, there were too few students enrolling in the years following and the problems of financial pressures combined with expanding staff needs due to increased enrollment nearly closed the school in 1971. That was avoided, Meshach explained, by the decision to shift the focus to preparing lay leadership for congregations. Insufficient student enrollment brought another threat of closure; in 1984 a crisis summit on Lutheran theological education brought together educators from throughout India and beyond. The result was a renewed direction of pastoral training at Gurukul that applied the traditional Biblical, systematic, historical, practical disciplines to the academic field of societal analysis of the communities in which Christians are called to live and serve. Contextual education has meant the introduction of women's studies in the curriculum, since over three fourths of the Lutherans in India are women, and 30% of the present students are women. Contextual education has also brought made room in the curriculum for the ramifications of the revolution in information technology that has made India a leading player in global field of this science, something Americans realize when finding themselves talking to India when calling for rescue from a computer glitch. Meshach made the point that Gurukul offers more than technical skills in communicating data, but enables students to gain a theological grasp of communication as a dynamic relationship of humans relating to others and to themselves by virtue of God's communicating to the world through his grace in Christ Jesus. Another aspect of contextual learning that Meshach stressed as Gurukul's mission is the inclusion of the study of the culture and history of the *Dalit* caste, some 300 million, or more than one quarter of India's population, belong to this lowest caste in which four our of every five Lutherans also belong. In this connection Meshach made a note to arrange a visit for us several days later with the head of the department of *Dalit* theology. And as all college presidents must, he touched upon the subject of finance. Congregations traditionally help students with costs; when a congregation is too poor to provide, scholarships are possible. Nearly 80% of the students, who pay $1,000 a year, receive scholarship aid through the College. 30% of the students are married and commute from home. Gurukul's standards are high; 90 applied for entrance in this year's first year class, 32 were accepted. Twenty students are studying for a Masters in Theology. A doctoral degree is offered in four academic disciplines; Gurukul is the only higher education institution in India that offers a doctorate in communication, which Meshach instituted four years earlier. He characterized the relationships among the eleven

Lutheran church bodies as generally good, with occasional exceptions in local settings. He emphasized how essential it is for Lutherans to work together in order to make a positive contribution as 2% of the twenty-six million Indian Christian population. The same holds true for all Christians,—Protestant and Catholic—to do the same as a minority of 1.6% (some claim 6% and more) of the total Indian population of 1.3 billion. He named as a chief burden in his work the scandal of disunity that blunts the mission of the Gospel in India with its spectacle of sheep stealing. In his view Pentecostals are often the most flagrant in this regard. As a Christian educator he is dismayed when he sees the gap between what the schools of the church offer and the rapidly changing nature of life in India today. What gives him joy in his work is seeing students maturing in faith as they learn to love God with their minds as well as souls and when he discerns in them a vision of their future in the church in India and beyond.

He spoke of a deep personal loss in his life before we concluded our conversation. Knowing we were Chicagoans, he spoke of the death of his wife a year ago when she was nearing the completion of her doctorate at the Lutheran School of Theology in Chicago. She appeared to be winning the battle against cancer after a long and demanding series of cancer treatments at the University of Chicago Hospital, but a sudden heart-related ailment took her life. When he quietly reflected on what it meant to lose his wife so suddenly—when she was so close to realizing her academic dream, so close to returning home to dear ones and a deepened vocation, our conversation took on what the Lutheran confessional writings call "the mutual consolation and comfort of the brethren." He recalled how much the immediate outpouring of support from the LSTC community meant to him and his younger daughter, Priscilla, who was with her parents in Chicago at the time He pointed to the symbols of Christian comfort and hope around us in his office as reminders of the mercies of God which surround and sustain him as he carries out his responsibilities of leadership at Gurukul College.

Monica Melanchthon welcomed us for tea in her third floor flat in the faculty housing building on campus, her hospitality intact despite the drain of spending hours waiting in line at the Indian Embassy for extra pages to be added to her passport needed for a forthcoming trip overseas. She explained that her husband, an Old Testament scholar from the Island of

Tonga in the South Pacific, teaches at a Protestant seminary in Sydney, making theirs a (very) long distance marriage at present. They manage to meet at conferences and have longer times together on sabbaticals that bring him to India and her to Australia. Thousands of Indian couples who are separated by distance because of work often go years without seeing each other, she added, making her grateful for the more frequent occasions that bring her together with her spouse. She is the daughter of a Lutheran pastor who later taught at the Serampore United Christian Seminary; thus she grew up in a family used to guests from the world over and this has helped her adjust to overseas living—especially

Monica Melanchthon

during the years when she completed her doctorate in Old Testament studies at the Lutheran School of Theology in Chicago. She teaches Bible at Gurukul College as well as courses in Women's Studies, one of the departments that Meshach highlighted in his commentary on contextual theological education for seminarians preparing to serve congregations in which women are numerically predominant. She spoke of women in the life of the church as measured by more than statistics, however. Although women's ordination is approved in nine of the eleven Lutheran churches of India, women are not fully accepted in proportion to their gifts. Few congregations support their studies at Gurukul; family support enables them to come. When they finish here, their assignments are more in diaconal ministries with children, the sick, and the elderly. I asked her whether she knew of a single woman who is serving as a pastor of a congregation, she answered that to her knowledge only the Gossner Lutheran Church has several, an indication of how much still separates women from their full potential in the ministries of the church. Melanchthon is not ordained. She said that due to the limits imposed on women's service she saw no reason for it.

Nothing that she is not now doing would be added by ordination, she said, "except for the sacramental stuff" and her conclusion was that she does not feel the need for it. Her views struck me as a realistic, thoughtful sense of herself and the path she has chosen to use her gifts in the Lutheran churches in India and beyond.

She added further insight into what the caste system means in today's India, especially the role of the Dalits in the church and society. There was no talk of caste in her family during her growing up days because caste thrives on shaming and no one likes to indulge in self-shaming. She continued: "Dalits are able to move freely in most areas of society, but when it comes to marriage the lines are drawn, hard and fast. She spoke of the constant cloud of caste awareness hanging over all of India. Though constitutionally abolished in 1950 the reality of the caste system is still unavoidable. The Brahmin and upper castes still hold tight to their power positions, and the next castes lower down do the same as they are able. Dalits are, functionally speaking, still the fifth caste, the outcast. This may not be seen in the ordinary course of daily life—Dalits can now own land, for example. But beneath the surface, the virus lingers. In her view, the caste system will continue to infuse every aspect of Indian life as long as Hinduism holds sway. And, she added, caste is evident in the life of the church, though she did not say how. Her estimate was that 90% of the Lutherans in India are Dalits, especially in South India. They can rise so far in political and other circles of Indian life, but no farther. Thus few Christians in India have political clout, and that will not change as long as the religious-sociological status remains as it is. In the space several hours' visit over a cup of tea, Monica Melanchthon gave us our first commentary on the role of women and the caste system in India, two subjects that were high on our list of questions, about which we would hear more.

At another time and place in Chennai I had two extended conversations with a Lutheran leader of unusual depth of insight gained as a sixth generation Lutheran whose keen theological mind (graduate degrees earned both in India and Germany) and rich ministry experience as pastor, youth worker, and professor, covered a lifetime. He understood my purpose well and gave me more than I could digest during our hours together. Because he is a controversial figure among Lutherans, he asked me not to include him by name in my narrative and with that understanding I took in all I could gain from him. In summary fashion, here is what he said:

While the official count of Christians in India is 2.4%, he places the number between 6% and 10%, and adds another 10% when figuring in the number of non-baptized Christians—a subject he advised me to study as fully as possible before writing on Indian Christianity. In response to my dilemma of being without time and resource materials during my visit, he plunged into the subject himself, as follows:

The issue of non-baptized believers is a hot potato that churches are not taking up. This is the result of a rigidity of doctrine and church tradition that fails to consider the plight of the person who has come to trust, love, and believe in Jesus but is not yet mature enough to handle public reactions to the rite of baptism. It grieves him that too many pastors of all denominations neglect those who find themselves isolated and without needed spiritual care. He also regretted the rejection of a well written book on non-baptized Christians written by an able Lutheran; he rescued the original manuscript sheets that were carelessly lost and saw them through to publication. But the book is largely ignored and the subject is left out of pastoral meetings, conferences, and mass rallies needed to publicize the value of such literature to congregations where it is needed. A theology of hope, patience, and trust in the power of the Holy Spirit must prevail, and Lutherans should provide it.

Attacks by Hindus on Christians are increasing. Political groups built on pro-nationalist extremism combine with Hindu radical groups to kill Christians and destroy churches and homes of believers. The top political officeholders know this but fail to speak out against it. There is a fear among traditionalists that Christianity will one day permeate all levels of Indian life, and persecution motivated by that fear will continue as long as India sees itself as a nation whose Hindu history and culture overrides its constitutional claims of freedom for all religions.

The mainline churches are going down. He did not elaborate on causes, but mentioned disunity among Lutherans as one example of mainline malaise. In contrast to statements I heard that Lutherans are generally unified, he spoke of the problems within Lutheran church bodies as more serious than malfunction between them. An example; one major Lutheran church has been unable to elect administrative leadership for two years for reasons of internal strife run amok, plus lack of transparency in handling funds. The missionaries who came in earlier times, both Protestant and Roman Catholic, managed to buy large segments of land which have now become enormously valuable. To the shame of unworthy leadership, such properties have too often been sold off for short term profit with no long range plan. That, too, has contributed to internal strife. The answer is repentance and renewal in the power of the Gospel.

Independent churches are growing, especially the Pentecostals. Instead of decrying their growth, too many Lutherans remain stuck in doctrinaire rigidity. He cited the example of a woman preparing for baptism by a Lutheran pastor, who required her to memorize parts of Luther's Small Catechism as well as the Creed and Lord's Prayer and in so doing discouraged her to the point of her inability to pass such a test. She works from 5 a.m. till 10 p.m. in order to keep her family together and has no capacity for memorizing doctrine. A Pentecostal pastor to whom she went asked her if she believed in Jesus Christ as her only Savior from sin and if she would join in worship as often as possible. She said Yes and was baptized. The problems Lutherans create stem from high doctrinal standards with no pastoral follow up. That is cheapening the grace of Christ which produces the fruits of sanctified living needed as the real measure of church growth.

Caste discrimination is a two way street. Where Dalits are a strong majority in a neighborhood or congregation, Dalits can discriminate against Sudnas, people of the caste above them. He knows from experience. He is one.

It saddened me that this distinguished Lutheran churchman requested anonymity. His grasp of problems among Lutherans, other Christians, and in India as a nation is well founded, and although his candor was unequivocal, it did not destroy his hope that God will have the last word on the church, nation, and world. In Christ, he said, we already know that that word is one of mercy for us all. The treasure of the Gospel is in earthen vessels, he said, and that is both the sobering reality and the abiding hope for the church in India. On that note we shook hands and parted.

The taxi ride through Chennai's streets, no less busy on the Saturday morning we traveled, brought us to Anbunathar Lutheran Church well before 10 a.m. Pastor Daniel Jayaraj was delayed by traffic; we were welcomed at the church door by an elder, Mr. Frederick Das. He is in his early seventies, a retired book publisher, who was happy to take a pew hymnal and show us the title page which bore the name of his firm. He was delighted to learn that we were Chicagoans; his daughter and family live in a suburb not far from our address. He and his wife have visited their children in the United States several times and promised to contact us when next he visits his family. The church interior is unique; its pulpit is shaped in the form of an ark, an ancient symbol of the church. Opposite the pulpit was the baptismal font, prepared for the baptism of two young men who were to be baptized that Saturday morning. Pastor Jayaraj arrived, apologized for not being on time to welcome us, and invited me to participate in the baptism. When he assured me that this would be welcomed by the two candidates whom he had instructed in preparation for their baptism, I was grateful to accept. The two young men, friends in their early twenties, arrived accompanied by their baptismal mentor, Joyce Victoria, who had an unusual story to tell regarding the events leading to this baptismal day. She is a graduate of the London School of Economics, but when unable to find work related to her field of study, began teaching English in her home where she lives with her husband and two children, a girl 9 and a son 4. A year earlier the two young men, Manuel Manikandam, 22, and engineer, and S. Rajkumar, 26, employed in quality control work, began taking lessons in the Victoria household which gave them the opportunity to become well acquainted with the children. The 4 year old boy was pleased when the older two English students took interest in his singing the songs he learned in the Sunday School of the congregation where his parents were active Christians. The child kept singing songs about Jesus at every chance, and speaking animatedly about the Savior as well. As this continued, Victoria saw that her students were taking the songs and chatter about Jesus seriously. She called this to the attention of her pastor, Daniel Jayaraj, and he responded to their interest by meeting with them regularly to tell the Jesus story as good news for people of every age. I learned about all of this as we gathered informally around the font—the two baptismal candidates, the pastor, the elder, the English teacher, and the two guests from Chicago. The baptism took place, with water poured over their heads in the name of the Triune of God; two young men became two new brothers, united in a covenant of grace that spanned continents and oceans, time and eternity.

Daniel Jayaraj knows the global scope of the church from experience. He spent three years in Sweden in a Lutheran congregation north of Stockholm, on loan as a missionary pastor from his Lutheran church in India. He learned Swedish, and the exchange experience was a boon to all, including his wife and two children who were with him. It is a sign of this new time in global Christianity whereby an Indian pastor, coming from a nation where many non-baptized believers are found, journeys in mission to highly secularized Sweden, where many baptized non-believers are to be reached. The once common notion that the church's mission goes from Christian Europe and America to heathen Africa and Asia has been fundamentally altered during the last half century; now the mission of the Gospel is everywhere. Jayaraj's aptitude for a mission assignment in Sweden began to form in his earliest years. He was born in a Christian family in southern India, and could remember the strong influence of two German lay women in encouraging him to study for the pastoral ministry. He served congregations in several areas of India, both in rural and town ministries, both of them among poor people. After returning from Sweden he was called to Chennai where he serves a congregation of 160 baptized, many of them well educated and prosperous. His strong belief that the church is always in mission, wherever it is planted, inspired the start of a partner congregation in a town an hour outside of Chennai and served by a young pastor whom he is mentoring. We met him later on the Saturday of the baptism. Alexander Sagayaraj is learning fast in his first pastoral assignment in a congregation of 50 families in a village of 350 Hindu families. He characterized Hindu-Christian relations as good in his area. People of both religions talk over the common problems and he has been surprised that Hindus come to him asking for prayer. He writes their names down in order to keep them and their requests clear in his mind and follows through in prayer for them as he continues contact. He described his pastoral rounds during the week: home visits, counseling, Bible studies, prayer gatherings, after school Bible classes for children, and organizing sewing classes for women. He sets aside time for preparation for Sunday preaching and teaching which take place at 9:30 and 3 p.m. With a hopeful grin he reported that his parents are about to conclude arrangements with another family whose daughter will become his bride, a reminder of another marriage tradition alive and well in another part of the world.

Sunday morning worship at Good Shepherd Lutheran congregation in Chennai was a déjà vu experience of preaching again from a pulpit I occupied twenty years earlier during a previous visit to India. Pastor Adiss Arnold is the son of a notable Lutheran theologian who taught and visited in the USA, Dr. B. H. Jackayya, including time with us in our home. The sanctuary, which seats 150, was filled to the last row—men and women seated on opposite sides, with a canopy stretched across the parking area immediately outside the door to shield the overflow congregation from the sun, already bearing down by 9:30 when the service began. The liturgy in the Tamil language followed the music and form of a Lutheran hymnal familiar to me from my childhood, which provoked nostalgia but also the question of whether newer music indigenous to Indians and fresh Scripture translations in Tamil were forthcoming. As part of the prayers of the people Pastor Arnold invited children to come forward to kneel for prayer and a blessing spoken over each one as they prepared for school exams in the coming week. It was a notable moment to see how youngsters in India learn early to seek God's grace for matters as real in their lives as school exams. The sight of their hands folded in reverence and their wide eyes gazing upward in anticipation made me humble and grateful to be in their presence. They had no qualms, teens included, about coming forward and kneeling. They are growing up in a land where spiritual awareness is everywhere, all the time, for better or for worse, and in this respect they have more to offer the western world than they realize.

That Sunday included a noon hour visit with James Reiff, who directs a micro-loan program of World Vision International in the region, and later in the afternoon, time for reading sociologist Dipankar Gupta's take on the caste system and its diverse hierarchies and multiple groupings which are fluid in all areas—except marriage. It was enough to remind me that what we foreign visitors to India can and should learn must teach us how much we do not yet know, and to depend on Indians themselves to interpret the present forms of what 3,500 years of tradition has produced. We can also ponder the fact that in the 500 years since the Jesuit missionary Francis Xavier set foot on Indian soil, the caste system has still made this saying plausible: "Hindu blood is thicker than baptismal water."

On two occasions during our Chennai days we met with Masilamani Azariah, a Presbyterian theologian and churchman on loan to the Lutherans at Gurukul College. He is a retired bishop of the Church of South India who communicates a hospitable spirit (he treated us to a splendid dinner on Beverly's birthday), a keen intellect, and endless drive in advocating the cause of Dalit theology among seminarians preparing for pastoral ministry. During the noon meal of a pastoral conference hosted at Gurukul, he cheerfully coached me on the proper way to eat in India— only fingers are needed—while telling me recollections from earlier days of working alongside Lesslie Newbiggen, a missionary theologian and churchman whose lifetime of service in India has left a profound legacy. Azariah speaks fast, pausing occasionally for my questions about the broad range of his work on the place and plight of the Dalits in Indian society. The central theme running through the three books he has published on the Dalits is this: they are both the challenge and the hope of India. He repeated an emphasis I had heard from every Indian with whom I spoke, that as long as Hindu themes and practice rule in India, the Dalits will remain outcasts—subtly or overtly. This is their destiny according to the texts of the Hindu sacred writings, and because the Dalits are destined to be the underclass, they suffer the psychological damage of being relegated to non-personhood. The church bears the primary responsibility of addressing this dilemma. However, as Indian Lutherans themselves told me, too often during the five centuries of Christian presence in India, the church has let the system stand. Conversion has been confined to the believer's inner life at the cost of nullifying the witness to God's power to transform society through those who are active as his co-workers for the larger good. All India suffers the blight of caste segregation. Those who flourish economically and socially as members of the upper caste maintain their superiority only because their privileged status rests on the backs of the poor and oppressed. The real genius of Hinduism is to divide, Azariah said; caste is the expression of the core belief that destiny prescribes an impenetrable fence between the Hindus and the untouchables.

Hearing these insights into the complex realities of Indian life, confirmed in every conversation with each Indian with whom we spoke, left us with impressions to sort out and interpretations to clarify. Hinduism teaches separation of castes, and yet Monica Melanchthon, a Dalit, has her doctorate, teaches in her field at Gurukul College, and keeps an international marriage intact. Daniel Jayaraj pastors a congregation of middle and upper middle class parishioners who hold well paying jobs and live in comfortable homes. The recently baptized young men, Manual and Samuel, are university graduates who participate in the Indian information technology boom that has propelled the nation into leadership in the cyber world, yet their spouses cannot be of a non-Dalit caste. Remi, the youth rescued from Chennai's slums, once the embodiment of the image of an untouchable, is a Dalit on the rise to a new life among Christians—how far can she go in non-Christian surroundings? A distinguished Lutheran theologian, himself a member of an upper caste, knows the bias expressed against him from Dalit caste Lutherans. Bishop Azariah, a Dalit theologian heading a department of Dalit studies, hosted us for a birthday dinner in a sophisticated setting in which no one questioned his caste status—nor his capacity to foot the bill. All of these people who received us graciously and shared their experiences and wisdom generously did not make caste their primary identity, but neither did any deny its divisive presence in life's most intimate relationships—of marriage and family. Amidst these anomalies and despite these complexities, we discovered that as two guests from outside, we could arrive in Chennai, experience days filled with contacts with varied people, squint to see what Indians see and cup our ears to catch every nuance and narrative of the ups and downs of being a practicing Christian in India, and leave with a sense of wonder, humility, and gratitude for the richness of so much received from those so ready to give.

PART 8

INTRODUCING
SOUTHEAST ASIA

Many of us have vague ideas at best as to which countries comprise Southeast Asia. Even lesser known is the varied religious makeup of these nations that stretch south and east from the Philippines through the more than 13,000 islands of Indonesia, then northward to include Thailand and Myanmar (formerly Burma). Vietnam, of course, is permanently fixed in the minds of those who fought a war there, but comparatively few are aware that this Southeast Asian nation is on the economic rise with its pragmatic mix of capitalism and communism. Southeast Asian peoples are alive and well in the human family and offer surprises worthy of note; Indonesia has more Muslims than the Middle East Arab states combined and the Islam that prevails here is largely benign. Christians have always been a minority in Southeast Asia, dating from 1323 when the Franciscans established a mission base in Sumatra, and later in 1521 when Magellan brought the first Catholic priest to the Philippines.

Lutherans are relative latecomers to Southeast Asia, beginning with notable missionary work among the Batak peoples of Sumatra in the 1860's and, more recently, in the 1950's when work in Singapore and Malaysia began. They are a minority in the region, numbering two million among Indonesia's 231 million population, 6,000 among the 22.6 million in Malaysia, and 5,000 among the 5.6 mlllion Singaporeans. In what sense do they see themselves as a vital minority? Philip Tan, a Lutheran pastor in Kuala Lumpur spoke for every Southeast Asian Lutheran with whom I met when saying that "the reason why Lutherans are here is to proclaim God's grace in Jesus Christ as good news to sinners trying to win Divine favor on their own." How do Lutherans carry that out? The means are varied, as the descriptions in these chapters show. However, one way mentioned by Gideon Chang, retired Malaysian bishop, was striking in its simplicity: "We sing our theology in the hymns of our tradition. Every one is a sermon in itself!"

Although not numerous in Southeast Asia, Lutherans contribute qualitatively to the theological and social ministry life of the larger body of Christians in this fourth largest nation in the world. An example is the actively retired bishop of one of the Lutheran churches in Indonesia, Armencius Munthe. He and his wife, Floriana, acquainted us with laity and pastoral leaders in congregations, seminaries, schools, and clinics in Sumatra, the northernmost island of the Indonesian archipelago, where Lutherans have served for a century and a half.

Floriana and Armencius Munthe

INDONESIA

Bishop Armencius Munthe met us at the airport in Medan after the short flight from Singapore across the equatorial waters of the Strait of Malacca. We were hardly out of the airport parking lot before he began a tutorial of background facts for us to digest prior to our work ahead. With staccato-like delivery, he informed us that 88% of Indonesia's 239 million population is Muslim, making it the largest Islamic nation on earth. There are some 13,000 islands comprising the Indonesian archipelago. One hundred and twenty of the varied languages spoken by Indonesians as yet have no translation of the Bible. On Sumatra, the island where Lutherans are concentrated, there are still thirty-two language groups among whom the Gospel is yet to be proclaimed. Munthe, a genial, wiry man in his seventies kept up this steady stream of facts—his high pitched voice never wavering—until we approached what I thought was our hotel for the night. Instead it was a banquet hall where a fund raising dinner was well underway. He escorted us in, explained that the event was a money raiser to boost funding for retired clergy, and suggested that if I wanted to add my name and pledge amount to the list appearing on a large screen on the stage I should not hesitate. Munthe's directness was not offensive. It introduced me to the cheerful intensity that marks his determination to get things done, a quality that grew in impressiveness as we followed him for a week of tightly packed daily contacts with people in congregations, seminaries, high schools, and clinics in the northern half of Sumatra.

Among the first things he had to sort out for us was the complicated picture of what Lutheranism looks like in Indonesia as a mix of Lutheran and Reformed traditions. The Huria Kristen Batak Protestan (HKBP), commonly called the Batak Church is a body of two million which traces its origins to the pioneering work in the 1860's by the visionary missionary from Germany, Ludwig Nommensen. Alongside it are another million believers of similar Lutheran/Reformed blend, gathered in ten distinctive Protestant Church groups which also trace their origins back to the latter half of the 19th century and Nommensen's work. What ties these churches together is a common theological bond through the use of Luther's Small Catechism. They also share ecumenical connections with other Protestants in Indonesia, and hold membership in the Lutheran World Federation and World Council of Churches. Munthe's own GKPS (Geraja Kristen Protestant Simalungun) church body, numbers 210,000 and supports joint seminary and other educational institutions of the church.

Early in our itinerary was a visit to a girls' middle and high school where the student body was outside the building, waiting to welcome us in a uniquely Indonesian style. They danced their hospitable greeting in graceful, rhythmic steps that combine delicate foot movements with similar gestures of arm and hand—performed with considerable skill and dignity. They got the giggles, however, when Munthe stepped into the circle, smiling and insistent that he and I join them in the dance—he far more practiced than I. As the group of a hundred girls crowded into one of the larger classrooms for Munthe's introduction of us as guests from afar, his gift for reaching kids showed as he explained our global travels and deftly mixed it in with suggestions that they sing some songs in English for an audience they rarely see—two guests from America. As our turn came to greet them we did so and added the Taize chant, "Jesus, Remember Me" to their repertory, a melody and ten word text that travels well worldwide. The next stop was at a technical high school where 700 students had been waiting outside at midday for nearly an hour, in orderly rows, all in uniform, boys on one side and girls on the other, an equal mix of Christian and Muslim youth who form friendships and get along well we were told. Munthe's message introducing us brought cheers and smiles, all the more impressive to us in the realization they had been standing under a hot sun for an hour. My brief greeting to them in English included invitations for them to respond in English as practice for their language skills. The school director gave us a look inside the computer lab and the motor mechanics shop where several boys were proud to start a gasoline engine they had repaired and assembled. The church serves well in providing such vocational education in rural Sumatra where work opportunities are ever more scarce than in the cities. Later in the day a visit to the Theological College serving Lutherans and other students in Pematang Siantar provided opportunity for a conversation with the director, Dr. Jamilin Sirait, who received us hospitably and made the hour count despite the fact that someone had failed to inform him of our visit. The school focuses on lifting the educational level for a student population from surrounding rural areas and offers an extension program for upgrading the theological level of laity who are congregational leaders. Nearby in the same city is one of the campuses of Nommensen University of the HKBP, begun a half century ago, and now ranks with the Lutheran University of Brazil as one of the largest Lutheran universities in the world.

En route to Lake Toba, a large inland lake in northern Sumatra where Nommensen translated the Bible and led whole villages and tribes to become Christian, the itinerary included a stopover at a medical clinic where Munthe's wife, Floriana, had served when she was a young deaconess, just back from five years of diaconal training at Kaiserswerth, Germany. She told us of her Christian family origins and that her father was among the first Indonesian pastors of the HKIP. She had come to know Armencius during his pastorate nearby the hospital where she was assigned to work, and knowing that he was single made her wonder if she might be a possible bridal prospect. She hesitated, however, because she had a slight limp from a leg impairment that came with her birth. At that point Munthe interrupted her story to say that the rare qualities of her faith and commitment to her calling made the limp irrelevant. She was with us throughout our days in Indonesia and the high regard in which she is held was evident in the welcome she received along the way and especially at the clinic near Lake Toba where she had served. Circling back toward Medan on the coast, two stops were notable in helping us get a feel for church life in Indonesia.

The first was a visit to the tiny village of Pangambatan where Munthe was born. It was an opportunity for a first hand look at a Batak family house typical of the sort in which he grew up—and in which people still live in remote rural areas. It was a large structure with a swayback, thatched roof and built upon a foundation of heavy wooden beams. A short ladder with several steps afforded a view of the interior, a dark area made smoky by a cooking fire smoldering on a bed of rocks. The living area divided into bi-levels, and what I presumed was a toilet was accessible somewhere below. I asked Armencius how it was when he was a boy—he lived in this house with four other families until he was twelve—and how he ever had enough light to do his school lessons after the sun set. His answer was instructive about how learning took place in an older Indonesian culture which still prevails in villages like Pangambatan. There was no light for lessons after dark. Instead the evenings were times for the family to gather and hear stories that the older ones passed on to the younger members. Story telling was the source of learning night after night, and the wealth of learning about life from the lore of preceding generations imparted a wisdom and a sense of belonging that he wished for youth in today's Indonesia. I thought of how such basics have formed him and stayed with him as he endured the Japanese military occupation as a young child, gained a high school education, went on to seminary, served congregations as a young pastor, went abroad for theological study in Hamburg, Germany, and then, as a churchman, traveled widely in the United States as well as in Asia, and then applied the fruits of these international experiences to his years as a bishop in his church in Indonesia.

Another experience that gave us a feel for life in a congregation in Indonesia was attending a wedding in a congregation of middle class parishioners in Pematang Siantar. The bride and groom, a strikingly handsome pair, arrived at the church together in a well scrubbed Honda borrowed for the occasion. The groom was a newly ordained pastor, dressed in a smart tan suit, blue shirt, and tie that would serve him well long after his wedding day. The bride was a striking young woman; her Indonesia dress was ankle length with a sari-like garment over her shoulder, her hair elegantly coiffured and her dark eyes tastefully eye-shadowed. The couple led the processional of several hundred guests and family members into the church with a seating capacity of 550. Prominent over the chancel was a cross painted bright crimson. In front were six large baskets of fresh flowers—readily available in this lush part of the world. Behind the chancel was a string of colored lights, blinking to accentuate the Indonesian love of color. The pulpit was front and left in the chancel, the podium to the right and the altar in the center. Around the sanctuary were pictures of the Savior in the vivid style of Protestant piety, together with one of the sacred heart of Jesus characteristic of pre-Vatican II Roman Catholic art. The church is just six years old, Munthe explained, with a white ceramic floor covering, walls with dark wood sections above the chancel. Fans were everywhere and welcome. The bishop of one of the Lutheran church bodies of a quarter million members, the Geraja Krisen Protestan Indonesia, preached and presided; another unusual feature was the participation of three choirs. After the ceremony, the couple came forward, each spoke their vows (looking not at each other but straight at Bishop Mangisi), the bishop then asked them to exchange rings, they knelt for the benediction, and arose—he with eyes still staring straight ahead and she with eyes demurely turned downward led the procession out to the accompaniment of the congregation singing a hymn to the melody of How Brightly Shines The Morning Star.

Weddings reveal both the happiest and sometimes the not-happiest of times in a congregation. Munthe explained that a kerfuffle had occurred about who would pay for the wedding. The custom here is that the groom's father pays for all, but in this case he was a recent widower still paying bills from his late wife's illness. The matter was settled by the agreement that an offering would be received—after the wedding service ended. As guests filed out to greet the newlyweds, each passed by an offering receptacle prominently displayed for that purpose. It was the suitable answer to a sticky matter that needed settling before all were out of sight. And it worked.

Church life among the three million Lutheran/Reformed Christians, the four million Roman Catholic Christians, and the rapidly growing number of Pentecostal and other Christian groups in Indonesia, could be only lightly touched in our days with Armencius Munthe as our guide. What we did experience is the sense that in this corner of the global community of Christians, embedded as they are amidst a huge Muslim majority (largely non-violent and distinctly set apart from their fundamentalist, fiery counterparts in the Middle East) there lies far more than we know, both in problematic divisions and questions of Lutheran theological identity as well as faithful discipleship and creative witness to the Gospel in ways that embrace rather than reject the long history of Indonesian culture. We hardly scratched the surface, but what we did experience in full was hospitality, warm acceptance, and unmistakable devotion to the same Christ who binds his own together in a bond no barrier can transcend.

In its tropical location just north of the equator, sunlit and washed by abundant rainfall, the four and one half million Singaporeans of this prosperous, multi-cultural city state live in a virtual garden of lush greenery. Here orchids spring up untended along the parkways and sidewalks are kept spotless by the notorious anti-spit laws. The skyscrapers that line the downtown business district symbolize Singapore's economic prowess. The upscale shops along Orchard Road, each competing with the next in brand name window displays, make it a paradise for affluent shoppers and a purgatory for those who can only look. A sense of arriving in a place of well-ordered prosperity settled in on us as we rode into the city with our host, Samuel Wang, a young pastor of the Lutheran Church of Singapore who had squeezed us and our bags into his mini-auto after meeting us at the Singapore airport (he later confided his consternation when spotting us at the arrival gate as "elderly giants"). Something from everywhere on earth seems squeezed into this city state holding its own at the southeast tip of Asia, and we— the elderly giants—were eager to take in as much of it as possible in days spent with people of the Lutheran Church of Singapore.

SINGAPORE

Queenstown Lutheran Church, where Terry Kee is in his eighth year as pastor, is a miniature of the demographic diversity of Singapore where 76% are Chinese, 15%, Malaysian, with the remainder scattered among Indians, Europeans, Australians, and Americans. The international make-up of the congregation became apparent as we entered the church on the Sunday morning of our visit. The faces we saw were Asian, Caucasian, and African, with hair colors to match. Pastor Kee began the service by inviting strangers to give their names and places of origin, a different country was named with each guest recognized. When our turn came, I gave our names and added a sentence saying that the music of the liturgy we were about to sing was written by Richard Hillert, a fellow member at Grace Lutheran Church in the Chicago suburb of River Forest, Illinois. There was just enough of an audible ripple of appreciative surprise to make the added sentence worthwhile. Though the thought of adding the informational note on Hillert came spontaneously, it was for the purpose of sharing something that those present would have no other way of knowing. The music and words of the Lutheran Book of Worship, heard in this congregation and elsewhere in the world Sunday after Sunday, come from a real person with specific gifts that reach across continents and oceans to where we were that morning. Even more to the point, the way we were welcomed at Queenstown Lutheran, by name and location, helped to highlight something exceptional about every Christian assembly for worship. Those gathered come together for purposes different from an audience in a theater ready to be entertained, or a stadium crowd itching for the kickoff or opening pitch. This is a gathering where Christ's welcome is received and shared—at Queenstown, the giving of names and places of origin. When this custom is thoughtfully observed it becomes to those present, a bond of belonging to each other for purposes of mutual encouragement and consolation because of belonging to Christ. To be sure, the Queenstown ritual of welcoming strangers by name and home location is not always and everywhere possible. But on that Sunday morning in that place it was. We who entered the church as strangers from an ocean away felt the power of the simple act of welcoming by name, and thereby were less strangers and sojourners and more fellow members of the household of God in that place. It was anything but superfluous. And, we hoped, the long-time members of Queenstown Lutheran Church did not simply put up with it as an annoyance.

Another thing happened in that welcoming moment. Several twenties-something youth rose to state their names and country of origin, then announced that they were part of an international crew of young adults aboard the ship *Doulos*, docked for several days in the Singapore harbor. They invited all present to come aboard for a look, and followed with a word about their mission of fanning out through the city to engage youth with the message about new life in Christ Jesus. Later that Sunday, we joined Kee for a for a stem-to-stern visit on board the *Doulos* to mingle among the 350 crew members—all youthful Christians from fifty different countries—as they welcomed hundreds of visitors to tour the vessel, hear music, relax in the International Café, and peruse books and magazines on Christian living which spread out on tables on the main deck. The *Doulos* (Greek for servant) way of global mission impressed me not only for what these youth gain during their two years of volunteer service as the ship drops anchor in ports around the world, but also for the long range impact on their lives thereafter. We would have missed all of this were it not for the two minutes of introductions at the opening of the liturgy that morning, and the congregation would have missed their connection with the musician who composed it. Hospitality counts in surprising ways.

Yet one more note on the morning service in Singapore. After the benediction the congregation remained to hear a report on the status of the budget. I noticed that the treasurer put the financial numbers into the perspective of the congregation's plans to expand the mission by calling a full time youth director, and he illustrated the need with a map showing the demographic growth of the youth population in the area. No one left. Pertinent questions were asked. A Yes vote to adopt the needed funding was unanimous. After hearing a budget appeal and its well-stated purposes, I felt even more at home at Queenstown Lutheran Church in Singapore.

After the service, the mission report, and coffee and conversation for members and visitors in a patio area, Pastor Kee and his wife, Sally (she edits the Asian Lutheran News publication of the Lutheran World Federation) sat with us to offer glimpses of their ministry through their eyes. Prior to coming to Singapore, they spent eleven years in northeast Thailand and contrasted their work among rural people there with serving middle and upper middle class Singaporeans of wide cultural diversity. Their individual story mirrored a wider historic pattern of Singaporean Lutherans. Lutheran work in this part of Asia dates back to a Southeast Asian Lutheran Conference in Penang in 1953, which in turn resulted in the arrival of the American missionary couple, John and Betty Nelson, in Malaya in 1955. From there the mission expanded southward to Singapore in 1960. Nelson continued to coordinate work in Malaysia and Singapore through the following decades, and Thailand was added in 1987 in cooperation with the joint mission work there by Lutheran mission agencies from Norway, Finland, and Hong Kong. Kee commented that the rapid expansion of Lutheran work through the region during the past half century without adequate pastoral training and support has resulted in too many Asian Lutherans who lack grounding in a real understanding of Law and Gospel and need help in weaving that essential mark of Lutheranism into preaching and teaching the faith. Furthermore, indigenous Lutherans in southeast Asia need time and maturity to develop ministries of the Word with a deeper feel for their Asian cultural and religious context. When I asked him for an example he cited the profound imprint of Confucius and Mencius upon the concept of religion as primarily ethical rules of conduct. That translates into the problem of turning the Gospel into a set of laws, a kind of moralism instead of a baptismal rebirth into Christ's redemption from sin and the resulting Christian life as an expression of the fruits of the indwelling Holy Spirit. In short, the task is to plant the Gospel of Christ's promise into a religious climate already filled to overflowing with Taoism, Hinduism, Islam, Buddhism and the most pervasive religion of all—consumerism in the booming Singapore economy. I heard some of these same reflections from Samuel Wang during our forty minute ride from the airport, and from Martin Yee, the keen minded young theologian who is the assistant to John Tan, the bishop of the Lutheran Church of Malaysia and Singapore.

Meeting with Bishop Tan widened our awareness of the demographic diversity of Singapore in which the church lives and serves. Roughly 76% of the population is Chinese, 15% is Malaysian, and the remainder are Indians, Europeans, Americans and a smattering of others from nearly every corner of the earth. Tan himself is an example of ethnic diversity. He was born of Christian parents and grew up in neighboring Malaysia. After finishing high school he heard God's call to ministry and went to Taiwan for his theological education. There he fell in love with a young Taiwanese Christian he met while doing his field education. He described their wedding that took place on the afternoon following his seminary graduation in the morning. The couple registered with the proper official in the local town hall, they bowed to each other, then to the official, then

John Tan

to their three witnesses, and "that was it" he said, smiling at the simplicity of the traditional ceremony. They then went through what became an ordeal of securing a visa for her to join him for his pastoral call to Kuala

Lumpur, Malaysia. At this point he went into lengthy detail in telling that story which also reveals the core of what he has learned and applied through his ministry in the years following. The visa saga was filled with sidebars of governmental red tape, temptations to bribery, impossible language requirements, and self-important immigration officials who promised much but delivered nothing. The real angel of God's providential working throughout that harrowing process was a modest, faithful woman of no political clout but who personally led John Tan and his bride through the serpentine clutter of obstacles and by her sheer strength of faith and gritty determination outwitted and outlasted bureaucracy. She taught him to see God's will at work in ordinary people who turn out to be extraordinary exemplars of faith, hope, and love. She remains the model and measure for his service as a churchman.

His subsequent path of continuing pastoral education took him to California for theological study in 1981, and two years later he returned to Malaysia where his theological and liturgical interests drew him toward the Lutheran ministry. It was not clear to me how he qualified for ministry in a Lutheran congregation; he nevertheless served a pastorate in his home area in Malaysia and then was transferred to Singapore where, as a pastor and bishop, he described himself "more Lutheran than many Lutherans." He provided this statistical overview: The Lutheran Church Singapore, affiliated with the regional Lutheran Church of Malaysia and Singapore, has six congregations with a total membership of 5,000 baptized. For two decades he had tried to begin a Lutheran school here but government permission has not been possible to date. Five of the six LCS congregations are financially independent; each has both a Chinese and English speaking congregation meeting and worshiping in the same building, the source of occasional friction but more often an amenable arrangement. An interesting surprise to me was the connection that Singapore congregations have established with mission congregations in Mongolia, China, and Thailand. Every year pastors and a lay group from Singapore go to each of these places to train people in evangelism and church planting. The witness is two way, Tan said. Poor but genuinely dedicated Mongolian Lutherans can teach Singaporean Lutherans much about discipleship and zeal in mission. Singapore is growing in prosperity. Consumerism is a huge challenge, prompted by the chic shopping malls on Orchard Street as well as in hundreds of other streets of the city crowded with the latest fashions and gadgetry. Singaporeans work hard and put in long hours, which takes its toll on marriage and family life. Drugs are a problem among youth, but the draconian policy of crackdowns on dealers keep the trade down. Two government-sponsored casinos feed the gambling craze to which, in his words, Chinese seem genetically disposed.

He spoke of these things as he and his wife, a gifted artist, hosted us for Chinese cuisine in a quiet restaurant where the ambience was conducive to talking of matters of the heart. Bishop Tan has arranged series of conversations with other Lutherans in Singapore, each with a slant on some aspect of the ups and downs of living the Christian faith in this city that is numbered with Hong Kong, Shanghai, and Seoul as one of the giants of commercial hustle, the so-called "Asian Tigers" along the Pacific Rim.

Ow Long Yang,—Mary is her adopted name—is 60, a teacher of high school chemistry for thirty-five years, who first heard the story of Jesus as a child of ten. She loved the story as told by her friend and began attending Sunday School in the neighborhood where she was born. As a dutiful child she had reason to be grateful that her parents did not oppose her growing fascination with Jesus, but they were of no help in answering the question that kept nagging through her teen years—"Is the story true?" She remembered how friends advised her to simply confess her sins and ask Jesus into her heart. But she could never find that to be simple. Her contact with Christian friends continued at Nanyang University where she majored in chemistry. She kept attending services in a congregation but still struggled with the truth question. Then, as she said, it was on a Sunday evening during her third year at the university that she heard a sermon on John 14 as Jesus as the Way, Truth, and Life. The preacher, she smiled when recalling the occasion, had a sore throat and his delivery was raspy. Moreover, during the service a heavy rainstorm hit, at about the time when the preacher asked "Where are the Christians? Raise your hands!" She held on to her stubbornness of the dozen years past and decided she would not be a Christian. As she sat with her hands folded she heard the scratchy voice from the pulpit turn to another Biblical text on the truth that God's ways are not our ways. She kept thinking of the many times people had urged her to just believe, as though it could happen by her own initiative. This time, however, as the truth of God's ways being other than her ways sank in, she sensed that no one was telling her what she must do. "And then and there I believed," she told me with feeling for the life-changing gift that had been given her some forty years earlier. She went on to say that it was not that she found the truth but that she was found by the truth. She was joyful, she added, greatly joyful and her tears flowed "like water from the rock" as in the Exodus story of Moses at Rephidim. It was a release into a new freedom, she explained, the freedom of not "having to" but "getting to" belong to God by his grace as the power that has kept her through her years. She found her way to Redeemer Lutheran Church not far from her apartment, and was glad to tell me that many in her family have followed her in her conversion, including both of her parents prior to their death. She has been active in teaching discipleship in her congregation over the past ten years as a cell group leader. She audits religion courses at Trinity Theological College to augment her faith life and at times finds things she hears unsettling. But the memory of that moment when God's ways were not her ways sustains her as she grows in loving God with her mind as well as heart and soul. She wanted me to note one more thing before she finished telling her story: "I have no problem working in the church as a woman, nor with the two ordained women who are pastors in the Lutheran Church of Singapore."

The Trinity College to which Mary referred is Trinity Theological College, founded in 1948 by Methodists, Presbyterians, Anglicans, with support from Lutherans added later. There are 215 students are enrolled at the Bachelor and Master of Divinity level. The faculty numbers twenty-three and represents a variety of denominations. Many Lutherans in Singapore have studied at Trinity, and with that in mind I was interested in listening to Jeff Truscott, a Lutheran from the United States under appointment to the Trinity faculty by the Evangelical Lutheran Church in America. He teaches courses in worship and liturgy and serves as chaplain to the student body. His way of describing the practical bent of Singaporean Lutherans when fashioning forms of worship from what others are doing went like this:

"If a man wakes up one morning and sees his neighbor selling limes from a lime tree, he goes out to buy a lime tree and adds it to what he has to sell'. Thus, some Lutherans have helped themselves to the popularity of the charismatic movement among churches in Singapore by borrowing ways of worship that have little to do with the Lutheran emphasis on Law and Gospel or the liturgy that has come down through the centuries in the Church catholic. The culture here, he said, is steeped in supernaturalism and abounds in mediums who mediate the spirits—for better or for worse—making it possible for the charismatic movement to become, in Truscott's words, a democratization of this tradition. He sees his role at Trinity as keeping faith with a theology well grounded in justification by faith without an "in your face" manner of presenting it. He is grateful that students have been accepting of his vocation here, and responsive to his introduction of practices they have not known before, such as chanting Psalms and prayers, foot washing on Maundy Thursday, and the remembrance of saints' days such as St. Bartholomew, missionary to Asia.

Nick Singh, a man in his middle years with the face and manner of a gentle saint, is on the pastoral staff of Redeemer Lutheran Church, a congregation which includes numbers of Indian Singaporeans who attend the Tamil language service. He was born in Malaysia, in a Sikh family whose roots were in the Punjab area of northern India. When speaking of his earliest contacts with Christians, he described the single thing he remembered from attending a Campus Crusade service when he was 16. It was the opening two words of the Lord's Prayer. Never before had he heard God addressed as "Our Father" and the words touched him deeply. He continued in secret contact with Christians until his baptism in an Anglican congregation at 21. He had finished his college degree in accounting in Kuala Lumpur and was working for Exxon when he sensed a call to the pastoral ministry and spent a year in New Zealand in a Bible College. When returning to Singapore he completed the four year course at the Singapore Bible College, another influential school where Lutherans have studied, and after serving an independent congregation for a dozen years found his way into contact with Lutherans and joined the pastoral staff at Redeemer Lutheran Church. It was the liturgy, he emphasized, coupled with the emphasis on justification by grace that draw him to the Lutheran tradition. In his pastoral work at Redeemer he spoke of his concern about the increasing consumerism that is the main form of attack on everybody's soul as "the demon that bedevils us all." Pastor Singh hosted an all day conference of lay and pastoral representatives from the six congregations of the Lutheran Church of Singapore, organized well ahead of my arrival so that I might share with them the highlights of what I have learned in visits to congregations and other ministries of the church in Africa, North Asia, South America, and Europe. As has been the case in all these places, so also in Singapore, I learned as much as I taught by receiving the hands-on witness of those who speak with authority as permanent residents of places where I can spend hardly a week as one who learns by listening.

Singapore's natural beauty and urban cleanliness are impressive, as well as beguiling. Lutherans know, along with others of The Way, that the Good News is truly good only for those who hear it with openness to a Savior from sin. The Lutheran presence has taken root here, and those tending its growth have an awareness of what they can give and receive as they join with other Christians in the daily challenge of living lives well centered in Jesus Christ amidst a widely diverse population tempted to choose material prosperity over the true treasure of the Gospel.

Eight years before the southeastern Asian nation of Malaysia was formed in 1963, John Nelson, a missionary from the United States, began Lutheran work among displaced Chinese migrant workers in the rural regions north of the capitol city, Kuala Lumpur. The city has now grown to a population of 1.5 million and has become, with Hong Kong, Singapore, and Seoul, one of the "Asian Tigers"— cities of aggressive commercial growth. I learned about the past half-century of Lutheran history in Malaysia when talking with Gideon Chang, the retired bishop of the Lutheran Church of Malaysia and Singapore, in the LCMS (Lutheran Church of Malaysia and Singapore) headquarters building in Kuala Lumpur. His story as a refugee from China who fled Mao's Communist Revolution in 1949 is representative of many Chinese Malaysian Christians who found among Christ's people a spiritual home when they had no other. As is the case with many Lutherans called to the pastoral ministry, he studied theology in Singapore, and then returned to Malaysia to serve. He suggested that I meet with Philip Tan, a younger Malaysian Lutheran pastor, for a sense of how ministry goes currently in this nation of nearly twenty-three million people, over half of whom are Muslim.

Philip Tan

MALAYSIA

I f I would have begun my conversation with Philip Tan by asking what it means to be a Lutheran in Malaysia, he might well have begun his answer with: "It nearly killed me!" Those four words summarize the incredible non-welcome he received twenty years earlier when he arrived at Christ Lutheran Church in Kuala Lumpur where he had been sent by the bishop for his first pastoral assignment. This trim, 49 year old Malaysian (neatly dressed in a tailored suit with blue clergy shirt and collar) chose to introduce himself to me by setting the stage for his rough beginning in ministry with a brief overview of early challenges he faced when growing up in a family steeped in traditional Chinese religion. Thus it was no surprise that his parents were cool to his conversion to Christianity which came through the witness of teen age friends. He had aspired to be a pastor soon after

he became a believer, but the objections of his family and his early affluence as a university graduate on his way up in the Caltex Corporation dulled
that aspiration. When, on one occasion, his pastor reminded him of his
earlier desire to do more than make money and enjoy the affluent life, he
acted upon his pastor's urging to study at Trinity Theological College in
Singapore. After completing his theological education there, he returned
to Malaysia, ready for ordination and assignment to a troubled congregation in Kuala Lumpur. Philip Tan was still in his twenties, inexperienced,
unmarried, disowned by his parents (who were counting on his Caltex salary
for their future security), with only a letter from the bishop in his hands
(but without his supportive presence) as he arrived for his first Sunday at
the door of Christ Lutheran Church where he was called to serve. His story
of what followed is as bizarre as any I have heard, anywhere, about obstacles faced when beginning a ministry.

The church council president was preaching that Sunday. He spotted
Tan as a newcomer and asked "Who are you?" Tan's answer startled him:
"I am your new pastor." An emergency meeting among the fifty members
present was held on the spot. Their decision was twofold, to complain to
the bishop for not sending an experienced pastor and to reject this newcomer standing at the door. After some further discussion, they reluctantly
handed Tan the key to the church building. Then the entire congregation
left. He told me that he spent the rest of that traumatic Sunday in a daze
of bewilderment, as he found nothing better to do than use some old rags
to clean up the rundown building. The pastor's apartment was empty, not
even a chair to sit on. The best he could do for a bed was to sleep on the
floor with his luggage as his pillow. That was how he spent his first night
as pastor of Christ Lutheran Church in Kuala Lumpur. The next message
to him from the council was "to keep a low profile" since he was not
welcome to serve the congregation and the leaders were beginning negotiations immediately for another pastor. Meanwhile the council members
did all the preaching. After three months of fruitless appeal to the bishop,
the former pastor (who had resigned) returned to sit in on the meetings
of the church council. His wife was the secretary. After several months of
this impasse, the bishop visited Tan and asked "How are things going?"
After hearing how things were going, he left in silence without offering

help or advice of any kind. Philip Tan endured this incredible situation for two years before the former pastor and his wife discontinued attendance at council meetings and left for good.

Astonished by what he told me, I asked Tan how he survived two full years of such total rejection, and whether the treatment he received revealed something about the Malaysian temperament that outsiders should understand. He answered No to the latter question; there was nothing generically Malaysian about the mistreatment he received. He put it down to a congregation that had lived too long in denial of the conflict that had silenced the Gospel and shattered every semblance of Christ-like relationships. With regard to the question of how he survived, he said that most nights he cried himself to sleep, and drew the strength he needed to outlast the meanness of the congregation and the ineptitude of the bishop by simply throwing himself upon the mercies of God and waiting for the congregation to do the same. Two years of waiting was a very long time under those circumstances, he said, because of the constant temptation to give up on God's timing and conclude that it was all a waste of his time and talents. Tan was at the top of his class in Singapore and had the offer to do graduate study at the University of Tuebingen in Germany. But he stayed on at Christ congregation with a dogged determination to outlast all the odds against staying. Another thing that sustained him was the Sunday liturgy which he was allowed to lead, with his voice as the only one heard in the otherwise silent congregation.

A turning point came for him when he picked up a book on prayer by the Korean evangelist, Paul Cho. It taught him to ask God in faith for what it took to meet specific problems and to be relentlessly consistent in begging for God's intervention, mediated in specific ways to overcome whatever obstacle stood in the way. He asked the council to meet with him for prayer every Saturday morning at 5:30, which they did for six months with no apparent results. The first signs of breakthrough began to appear when the leaders of the opposition began to ask for forgiveness for their sins of hard-heartedness and all the damage done. Tan and the penitent leadership then realized that such honesty before God had to spread through the congregation. With that in mind he set aside times for prayer and fasting in which the whole congregation was asked to join.

The leaven of penitence and renewal spread among the congregation, and with it a new sense of what the Lord was preparing them for—outreach to the surrounding community.

He spoke of that turning point toward mission as the result of a vision given him. He saw a brilliant light shining down from above upon muddy ground that was slowly moving toward the light. He prayed to understand what the vision meant and perceived its meaning as Christ's teaching him that the turgid mass of moving mud meant people struggling to break free from drug addiction, lives of poverty, broken marriages, broken lives of every sort who were—as he put it—"not the *good* sinners easily reached but the worst kind who, despite all, were not lost to God." Revival at Christ Lutheran congregation followed with signs and wonders heretofore not known by the much-tested pastor and congregation. Within the familiar cadences of the Lutheran liturgy people would break down in tears as they experienced the depth of what they were doing when confessing their sins and receiving the liberation promised by the Gospel announced in the absolution. Miraculous healing also occurred, and speaking in tongues as well. When another pastor warned: "Be careful, Philip, you are walking on thin ice!" his response was that he sought none of these things nor did he assume that these manifestations of the Holy Spirit would continue unabated. The lasting gift of the Spirit upon which he depended was the power of the Gospel to unify the varied charismata of the Spirit and keep the congregation, once so astonishingly divided and mean spirited, reconciled in Christ's love and thus united in the bond of his peace.

Philip Tan is now in his twenty-second year as pastor of Christ Lutheran Church. Sunday attendance runs between eight hundred and a thousand. He oversees a staff of fifteen, including teachers in the daily preschool and kindergarten program which Tan values highly as a building block for young lives and outreach to their families. His average day begins at 7:30 with worship, followed by visiting the sick, counseling, meetings, study, and planning the congregation's mission trips that take lay members to evangelize in Vietnam, China, and Myanmar. After our conversation he introduced me to a young woman who had been badly burned by a terrorist explosion in Yangon, Myanmar, on a congregation mission there two years before. She spoke of the pastoral visits Tan made to her that required traveling hundreds of miles to reach her when she was fighting for her life in the hospital, and the support of the congregation for her and her family during her long months of recovery in Kuala Lumpur. Tan spoke of her as a living sign of the healing grace that reaches the total person as well as its promise for healing the ills of urban and rural society in Malaysia. Philip Tan's story bears witness to the grace of Christ at work in turning a woefully sick congregation into a renewed body of believers with its doors and hearts open to the least and the last in its surrounding community and beyond.

Signs of that larger sphere of mission were evident in the diaconal work of Yap Lee Cheng whom I met in the LCMS headquarters building in Kuala Lumpur. I had read about her in a national magazine article which described her as a Mother Teresa of Malaysia. She looks nothing like the late celebrated nun of Calcutta, however; her long black hair framed distinctly Chinese features and the fashionable blue and white dress she wore was not the simple garment worn by the Sisters of Charity. Known widely in Singapore by her nickname Wendy, she is a social worker in her late forties who recalled that when she prayed as the lone Christian in her family she was shouted down by parents and siblings. When Beverly asked her why, she quoted their reason: "because it will hurt our chances at the lottery!" Undaunted, she persevered in her determination as a self-taught, self-made, self-supporting Christian who served orphans, the homeless aged, the diseased, the mentally ill, and other who fall between the cracks without a safety net. She paused long enough in her case-after-case recitation of people who are poor, have no savvy, cannot read, and live in isolation on less than $175 annually, to describe how she came to her calling. Her mother's illness and death put her into a deep depression that made her suicidal. She prayed to God for release and his answer took her out of herself by directing her toward others in need. Her husband, himself handicapped by polio early in life, had empathy for her new-found calling and encouraged her as she began to go from door to door in poor areas, seeking out people in crisis. From this beginning she broadened her work to starting up orphanages, homes for the aged, a home for special needs children, a center for drug addicts—all this as a wife and mother of four children of her own. This frenetic pace changed, however, when her 9 year old daughter came home from school one day saying that the teacher had asked the class to draw a picture of their mother. She showed her mother a blank page. She took it as a wake-up call of realization that she could not serve others if her own children were neglected. She began training others to join her lay ministry and continues to do so with close ties to the Lutheran Church of Malaysia and Singapore, but not under its direction or support. She gets funding for her work on her own without depending on the LCMS because, as she explained, so much of her work is with people whose daily struggle is not about being Lutheran or Catholic but simply to stay alive.

Erik Lai represents still another facet of the active role of laity in Malaysian church life. He is in his 40s, married, the father of three children; his flawless English and ready grasp of my purpose made him particularly valuable to listen to. Like many, he is the first Christian in his family line and his introduction to the Christian faith came through a teen age friend who invited him to a youth gathering in a Lutheran congregation. His mother was wary of his growing involvement, fearing it would lead to baptism which, in her mind, was identified with alienation from everything it meant to be a Chinese Malaysian. As his new found faith deepened, however, his mother discovered that her son's attitude and actions of filial piety toward her and his older siblings were all the more heartfelt (his father had died when he was 13). By age 21 he was a baptized confessor of Jesus Christ as Lord, and showed maturity in handling the delicate balance of his Christian faith with family occasions when ancestral rites were followed. On days of remembrance of his father's death he would join the family at the graveside and present flowers, but not pray to his father—which drew resentment from his relatives. His mother, however, did not take offense because she had seen how his convictions made him a better son. He could not eat food offered to idols but prepared his own food for ceremonial occasions. Gradually his family saw that his walk with Christ did not cut him off from them and the culture they valued, and in telling these memories he kept stressing the importance of strong pastoral support (from the pioneer Lutheran missionary, John Nelson) as he grew in integrating his faith with being fully Chinese Malaysian. He graduated from university with an economics major, trained in Japan for work in a marine insurance firm, and married his wife whom he met when both were active in the congregation. Their church wedding was another instance of faith joined creatively with tradition. The church ceremony was followed by a Chinese tea ceremony at home in which the younger served the family elders.

At 38 he took over a struggling Christian bookseller company deep in debt and used his business acumen to reorganize it and reach out in direct contact with pastors and congregations. He relocated the previously separate stores in new sites strategically placed in well established bookstores in Kuala Lumpur. In two years he accomplished a successful turnaround of his firm by making it into Malaysia's largest Christian bookseller. A key to this, he explained, was creating book displays in congregations (only 5% of which were Lutheran) and direct mail sales. As president of Glad Sounds Inc. he sets aside 30% of the profits from certain segments of his business for mission purposes of the LCMS and other churches of Malaysia. He travels abroad extensively for leadership training, youth ministry, stewardship workshops, and in his duties as a member of the Editorial Board of the Asian News publication of the Lutheran World Federation. Listening to him I could not miss his passion for the promise of strong Christian leadership in swaying the destiny of nations, especially in his own Malaysia today.

Lutherans have a voice in the Malaysian national legislature in the person of Hoh Hee Lee, who went out of his way to meet me in our hotel and give me his time for an interview on his faith at work in serving the public good as an elected member of the state assembly. He is 46, married, the father of three young children ("I need to spend more time with them" was a postscript he added when showing me their picture), and a man with a natural *gravitas* that inspires voter support. His story, like virtually every other Malaysian Lutheran with whom I spoke, began with memories of growing up in a home where traditional Chinese folk religion prevailed. He explained what that meant: high regard for parental authority, praying to the spirits of deceased ancestors, making offerings to them, keeping idols in the household, and burning incense in homage to their sould. He was born in a village where a church was located close to his house and at age 14 he became interested in the games, camping outings, and fellowship activities that included Bible study for youth. It was the prospect of fun that attracted him initially, he said, but he found more than fun as his participation increased. He was baptized at 21, an event which his parents and family opposed because of their fear that as a Christian their son would not support them in their old age, nor would he honor their souls as they moved to the vague realm of the spirit world after death. He has supported them faithfully and will continue to do so, he assured me, and in this regard he shares a concern common to all first and second generation Christians in the LCMS and other Christian bodies in Malaysia. He graduated from college with a degree in management and worked for some years in various sales jobs, ranging from t-shirts to books to mutual funds. His respect for the system of British law as a positive legacy from the days of British colonization in Malaysia motivated him to turn from business to a career in law and government. After finishing law school in Kuala Lumpur he began his private practice and then was successful in his first run for election to the state assembly. He gave me a brief explanation of the governmental system in Malaysia in which his party has been predominant in choosing the prime minister for terms of five years. He was about to answer my inquiries about his own experience in the legislature when our conversation was interrupted by a team of dancers and acrobats entering the hotel lobby with drums banging and cymbals clashing loudly as the troupe danced in tribute to deceased ancestors, all this to the delight of guests in the lobby. This stopped the civics lesson short, but he did insist on telling me—in words shouted above the impromptu cacophony of dancers and drums— that his Lutheran grounding gives him a good base for his calling as a Christian in the legislature, that Lutherans in Malaysia do well to pay attention to Pentecostal mission methods without adopting the theology of a prosperity gospel, that the challenge to reach the Malaysian youth generation today is immense, and that his own congregation of the LCMS is growing. Yes, he added, the traditional worship has given way to contemporary music and the hymnals stay unused in the pews. More important to him than how one worships God on Sundays is that believers put a sound faith to work on Mondays and the weekdays following. For him that meant demonstrating that politics is not dirty but a holy calling in which he is responsible to God and to the people he serves. Our time was up. The acrobats were setting up a wooden bar contraption for more acts. The drums were deafening. We shook hands. I mouthed my thanks for the time he gave me.

And he was off through the main doorway of the hotel lobby before dancers and acrobats took over.

A luncheon visit with LCMS Bishop Philip Lok concluded the days in Kuala Lumpur as he told us of the work of the seventy pastors serving the 10,000 Lutherans in sixty-one congregations of the church body. He is youthful in appearance—all Asians seem so to western eyes—but well experienced and well respected as the servant of the servants of God, a traditional description of bishops at their best. He said that in the Malaysian population of twenty-six million, 8% are Christian, with Islam as the dominant religion of more than half the population, Buddhism next, then Hinduism. In his own church body of the Lutheran Church of Malaysia and Singapore there is currently a pastoral shortage. We parted with words of interest in continuing contact via the internet, and his parting words about Southeast Asia as one of promise for the course of the Gospel in a nation in transition was symbolized by the Petronas Towers within sight through the restaurant window. These twin structures, the highest in the world when built, direct the eye upward, a suitable symbol for what the church is called to be and do in this land of diverse peoples, problems, and promise.

PART 9

INTRODUCING
PAPUA NEW GUINEA & AUSTRALIA

Hardly a hundred miles separate the South Pacific island nation of Papua New Guinea from the northernmost tip of the mainland of Australia. Yet the social and cultural distance between the two nations is huge. The same might be said of the nature of Christianity in each place, if the Papuan version, when viewed through western eyes, is regarded as primitive, while the Australian form is taken as modern because of its western dress. A deeper look, however, reveals surprises and complexities. Christians, both Catholic, Protestant, and Lutheran missionaries came to Papua New Guinea in the 1880's. By 1900, Christians of the three traditions numbered 4% of the population. By 2000, 96% of the people of Papua New Guinea professed the Christian faith, an astonishing pace of growth unmatched anywhere throughout that century. Australia presents a different story. In 1770, when Captain James Cook claimed the east coast for Great Britain, the growth of congregations formed by Anglican settlers was slow due to the fact that Australia had also become a penal colony of the British crown. Though that practice ended in 1868, Australia's strongly secular culture, shaped by the rugged individualism necessitated by its unique geography, has been a stiff challenge to Christians of all traditions. The Anglican Church has declined in number from half the population in 1851 to one third by 1971. The German Lutherans who came in 1834 maintained their ethnic identity, as did successive waves of others throughout the 19th century, which meant institutional stability, if modest growth, based on immigration. Australian Lutherans have been exemplary in establishing mission beginnings in Papua New Guinea and fostering its phenomenal growth thereafter.

Wesley Kigasung, Lutheran bishop in Papua New Guinea, wanted to learn to fly as a high school boy in the late 1950's. When he asked his father for permission to apply for training as a pilot, his father answered with a question of his own: "What's a pilot?" He had never seen an airplane nor was the word pilot anywhere in his vocabulary as one born in a tribal society closer to the Stone Age than to the era of airplanes that fascinated his son. Kigasung did not become a pilot. Instead he used his gifts to become a Lutheran pastor, educator and bishop of the Evangelical Lutheran Church of New Guinea. He told me this story to illustrate the astonishing leap from his father's generation to his own. Another symbol of rapid change during the past fifty years is the growth of the Christian faith in Papua New Guinea from less than 5% to the present 96% of the 5.5 million population, 1.2 million of whom confess Jesus as Lord in the two Lutheran church bodies in the land.

Dean Lueking and Wesley Kigasung

PAPUA NEW GUINEA

I had met Wesley Kigasung on several earlier occasions, in 1983, when he was president of the Lutheran seminary in Lae, and prior to that when he was completing his doctoral studies at the Lutheran School of Theology in Chicago. My first impression when meeting him again was that he had lost none of the down-to-earth quality that makes him equally at home with village grannies as with international dignitaries who come visiting. He is a man big in body as well as capacious in mind, and his good humored mix of local ways with his sophistication as a global churchman shows in his fondness for chewing the reddish Betel nut for its nicotine kick while dressed in the full dignity of his clergy suit with pectoral cross.

In the first of two lengthy conversations with him in Lae, the city in eastern PNG where the church headquarters, the major theological seminary, and the teachers college of the church are located, he spoke of things that both cheered him as well as put gray streaks among the thinning strands of hair left on his head. He mentioned first the satisfaction of having completed a year of extensive travel to pastors and congregations throughout PNG to hear their concerns, share their joys, and mentor them with his wisdom, experience, and theological depth gained through the years. It had been exhausting, taking its toll on his health (he spoke of some heart setbacks that made him pace himself) and it meant less time at home with his wife, Susie, their three children and the grandchildren. He counted it altogether worthwhile, however, in the realization that a church growing so rapidly needs internal growth at all levels, especially at the crucial point of congregational leadership. He knows he cannot do all the mentoring himself and described continuing education opportunities he has established in each district so that he might retire in good conscience, or at least remove his name from eligibility for re-election as bishop. His brethren, he said, are prevailing upon him to continue nevertheless, some even saying that it would be to the honor of God if he were to die in office. He said he preferred to put that honor off until sometime later in the future.

He went on to point out one factor behind church growth that he regarded as unique to the current Christian scene in Papua New Guinea. It is a laity-led initiative in various areas to relocate whole groups of Christians from one neighborhood to another where they function as a community in mission to their neighbors, seeking to live the Gospel preached and taught in their midst and thus draw converts to the faith, who then are trained to pass the faith on. Another reason for growth he cited was one I had not thought of before. In PNG the absence of world religions such as Hinduism, Buddhism, and Islam (lightly represented by Indonesian immigrants on the northern coast) made for a clearer path to reach people steeped in a folk religion that also offers more connecting points to the salvation history revealed in Scripture. He spoke of the leavening work of the Holy Spirit through schools (8 high schools and more than 180 elementary schools), several hospitals, numerous health centers, medical aid posts, and maternal and child health care programs introduced where none existed before. The church has an active Women's Department for purposes of leadership training of women and girls who are reached with the Gospel while instructed in hygiene, nutrition, and child care. Women are not yet ordained, he added, since it is not asked for, at least not yet, in the church he knows well from his lifetime experience.

All of these things take money, he added, and teaching stewardship to converts, who in many cases are new to a cash economy, is a long term task. In his role as bishop, however, Kigasung emphasized that he has not made money a top priority. The greater challenge is to begin with what God calls people to be as his children and then to trust him to bring results far beyond all expectations. Wherever he has gone in his mentoring role as bishop, he has not wavered from emphasizing, as he put it, that "cash cannot buy visionary leadership"—though he acknowledged ruefully that others are better at raising money than Lutherans and they offer lessons to be learned. Kigasung cited the real wealth given to Lutherans to share as the treasure of Christ's grace for sinners as the heart of the Bible's message and trusting God to do great works in the face of huge obstacles, self-doubts, and the temptation of schemes for rapid church growth at the expense of depth in discipleship. He credited exceptional missionaries who mentored him with these truths when he was a young pastor starting out, many of them sent from the United States during the 1950's by the Missouri Synod Lutherans. He spoke with respect for their aptitude in recognizing the importance of sensitivity to Papuan culture as theologically necessary and essential to their love for people radically different from themselves. He drew upon his gift for putting the theology he learned from missionaries into plain talk when counseling Papuan pastors in their approach to people: "Don't let your people go for the fast food stuff,—'fish and chips religion'—but feed them with the solid yams and taro from the land—the good news of Jesus the Savior from sin."

The image of solid food from the land as analogous to the solid food of the Word became more real than we expected when Kigasung re-arranged his weekend schedule to take us personally to a Sunday in Binimamp, a village two hours out from Lae. We had been invited by Nari Gawebing, a villager whom we had met while he was in Lae for a church conference, to return with him for a two day taste of life in his village. Kigasung learned of the plans and made the better suggestion to take us to Binimamp himself, knowing much better than we what we would be in for, and it was to our benefit that his wisdom prevailed. He fetched us from our quarters in the church guest house early on Sunday morning and, with his wife, the church secretary, and Beverly in the jump seat of the church pickup truck, drove gingerly around highway potholes for the two hour ride from Lae to the village. The surrounding countryside was strikingly beautiful, with lush green covered flatlands spiked by sharp edged ridges giving way to low lying hills along the way. Our arrival in Binimamp was an event. The news had spread that the bishop was coming bringing a foreign couple along. him. The village itself is set back a mile or more from the highway, accessible by a dirt road. There, some 500 people live in scattered clusters of thatched roof huts raised several feet off the ground ("to keep out snakes and other animals" was the explanation). The walls of tightly woven palm leaves were artfully decorated in various patterns to make the huts weather proof, and the grass thatched roofs were another sign that all materials needed for a dwelling were within easy reach. Adding to the self-sustainability of village life is the fact that the skills needed for building homes have been handed down in families from generation to generation; everyone has a specific part and knows what to do. Our arrival was announced by the sound of drums as well as by the shouts by excited kids running alongside as the pickup truck pulled slowly into the center of the village. Women were already outside preparing food in cooking fires burning within hollowed out logs, lined with stones and mud to keep them intact from the smoldering coals. Younger men were busy shredding what looked like strips of coconut and other spices for the main menu of chicken, yams, and vegetables from nearby gardens. The elders attended to their role of welcoming us with handshakes and smiles, as well as providing folding chairs for our entourage while other leaders sat comfortably on standard seating—large palm tree leaves spread over well swept, hard packed earth under the branches of mango trees. As Bishop Kigasung was brought up to date on village matters, I walked around to chat with people young and old, take pictures, and simply savor the hospitality of this unique Sunday morning.

By mid-morning families were gathering to join the procession toward the large, open, grounds of the center of the village where the worship service took place, an area well sheltered by a grove of sturdy trees. At the sound of drums all took their places in the processional line, led by the evangelist, along a pathway lined with orchids and other brilliantly colored flowers, then through an archway framed with woven palm branches, and finally into the open clearing where the worship service took place. Behind the evangelist were six lithe young men dressed out in feathered headdress, with beads strapped across their chests, their legs banded with more colorful feathers and straw decorations, and a brightly colored skirt wrapped around their middle. In slow, graceful movements suggesting gestures of reverence, they criss-crossed each other as they ushered the column of several hundred people toward an altar table, who then fanned out and sat down on woven palm mats to form a circle of worshipers. It was impressive that such an open, impromptu sanctuary could be created on the spot, without roof or walls, well shaded from the sub-equatorial sun, wonderfully cooled by a refreshing breeze, without electrical power for lighting or organ, open to everyone, including an occasional dog, pig, or chicken wandering through without censure from the congregation. The liturgy was sung in Pidgin, a practical language combining PNG dialects with English, and, as the hymns were added, the power of the worship was palpable. A guitarist sounded an opening note. Then a solo voice sang the first line of liturgy or hymn. A chorus of a half dozen would follow to establish the melody line. Then the entire assembly joined in harmonized singing from memory the full liturgy and all of the verses of all the hymns. The hymn texts, I was told, were rich in images drawn from PNG culture and are chosen with care for theological soundness in proclaiming the salvation story from the Bible. Since both liturgy and hymns were known by young and old from memory—I saw no printed hymnbooks around the circle—both the liturgy and hymns are the main channels of instruction in the faith. The three lessons for the Sunday were read, each by a lay person who stood to read the appointed Scripture; the entire assembly rose to hear the Gospel reading, followed by speaking the Apostles Creed in unison.

As Bishop Kigasung interpreted my sermon I recognized that he was adding his own sentences needed to connect my words with the thought world and lived faith of those gathered. At the offering, all were invited forward to present their offerings in receptacles which were hollowed out coconut shells placed on the altar table for that purpose. A second offering followed while hymns were sung, and most of those in the congregation returned to support the special purpose for designated that Sunday. After the prayers of the people, the Our Father, and the Benediction pronounced by Bishop Kigasung, selected members came forward to speak the gratitude of the village for the visit by the bishop, followed by another group for a ceremony we did not expect. Kigasung explained that each one who approached us brought a gift of friendship individually crafted from materials available from Binimamp and its surroundings. Four women presented us carrying bags made of netting, several more brought leis of fresh flowers, one girl brought a shell necklace, an older man brought wooden spoons he had carved, another brought a cooking pot he had molded from clay, and the presentation of the final gift of a grass skirt that Beverly brought delighted smiles and applause as she tied it around her waist. Their generosity was all the more moving because each gift was a personal expression that took time, effort, and skill to make as a sign of hospitality to two strangers from half way around the world. As each presenter came forward to put their gift into our hands the question came to mind of what their experience would be if the occasion was reversed. How would North American Lutherans handle a Sunday morning liturgy introduced by colorfully garbed guests from PNG, dancing their way down the church aisle through an orchid-laden archway to the altar, accompanied by drums pounding out the beat? That question ought not be rhetorical. More and more there are channels of international exchange that bridge the gaps of isolation, indifference and parochialism that block awareness of what Christians mean when confessing the church as one, holy, catholic and apostolic. The temptation is to caricature the congregation in Binimamp as quaint, if not primitive people who live in thatched roof huts, do liturgy with dancers in feathered headdress, and worship in open air spaces. The better view is to envision them as fellow members of Christ's global body who show the grace of hospitality in ways that are all the more unforgettable because they come from their own hands and hearts.

The spirit of community did not end with the presentation of gifts. It progressed to the enjoyment of the food served to the villagers: yams, taro (edible roots of a starchy plant), cooked bananas, coconut dressing, chicken and other items not known to us. While kids romped about, the adults remained seated on palm leaves around the circle (men with men, women with women) for conversation and the sheer enjoyment of Sabbath fellowship. By 2 o'clock the mealtime was finished. Bishop Kigasung took over to report on local and national church doings, as well as to comment on issues coming before a Lutheran World Federation meeting in Lund, Sweden which he was preparing to attend. He held forth for an hour. Though I could not understand his rapid-fire Pidgin I could sense that he was getting through to his mostly male listeners as they responded with exclamations of concern, surprise, or applause. Again, my mind turned to the question of how a congregation at home would engage in a post-service presentation on vital church matters with the same interest and patience. Obviously, it was Kigasung's presence and his pastoral gifts that were working in Binimamp. When the bishop comes, everyone attends worship and stays on to listen to his report. The distractions that diminish too much of Sunday elsewhere in the world, draining it of worship, fellowship, and table fellowship, were not present on this rare Sunday in this remote place.

Nari Gewebing, the Binimamp villager we met in Lae, is a person whose life story enlarges the picture of village life beyond the limits of a one Sunday visit. He was born in Binimamp and remembered the stories told him by his grandfather who was the first Christian in the family line, including accounts of the horrors of the Japanese occupation during World War II and the unspeakable atrocities committed especially against PNG women. His father, also a native of Binimamp, was a teacher who had been trained in the Lutheran teachers college in Lae. As a young student whose father took interest in his study habits, Nari passed his school examinations successfully, then left the village after high school in a larger town nearby to study electrical engineering. He prospered in his working career in Lae, where he and his family established themselves as city people. When his father's health failed he felt duty bound to return to his village to assume the care of his father. In this time –"out of the blue" as he described it, he was named as a youth coordinator in the congregation (everyone in the village is Lutheran), something he knew little about but became a calling for which he had natural talents as a leader. He coordinated youth work under a government program for nine years, working also with the evangelist and church members. He bought a generator and projector for showing film strips to attract youth and help them understand themselves and their need for the

Word of God. He was clear in his theological understanding that no behavioral change can take deep root without the inner working of the Holy Spirit through the power of God's love revealed in the Gospel. He spent time in Australia in continuing education for his increasing duties in the church, which moved from local youth work to coordinating youth ministries among congregations of his district. This was followed by his election by his area synod to the board of Lutheran Health Services, a position which made him responsible for finding and organizing the training of volunteers (most of whom are women from area villages) in health care services throughout the region. It was in that connection that he had come to Lae for a week of meetings with other board members which enabled us to meet him and receive his invitation for a weekend visit to experience what he rightly called the real Papua New Guinea. In telling us his story he illustrated how a boy from Binimamp can do well in school, continue his education through college, relocate in the city and finish further higher education, marry, enter a career, gain international experience through church connections abroad, and then act upon strong filial bonds to move back to his village roots to care for an ailing parent. The values underlying that story are universally valid and suggest a staying power needed everywhere.

Gerald Mangiri, 52, directs the theological training program of the Evangelical Lutheran Church of Papua New Guinea which includes the major theological seminary in Lae, another seminary for practical pastoral education at Logawing, on the southeast coast of PNG (in one of the most beautiful campus locations anywhere, atop a thousand foot cliff overlooking the Coral Sea), and Balob Teachers College in Lae. His duties are to oversee staffing and funding of these institutions, including the placement of lecturers from overseas. He received me in his office in Lae, and began our conversation with comment on the tasks facing the 150 students when they finish their training in the two seminaries of the church. First, he explained, there are between seven and eight thousand dialects in the country which are confusing beyond description in their diversity and for which the only solution is the unifying effect of the national language, Pidgin. The other factor is one that Kigasung had described from his experience with the gap between his father's time and his own, the leap in just forty years from a Stone Age life to that in PNG today. He cited the inevitable problems of urbanization: rising crime rates, especially among high school graduates who seek employment in towns and cities but find none, cultural dislocation and social isolation in adjusting to urban life which sever the family and tribal ties found in rural settings, and the increase in disease, especially AIDS, in the larger cities.

Mangiri's personal life story began with his birth and upbringing in a Christian family in a village. He did well in school, studied business at the university, and worked in a bank for three years in Port Moresby. He was restless, however, with a life that was outwardly affluent but lacked inward purpose. He enrolled in Martin Luther Seminary in Lae, finished the four year course with distinction, served his first pastoral assignment in what he described as a caring-sharing ministry, an adaptation of the PNG cultural concept of the extended family to a congregation ministry. I asked for an example. He cited the custom of the bride price whereby the groom and his relatives must contribute financially to the bride's family as well as to cover wedding costs. Applied to a congregation, the concept means that as new people come as strangers to the town or city, members of the congregation take on the role of a spiritually supportive family, helping find housing for those without relatives, and above all, helping newcomers find a spiritual home among Christ's people. Mangiri is married, the father of five children, and though his pastor salary is modest, he and his household open their home to newcomers on weekend occasions as an example of the ministry of hospitality to the congregation.

He touched upon varied problems encountered in pastoral ministry, one of which is polygamy, which is still practiced despite the church's constitution which declares it contrary to the Word of God. Despite that stated conviction, he knows Lutherans in political life who have two wives. The problem is acute when one wife and set of children are abandoned. Then the church must become active as a haven of care for such women and their young. There is still the lingering mentality in PNG culture that many wives are a sign of material possessions which mark the Big Man. Mangiri said that the church must counter this with the example of the New Man in Christ, faithful to one wife, devoted to his children, and aware of his daily work as a calling under God. He spoke also of the rapidly changing role of women and the status of the question among Lutherans of ordaining women. Mangiri favors it. But his wife urged him not to take a leading part in the debate because she felt the church is not yet ready for it. In her view, women are by nature a shepherding presence in congregations and need no ordination to confirm that gift. He sees the wisdom of her gradualist approach, since women are already leading Bible studies, literacy and health programs in and beyond congregations, and do much of the visitation to single women and widows. Furthermore, in the nation at large, women are already teachers and office holders in government, in fact the first woman elected as premier of Papua New Guinea was a Lutheran. Urban congregations are better prepared to accept the ordination of women but this is not the case in rural areas. He said he did not expect to see it in the church in his lifetime.

Mangiri spoke appreciatively of the value of continuing service by non-PNG persons in the church, particularly those who come as visiting professors in the seminaries and other short term specialists needed in medical work, leadership training, and youth ministry. On the subject of relations between indigenous PNG clergy and overseas church workers, he told of a personal experience that taught him to trust God's providence to prevail in the long run over hurtful conflicts that occur. In his teens he had been bitterly disappointed when an American missionary, a director of the Lutheran high school that had accepted him, then turned him down because he arrived late due to transportation delays beyond his control. After tears of angry disillusionment he entered another high school where he flourished in his studies, then went on to graduate with a university business degree and enter a successful banking career. That, in turn, was interrupted by his midlife call to the seminary in Lae and service as a pastor in a congregation. After some years of experience he was selected to spend a year in the United States as a guest pastor in partnership with American clergy serving several congregations in the mid-west. When he discovered, to his astonishment, that one of the pastors with whom he was to work was the former missionary who had refused him admission to the high school years before, he dreaded going to the parsonage door to present himself, but went anyway. He met the pastor who was equally surprised to recognize who it was that had come thousands of miles to serve. A long simmering grievance, never acknowledged, was faced at last. When the offending pastor apologized for his mistreatment of Mangiri and asked for his forgiveness. Mangiri offered it gladly, and saw this reconciliation as the sign of the Divine providence working in hidden ways all along, now surfacing to give his time of service in America a deeper dimension. He learned much about pastoral counseling of those in troubled marriages and families that helped enrich his calling when back in PNG, and found particularly good rapport with poor black families with whom he could empathize because he, too, was black and served an underclass back home. He showed me an example of highly productive collaborative work with another American missionary, Willard Burce, with whom he worked in revising Luther's Small Catechism to make it "speak Pidgin" in the PNG context.

A serendipitous breakfast table conversation enabled me to meet Don Kuban, a poised, outgoing man in his early 50s who was attending the Lutheran Health Services conference at the church headquarters compound in Lae. With his fluent English and considerable experience in conversing with overseas guests it was possible to engage him quickly in the purpose of our coming to learn from the stories of people like himself. He was born on Karkar Island, off the coast of north central PNG, into a family in which his paternal grandfather, the first to become a Christian, was one who had been trained for his life work as a medical orderly by the legendary pioneer doctor of medical work in PNG, Dr. T.G. Braun. Kudan was encouraged by his father to do well in school, and although the stories he had heard about his grandfather's experiences as a medical orderly were part of his growing up, he became a teacher and was well on his way in that career. Then, one day, "out of the blue" as he said, he received a letter from a hospital in Medang asking him to consider becoming the director. He left it unanswered for months, at a loss as to how his educational degree could qualify him to be a hospital director. Without explaining what followed in detail, Kudan told of how the conviction grew in him that the unanswered invitation was a call from God which he accepted. He and his bride moved from Karkar Island to Medang where he found his way into his new position and flourished in it for several years. From this post he moved on to regional leadership with the church based Lutheran Health Services in which he continues to serve. Among other things, he told me that 52% of the health services in the nation are supplied through the agency of the church, 100% of the training of volunteer health workers throughout PNG occurs through the congregations of the church, and 60% of nurses training is carried out through the medical and educational offices of the church. Things that vex him: dishonesty in channeling government funds through the church for health care service nationwide, a process where transparency is lacking in both the church and government. He was careful to avoid confrontational approaches when dealing with this problem, instead "I would sit quietly in the corner and say nothing until it was time to speak up—and then speak plainly to the problem." His persistent call for transparency in handling funds made him an enemy in the eyes of many, but he has persevered and finally has established a transparent system of delivering PNG currency to local congregations. Malaria is the greatest health threat in PNG he explained: "everyone has it in their blood, including me." Early detection—made possible primarily through volunteer health workers in congregations—can mean control against full blown malaria through medication. Failing that, the chances for survival diminish rapidly. We talked of other health problems, including the effects of urban loneliness and dislocation from family ties. I told him my immediate impressions in our first days in PNG of noticing the predominance of people gathered in pairs and clusters rather than alone. He responded that PNG culture places primary importance on belonging, having someone in the immediate or extended family with whom to join, whether at home or in a new place. The absence of such ties is at the heart of the huge problems of gangs, comprised of both boys and girls, who are causing the crime rate to surge.

An instructive lesson in relating the complexities of PNG primal religion to Christian thinking was provided in a visit with Daniel Watato, the deputy director of the Martin Luther Seminary in Lae. In Melanesian religious thought the central place of ancestors is essential in three ways: every person's identity and actions come down to him through the flow of the generations, the present human community is made up not only of the living but also the hovering ancestors who are equally alive and even more powerful than before their death, and that the good life depends on maintaining right relationships with this dynamic community of the living and the ancestral spirits. Other aspects of the breadth and depth of primal religion were beyond the scope of our discussion, but not beyond the importance of respect on the part of Christians when approaching this vast realm in which primal religion and PNG culture are inseparable.

The one practical point he emphasized to me was that Christians, he meant Lutheran Christians here, have yet to incorporate into liturgical worship the lively sense of celebration of life that primal religion contains. To this end, he added, the need is not to mimic primal religion but to recover from the Bible, and especially from the Old Testament, the reality of *shalom*, that all-embracing peace, happiness, and well being that can be expressed— among other ways—through religious dance and ecstasy (a remark that made me think of the Binimamp Sunday experience a few days before). PNG Christians hear such New Testament passages as Hebrews 12: 1-3 ("since we are surrounded by so great a cloud of witnesses…:") with ears more readily attuned to how that includes their own forbears, and thus finds a connection to Jesus Christ, to whom all the witnesses point. That led him to say that the best thing PNG Lutherans bring is faith alone, grace alone, and Scripture alone as the pillars upon which the many and varied ways of God's coming of old becomes the good news of God's coming now in the crucified and risen Christ. Baptism and the Eucharist are sacramental means of proclaiming the Word made visible, a term of Luther's that has powerful resonance in the PNG mindset which is tangible rather than abstract. Presently, the Pentecostal movement carries a strong appeal to the senses, but without the underpinning of God's grace, a problem especially for Lutheran youth who are fascinated by emotional spectacle but lack the maturity to grasp its limits. In view of these inroads he saw no reason for two Lutheran churches to remain organizationally separated. Together, the 130,000 member Gutnius Lutheran Church and the Evangelical Lutheran Church of New Guinea with more than a million baptized, can be a more effective witness to sound Christian faith and practice.

Currently there is a shortage of pastors in the Lutheran congregations. Although fifty apply for admission annually, an average of around twenty meet the standards for the six year course of study. Congregations and their pastors must approve candidates, who also are required to have completed high school. The average age of the seminary student is 24, though the age range can reach as high as 40. Married students are eligible. Financial support for seminary study comes from the congregation and families of the students. In addition to theological education in preparation for the pastoral ministry, the seminary in Lae offers a three year parish worker program for men and women, with six women currently among those enrolled.

Lutherans have been in Papua New Guinea since 1886, when a German missionary sent first to Australia by the Neuendettelsau Mission Society in Bavaria, realized his dream to serve where there were no Christians. Johann Flierl came up from Australia to the northeastern tip of Papua New Guinea in 1886 to begin the Lutheran witness in proclaiming the Gospel. In the century and a third since, hundreds more have come from Germany, Australia, and the United States as evangelist missionaries, teachers, professors, educational administrators, doctors, nurses, pilots, carpenters, builders, farmers, and suppliers of varied technical services in support of PNG leaders of the two indigenous Lutheran church bodies formed in the late 1950's. Some of these missionary servants served lifelong in PNG and some lost their lives there. The emergence of gifted PNG church leaders in the past half century signifies the fruit of the labors of those who planted the seed of the Evangelical Lutheran Church of Papua New Guinea and the Gutnius Lutheran Church of the Enga Highlands. This sketch of five Lutherans offer a glimpse of who they are and what they see through their eyes. Brief though these are, they yet point beyond to the vast, growing, complex, sometimes failing, sometimes succeeding remnant of God's faithful people at work in a part of the world that has been catapulted in hardly more than a generation from a primal culture with all its complexities into new complexities that are part of modern civilization. Few places elsewhere on earth tell such a story with the compelling force of God's mysterious, surprising, transforming love at its heart.

When German Lutherans settled in south central Australia in the 1830's, they brought not only their Lutheran convictions but a talent for wine making as well. As many would agree, the combination has aged well over the decades since, as we learned when meeting Norman Habel in Adelaide. He comes from Lutheran roots of long standing, loves good wine, and is a Biblical theologian with a keen mind and a sense of humor. He once wrote a serious study on an Old Testament prophet with the whimsical title "Are You Joking, Jeremiah?" which caught on well both in Australia and the USA. Nowadays he not only writes on the Biblical prophets, he looks like one. His white hair goes in all directions, his lengthy beard frames a face of granite-like integrity, and his eyes sparkle with a warmth and humor not commonly associated with Jeremiah, nicknamed the Weeping Prophet. As he served us a glass of vintage Australian merlot he was off on yet another impassioned discourse, this time on caring for our fragile earth and denouncing its scandalous misuse. It was vintage Habel, an Australian who is fully alive, totally concerned, altogether persuasive about things that count—qualities that make him both an asset and a sometimes rambunctious rebel among the 255,000 Lutherans of the Evangelical Lutheran Church of Australia.

Norman Habel

AUSTRALIA

If it is true that an Australian Lutherans can sometimes be a bit of a paradox, a kind of Crocodile Dundee with clerical collar, Norman Habel qualifies convincingly. He trained for the ministry at Concordia Seminary in Adelaide, which makes him typical among the 400 Lutheran pastors in Australia who studied there. His three year service as a pastor in Brooklyn, New York, coupled with Old Testament graduate studies at Union Seminary during that time, makes him atypical. He takes Biblical theology seriously, typical of Australian Lutherans. When he shook up a group of ultra-conservative mid-western Lutheran clergy in the USA with a lecture challenging their fundamentalist view of the Bible, one was so upset that he mailed Habel a razor blade in an unmarked envelope—surely an atypical way to object. When he initiated the first department of Old Testament studies at the University of South Australia where he taught for years, the high academic standards he established were typically rigorous. When the conservative element of the Lutheran Church of Australia put him under a fourteen year ban that forbade him access to preaching, even the funeral sermon when his father-in-law died, that was atypical. It was typical of his Australian Lutheran missionary spirit (Lutherans have an enviable record of serving aboriginal peoples in the Australian heartland, even more as missionary pioneers in Papua New Guinea) to go off to India for four years as an innovative mission school principal. It was atypical that when he and his wife found an abandoned infant barely alive on their doorstep, they raised her to adulthood as their own daughter. It is typical that Habel has his mind set on writing another book. An atypical title he is considering is "Why The Hell Are You Still A Lutheran?" People like us who come visiting to Australia looking for what is distinctive here are not led astray when finding Habelian typical/atypical qualities in Australians in general, Lutherans in particular.

This was evident throughout an evening of listening to four Australians who came together from varied backgrounds. Dorothea Prenzler, a teacher, was the first to tell her story. She was born in Germany and came with her parents (her mother a doctor and father a pastor) as a 12 year old to Australia where her schooling took her eventually to Brisbane for a degree in education. During her university years her parents went from Australia to Papua New Guinea as a missionary team. Following further studies in teacher education in Germany, she found her way to PNG to teach in a school for missionary children, met and married her husband, and served with John Prenzler for years, both in PNG and Australia. Her story of how she came to her missionary calling was unusual. She had intended to serve in the teaching mission somewhere beyond Australia, a desire that grew as she was studying the Bible in the Crossways program developed in Australia and now used widely in the world. In a dream one night she saw something like a white plastic basket, descending as if to transport her elsewhere. But it was falling apart and she was terrified to think of it as a prophetic omen that her desire to serve in the church would end in disaster. But the weird image disappeared, leaving only an angel telling her that God's grace was sufficient and that she should not draw back in fear. She awakened, weeping, but also comforted, and a half year later took the call to PNG for years filled with blessing beyond her imagining, as well as inseparable from the demands of living in places where the amenities of life in Europe and Australia are lesser known.

Next to Dorothy sat Margaret Hunt, a nurse who had served in the remote town of Hermannsburg (one can travel 500 miles in any direction to find much of a town) in the desolate area the Australians call The Outback. She had taken her studies for her nursing profession in Adelaide and Perth, after which she gave serious thought to becoming an ordained Lutheran pastor well before the issue of women's ordination was debated among Australian Lutherans (it is still unresolved). She returned to Hermannsburg and came into contact with aboriginal peoples—baptized Christians—and was motivated to learn more from them. She was put off by conventional attitudes that dismissed aboriginal medicine as worthless consorting with witch doctors who mixed magic with evil. What she saw was more than that, she contended, as she continued to observe respectfully and listen carefully to those she knew well enough to gain their trust. In ways unconventional to western concepts, she looked for signs of the intervention of God's care and healing hidden amidst aboriginal belief in spirits, dreams, incantations, and herbal remedies. Lutherans have been at work among such people for 125 years, she told me, strong in zeal but lacking in knowledge. The inroads of alcoholism and government welfare programs that stripped away the traditional tribal male hegemony left the aboriginal family systems in ruins. Women now had to support most of the men. Children grew up without the coherence of tribal discipline. In this long, downward slide, the practice of western medicine was ineffective at best and injurious at worst. Government efforts to impose a way of life foreign to the aboriginal culture were useless, and missionaries were too blind to see the results of trying to serve people without sufficiently understanding their ancient ways. She recognized her own lack of theological grounding for what she wanted to do, and in 1990 took a bold step by enrolling at Concordia Lutheran College in Adelaide to study theology. She loved it, but as she progressed the more conservative men in her academic surroundings were scandalized by her theological acumen. Increasingly frustrated, she transferred her studies to the Biblical department of the University of South Australia where she encountered Norman Habel and a learning atmosphere where questions were accepted as essential to learning. A turning point came for her when she attended a retreat led by a Catholic nun who chose the New Testament story of the woman who came to Jesus for healing after years of spinal paralysis. She began to weep when she recognized herself in that woman, bent over by the need to justify her zeal before men who claimed an overbearing authority. Having found herself in Habel's classes she pursued her discomforting questions openly, taking issue with the Old Testament accounts of God's acts of what struck her as wanton killing and biased selectivity. She told me about Habel's teaching method of hearing her out and then pushing her beyond her presuppositions with his standard phrase, "But now Margaret…" and then not letting her solve matters by simply cutting out controversial passages. Instead, she described his Lutheran pathway of facing confounding passages by drawing them to the interpretive key to what the Bible itself holds forth as its center—God's suffering love in the Christ of the cross and resurrection. She is now pursuing a doctoral degree under Norman Habel's tutelage while continuing her nursing profession in community care. Her stories touched upon strengths and weaknesses of the Australian Lutheran tradition and the tenacity of her pursuit of theological depth, coupled with learning from aborigines while serving community needs, make her a notable example of an Australian Lutheran who is a work in progress.

John Pfitzner told me that the reason he wrestles with bouts of disaffection with his Lutheran church is because of his commitment to its theology, not disregard for it. The context for his story, he pointed out, is the fact that Australia is a highly secular nation. The Gospel is needed everywhere in this land of nearly twenty million population. Although the issues of women's ordination and the status of homosexuals are important, his main concern is that the Lutheran church that he knows and loves is not fully present to the modern world as it exists in Australia. He has been active in Amnesty International for twenty years, but has found too often that Lutherans fail to see the integral link between their theological tradition and the urgency of such issues as human rights for people who suffer greatly. In his view, the church is too defensive when it ought to be in the forefront of where Christ calls his people to be in the world. His hope for Australian Lutherans lies in greater alliances with other Christians who have gifts of ministry that are needed. Only as the church lives out its role more actively in seeking justice for those marginalized in Australian society will it discover the power of its faith heritage, he said. He spoke of how much it meant to him recently to hear a Lutheran church leader speak openly of the need for repentance for the neglect and mistreatment of aborigines. That repentance, he said, must lead to active strategies for advocacy in public affairs. He cited his 15 years of pastoral ministry in Hermannsburg as the background for his concerns—and his hopes. In more recent years he has moved in a new direction in taking his call to vocation outside of the Lutheran church to the book publishing industry, working for secular publishers with a wider influence in Australia. He regards himself as no less Lutheran because he serves outside conventional church channels and when I asked him whether his pastoral colleagues see him as faithful to that widened calling, his answer was short: "it depends on who's asked."

James Winderlich has had 16 years of pastoral experience in several congregations, including service on the board of the Lutheran Church of Australia mission among some 6,000 aborigines scattered throughout the vast outback that comprises two thirds of Australia. His story shed a different light on the complex situation of failed governmental programs among aborigines in the area around Alice Springs, near the famed Ayers Rock. He described ways in which the church has taken over faltering government educational efforts and has started anew by methods of intensive individual interaction with aboriginal people who show an aptitude for church related service. This has led to the ordination of 26 Lutheran aboriginal pastors since 1964. The participation of these ordained clergy in the larger life of the LCA is voluntary. The reason is that participation must be their choice rather than enforced conformity, a policy that incorporates respect for the integrity and wisdom of aboriginal pastoral colleagues. The tone underlying Winderlich's commentary was one tinged with white guilt for discrimination in general, heroic efforts by few, and frustrations felt by many—a pattern much like that of the Christian mission to native Americans in the United States. He went on to sketch out some interesting historical details which are part of the Australian Lutheran story. When the pioneers came from Germany in 1830's they brought their pastor with them. When the second shipload arrived some years later they came without a pastor, and when invited to join the founding settlers as one congregation, they first conducted a doctrinal inquiry. Their decision was that the pastor on hand was not Lutheran enough and refused to join. Instead they appointed one from their own settlement to become their elder. Ironically, they later sent him off to a local Congregational Church to be ordained, then took him back as officially qualified. This was the origin of St. Stephens Lutheran Church in Adelaide, a leading congregation in the Lutheran Church of Australia despite its odd beginning as too Lutheran for a merger with an existing Lutheran congregation but content with non-Lutheran hands laid on their elder to be their shepherd. Winderlich's point was that Lutherans, like other Christians in Australia, were too preoccupied with their internal matters to reach out to those living in the nation's outback for countless aeons. He was happy in his present calling as pastor of St. Stephen's, Adelaide, and characterized it as "joyfully shaping up" the 650 faithful in his care. As one born and raised in the beautiful and fertile Adelaide area (the city has been voted the most livable place on earth), his conscience is not only stirred by the challenge of the aborigines but by the increasing environmental problems that affect Australia, where its slender urban rim of coastal areas encircle the huge, arid outback that spreads for hundreds of thousands of square miles within that rim.

In one form or another these four Australians told stories that evoked a sense that each is a maverick within the Aussie Lutheran fold, in the original sense of maverick as an unbranded calf in a herd branded to graze the open prairie. That's my term, not theirs, and it in no way suggests that as mavericks they are less faithful heirs of Martin Luther who was anything but a standard brand churchman of his day. Certainly in their hospitality shown us they represent the warm welcome we received throughout our Australian itinerary. Their open, critical, liberal outlook in theological matters and the mission of the church gave me the feeling of being with Lutherans in transition from the settled comforts of a traditional past toward something not yet clearly defined as a church in mission to a nation where golf courses and tennis courts are more crowded than churches on Sunday mornings.

Dean Zweck, a seminary professor at Concordia Seminary in Adelaide, and our congenial host in Adelaide, took me along for a morning conference of pastors serving congregations in the Barossa Valley north of Adelaide, an area rich both in Lutheran history and vineyards that produce world famous wines. After a drive of more than an hour we pulled into the parking lot of the Lutheran church in Ingeston where the sturdy stone church building with a tower visible for miles around stood as a testament to those who had built this sanctuary and made it their spiritual home throughout previous generations. The dozen pastors who gathered to hear Zweck's presentation welcomed me for a brief summary of my global travels, but my purpose was to listen more than speak. The pastor of the Ingiston congregation, Vernon Kleinig, has 33 years of pastoral experience behind him. He is the sole pastor in this congregation of about 400 baptized, which makes it larger than average among the 600 congregation of the Lutheran Church of Australia. Like many clergy of the LCA he was much influenced during the formative days of his seminary studies by Herman Sasse, considered by many to have been the most influential theological mentor of Australian Lutheranism in the first half of the 20th century. Kleinig said that to understand the impact of Sasse on Australian Lutheranism, and what makes it distinctive, two words are necessary: evangelical catholic. Evangelical means centering the whole of theology in what the Lutheran confessional documents of the 16th century speak of as the true treasure of the Gospel, the great *sola* affirmations of grace alone, faith alone, Scripture alone as the foundation of the church's message and life. The term catholic means universal, the whole body of believers called by the Holy Spirit to faith and discipleship through the Gospel. Kleinig was quick to add that because he is Lutheran in the sense of being both evangelical and catholic, this by no means infers that the quarter million Lutherans listed as affiliated with the Lutheran Church of Australia are firm in this understanding. He cited how some in his own Ingiston parish congregation are buffeted with problems of family dysfunction and broken marriages. Farmers in the area have been hard hit by several years of drought hand running, and must draw upon their pastor's counsel as well as those of Lutheran Community Care for support in working through their problems. In the face of such things, however, he stressed the positive and named experiences that give him joy in the work. Congregations in this area, his own included, are growing. Small country congregations are close knit communities of faith where people reach out to each other in times of need. The sick and elderly are visited. Congregations find ways to extend their witness and care to people outside their membership. He has been invited to speak to Lutheran students on the campus of the nearby Ballarat Catholic University where he found a positive response to his presentations on Lutheran theology, adding that his Catholic faculty friends cautioned their students against becoming "Luther addicts." This was meant with some degree of respect, Kleinig said, since the Catholic university leadership welcomed Lutheran presenters more than other Protestant because of the coherence of its doctrinal center in the Biblical Gospel, the sacraments, and a liturgical worship tradition that reflects the catholic heritage through the centuries. More than most pastors in Australia, Kleinig has taken opportunities to further his theological education abroad. He traveled to the Lutheran Church Missouri Synod's Concordia Seminary, St. Louis, for a master's degree in systematic theology under the renowned specialist in the Lutheran Confessions, the late Arthur Carl Piepkorn, and has shared the benefits of that experience with congregations and colleagues since his return.

Malcolm Bartsch is another Australian with strong ties to the USA Lutheranism of the Missouri Synod through the sabbatical year of graduate study he spent at Concordia in the Chicago suburb of River Forest, Illinois. He is a graduate of the seminary in Adelaide who, with his wife, Ann, spent eight years in Papua New Guinea as part of an ecumenical team of Roman Catholic and Anglican educators in developing the religion curriculum for use in teacher training and in schools there. When meeting the Bartsch's during our days in Adelaide, we renewed our friendship at a dinner in their home which featured the Australian staple items of lively theological discussion and good wine. Like Kleinig, Malcolm Bartsch told stories of Lutherans working well with Catholics. On one occasion in PNG

Malcom and Ann Bartsch

the pressure was on to produce in the space of two weeks a supply of religion curriculum materials that covered a three year period—an accomplishment made possible, Bartsch thought, "because we were prayed for." A Catholic nun had gathered others to join her in a round the clock cycle of prayer during the two weeks. The French nuns also hosted him in the Franciscan convent where they lived, posting a sign over his room reading "Male—married" and during mealtimes including him in their practice of hearing a Biblical passage read and following it with twenty minutes of silence for reflection on the text. "What do Lutherans do with that?" he remembered asking himself at the time, a reminder of what pragmatic-minded Australian Lutherans can learn from the long Franciscan tradition of meditative mealtimes.

A further benefit Bartsch took from his years as a missionary educator in PNG was cutting away cumbersome theological jargon from his language of faith. Pidgin is a language without abstractions; it requires one to think and teach through concrete images which reflect what people experience, and does so with daring imagination. Thus in Papua New Guinea where there are no sheep, Jesus is known as the Pig of God, since the pig is the animal of sacrifice both in religious ceremony and daily life. The larger lesson from his PNG years is that Christians, wherever they are, inevitably live and work in a cross-cultural milieu. What that means in Australia, an increasingly culturally diverse nation, is that the white ethnic population is no less in need of the Gospel in a culture-sensitive manner than are the aborigines of the land. When Lutherans heed their theological heritage, which teaches that all cultures are tainted by human sin, they have the necessary starting point to diagnose the cultural idolatries that must be addressed with God's law—Australia included. When Lutherans live out the primary theme of their heritage, the grace of Christ's saving cross and resurrection as power for daily living, they offer saving truth needed by every person and community in every place—Australia included. Bartsch cited an example from a recent conference he attended on challenges to the Australian church. The theme was whether the church is a sheltering harbor that keeps ships tethered at anchor, or whether it is a place for repair and re-fuelling ships to endure storms en route to destinations. In the Australia that he knows from his birth, people are not moved by popularized religion which approaches people—in pungent Aussie idiom—as "tall puppies cut off at the knees and stuffed a religious box." Faithful mission reaches deeper into the human dilemma and offers God's renewing power alive in the church as the beloved community, open to all. In Bartsch's view, discipleship is a constant journey of learning to know Christ ever more fully in the body of all who profess his name.

Christianity is shrinking in numbers and influence in Australia. Why is that? I asked. He answered that one reason is that Lutherans have been a predominantly rural church and have not kept pace with an increasingly urbanized nation. Furthermore, as in the USA, there is a rising interest in loosely defined spirituality, but not in the Christian message of human sin and Divine grace. His interest in education and schools prompt him to continually seek ways to prepare teachers who are gifted in connecting the Biblical salvation story by sharing it with the life stories of people open to receiving it. It won't happen by pastoral imposition of answers from the top down. The more promising connection is through lay persons whose manner of life is such that secularized Australians see in them something that makes them take notice and want to find out what that something is.

How do students preparing for church vocations as pastors and teachers view these matters? Answers came during a day spent on the campus of Concordia Lutheran College engaging in discussions with a variety of students. Leon Krieg is an honor student in the Concordia lay theological training program with a career background as a former mapmaker for an arm of the Australian government. He is now in his fourth year of this intensive program, having first heard of it through a note in the church bulletin of his congregation. "Sometimes God doesn't tell us why; we just get interested in something worthwhile and let him answer later on" was his summary of how that note led him to where he now serves as a pastoral assistant in a congregation. Women also participate. His present experience has broadened his opportunities to advocate the program to others. He noted how an increase of trained laity in congregations can bring about greater tolerance for church problems and add significant lay contributions to solutions. Krieg is married and the father of three; his retirement income is sufficient for the support of his family.

Brian Van Wageningen is tall, with a streak of gray befitting his retirement years, and a ready smile that often crossed his face during our conversation filled with thoughtful commentary on his past and present as an active layman. When he retired from his position as an administrator in the Australian school system he planned to form a small educational management program in Adelaide and make it useful to the church educational system. When Malcolm Bartsch, then dean of studies at Concordia College in Adelaide, heard through Leon Krieg of Van Wageningen's experience and interests, he brought him on as an interim dean of studies, the position in which he is currently serving. His contact with Lutheran schools began in his youth, when his father, a Christian Reformed pastor, enrolled him in the Lutheran school system where he was immersed in Luther's Catechism for five years. He later entered a college of the Reformed Church with a pastoral ministry future in mind, but was disillusioned by what struck him as a theology and practice too compromised by an adaptation to watered down mainstream Protestantism. He defined that as putting human efforts over what God does, church growth methods aimed at increasing numbers by catering to what the public wants, disbanding the Apostles Creed as outdated, and gutting the liturgy with substitutions for the Aaronic benediction with such novelties as "Have a good one, mate." He changed from theology to an education major and spent years in a career of educational administration and along the way found a church home for himself and his family in a Lutheran congregation. Now, at 63, he is fully engaged in a program of theological studies at Concordia College, and is amplifying his gifts for lay ministry by studying organ. Given his experience of a conscious choice of becoming a member of a Lutheran congregation, he confessed to moments of being judgmental when seeing parishioners around him apparently doing little more than going through the motions of the liturgy when at worship. In his words, his instinct at times was to stop everything and announce—"Think about it, people!"—but instead of carrying through that disruption, has found it enough to keep his own attention centered on what it means to tremble in reverent awe when addressing the living God.

Louise Thomas opened our conversation with a surprising comment. She cited the date of her baptism as a newborn infant as the reason she had something to say about what it means to be a Lutheran Christian in Australia today. Her point was the immense difference it made that she grew up in a household where her parents regarded baptism as more than a tribal rite with little consequence. Having parents who took their vows seriously by teaching her to pray, hear the stories of Jesus, and themselves live the faith into which they were baptized, made all the difference. The quality of her spiritual upbringing, she soon discovered as a youth, set her apart from the majority of her friends and fellow students attending her school in Adelaide. It was at that time the largest public school in Australia, well filled with youth from non-Christian religions, as well as from Australian families of religion lite. A maternal grandfather had also helped her parents as formative religious influences during her early years. He was a pastor given to quoting Shakespeare as often as quoting Scripture, a gift that increased her love for literature as well as her being at home in the Bible. He took her and her siblings along on pastoral visits to those who were patients in mental health institutions he served. He taught her to memorize verses from hymns of the Lutheran tradition and made it a point to attend Christmas pageants in which she and her brothers took part. She recalled her memories as a 12 year old of church services where her boredom during sermons she could not understand was relieved when it came time to sing hymns, many of which she had learned earlier. She attended Lutheran high school "where it was cool not to sing in chapel," but she came to realize that being un-cool by singing anyway was a way of witnessing that worked for her. She went on to major in education at Concordia College where she met her husband, became a teacher, and broadened her ecumenical awareness of the wider church by doing further studies at an Anglican college. For six years she taught elementary grades in a new Lutheran school that had opened in Sydney. After that she postponed graduate studies toward a goal of leadership in Lutheran schools to bring her three children into the world. She characterized this time in her life as a battle within herself against a cultural devaluation of the teaching role of a stay-at-home mother with her children as less than a professional career of classroom teaching and school administration. She resolved it by combining her priority placed on time with her three children with directing the Sunday School in her congregation where she could apply the full range of her pedagogical training to develop a first rate learning experience for children from 4 to 14 task too often relegated to anyone willing to take it on, regardless of qualifications. This was the latest commentary on her opening comments on baptism as the beginning of lifelong growth in discipleship.

As acquisitions librarian of Concordia College, Helen Schubert did not come from a sophisticated family accustomed to the hushed atmosphere of a library lined with books. She recalled her rural childhood in a family household in which she was both frightened as fascinated by "aunties who were wild women interested in feminist ideas—one ran a pub and another even married a Catholic." Her father worked on Sundays. The reason she started in Sunday School was that her mother learned to drive and took her to the nearest church. Helen was not baptized till she was 7, and that came about through the influence of her maternal grandparents who were church people. When as a teenager she lapsed for a time, her sister told her she was headed straight for hell. It was, she said, enough to scare her into attending church again. Despite the rough-edged family life and muscular Christianity in the church of her youth, she discovered a love for books when attending college in Adelaide, an experience that served her well when teaching reading and literature in a Barossa Valley school. Meanwhile she had met and married a man who came from a religious background such as she had never known. One of the things that surprised and impressed her as a young wife acclimating herself to her husband's family was, as she widened her eyes when recalling it, "they actually talked about God around the dinner table." Her husband, David, had an ear for language and music, and in his spare time as a teacher began composing liturgies for Vespers and Matins, using what she described as precise and elegant words that were set to contemporary music of quality. To his surprise, she said, his creative efforts proved more than an experiment; the worship materials he created are still used in congregations. Helen was asked to do substitute teaching at Concordia College from time to time and when asked to consider taking on librarian responsibilities at the school, she went back to the university for a library degree. There she sat in on tutorials on literature and found satisfaction in discerning nuances of Christian symbolism that other students missed. Now, as a mother of two sons and a grandmother twice over, she is grateful for her varied life experiences which have enabled her to welcome into her heart her daughter-in-law, an aboriginal woman of whom the wild aunties of her childhood would surely approve.

Conversation with these four adults, Australians of widely differing backgrounds who found common ground through serious continuing theological education, enlarged my view of Lutheranism here that is both grounded and open to creative thinking, marked by a barley-bread plainness of manner that is neither shocked by the exotic nor swept away with it, and comfortable when described as people of the Tradition (in the sense of the living faith of the dead) but uncomfortable with insinuations of traditionalism (the dead faith of the living). Michael Hassold, Concordia College administrator and professor of pastoral theology, systematic theology, "and everything else"—as he added with humor, provided this overview of theological education in Adelaide. There are thirty-five candidates for ordination currently on campus with a larger cohort who are off campus on internships and other assignments, a drop from earlier years and a source of concern over a coming shortage of pastors in the Lutheran Church of Australia. Normally the incoming class numbers between ten to twelve; this year the number is five. Hassold regards the next ten years as critical for pastoral training, not only in the quantity needed but especially the quality of men with aptitude for preaching and teaching. There are those, he added, who say that the shortage would be remedied promptly if the church would ordain women to the pastoral ministry. That day is not here, he said, at least not yet. More than that he did not say. Another form of solution is already taking place in remote areas of Australia where twenty Lutheran school principals have been ordained for pastoral work in congregations without a pastor. Regarding teacher education, I was surprised to learn that 300 teachers are needed to fill vacancies in Lutheran schools throughout the nation; currently 350 are now preparing but that number was 500 only three years previous, a sign of another shortage looming. "We are a small church surrounded by militant Assembly of God, Pentecostal, and Emerging Church programs" he observed, "with the temptation for people to wander off to these groups, or for Lutherans to imitate them." At the heart of that problem, he said, is separating the work of the Holy Spirit from its central Scriptural theme of preaching the Gospel and administering the sacraments. Lutherans bring needed leaven to the spiritual life of Australia by keeping the fruits of the Spirit inseparable from the good news of the crucified and risen Savior who forgives sinners and gathers them for mission in the world.

This calls for ecumenicity. Lutherans can't do it alone. He was encouraged by what he sees as lively dialog with Roman Catholics and Anglicans, who together comprise one half of the Christians in the land. On another positive note, he is glad to see the doctrine of justification by faith much more in focus in ecumenical dialog. His potpourri of current matters included what is widely called "worship wars" over traditional and contemporary worship among Lutherans. Such mixing and matching goes on, with many congregations offering two services on Sunday, one traditional, the other contemporary. His summary word about his present calling testified to the lasting satisfaction he finds in applying the central Lutheran theme of justification by faith to the educational programs for laity, a truth he sees not as one doctrine among many, but the very center of God's power to equip his people for daily ministry in the world.

An unusual set of circumstances surrounded the person with whom we had our final conversation on the Concordia campus. Maria Gramm is nineteen, a tall and attractive young woman who told us of her birth and up bringing in Leipzig, Germany, the only child in a family where, as she said, "there was no religion of any kind except the failed promises of Communism which nobody believed anyway." She did well in school, and at age 18 began to travel the world. When reaching Australia she found her way to Adelaide, and on a walk one weekday happened by Bethlehem Lutheran Church. Her curiosity led her to do something she had never done before—enter a Christian church. She tried the church door, found it open, and worked up nerve to go inside where she was greeted by members who showed her hospitality. She told them of her curiosity over what went on inside of churches; they invited her to return on Sunday and find out more. She did, and was not prepared for the impact of being present in a service of worship, surrounded by people at prayer, singing, and listening to what was said from the pulpit. She kept attending, and after some months of exploring her spiritual curiosity further, she began meeting with the pastor regularly. She informed her parents in Leipzig about what was happening to her, and although they appeared to give her wide latitude in choosing such a course, they expressed concern when she told them she was ready for baptism. Their impression was that baptism had to do with a cult of some sort and this worried them. Her mother surprised her by coming all the way from Germany to be present at her baptism in order to meet those who were part of her daughter's new spiritual family. Her next step was to enroll in the lay theological study program at Concordia College, with a view toward a future vocation of service in the church. What form that might take and where it might lead she did not yet know. While listening to her story I thought of her need for protection from overly zealous assumptions as one newborn in Christ. The image that came to mind fit well for Maria among her mentors in Adelaide, that of a mother kangaroo protecting her newborn in her sheltering pouch. Maria needs the nurture she is receiving from Australian Lutherans. And Australian Lutherans need the renewing breath of the Holy Spirit breathed upon them through this young woman who happened to walk by Bethlehem Church one day and found more than an open door.

What can one learn from these dozen men and women about the blessings and burdens of living the faith, "down under," as Australia is popularly nicknamed? These cannot speak for a quarter million other Lutherans who are there, nor did they presume to do so. One truism, however, about Australian Lutherans that might apply widely and find acceptance both as a promise and a peril. It lies in a word play on Tradition and traditionalism learned from the late theologian Jaroslav Pelikan: Tradition—in the sense of the living faith of the dead which is centered in the Gospel handed down through the centuries—is alive and honored among Australian Lutherans. Traditionalism—in the sense of the dead faith of the living—is a blight on Australian Lutherans that is painful to recognize but can be overcome as the Holy Spirit moves the church from maintenance to mission.

AFTERWORD

Responding to the promise and perils of the global church as seen through the eyes of those described in these chapters can lead to any number of practical actions. Among them are these:

First, and most easy to overlook, is the action of intercessory prayer. "Thy will be done on earth as it is in heaven" is a missionary petition of our Lord's Prayer. Praying it with that awareness can be done by naming before God the known individuals who are distant in miles but not in spirit. It can also be a part of the prayers regularly offered in congregation worship as particular churches in particular places are lifted up before God. Prayer is the common language of our partnership in the whole family of God that reaches everywhere.

The global family of humankind is down the street as well as across salt water. Think of what it would be like to be recently arrived in a land totally new, struggling to speak a new language and wondering how to find friendships that can surmount the barriers of loneliness and a homesick heart. Something as simple as hospitality, offered in tactful ways that hospitable people will always find, can be—literally—a Godsend.

Mission tourism is a whole new category of travel. The experience of meeting people of the faith in another land can put a face on an otherwise strange place. When planning an itinerary abroad, why not check with the local congregation or denomination to get needed details on where to find fellow believers who will provide a welcome at a church service, or better, a welcome in a household that can transform a place on a tourist map into an unforgettable experience with people? It's a two-way street; blessed is the congregation that makes itself known as a welcoming member of the Body of Christ to those who seek that welcome.

Service projects, involving youth as well as retirees, and lots of age groups in between, are available through myriad sources—most often through denominational offices and publications, congregations which have sponsored service projects that are well planned, and by word of mouth from those who have stories to tell from their own experience. Blessed are those who seek; they shall find.

Education materials, videos, curricula for youth and adults, and information on local and regional meetings on the global mission of the church are readily available from denominational offices. Often it is through such means that the initial interest in the global church is begun. Finding speakers who bring personal witness to the excitement and challenge of the changing world Christian scene is not hard. Begin by consulting available church sources, and keep an eye on scheduled events which feature people who can inform and inspire by what they have seen and done.

Pastoral sabbaticals are golden opportunities both for the minister and the congregation. Everyone gains when the vision of the world church is widened, and the pastoral leader returns with faith and insight refreshed and deepened. Sabbatical purposes vary widely; keep open to including some ways of networking with the global church as one possibility. Congregations need to learn the value of a sabbatical for their pastor. That happens because pastors provide the initiative and can clarify the overall good that results.

In his Foreword, Martin Marty suggests that this book is but a beginning of what we both hope will be more globe-trotting by others of other traditions to track what is going on in their global church connections and bring that witness home to enlarge the vision of what God is doing in his world. There is never a lack of bad news making the rounds in the world; there is so much of the Good News at work in the lives of faithful people that can be seen, heard, and told. I believe there are many who long to hear that Good News, and in so doing, come to know a deeper joy and wonder for the global reach of the Savior. There is nothing better than to respond to his call to make that happen.